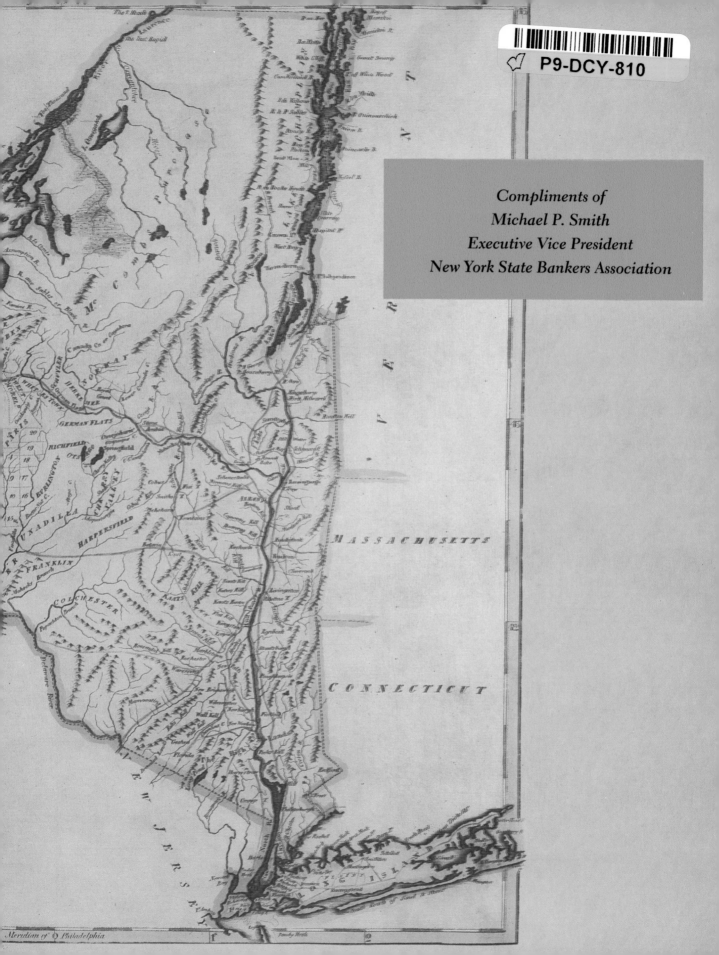

P9-DCY-810

For Each, the Strength of All

Other Books by J. T. W. Hubbard

Banking in Mid-America

A History of Banking in the State of Missouri

Magazine Editing for Professionals

*How to Acquire the Skills You Need to Win a Job
and Succeed in the Magazine Business*

The Race

*An Inside Account of What It's Like to Compete
in the Observer Singlehanded Transatlantic
Race from Plymouth, England, to
Newport, Rhode Island*

For Each, the Strength of All

A History of Banking in the

State of New York

by

J. T. W. Hubbard

New York University Press

New York and London

in association with the

New York State
Bankers Association

NEW YORK UNIVERSITY PRESS
New York and London

Library of Congress Cataloging-in-Publication Data

Hubbard J. T. W., 1935–
For each the strength of all : a history of banking in the state
of New York / J. T. W. Hubbard.
p.   cm.
Includes bibliographical references and index.
ISBN 0-8147-3514-2
1. Banks and banking—New York (State)—History.   I. Title.
HG2611.N7H83   1994   94-17952
332.1'09747—dc20   CIP

New York University Press books are printed on acid-free paper,
and their binding materials are chosen for strength and durability.

Manufactured in the United States of America
10   9   8   7   6   5   4   3   2   1

Front endpaper: Map of New York State, 1796. (Engraving by
David Martin; published by J. Reid, New York, 1796, collection
Arents Research Library, Syracuse University)

Back endpaper: Map of New York State, 1829. (Compiled by
D. H. Burr, 1829; engraved by Rawdon Clark, and Co., Albany,
N.Y., collection Arents Research Library, Syracuse University)

This book is dedicated to my children
STEPHANIE, RUFUS JOHN, KATE and CLARE.

And to a real lady and a real gentleman
AMF and RHF.

To the more than 170,000 bankers of New York State . . . and to their predecessors, whose vision, energy, and initiative have made our State the banking capital of the world.

The longer you look back, the farther you can look forward.
 —Winston S. Churchill

We need history in order to breathe. To be without a history is to be without some essential element of one's own reality. —Page Smith, *A People's History*

Contents

List of Illustrations

List of Illustrations

List of Illustrations

List of Illustrations

Foreword

ONE HUNDRED YEARS AGO, Buffalo banker William Cornwell called
his colleagues to unite in political action. Politics and publicity typically were
anathema to the scions of banking; but a financial crisis was gripping the
nation and unemployment in the state had risen above 30 percent. From the
canyons of Wall Street to the shores of Lake Erie bankers recognized that the
times called for action; current laws and institutions simply weren't responding; and New York was, after all, the largest banking state. And so they
heeded Cornwell's call, coming together to form the New York State Bankers
Association. Cornwell's vision of unity and reform is as compelling today as
it was in 1894.

Professor Hubbard's lively narrative chronicles the history of banking in
New York State through the key events, and most important the colorful
and vivid characters—some familiar, some not—who shaped these events:
Hamilton, Burr, Morgan, Glass, Steagall, Strong, Davison, Baker, Aldrich,
Rockefeller, Roth, Volcker, and Wriston, to name just a few. The Erie
Canal, the great wars, the Great Depression, the Roaring Twenties and the
explosive Eighties all had their part in shaping New York banking. This is
not a history of the New York State Bankers Association as such, nor is it a
book just for bankers. It can and should be read by anyone interested in the
role of New York banking in the development of the Empire State and
the nation.

Here is the story of how Alexander Hamilton, the nation's first Treasury

Secretary, brought the Bank of New York into being to "discount" the notes of storekeepers issued to pay for merchandise, and thus fuel the growth of the mercantile class. Hamilton's vision was the beginning of commercial banking in the state—and a brilliant counterstroke to the "elitist" Robert Livingston, chancellor of the New York courts and a major landowner, who proposed to lend money only upon the security of land. Then there is Hamilton's one-time law colleague and later deadly rival, Aaron Burr, who chartered the Manhattan Company to bring "pure and wholesome water" into the City—and cleverly slipped into its bylaws a provision that made possible the creation of another great banking organization, today the Chase Manhattan Bank. Typifying the Roaring Twenties was the flamboyant, "Gatsby-like" George Mitchell, who drove fast cars, speculated heavily in the stock market, and assumed the presidency of the giant National City Bank at age 42.

Professor Hubbard vividly depicts the tragedies as well as the triumphs. Here is William Cornwell, NYSBA's first president, and a man of letters as well as a brilliant and foresighted banker. But a few incautious loans, a zealous examiner, and his once-great City Bank of Buffalo came crashing down around him. The more things change, the more they remain the same: turn the pages and we read of the spectacular growth of the Franklin National as a prosperous suburban bank—until it was attracted by the bright lights of the big city. Not long after came the "LDC" crisis, as bank loans to lesser-developed countries turned sour.

But always the courage and ingenuity of New York's bankers shine through. In the depths of the Great Depression, George W. Hamlin allayed the fears of his depositors—and saved his Canandaigua National Bank from a potentially disastrous bank run, following the failure of its less-sound neighbor—by stacking $1 million in cash "in plain view" behind a teller's window. At the other end of the size spectrum, Walter Wriston built Citicorp into the nation's largest bank, a presence in every part of the world and an aggressive innovator of new products and lines of business.

By showing us our origins, Professor Hubbard gives us cause for comfort. Even as our industry grapples with the problems of declining market share, overregulation and fierce resistance from other financial service providers to level the playing field, we are emboldened by the great challenges that we have met and overcome in the past. The LDC debt crisis was painful—but hardly comparable to the trauma of the Great Depression. The recession of the 1990s ate into profits—but how much more trying was the banking panic of the 1890s? The shifting political winds are ever worrisome—but this is hardly new. In fact, they are the very reason New York's bankers responded to the "Call" and formed the New York State Bankers Association.

Throughout the century of its existence, the activities of the Association have been inextricably entwined with the growth of New York's commercial banks and their rise to preeminence in the nation and the world. Its members have heeded the call to political action, and have been instrumental in every major piece of legislation affecting the industry, from deregulation of interest rates on deposits to the permanent extension of New York's consumer credit protection laws, successfully completed in 1994. Through the efforts of the NYSBA, New York State pioneered interstate banking legislation in 1982, and ten years later enacted the nation's first interstate branching bill.

Where necessary, the NYSBA has carried the legal fight from the legislature into the courtroom. In the 1950s the Association helped overturn the laws prohibiting commercial banks from advertising their savings accounts. In the 1990s it won the right for New York State-chartered banks to sell annuities, and led the way in defeating a fee imposed on banks, and only on banks, to pay for the cost of their own tax audits. Both of these actions were upheld unanimously by New York's highest court, the Court of Appeals. These successes were possible because NYSBA's members stood together— "for each, the strength of all."

In addition to providing an array of services to its member banks, the Association continues to be a leader in banking education—fueled by the spirit of William Cornwell, who, among many other achievements, founded the American Institute of Banking to educate further generations of bankers. On the occasion of its Centennial the NYSBA is proud to sponsor this book as an educational tool in furtherance of its primary mission: the well-being of the State's commercial banking industry.

But the past is prologue; our Centennial is a time to look forward as well as back. Professor Hubbard reminds us that George F. Baker, president of the First National Bank of New York, once was asked why a person of his experience could not predict what lies ahead. "You can't know," he replied, "because *every time is different*." Fortunately, New York's banks have the unparalleled wealth of talent—the greatest resource of all—to meet whatever the future may bring. And thanks to this book, we can better see the road before us as we plan our trip for the next one hundred years.

Michael P. Smith
Executive Vice President
New York State Bankers Association
April 1, 1994

Acknowledgments

THIS BOOK is the story of banking in the state of New York, and my biggest "thank you" goes to the bank presidents and chairmen throughout the state who took the time to complete our questionnaire on how things were four and five decades back, and how they got to be the way they are today. These CEOs also devoted numerous hours, and much energy, to explaining how their individual institutions worked, and how they made their way forward through the years. Special thanks go to Arthur Roth, former chairman of Franklin National; Hollis Harrington, former chairman of the State Bank of Albany; and Henry Pomares, former comptroller of the Empire National Bank of Middletown, all of whom spoke to me at length on the telephone.

Special thanks also go out to all those working in the state's libraries, museums and photo collections who helped me to exhume and illustrate the financial history of New York. Village and town historians, often holding office without any form of remuneration, also provided details that would have taken years to discover by myself. Warren Moffett, the village historian of East Aurora, consulted his amazing files and identified the house that William Cornwell built more than a century ago. Mary Bell, director of archives at the Buffalo & Erie County Historical Society, helped find people and scenes from Buffalo's past. I want to thank Dr. David Stam, director of Syracuse University's Bird Library, for helping me approach other libraries around the state. Thanks also go to Antonio Bell, associate librarian, and Paul Barfoot, library assistant III, who helped me crack several of Bird

Library's more opaque computer codes. Carol Hamilton and Betty Reid, working under associate librarian Dorcas MacDonald in the University's Interlibrary Loan office also did magnificent work, while associate librarian Randolph Bond in the Fine Arts division helped immeasurably in my search for appropriate illustrations. Special thanks also go to Dr. Mark Weimer, map enthusiast and curator of Bird Library's Special Collections, for his help in unearthing our endpaper maps; thanks, also, to David Broda for photographing them.

I also wish to thank Carolyn Wilson and chief curator Tammis Groft of the Albany Institute of History and Art, and Kathy Stocking, registrar of the New York State Historical Association of Cooperstown, for help in finding and obtaining images of life in New York in earlier centuries. Adam Gonnelli of the Federal Reserve Bank of New York provided valuable information concerning currency and the operations of the bank. The Museum of the City of New York's Tony Pisani researched and provided images of several of the city's old buildings. Kevin Murphy of the Bettmann Archive uncovered some fine images of citizens at work and play over the years. Jim Francis of the New-York Historical Society worked amid difficult conditions to produce some fine images, as did Wayne Furman and Ms. Glover of the New York Public Library. Nancy Schmugge is to be thanked for her work at the Pierpont Morgan Library. Thanks also go to the Union Club of New York and to Eric Widing, chairman of its Arts Committee, for kind permission to reproduce Frederic Chapman's fine painting of Washington's Headquarters at Newburgh. Martin Gengerke of Stack's Rare Coins, New York, made available some fine images of early currency. Thomas Croft, vice president of Morgan Guaranty, provided us with a fine image of the controversial Anglo-French bond of 1915.

Thanks also go to Steven Rautenberg, vice president for corporate relations at Chase Manhattan, and to Dr. Jean Hrichus, archivist, and Jim Moske, assistant archivist at Chase, for providing invaluable help in the acquisition of illustrations concerning the bank's earlier years. Similarly, Michelle Biondi, assistant archivist at Citibank, dug through mountains of material to find the pictures we sought. Charles Long, Alan Goldstein, and Jack Morris also opened many doors for us at Citibank. John Herzog, director of the Museum of American Financial History, produced images of many historic documents. Dr. Karl Kabbelac of the Rare Books Room in Rush Rhees Library, University of Rochester, uncovered some fine pictures of that city and its people.

Hank Schramm, a former bank executive and author of numerous books on the history of central New York, proved to be an unfailing source of information and encouragement; he read and commented upon several of the book's chapters. Robert Lisbeth of the Photo Restoration Directorate at the Library of Congress provided some invaluable pointers, and encouragement, in obtaining access to illustration materials. Lisa Hartjens and Athene Angelus of Imagefinders of Washington also helped us locate many fine images. Judith Haven and Thomas Hunter, curators at the Onondaga Historical Association, helped us find painted and photo portraits of many early New Yorkers. Melissa Forgey, assistant curator of collections at the Jekyll Island Museum, Georgia, kindly provided us with a photo of the old club-house. Lois Oglesby, director of collections at the Mariners Museum in Newport News, helped us obtain an aquatint of old New York's waterfront. Professors Tony Golden, David Sutherland, Tom Richards, Jay Wright and Randy Grimshaw, my colleagues at Syracuse University's Newhouse School, gave me invaluable insights concerning the mysteries of photo reproduction, as did Sharon Pickard, manager of the Burnet Road office of Syracuse's Industrial Color Labs. Joshua Nefsky, highly competent photographer based in New York City, helped turn some of those insights into reality. Professor Richard Sylla, the noted economic historian at New York University, led me to many important sources on the early years of American banking, as did Professor Roger Sharp of Syracuse University.

Special thanks go to the New York State Bankers Association and its member banks, who commissioned this project. In particular, I want to acknowledge the unflagging support of the NYSBA's Centennial Committee, who first conceived of this project as a unique and special way of commemorating the Association's one hundred years of service to New York's banking industry: Robert H. Fearon, Jr., chairman of the Centennial Committee and of Oneida Valley National Bank, and a past president of the NYSBA; Dr. William L. Bitner III, then chairman of the First National Bank of Glens Falls and also a past president of the NYSBA; Ernest Ginsberg, vice chairman of the Republic New York Corporation and president of the NYSBA for its 1993–94 centennial year; George W. Hamlin IV, president and chief executive officer of the Canandaigua National Bank and Trust Co. and a past president of the NYSBA; James Whelden, chairman of the Ballston Spa National Bank; and Michael P. Smith, executive vice president of the NYSBA. Thanks also to James P. Murphy, executive vice president of the NYSBA when this project was born and now executive vice president of Fleet Financial Group, Inc.; David L. Glass, the NYSBA's General Counsel, who along with Mike Smith lived and endured with this project from the beginning; and Robert H. Cole, the NYSBA's former vice president.

My profound thanks to all these people for keeping their nerve—and their good humor—in our prolonged effort to bring this unusual venture to a happy and successful conclusion.

Bluff Island,   J. T. W. Hubbard
Clayton, N.Y.   May 1, 1994

1

Signers of the Call

FOR STUDENTS of classical literature, the Ides of March is a day fraught with peril and ill-omen. This fact cannot have been lost on the five men who assembled around the mahogany table at 10 A.M. in the boardroom of the City Bank in Buffalo on March 15, 1894.

In the seventy years since the completion of the Erie Canal, Buffalo had grown from a remote trading post into the nation's great western entrepôt for wheat and lumber. Its population—now amounting to some 340,000—had until recently been welcoming new residents at the rate of 16,000 a year. It was the terminal of fifteen shipping lines and more than a dozen railroads. According to the city directory of 1894 it was also home to three telegraph companies, five detective agencies, six major hotels, seventeen horse traders, twenty-four breweries, three hundred and twelve saloons and, in a nice touch of refinement, four dancing academies and no fewer than one hundred and ninety music teachers. Grover Cleveland, the product of Buffalo's crude but supremely efficient political machine, now occupied the White House in Washington.

But even friends in high places were not enough to assuage the fears of the men who assembled in the City Bank's upstairs boardroom at 319 Main Street on the morning of March 15, 1894. Here William C. Cornwell, the president and chief executive officer of the bank, introduced his guests to one another. The group included Henry C. Brewster, a genial white-bearded man of 49, who served as the cashier of the Traders National Bank in

Main Street, Buffalo, in the 1890s. Offices of the City Bank can be seen just above the streetcars to the right. (Buffalo and Erie County Historical Society)

Rochester, New York. D. A. Avery, cashier of the Second National Bank, journeyed up from Utica for this meeting. Also present was Frederick W. Barker, a tall, thin-lipped individual who was the cashier of the Robert Gere National Bank in Syracuse. Barker, noted for his meticulous accounting skills and his ability to size up the condition of a bank within minutes of walking through the door, would one day become president of the Syracuse Savings Bank. And finally, there was Charles Adsit, cashier of the First National Bank of Hornellsville in Steuben County. He worked for his father, Martin Adsit, who had operated a private bank before the Civil War and was now president of the First National.

Perhaps Cornwell—a brisk, dapper man with a short, neatly trimmed beard—believed that he himself needed no introduction. The son of a distinguished Buffalo attorney, he was directly descended on his mother's side from one of the Hudson Valley's great landed patroons, Chancellor Robert Livingston of Clermont Manor, a man who had once vied with Alexander Hamilton for the privilege of starting the first bank in the state of

New York. After service as the chief cashier of the Bank of Buffalo, Cornwell had realized the dream of many cashiers and founded a bank of his own. Situated in a rambunctious, expansive community like Buffalo, his new City Bank proved an immediate success. With an initial capitalization of $300,000 it had, by the end of its first year in business, accumulated new deposits worth more than $1 million. But despite his stern demeanor and his well-filled waistcoat, Cornwell was no ordinary banker. He quickly acquired a wider reputation as the founding chairman of the Buffalo clearinghouse. He was, as any successful businessman ought to be, good with figures. But he also had a great way with words. He was the author of numerous books

In the 1870s, obscure painters like Eduard Manet and Edgar Degas congregated at the Café de la Nouvelle Athènes in Montmartre. (Watercolor by William DeM. Rolland)

about the problems of banking. He was the creator of the so-called Buffalo Petition, a document used to good effect by bank managements across the country in the bitter struggle to repeal the Sherman Silver Purchase Act of 1890. In the fall of 1893 Cornwell had delivered a learned disquisition on "Currency Reform" to the American Bankers Association at its annual convention in Chicago. And only the previous month he had spoken to Buffalo's prestigious Liberal Club on the importance of the gold standard.

Yet for all his conventional success there was also an unorthodox—some might say Bohemian—streak in William Cornwell's character. He was interested in literature, and in art. Though born and raised in Buffalo he had traveled to Paris as a young man in the early 1870s, at the termination of the Franco-Prussian war. There he had enrolled in the Académie Julien, a noted school set on the upper heights of the Passage des Panoramas, and studied painting under some of the masters of the time. After a hard day's work with palette and brush at the Académie, it was the custom of Cornwell and his fellow students to stroll down through the alleys of Montmartre for a glass of wine at the Café de la Nouvelle Athènes, where they might converse among themselves and with obscure artists like Édouard Manet, Edgar Degas and Paul Cézanne. The work of these provocative "impressionist" painters had been banned from the walls of the city's most influential galleries. Cornwell and his friends found such outcasts eager to sell some of their finer paintings for a bottle of Montrachet and perhaps fifty American dollars, cash on the bar. Even now, at the age of 43, Cornwell occasionally surprised his acquaintances in Buffalo by conversing with foreign visitors in fluent French.

Today, however, Cornwell spoke to his visitors in plain English. The minutes of this meeting in the City Bank's boardroom survive. Though they do not yield a verbatim account of every statement made, they undoubtedly reflect the general tenor of the discussion that took place. All was not well with America, Cornwell noted. Since the panic of the previous spring some 15,000 businesses and 94 railroads—constituting more than 30,000 miles of track—had collapsed, together with 158 national banks, 172 state-chartered banks, and 177 private banks. Many savings institutions had also been pulled under. During the last winter unemployment throughout the country had risen to at least two and a half and perhaps three million. In the state of New

York conditions were even more severe, with one man in three out of work. Just last September Governor Flower had noted at the New York state fair that, while surrounded "by the best products of the harvest season," it was difficult for his audience to understand "that in other parts of our state men and women, deprived of work, see destitution and misery confronting them."

Many of the poorer people of the cities had gone hungry and cold while farmers, unable to market their products due to depressed prices, were feeding their fresh milk to the hogs and using their corn crop—now selling for a paltry 30 cents a bushel—as fuel to heat their homes.

The nation had not endured such anguish since the catastrophe of the War between the States. Yet with little or nothing being done to resolve the crisis, matters could only get worse. The United States, Cornwell told his visitors, was "pounding along like a great ship on the ocean, with the engines at their utmost, politics at the wheel, ignorant of our bearings, and liable at any moment to collision and disaster." If matters were not put upon a saner course, the country could soon find itself thrust into a second—and perhaps far more bitter—civil war. This time region would not be pitted against region, but class against class, those who have versus those who have not.

The signs were everywhere. Labor disputes, once susceptible to reasonable discussion, now often erupted in violence. Anarchist bombs were detonating in parks and public meetings. In Ohio a popular agitator named Jacob Coxey was assembling an army of unemployed men to march on Washington. There were ugly rumors of trouble brewing in the coal mines of Pennsylvania, and in the factories of the Pullman Company, which made railroad cars in Chicago. Just last year a fanatical anarchist named Alexander Berkman had nearly taken the life of Henry Frick, the president of the Carnegie Steel Corporation. Only the intervention of two carpenters, who happened to be working in the next office, broke up the bloody melee. Today's street ora-

Waters of the barge canal and Lake Erie join in the foreground of this nineteenth-century skyview of "rambunctious, expansive" Buffalo. (Lithograph by J. H. Colen; Stokes Collection, New York Public Library)

tory—Marxist, populist, anarchist—frequently advocated outright revolution. A charismatic young speaker named Emma Goldman had recently exhorted a crowd of thousands down in New York's Union Square to demand work, and food. And if the members of the assembled crowd could not obtain them peaceably, then, she said, they should launch a direct assault upon "the citadels of money and power." The young *pasionara*, aged 24, went on to tell the wildly cheering crowd that "necessity knows no laws."

Necessity knows no laws. Perhaps Cornwell repeated the ominous words for emphasis. He had heard that kind of talk before, when he'd been a student in Paris in the 1870s, during the days of the Commune. The young banker-to-be had witnessed numerous skirmishes around the barricades, as citizen fought citizen. Eventually, when the government's troops forced their way back into the City of Light, more than 17,000 French civilians perished at the point of a bayonet.

Were the people of America now about to suffer a similar fate? Hadn't Henry Adams, the celebrated historian who was also the grandson and the great-grandson of presidents, recently declared, "For a thorough chaos I have seen nothing since the War to compare it with. The world surely cannot long remain as mad as it is, without breaking into acute mania. Everyone looks on his neighbor as a dangerous lunatic."

Would crowds like those in Union Square, and inflammatory speakers like Emma Goldman, soon be gathering in the squares and parks of upstate

This baroque two-dollar silver certificate, created under act of 1886, was "receivable for customs, taxes and all public dues." The cherubs, representing electricity and steam, are presenting their gifts to the matriarchs of commerce (left) and manufacture. (Martin Gengerke, Stack's Rare Coins, New York)

New York? Would the orators conclude their speeches with an exhortation to assault the premises of nearby financial institutions, always a ready target in the minds of the dispossessed?

Surely, said Cornwell, looking at each of his visitors in turn, this was the time for all the banks of New York to stand together. They must form an association—call it the New York State Bankers Association, if you will—that would enable each bank, when in trouble, to have the influence and the strength of all. For a moment Cornwell glanced down at the notes before him. At present there were 534 state and national banks doing business in the state of New York. Together, with the private banks, they had a combined capital and surplus of $200 million. The amount of business done each year, he declared, just about equaled the business done by banks in *all* the other states combined. Such an association could, if its members were able to agree upon a common program, work to change the nation's financial structure.

Cornwell's visitors must have asked him about the American Bankers Association, founded back in 1875. Why establish a new group when an organization capable of speaking for bankers throughout the country already existed? In response Cornwell probably pointed out that this was precisely the problem. For all its merits the ABA—and he was himself a regional vice president—represented all the bankers in the country, many of whom endorsed the idea of "free silver." Cornwell and George Levi, a distinguished banker from Texas, had presented the case for sound money on numerous occasions, including an address to the entire convention in 1893. But no agreement on a clear course of action had emerged. Indeed, the feeling among many of the more thoughtful members of the association was one of exasperation. Here Cornwell smiled. This exasperation had grown so pronounced that his old friend George Levi had taken to calling the ABA "simply a mutual admiration society" and "an autocratic . . . star chamber organization" only marginally interested in the concerns of its membership.

The present state of social unrest and its underlying economic dislocations

could, in Cornwell's view, all be traced back to the flood of "fiat money"—artificially created currency with no direct basis in real value—that now sluiced through the foundations of America's financial system. "The Fiat principle," Cornwell told his visitors, "is to a nation what the whisky habit is to men." For how long could this drunken rampage be allowed to continue? In the three decades since Abraham Lincoln's death, the Congress and the U.S. Treasury had between them created, by government fiat alone, more than $900 million of circulating currency. Most of the new money was composed of paper greenbacks, legal tender notes not fully backed by gold,

and coins, each of which contained a quantity of silver worth less than 60 percent of its face value.

These artificial dollars, maintained Cornwell, were not merely inflationary. They also provided a classic example of Gresham's Law: bad, or unsound money, drives out good money. While American debtors had for years insisted on paying their bills in the inflated paper and silver currency, their creditors—including many European investors in American securities—had been equally determined to collect in gold, or its equivalent. The Treasury had been caught squarely in this monetary vise. As Cornwell's visitors were well aware, the drain on bullion had, on April 22, 1893, pushed the U.S. government's gold reserve below the $100 million minimum mandated by law. Eleven days later, on May 3, three Wall Street brokerage firms failed. Their collapse was followed by a sharp drop in the price of industrial stocks, and a nationwide run on banks.

"It was fear about the Gold Reserve that made the panic of 1893," Cornwell told his listeners by way of summary. "The Reserve is the big barometer of the commercial atmosphere. Everybody in this country and in Europe is forever anxiously watching it; the capitalist, the money lender, the bank manager, the business man—always looking in the newspaper to see how the Reserve stands; and all smile or look sorry as it shows high or low. If below the limit the question from day to day is, 'What shall be done?' Enterprize wilts; business stops short; Europe sells our securities; we are in the gloom of coming storm."

True, President Cleveland and Congress had, after a bitter battle, repealed the Sherman Silver Purchase Act in November of 1893. But that did not alter the fact that nearly $900 million worth of "fiat money"—mostly greenbacks and silver dollars—was still circulating in the nation's bloodstream; another panic could occur at *any* moment!

Such a ramshackle system must be changed. It was an embarrassment. Last year the influential *Bankers' Magazine* of London had looked down its nose at the United States and declared that the "Americans are a people of magnificent achievements and of equally magnificent fiascoes. At present they are in the throes of a fiasco unprecedented even in their broad experience."

The financiers of the world, said Cornwell, gaze at the United States "in mild amusement at the spectacle of a great people, tolerating, nay clinging with childish affection to such a system; they look on, but since 1890 the capitalists of Europe have taken good care to avoid investing with us, and this they will continue to do until our temporary insanity is permanently cured."

Today, signs of such insanity were everywhere. Of those present in the boardroom, Frederick Barker of Syracuse was probably the most firmly opposed to the idea of mixing politics and banking. Yet he acknowledged that, in moments of great crisis, the two could not be separated. Back in 1879, as a young man of 28, Barker had been called upon to act as the court receiver of the recently suspended Oswego City Bank. He vividly recollected the anger and the bitterness of the depositors, who had lost their all, and the manifest shame of Mr. DeWolf, the bank's president. As Barker's examination later proved, DeWolf was neither a fool, nor a criminal. Indeed, he had been described by a local newspaper as a man "of large means and a shrewd business capacity." And yet his bank had failed. The incident had reinforced Barker's inclination to go "by the book" in everything he did as cashier of the Gere bank. But the collapse of the Oswego institution left him with the apprehension that even the most punctilious adherence to the book might not be sufficient to prevent disaster. By their very nature, panics and crashes struck like a bolt from the blue upon the heads of the incompetent and competent alike. Perhaps, if the bankers of the entire state coordinated their efforts, it might be possible to devise a system that would be less hazardous to men of sound judgment.

William Cornwell's proposal for a separate—and perhaps competing—statewide organization doubtless provoked additional questions from his visitors. How much would it cost to get such a group established? And how could the members of an organization, spread as they were over such an immense geographical area, meet together on a regular basis? Yes, the Empire State Express had recently made the run from Grand Central to Buffalo in the record-breaking time of seven hours and six minutes (average speed: 61.4 mph). But many sizable communities throughout the state still had no railroad connection. Unless a man saddled his horse, contact with the outside world depended on the dilapidated stagecoaches, which were frequently hard pressed to make more than two miles in an hour over back-country roads.

But, as some of Cornwell's visitors undoubtedly pointed out, there was an even greater difficulty. Such an association could hardly succeed without the active support of the major financial institutions in the city of New York: why would the presidents of the lordly First National, and the Hanover, the Manhattan, and the Chase wish to attend monthly meetings and rub shoulders with the officers of such marginal operations as the Bank of Antwerp

The "Big Three" of American Banking:

Left, James Stillman, president of National City Bank of New York, inhabited "a Temple of Silence." (Citibank Archive)

Center, George F. Baker, president of the First National Bank of New York, was known as "the Sphinx of Wall Street." (Baker Trust)

Right, Pierpont Morgan, senior partner of J. P. Morgan, "harbored an abhorrence of notoriety." (Pierpont Morgan Library)

near the Canadian border, and the Lumberman's Bank of Wilmurt, up in the wilds of Herkimer County?

The big banks had little to gain from such an arrangement. And for their part the smaller upstate banks frequently viewed the city banks with suspicion. Indeed, those suspicions often extended to all banks outside their immediate community. As things stood, bank presidents in neighboring counties were often ignorant of each other's names. Even when institutions were situated in adjoining townships their cashiers might go for a lifetime knowing each other, as the quaint phrase had it, "by signature alone."

Perhaps that was just the point, replied Cornwell. If the individuals in remote areas had a forum in which to meet, they could confer on such common interests as the establishment of uniform procedures, prevention of crime, and—this was the topic of the hour—what they felt were unjust rates of taxation in comparison to those levied on the new bank trusts. By meeting face to face they could also establish fraternal contacts, and exchange views on the political and economic issues of the day.

A lively discussion ensued. It is highly probable that at some point Henry Brewster, cashier of Traders National, intervened. A contemporary portrait shows him to be a man with a full and somewhat shaggy beard. The eyes, framed in gold-rimmed spectacles, were those of an individual who, while capable of firmness, had experienced a measure of sorrow. Back in 1863 Henry, then aged 18, had been drafted by lot into the U.S. Army. However, Simon Brewster, the young man's father and, incidentally, president of the Traders, had a different idea and ordered the butler to keep Henry locked in his room until the youth—to his abiding humiliation—agreed to pay a substitute to serve in his place. Three decades later, old Simon still ruled with an iron hand. But as cashier Henry, at the age of 49, now held responsibility for most of the day-to-day operations of the bank.

The only way to ascertain the appeal of a statewide organization, Henry Brewster told Cornwell, was to canvass the presidents of banks throughout New York. Let us send out a letter over our joint signatures asking them if they wish to participate. If there was a strong response in favor, said Brewster, then he would be prepared to hold a second meeting at his residence, a palatial establishment on Rochester's fashionable East Avenue, sometime in April or in May; at that time Brewster would also endeavor to persuade one or more of the big Manhattan banks to send a representative to confer with the members of the present group.

No suggestion could have delighted Cornwell more. Traders National had substantial dealings with most of the major Manhattan banks. Brewster was himself a member of New York's prestigious Union League Club. This, together with the fact that the Brewsters of Rochester were directly descended from the Brewsters who arrived on the *Mayflower*, ensured that Henry would receive a full hearing in the executive suites of the city's largest banks.

Brewster would undoubtedly experience his trickiest moments in the office of James Stillman, president of the giant National City Bank at 52 Wall Street, and that of George F. Baker, president of the First National Bank at 2

Wall Street. The popular press frequently referred to these two men, together with the merchant banker J. P. Morgan, as "The Big Three of American Banking." Both Cornwell and Brewster knew that without the blessing of this close-knit triumvirate the proposed association had little chance of acceptance by the other major city banks.

Getting the approval of Stillman and Baker, however, would not be easy. Like their friend Morgan, they viewed anything that smacked of "politics" and "publicity" with abhorrence. Such apprehensions would eventually drive the ascetic and cerebral Stillman to cultivate a wraithlike anonymity; now, though in the midst of a quiet but relentless campaign of merger and acquisition that would make the City the largest bank in the U.S., he seldom attended public functions. Much of his work was performed not in the office but alone, late at night, in his palatial brownstone at 9 East 72nd Street. Though an early riser, Stillman seldom entered the bank before eleven in the morning, and his arrival was sometimes so unobtrusive and diffident that it went unrecognized by even his most senior employees. Following a boisterous childhood in Brownsville, Texas, and a successful career as a cotton broker, it seemed that Stillman had finally found his calling. "After 1893," declared an early biographer, "it is the truth that the Bank, in James Stillman's mind, had become an article of religion." His new mode of worship was neither rowdy nor demonstrative. Indeed, noted the same admirer, it was much like that of a mystic, for the eminent banker now "made his home in the Temple of Silence."

The robust and cheery Baker was clearly the most accessible of the three financial triumvirs. On warm summer mornings it was his pleasure to ride to work down Broadway in the back of an open carriage, accompanied only by a brown and white terrier called Peggy. When he reached the corner of Wall Street a waiting city policeman would halt all traffic as the carriage made a U-turn in front of the First National. Each day many pedestrians stopped and marveled as the great man, walrus mustache bristling, stepped down onto the sidewalk and made his way into the bank that would, after 1899, pay stockholders an annual dividend of 100 percent on their invested capital.

Getting in to see the genial Baker would not be difficult. But persuading him to say anything that might constitute a pledge of support would be a major challenge for he, too, had made a career of taciturnity. Widely known as "the Sphinx of Wall Street," the president of the First National Bank was said to have made only two public speeches in his entire life, both no longer than a single paragraph. Even when relaxing among family and friends, Baker was against idle chatter. "Everyone should reduce his talk," he once advised a garrulous visitor. "Silence uses less energy. I don't talk because silence is the secret of success."

Up in Buffalo, the strategists around the boardroom table of the City Bank decided that if Henry Brewster could use his connections and his gruff charm to track down the elusive James Stillman and persuade both him and George

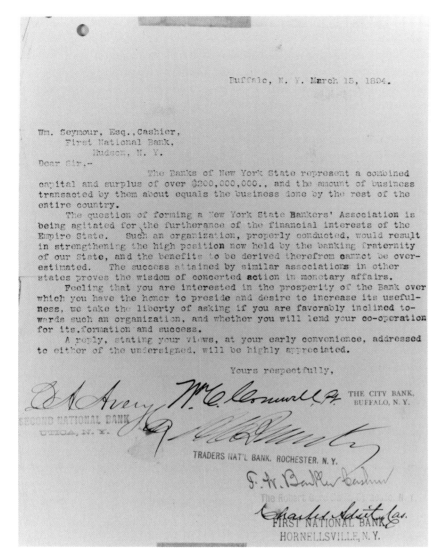

"The Call" for the formation of the New York State Bankers Association was signed on March 15, 1894. (Photo by Joshua Nefsky; New York State Bankers Association Archive)

Baker to utter a few words of benediction, then the idea for a New York State Bankers Association had some chance of succeeding.

After Cornwell had entertained his visitors with an ample lunch at a nearby hotel—perhaps the Robinson or the White Elephant, just across the street—it is likely that the party returned to the boardroom to work out an appropriate wording for the letter that would go out over their five signatures to some two hundred bankers across the state (see above). This founding group of bankers would, in the minutes of all subsequent meetings, be respectfully referred to as "The Signers of the Call."

Later that afternoon, after the departure of his guests, William Cornwell locked up his papers and closed the door of his office. He bade porter Harry Lewis and bank detective Alf Winkleman good day and then strode off down

Main to the Pennsylvania Railroad terminal. Unlike many of the city's successful executives, Cornwell chose not to reside in the fashionable Colonial Circle district on Buffalo's north side. Instead he and his wife Marian decided, at a time long before "commuting" became commonplace, to make their home at Rushing Water, an elegant 57-acre country estate situated some 20 miles out of town, near the leafy village of East Aurora.

In all probability, Cornwell purchased a copy of the *Buffalo Evening News* to read on the train. Not all the news was good. The warm weather, declared the headlines, had fomented a new outbreak of typhoid fever in the city's south-side slums; the cause, said the city's health commissioner, was probably the drinking of contaminated water from the Bird Island Reservoir. In other news a court ruled that a Buffalo clergyman named Pfitzinger could not be charged with libel for calling his bishop "a bad egg" in print. Further afield, Governor Flower had issued an order requiring the mass resignation of the entire Troy, New York, police force which, the *Evening News* said, was composed of known "thugs and murderers." A series of lectures on women's suffrage in Albany had concluded with an address by a Mrs. Howell. The paper noted that Coxey's army of unemployed, now gathering in Ohio, would begin their march on Washington in about ten days. It also noted that a band of thirty "desperadoes" in Marfa, Texas, had chosen a less peaceable way of keeping the wolf from the door by boarding and driving off with an entire freight train belonging to the Southern Pacific Railroad.

On the far side of the Atlantic ocean, Queen Victoria serenely embarked on the royal yacht for an extended holiday in Florence, where her party would reside at the villa of Count Faffricotti. In Russia, the czar's special police had broken into a house in St. Petersburg and surprised some Nihilists hard at work "manufacturing infernal machines." In the ensuing struggle a young female Nihilist shot two policemen dead. Three Nihilists also died in the shoot-out, and the remainder, including the young woman, were "bound and taken to the Citadel."

A horse and trap customarily awaited William Cornwell when he stepped off the train in the little station at Whaley and Main in East Aurora. A few minutes later he rode through the gates of Rushing Water.

Marian and William had built the house in 1885 for use as a summer place, but it soon became their year-round residence. Its commanding feature was a great stone tower, three stories high and some 30 feet across, attached to the southeast corner of the building. This massive structure, with echoes of Lord Tennyson's Camelot, stood high upon the cliffs overlooking the river. Behind the tower lay the main part of the house, its steep roof buttressed by two large stone chimneys in the French provincial style. A broad wooden porch, open to the summer breezes, extended from the western end of the building. Off to the north, beyond the circular gravel driveway and the extensive fish pond, lay a carriage house capable of accommodating four large horse-drawn vehicles side by side. On the villa's southern prospect a wide lawn ran to the edge of the wooded gorge where, more than 60 feet

below, the waters of Cazenovia Creek roared by on their way down to Lake Erie.

It was the sight, and the sound, of this torrent that inspired the Cornwells to name their house "Rushing Water." It was the first sound they heard when they awoke in the mornings, and it was the last sound they heard when they fell asleep at night. The house not only gave William a welcome respite from the clangor and confusion of the city; its serene atmosphere also afforded him an opportunity to paint, and to research and write such volumes as *The Currency and the Banking Law of the Dominion of Canada*, subsequently published by G. P. Putnam & Sons. Here, also, he wrote *What Is a Bank?* and *Greenbacks, the Source of Our Troubles*, pamphlets that sold tens of thousands of copies nationwide.

The house still stands today. Perhaps the book-lined study, entered through a door set just to the right of the mansion's huge main hearth, should be viewed as the true birthplace of the proposal that would eventually culminate in the formation of the New York State Bankers Association.

Life at Rushing Water was seldom dull. Marian Cornwell, the daughter of a prominent physician, was noted for her hospitality. The Fourth of July was generally celebrated with a champagne party on the lawn. As president of the Buffalo Society of Artists, William welcomed many sculptors, musicians, and actors to the house. Dinner parties were noted for their intellectual ferment. Bankers and successful businessmen might find themselves seated across the table from painters, and writers like Elbert Hubbard, the founder of East Aurora's Roycroft Community. Topics of discussion might range from the brilliant but controversial essay written by a young professor named Frederick Jackson Turner entitled "The Significance of the Frontier in American History" to the economic impact of the huge new electrical generating plants that had just been installed at Niagara Falls. Guests might also expect to be asked their view of Thomas Edison's new invention, a "kinetoscope" that allowed audiences to watch moving pictures. An enterprising mechanic named Henry Ford had just road-tested his newfangled "auto-mobile." The revelations of the Lexow Committee, investigating police corruption in New York City, must also have been a topic of concern, as was the "revolution" fomented against the queen of Hawaii by the Machiavellian U.S. envoy to those islands, John L. Stevens.

The only dinner topic likely to be even more controversial than the parlous state of the American economy was the validity of the fashionable yet disquieting credo of "social Darwinism," as espoused by Herbert Spencer and his wealthy American followers. Society was a jungle, they claimed. Only the fit can—or ought to—survive. The poor, the sick, and the unemployed were "unfit" and must therefore go to the wall. Spencer's teachings about the elimination of the weak inspired John D. Rockefeller to compare his oil trust to a rose in that it could only "bring cheer to its beholder by sacrificing the early buds which grow up around it." These teachings also hardened the attitude of many other businessmen toward the plight of manual laborers.

At Rushing Water discussion of such controversial topics was always forthright, and sometimes vehement, much in the style that Cornwell had learned—and mastered—as a student in the cafes and bistros of Montmartre. After the crash of May 1893 the leading topic of conversation became the troubles that beset the American economy.

Why was it, Cornwell and his friends wondered, that times of prosperity were *inevitably* interrupted—as surely as night followed day—by times of panic and depression? In the present century alone New York's banks had been struck by major "panics" in 1819, 1837, 1857, 1873 and now again in 1893. Surely the advent of these disasters, with their awful cost in human and economic terms, could not be purely arbitrary? Somewhere, lurking in the mountains of data assembled by the economists, there must be a logical explanation, a predictable pattern that might be used to eliminate—or at least to soften—the impact of future panics and crashes.

What were the true causes of these terrible downswings, and how could they be averted? That, certainly, was the root question. Every visitor seemed to have his or her own pet solution to the problem. Get government into banking. Get government out of banking. Take all the national banks' paper currency, and replace it with a federal currency that could be expanded, and retracted, at the behest of the Treasury. Retire the greenbacks. Withdraw the silver. Bring back the Bank of the United States, the "great hydra-headed monster" that President Andrew Jackson had slain back in 1836 . . .

After all the visitors had gone home, Cornwell often sat in his study, the sounds of the creek in his ears, and read deep into the night. Like researchers before him, and those who would follow him, Cornwell pored over a maze of graphs that plotted every conceivable variable—bank deposits, prices, velocity and amount of currency in circulation, gold reserves—against every

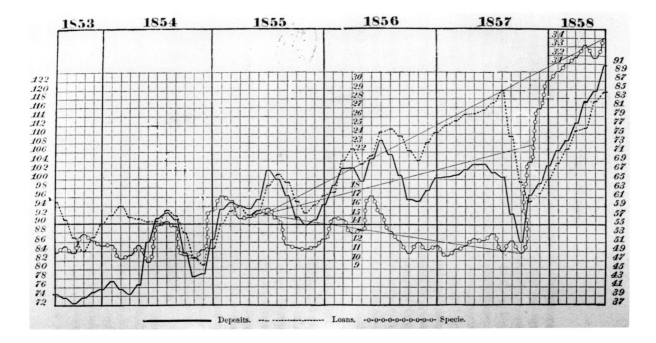

——— Deposits. --- ------------ Loans. -o-o-o-o-o-o-o-o-o- Specie.

other conceivable variable—levels of investment, unemployment, inflation, tariffs, taxes and foreign trade.

Somewhere, lurking among these jostling data, lay an explanation that could clarify the similarities and connections between the panic years of 1819, 1837, 1857, 1873, 1893. Cornwell did not believe such crashes were inevitable. Nor did he accept the fatalistic logic of the French writer Clement Juglar who argued in his new book, *Of Commercial Crises*, that "the riches of nations can be measured by the violence of the crises they experience." Juglar's topsy-turvy reasoning seemed to suggest that the road to ever greater riches lay in a nation's willingness to endure crises of ever greater violence.

Panics and crashes were, by their very definition, unpredictable. No matter how many economic data were assembled in the wake of the previous crash, the next crash always came as a surprise. In many ways the future crash, the one that had yet to occur, resembled a great Bengal tiger stalking its prey through the forest; when the tiger finally pounced it always—*always!*—caught its victim unawares. George F. Baker, president of the fabulously successful First National Bank of New York, had once been asked how it was that a person of his unrivaled experience could not, somehow, predict the economy's peaks, and its valleys. "No," replied the great financier, "you can't know because *every time is different*."

Bank presidents and cashiers were the soberest and most level-headed of men. Yet most of them would admit that, at one time or another, they had felt the presence of the tiger lurking nearby, awaiting an opportunity to strike. William Cornwell had himself felt the creature's breath upon his shoulder on a number of occasions. Just last summer many of the biggest banks in the

Could the cause—and the cure—of the nation's periodic panics and disastrous crashes be divined from a close study of charts like this? (James Gibbons, The Banks of New York, 1858)

city of New York had been thrust into a state of partial suspension when they adopted "the extreme measure of refusing to cash the checks of their own depositors." Only the intervention of the New York Clearing House, and its decision to issue $38 million worth of its own certificates, had prevented the collapse of the nation's financial system.

Like most bankers in the eastern states, William Cornwell believed that the federal government—with its flood of greenbacks, its debased silver and its penchant for political log-rolling—was quite incapable of maintaining a sound banking structure. From its very nature, he argued, the government "is as unfit to issue the circulating medium required by commerce as would be the faculty of a young ladies' seminary to conduct a great war." Only banks could effectively manage a currency that would be both secure, i.e., convertible to gold, yet elastic enough to accommodate unexpected surges in demand without panic and collapse. With such a currency the banks would curtail both inflation and the wilder flights of speculation. They would not, of course, be able to eliminate panics altogether, but such a currency would dampen their impact; it would, in short, impose a sharp limit upon the size of the forest in which those great beasts might stalk—and ambush—their victims.

Since Washington was unlikely to surrender such authority of its own accord, it would also be necessary to create a political constituency—like the New York State Bankers Association—powerful enough to thrust any proposed new structure into law.

On June 16, 1894, Henry Brewster assembled the Signers of the Call—as they had come to be known throughout the state—at his residence in Rochester. The news was good. Of the 171 responses received by that date, 4 banks were unfavorable, 14 were favorable if the proposed association "could be made a success," and no fewer than 153 were downright enthusiastic. The big banks, after some initial foot-dragging, also approved. James Stillman's National City was in, as was George Baker's First National. The Big Two seldom spoke for attribution. But in the elephantine body language of the day, the message from the granite fortresses at No. 2 and No. 52 Wall Street was clear: the idea of a new organization, wholly independent of the American Bankers Association, was *sound*. In the upshot more than eighty big city banks, including the Chase National, the Bank of New York, the Chemical and the Manhattan Company Bank, approved the proposal to form a statewide banking association.

In addition James M. Donald, chief cashier of the Hanover National, had come as an emissary from the city to present a proposal to the meeting in Rochester. After some deliberation, Mr. Donald declared, the downstate banks had concluded that their huge conglomeration of resources might have the effect of overwhelming some of the smaller upstate institutions. Therefore, he said, the city banks wished to present a proposal that the banks of the state be divided, depending on their location, into eight, or perhaps nine, geographical regions. Each area would be made up of five or six neighboring counties, thereby permitting the bankers of a particular area to meet, if they chose, on a frequent basis throughout the year. After some discussion a subcommittee was appointed to draw up a constitution. And it was also decided to hold the first convention on August 15 and 16 at Saratoga Springs.

J. H. DeRidder, cashier of the Citizens National Bank in Saratoga Springs, then undertook to arrange accommodations, with the convention's headquarters at the Grand Union Hotel. Guest speakers at the Saratoga convention would include James H. Eckels, comptroller of the currency, and Charles M. Preston, superintendent of the New York State Banking Department. Even those who had not yet resolved to join the new organization were invited "to come to this meeting and consider the matter." August 15, 1894, was a mild, cloudy day in Saratoga, with patches of sunshine occasionally cutting through the overcast. Temperatures, though warm (high: 76 degrees Fahrenheit) were not oppressive. While almost three hundred banks had indicated their interest in joining the NYSBA, only seventy-five were able to send a representative to this first convention. Rooms at the Grand Union and the United States Hotel would be $5 a night, $4 a night at the Windsor and Congress Hall and $3 at the Worden, the Adelphi and the American. Special railroad tickets, at two-thirds the normal rate, could be secured through the Trunk Line Passenger Association.

In his opening address Eckels launched a frontal attack on the notion of a silver-based currency. If it is to serve the nation, he said, all currency must "be worth the full face of the value which it purports to carry." Silver was the

root cause of today's social unrest, and so long as it remains in circulation "so long will the springs of populism and socialism be fed, and the country's welfare menaced, and the earnings of capitalist and laborer made the constant prey of legislative folly." This sally stirred the listening bankers to prolonged applause.

Unlike William Cornwell, Eckels seemed to entertain an almost fatalistic attitude toward panics; hardship and an element of financial chaos were, he asserted, "inevitable." Eckels believed the people themselves were often responsible. When panics were caused by "overtrading, undue speculation and extravagance" they could not be avoided "as long as the people set in motion the forces in which they have their origin." Indeed, the bankers themselves were often responsible for the trouble since, "by granting credit too liberally" they were setting afoot "a thousand schemes that must end in ruin." The audience apparently greeted these remarks with stony silence.

A partial solution to these problems could be had, said Eckels, by strengthening the powers of the U.S. Treasury; this would, at least, ensure that no panics occurred as the result of "vicious monetary legislation" by the Congress. At the same time, such a move would enable the Treasury to forestall the present raids by European banks upon the dwindling U.S. gold reserves. The government's financial strength should be beyond question, Eckels declared in conclusion. It must be second to none.

In his inaugural address as the newly elected president of the NYSBA, William Cornwell echoed Eckels's somber theme. The U.S. government, he said, must somehow create a central banking authority that would be able to hold its own with the central banks of Europe. Neither Cornwell nor Eckels chose to tackle the difficult question of just how this authority was to be constituted. Nor did they speculate on how its power would be asserted in a way that did not antagonize the people, as Nicholas Biddle's Bank of the United States had antagonized them in the 1830s. But, like Eckels, Cornwell clearly believed that a central authority must be preeminent. "No one ever accused the Bank of England of being too strong," he said. Yet the paradox remained. How could one create—without the lapse of centuries—an institution that, while dispensing wise and timely prescriptions in the economic arena, had the objectivity and the stamina to survive the most bitter criticism in the political arena?

The primary concern of the new bankers association, he asserted, was to increase its membership, and therefore its power to effect favorable legislation. The result would be for the benefit of everyone "for who does not drink in new life when the golden sun of prosperity is shining?"

The superintendent of state banking, Charles M. Preston, then gave the bankers a stern lecture on the Do's and Don'ts of sound banking in the state. If his examiners did a careless job when they came around to look at the books, the bank's officers must not hesitate to inform the superintendent's office. Likewise, the bankers must take care not to make loans secured by their own stock. State banks must standardize their methods of keeping accounts and rendering monthly statements to their customers. Preston's audience did not applaud when he warned them that they must not, lest they wished to suffer great embarrassment, borrow "large amounts of money on their own personal account" from their banks.

After these admonitions Preston went on to point out that while New York's 331 federally chartered banks had the right to issue national currency notes, the two hundred-odd state chartered banks had no such right. While he did not favor the repeal of the 10 percent tax on the old state-issued notes, he did believe that state banks, with a total capitalization (plus surplus and profits) of more than $60 million should, upon depositing appropriate security, also be permitted to issue federal notes. Since passage of the National Bank Act in 1864, the tax—now one percent—imposed on circulating currency by the Comptroller of the Currency had produced a surplus, after all expenses had been paid, of $42 million. This fund, he maintained, should be used to secure the currency of both state and national banks alike. "Under this arrangement," argued Preston, "the currency would not only be uniform, but it would be elastic, and every incorporated bank in the country would receive it, State as well as National."

Like Eckels, Preston left his listeners in a somber mood. The only light touch was probably unintentional. Toward the end of his speech Preston announced that recent events in Europe had revealed the existence of a nefarious conspiracy among the monarchs of Germany, England, France

The bankers assemble, August 15, 1894. William Cornwell, with cravat and long dark coat, is standing in front of the garden seat to the right. Henry Brewster stands on his left. In all likelihood the craggy-faced man in the tweed suit to Cornwell's right is the convention's guest of honor, Comptroller of the Currency James Eckels, while the youngish man in the light suit on Brewster's immediate left is probably State Superintendent of Banking (and archconspiracy theorist?) Charles Preston. (Photo work by Joshua Nefsky: New York State Bankers Association Archive)

and Russia. These conniving gentlemen, Preston claimed, had become bitterly jealous of the United States. The success of American commerce "has stupified every king and courtier of Europe." Now, Europe's central bankers believed the time had come "for suppressing this great influence of United Statesism." The royal conspirators, it seemed, planned to drain away more than $300 million of America's gold reserves "by accumulating the yellow metal on an extensive basis."

Such a dastardly plot might have come straight from the pages of the popular novelist E. Phillips Oppenheim. "The shipments [of gold] have been made to England for a while; then of a sudden there has been a change to France; then unexpectedly to Germany, Berlin and Vienna has been the drawee, between whiles Russia has loomed up." All this sinister activity had convinced the superintendent that "there has been a well understood plan of campaign against the United States."

Talk of such a conspiracy emphasized the helplessness and bafflement with which Preston and Comptroller Eckels—both known for their sound and sober judgment—viewed the panic and crash of 1893, the latest in what seemed to be an unending series of devastating panics and crashes. Both men appeared to have resigned themselves to the idea that such phenomena were inevitable and beyond the realm of human control. Though he said nothing at the time, William Cornwell clearly did not agree.

In the weeks after the convention the new Council of Administration under the chairmanship of Cornwell met repeatedly at the Windsor Hotel in New York. The Council, forerunner of the NYSBA's Governing Council today, comprised the association's four top officials, elected statewide, and the chairmen of the nine regional groups. The Council's concerns included the creation of a uniform monthly statement for bank customers, the elimination of the tax advantages granted to trust companies, and protection against crime. However, at this point the council's primary concern remained the challenge of expanding the membership. Printed copies of the convention speeches were circulated to all banks in the state. By November, 311 of the 534 eligible banks had joined, in addition to 14 private banks.

Predictably, the strongest interest came in the urban areas at the eastern and western extremities of the state, with the Buffalo area (Group I, with 62 percent), Rochester and Finger Lakes (Group II, with 77 percent) and Manhattan and Staten Island (Group VIII, with 82 percent). The lowest level of interest came in Long Island (Group IX with 40 percent) and the huge center strip of the state, running from Ogdensburg on the St. Lawrence to Delaware County on the Pennsylvania line (Group V with 37 percent). Over the winter of 1894–1895 the association picked up another 25 banks, which brought the overall total to 350. By the convention of 1895, the total had jumped to 389.

On December 29, 1894, William Cornwell delivered an address before the Reform Club of New York entitled "A Way Out." This moment was, in many ways, to be the high point of his career. The speech, in which he outlined his proposals for the restructuring of the nation's financial system, was extensively covered by the major newspapers. The U.S. Treasury, he suggested, should issue $500 million worth of 2½ percent Gold Bonds. Banks throughout the country would be encouraged to purchase these bonds. As they were sold, the Treasury would use the proceeds to retire the so-called legal tender currencies of greenbacks and silver dollars. Then, on depositing these gold bonds with the Treasury, a bank would be permitted to issue its own notes up to 150 percent—a significant increase on the current 90 percent—of the value of the bonds deposited. The proposal was roundly applauded by the members of the Reform Club. Two days later the *New York Times* wrote an editorial in which it declared that "Mr. Cornwell's plan has great merit of being the first that embraces the essentials of a sound system of bank currency, ultimately independent of the Government, and, with this, the sure disposal of the legal tender notes."

In the months that followed, Cornwell worked hard for the acceptance of this proposal. When the NYSBA held its second convention, in July of 1895 again at Saratoga Springs, he included in the roster of visiting speakers an address by B. E. Walker, the general manager of the giant Bank of Commerce in Toronto.

Walker, perhaps at Cornwell's urging, performed a courteous but lethal dissection of the current American system of banking. The chief problem, Walker told his audience, arose when President Jackson "ruthlessly destroyed" the second Bank of the United States under Nicholas Biddle. Since then banks of the United States "are numbered by the thousands, have individually small capital and no branches." At this very moment, he told his American audience, their southern and western banks needed capital for all manner of enterprises. And the eastern banks had the necessary funds "but there is no machinery for bringing them together." The system was absurd. In contrast, the major banks of Canada, including his own, had forty or fifty branches across the country. The Bank of Commerce "gathers deposits in the quiet unenterprising parts of Ontario, and lends money in the enterprising localities" thereby permitting both the quiet and the enterprising communities to prosper.

As required by the NYSBA's constitution, Cornwell stepped down as president at the end of this meeting, to be replaced by James G. Cannon, vice president of the Fourth National Bank of New York. In the months that followed Cornwell returned to his desk at the City Bank in Buffalo, changing its charter to make it the City National Bank in 1899; he and Marian resided at Rushing Water where William continued to paint and write books and pamphlets that advocated banking and currency reform.

Alas, William Cornwell's story did not have a very happy ending. When Buffalo was chosen as the site for the Pan-American Exhibition of 1901, the City National Bank made some loans for the speculative purchase of certain tracts of real estate near the exhibition grounds. In its statement of June 1, 1901, the bank declared deposits of $3,872,584 and total resources of $4,695,859. Yet some two weeks later the federal examiner sternly warned the bank that it had made a number of individual loans each amounting to more than 10 percent of its capital, and that it had thereby "over-stepped restrictions imposed by law." City National, wrote the examiner, must take immediate steps to set things straight.

Despite its best efforts, the bank had not extricated itself from the questionable loans by Friday, June 28, 1901, and the comptroller of the currency ordered the bank placed in receivership. For William Cornwell the tiger that stalked through the nightmares of every banker had finally leapt from the shadows. On the following Monday, City National's offices on Main Street were crowded with anxious depositors, seeking the return of their money. Several policemen stood at the door but the crowds of account holders were, for the most part, orderly. The scene, wrote an *Evening News* reporter, was one of "suppressed excitement" and "the atmosphere of the place was the peculiar, indescribable condition which always follows an affair of this sort." William Cornwell, the bank's president, "could be seen in his private office, next to the street, but denied himself to everybody."

For Cornwell the humiliation was complete. The noted apostle of sound banking, the man who had "gained a very high reputation for mastery of correct principles of finance through his published writings" now sat, caged in his office, as a crowd of sullen depositors glared at him through the front window of his collapsed institution.

Cornwell made no attempt to reopen the bank. But the harsh experience reaffirmed his conviction that all banking, to be sound, must rest squarely on the established value of gold. When the affairs of the bank were finally settled, he retired, at the age of 50, to the sanctuary of Rushing Water. During the winter months he and Marian traveled to France and England. While in London Cornwell became a member of the Athenaeum Club. Four years later, the Cornwells put Rushing Water up for rent and moved to New York, where William began to edit a weekly journal entitled *The Bache Review* for the J. S. Bache Co. The publication became an eloquent and forceful advocate for the retention of the gold standard. Cornwell followed the proceedings of the fledgling New York State Bankers Association closely. In the wake of the so-called Bankers' Panic of 1907, he helped establish a group called the National Reserve Association. In 1911 Cornwell wrote a widely circulated pamphlet for this group that argued for "a cooperative organization of banks that will give us the results of European experience without the creation of a central bank." In many ways this association represented an embryonic Federal Reserve System, with banks across the country clumped together in fifteen independent regional associations, loosely connected under a national headquarters with offices in Washington. The directors of the regional and national boards would be elected by the member banks, each of whom would become a part of the association by subscribing an amount equal to 20 percent of its capitalization.

Though little is known about the final days of the preeminent Signer of the Call, it is clear that he retained a lifelong concern for the future of banking. He was free with his time, and his advice, for the younger men coming up in the profession. In 1900 he requested, and received, a grant of $10,000 from the American Bankers Association to establish an organization he would call the Institute of Bank Clerks. The purpose of the group, of which Cornwell became the first president, was "the educating of young banking men." Later, at his suggestion, the name of the group was changed to its present title of the American Institute of Banking. From its founding to this day the institute has provided graduate and postgraduate programs of the highest quality for those working in the profession.

William Cornwell, by now a widower, acquired the handsome mansion at 41 Washington Square where he is known to have resided until his death, at the age of 80, on May 11, 1932. Besides helping the profession improve its skills, Cornwell also retained more than an academic interest in painting. Indeed, shortly after the conclusion of the Great War, it is known he sought a patent for a process called "Lumina," which achieved artistic effects by presenting arrays of colored paper on a glass screen. As a point of pride he used to attend the annual meetings of the New York State Bankers Association whenever his health permitted.

2

The Speculators

THE SUMMER of 1783 was a time of feverish activity for the leaders of Europe and one of suspense for those of America. King Charles III of Spain put aside his customary torpor and initiated an intrigue to acquire Gibraltar and the distant territory of Florida. After years of prevarication, Catherine, empress of Russia, decided to abolish serfdom among her people and—in the same rare mood of liberality—extend diplomatic recognition to Britain's thirteen rebellious colonies. Her gesture was not appreciated by King George III of England who, despite a painful attack of gout in his right foot, bestirred himself in a last-ditch effort to discredit his own government in its efforts to negotiate a treaty with the American peace commissioners in Paris.

On the far side of the Atlantic, however, George Washington found he had time on his hands. The fighting was over. He and his officers had no more campaigns to plan, and no more charges to lead. The negotiations in Paris had dragged on for months now, with no end in sight. Each day, despite the summer heat, the commander in chief gamely shuffled through an unending stream of paper at the army's headquarters, situated high on the cliffs above Newburgh, New York. But enough was enough. Sometime in the middle of July Washington wrote to a friend that he had "concerted with Governor Clinton to make a tour to reconnoiter . . . the northern part of this State."

The expedition would enable him to check on frontier defenses against the distant—yet provocatively situated—British garrisons still occupying the

strategic lakeshore port of Oswego and the lower reaches of Lake Champlain.
At the same time it would permit the general and the governor to explore the
new lands, with their vast commercial possibilities, that the state of New
York was about to acquire from King George III (see front endpaper).

The great tour began on July 18 when Washington, Clinton and a small
party took their mounts across the river on the Newburgh horse ferry and
rode up the eastern bank of the Hudson. The bristling pace set by Washington did not surprise his aides, but it must have presented a severe test of his
friendship with George Clinton; despite the summer heat the group was to
travel, in the next eighteen days, a distance of more than 750 miles, some of
it by boat and much of it over wilderness trails or narrow forest "traces" from
which only the underbrush had been cleared.

Washington had first met George Clinton back in the spring of 1775,
when the future governor had journeyed to Philadelphia as one of his
state's representatives to the Continental Congress. In many ways Clinton
resembled his fellow delegates. He was in his thirty-sixth year—four years
older than Thomas Jefferson and three years younger than Patrick Henry—
and, as a direct descendant of the second Earl of Lincoln, he had some blue
blood in his veins. But unlike many of his colleagues from the South,
Clinton had been forced to make his own way in life, first as a land surveyor
and then as a lawyer in his native Ulster County, on the west bank of the
Hudson River. Ever since he stood up to defend a radical pamphleteer
named Alexander McDougall on the floor of the New York provincial
assembly back in 1770, Clinton had harbored no illusions about the sanctity

of the British Crown; King George, and all his posturing toadies, must be sent packing. Indeed, he swore at the time he'd "rather roast in hell to all eternity than be dependent upon Great Britain or show mercy to a damned Tory."

While in Philadelphia it was clear that the burly, outspoken Clinton was no intellectual, prepared to challenge Adams or Madison on the finer points of constitutional law; but his warm heart and his forthright manner had made him a firm favorite with the small landholders and tradespeople of New York. From the beginning Washington and Clinton—both straightforward men of action—had taken a liking to one another. When Clinton was appointed to the post of brigadier in New York's militia, they worked together on plans for the defense of the Hudson valley. Now, six years later, the two men rode side by side up the eastern bank of that same river. Their friendship, forged in the flames of war, would endure for the rest of their lives. But their differing visions of how the brave new world that unfolded before them should be settled—and developed—were destined to involve succeeding generations in wrangles so profound and so far-reaching that they would not be resolved for half a century, and more.

The party crossed the Hudson again two days later at Cohoes Falls, just above Albany. They paused for a while beside "the Mineral Springs at Saratoga"; indeed, both men were so impressed with the possibilities of developing the spring that they laid plans to purchase it for themselves, along with thousands of adjoining acres. After surveying Bemis Heights, the site of the great victory over Burgoyne in 1777, the riders continued north to Lake George, where they left their horses and embarked in "three light Boats" to paddle and sail down to Fort Ticonderoga and then on to Crown Point on the wooded shores of Lake Champlain.

It is difficult for modern travelers to appreciate the raw, untouched splen-

dor of the scenes that greeted the eyes of Washington and Clinton. Some hint of their pristine grandeur, however, may be conveyed by the descriptions of a young Harvard historian named Francis Parkman, who trekked with knapsack and canoe through the lakes and forests of the upstate region sixty years later, long before the advent of the smokestack and the souvenir stand. A visitor, Parkman noted, might glide in his canoe on the waters of Lake George "under a silent moon or in the languid glare of a breathless August day, when islands floated in a dreamy haze, and the hot air was thick with odors of the pine."

Washington and Clinton were awed by the pristine grandeur of Lake George, "where islands floated in a dreamy haze, and the hot air was thick with odors of the pine." ("Dawn of Morning, Lake George" by Jasper Cropsey, 1868; Albany Institute of History and Art)

Lynx and brown bear still roamed freely through the virgin forests to the north and the west, and at night the spectral howl of the timber wolf might cause even a seasoned outdoorsman to push back his blanket and reach for the bayonet or the loaded musket that lay ever at his side. For all their lurking peril, however, such scenes were a world away from the carnage of war. Washington and his party were entranced.

On arriving at Crown Point, the commander in chief issued a few crisp orders as to how the dilapidated fort and that at Ticonderoga could be strengthened and supplied more effectively. Then he turned the little convoy south again to Putnam's Point, where the grooms had brought the horses. The party disembarked and rode overland to the village of Schenectady, and then west up the northern bank of the Mohawk River to Fort Stanwix, which stood in the wilderness just a dozen miles to the east of Lake Oneida. Four years earlier Clinton had ordered the Mohawk surveyed in the hope that a

The Speculators

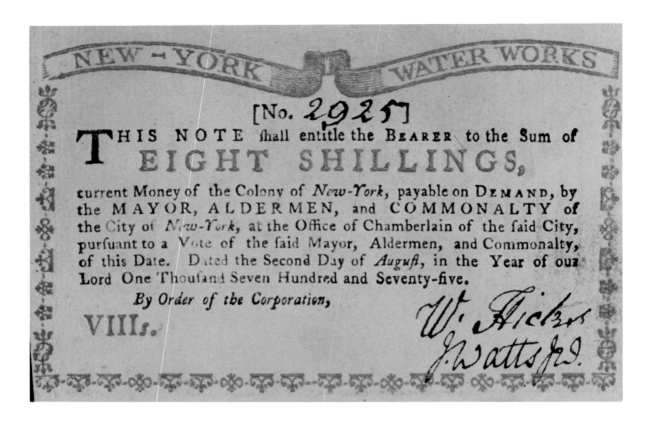

NEW - YORK WATER WORKS

[No. 2925]

THIS NOTE shall entitle the BEARER to the Sum of
EIGHT SHILLINGS,
current Money of the Colony of *New-York*, payable on DEMAND, by
the MAYOR, ALDERMEN, and COMMONALTY of
the City of *New-York*, at the Office of Chamberlain of the said City,
pursuant to a Vote of the said Mayor, Aldermen, and Commonalty,
of this Date. Dated the Second Day of *August*, in the Year of our
Lord One Thousand Seven Hundred and Seventy-five.

By Order of the Corporation,

VIIIs.

By the end of the war this eight-shilling colonial note, issued by the city of New York in 1775, could have purchased a dozen acres of prime real estate for George Washington and Governor Clinton. (Martin Gengerke, Stack's Rare Coins, New York)

canal might be built to bring fresh water to the growing community at Albany. Now, as he and Washington rode along the river's banks, they discussed the possibility of a larger canal project that would permit the passage of vessels carrying heavy cargoes.

"Prompted by these actual observations," Washington later wrote enthusiastically to a French nobleman, "I could not help taking a more contemplative and extensive view of the vast inland navigation of these United States." He went on to speak of the importance of improving the network of natural waterways already dealt to the region by the hand of Providence. Then the former land surveyor and future president concluded his letter with these fateful words: "I shall not rest contented until I have explored this Western Country, and traversed those lines (or a great part of them) which have given bounds to a New Empire." It is said that this avowal by Washington caused New York to be known, henceforth, as the Empire State.

Fort Stanwix (situated in what is now Rome, New York) also intrigued Washington. Up until now it had marked the westernmost limit of the territory of what was generally called "Old New York." Under a solemn agreement made in 1763 between the Iroquois Indians and the agents of George III, Stanwix marked the line beyond which land speculators and settlers of European origin must not venture. Soon—if all went well in Paris—those restrictive royal compacts would be worth no more than the parchment on which they were written.

Washington and Clinton were so intoxicated by the sight of these new territories unfolding before them that they discussed yet another joint enterprise; this time they were to purchase the land on which Fort Stanwix itself stood, together with much of the surrounding acreage. After resting a day or so on the uppermost reaches of the Mohawk, the party rode down to what is now Cooperstown at the foot of Lake Otsego, and then made its way up through Cherry Valley—still badly scarred from the Indian attack of 1779—before returning to Newburgh, which Washington reached on August 5. It is not surprising, after such an equestrian feat, that he found his poor horses to be "so much Fatigued that they will need some days to recruit."

When the American peace commissioners eventually signed the Treaty of Paris in September 1783, it inspired an immediate "rage of land speculation" throughout America. The acquisition of the territories to the west and to the north of Albany more than tripled the size of the state of New York. Washington and Clinton failed to purchase the Stanwix tract and the mineral springs at Saratoga, but they did jointly acquire a spread of some 6,000 acres on the southern bank of the Mohawk, just below what is now Utica, New York. Unlike many of those that followed, both men were experienced surveyors with a shrewd eye for land, and the investment proved very profitable. Purchased for about eight pennies an acre, the undeveloped woodland was divided into lots of 100 acres, and resold for between one and ten New York shillings an acre, depending upon quality of the parcel. Before his death in 1799, Washington had received back more than double his original investment while still retaining 1,000 acres of prime property, estimated to be worth 5,000 American dollars.

Major investors from Paris, Rotterdam and London were quickly drawn into the game by the prospect of such returns, as were some of the most

The Speculators

prominent Americans of the day. These included Robert Morris, the shrewd superintendent of the nation's finances during the years of war, Aaron Burr, and Alexander Hamilton. Baron von Steuben, Washington's drillmaster, acquired 16,000 acres in Oneida County. The Livingston family already held large tracts in the Mohawk valley, and were now eager to expand their holdings in the new territories. William Bingham, a rich merchant in Philadelphia, acquired thousands of acres in what is now Broome County, where he laid out the city that would one day bear his name. Two Englishmen, David Parish and Sir William Pulteney, also bought thousands of acres in the northern and western parts of the state, as did Judge William Cooper, father of the novelist James Fenimore Cooper. In all, the Board of Land Commissioners sold speculators and their wholesale agents, the so-called land jobbers, more than 5.5 million acres between 1786 and 1791.

The state also granted 1.5 million acres to military veterans. Some soldiers attempted to clear and settle these 600-acre tracts but more often they gave an additional thrust to the speculative fervor by selling their warrants to the ever-acquisitive land jobbers. The Holland Land Company, financed by four Dutch banking houses, acquired all the 3.3 million acres west of Batavia in addition to some sizable tracts in Madison and Oneida counties. At the same time many of the larger estates along the Hudson, previously owned by Tory magnates, were broken up and sold to the hundreds, and sometimes thousands, of tenant families who had worked them over the years.

But the boom was short lived. The loose confederation of states—symbolized by its grossly debased currency, now worth but two cents on the dollar— seemed to lack both the authority, and the resolve, to thrust American

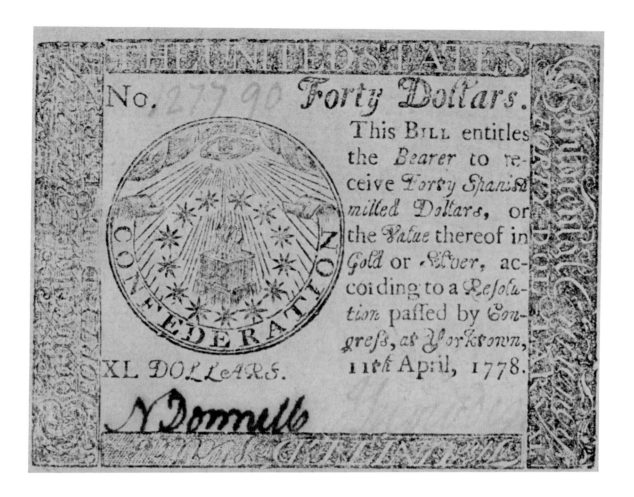

This forty-dollar Continental bill, issued in 1778, would be worth a mere eighty cents by the end of the Revolutionary War. (Martin Gengerke, Stack's Rare Coins, New York)

merchants into the more lucrative postwar markets of Europe and the West Indies. New York City, with its dependence on mercantile trade, was particularly hard hit. The departing Loyalists depleted the local economy further by taking with them an estimated £1.5 million in bullion and gold coin.

But the Americans were not without resources. On February 22, 1784, in a bold search for new markets, the 360-ton clipper *Empress of China* tacked her way through the ice floes in the East River, outward bound for Canton, China, via the Cape of Good Hope. The crew of the heavily armed vessel, commanded by the formidable Captain John Green, included "many young gentlemen of good family" whose seamanship had been "tempered by the exigencies of the privateering service." In the years ahead this epic fifteen-month voyage to the Orient—launched amid the devastation of war—came to typify the optimism, the hard-headed perspicacity and the unbounded enterprise of the banking community of New York. The *Empress* traded a cargo of small manufactures, ginseng, and Spanish silver for a hold filled with elegant china crockery, cases of tea and boxes of fine-spun silks for the ladies of Europe and America. Total expenses for the momentous venture

amounted to some $120,000, an investment that would eventually yield its financial backers a net profit of $30,700.

The state's merchants and financiers also sought to subvert the embargo on the West Indian trade by having their ships surreptitiously unload in harbors under the control of Dutch and Danish authorities. Later a small fleet of vessels from New York, bearing skillfully forged English documents, were to develop a prosperous trade with a number of Britain's Caribbean possessions.

Back in New York, wealthy citizens put a further drain on the state's hard currency by indulging a craze for English manufactured goods. True, the soldiers were gone, but after the drab years of war high society now demanded that its homes be filled with English furniture, English china, English books and English fashions. "In the dress of the women you will see the most brilliant silks, gauzes, hats and borrowed hair," declared a somewhat caustic observer from France. What their husbands lacked in fashion sense, he decided, they made up for in gluttony. "The men have more simplicity in their dress; they disdain gew-gaws but they take their revenge in the luxury of the table."

For the dirt-poor settlers flooding into the northern and western territories, however, it was a different story. Most of the new tracts were divided into townships 10 miles square. The cost of an uncleared parcel of 100 acres would typically run about £20 (or some $50), with a quarter of the money down and the rest due in 60 days. Some land jobbers, in a process known as "hothousing," sought to attract settlers by laying out roads, sawmills, schools, gristmills and even taverns. Inevitably, this would double or even triple the

initial cost of the new land. Many pioneering families lacked the acceptable currency with which to make the initial purchase, while others—no matter how hard they worked—lapsed into insolvency long before they could make their virgin acres produce a single crop. As the postwar economic slump deepened, many speculators, like Parish and Pulteney, lost a fortune. Judge Cooper became entangled in numerous lawsuits, and Robert Morris, after several disastrous years, saw his last 500,000 acres go at a sheriff's auction.

A leading cause of these speculative plunges was the absence of a stable, commonly acceptable medium of exchange. Each day New Yorkers were forced to settle accounts in a bewildering array of currencies that included everything from ducats, pistoles and dubloons to French Louis d'or, milled Spanish dollars and British guineas. Governor George Clinton, with the approval of the legislature, had issued £165,000 and then £200,000 worth of

state-backed bills in small denominations, but even these did little to dispel the monetary confusion and the general lack of credit in the state's postwar economy. Early in 1784 Chancellor Robert Livingston of Clermont Manor and several other major landholders called upon the New York legislature to approve an exclusive charter for a new institution, to be called the Bank of the State of New York. Its capital of $750,000 would be subscribed in shares of $1,000; each stockholder would pay one-third of his subscription in cash, with the remaining two-thirds to be secured by the pledge of land, appraised at no more than two-thirds of its market value.

At first glance the proposal seemed to have an excellent chance of passage. Though only thirty-eight years old at the time, Livingston was a figure of renown. Besides holding title, with his family, to more than 100,000 acres of land in Columbia and other upstate counties, he was known as a formidable lawyer, and had served with Jefferson on the committee charged with drawing up the Declaration of Independence. After his appointment as head, or chancellor, of New York's civil courts, Livingston had served a term as the country's first secretary of foreign affairs. He was also known for his disdain of ordinary mortals, and for his abrupt changes of mood. A contemporary described him as being "tall, handsome . . . with an abundance of hair, already grey, which fell in ringulets over a square high head."

The bank could be expected to offer farmers and other rural residents long-term loans, secured by land, at the rate of 4 to 5 percent per annum. This contrasted sharply with the 6 to 9 percent customarily charged by the few private bankers in the state. Predictably, when word of Livingston's proposal leaked out, it aroused considerable enthusiasm among the "country" members of the legislature, but others, particularly the wealthier residents of the city, were skeptical. Land, as future generations would learn to their cost, was an illiquid asset that might, with a small change in economic conditions, experience a sharp depreciation in value.

Alexander Hamilton, a young lawyer who had already made a name for himself defending the interests of Loyalists in the city of New York, cast a shrewd eye on Livingston's proposal and found it to be filled with "absurdity and inconvenience." Since the matter was already before the legislature, Hamilton quickly decided that it was necessary "for the sake of the commercial interests of the State, to start an opposition to this scheme."

At 6 o'clock on the evening of February 24, only twelve days after the proposal for the Bank of the State of New York first became public, Hamilton assembled a group of merchants and prosperous fellow lawyers at the Merchant's Coffee-House, situated on the southeast corner of Wall and Water streets. The gathering included many of New York's most prominent citizens, including John Vanderbilt, Nicholas Low, Joshua Waddington, Rufus King, Isaac Roosevelt, forebear of two future presidents, and Alexander McDougall, the fiery Scots pamphleteer whom George Clinton had single-handedly defended fourteen years earlier against the Royalist majority in the provincial assembly.

Also seated at the gathering was a young lawyer named Aaron Burr who, though Hamilton's friend and colleague at the time, would eventually become his deadly rival. The careers of the two men had run an eerie parallel. Both were in their late twenties at the time of the meeting in the coffeehouse. Both had outstanding war records. Both stood five-foot-six in their socks and both, it is said, held a magnetic appeal for women. Their courtroom styles, however, were quite different. "Of the two, Hamilton was perhaps the more profound, the more erudite, the more long-winded; Burr the more superficial, the more concise and the more successful." Burr, the son of the president of Princeton College, had an easy way with all classes of society while Hamilton, the illegitimate son of a merchant, had a thin, rasping voice, and his manners, noted a contemporary observer, were "tinctured with stiffness, and sometimes with a degree of vanity that is highly disagreeable."

When all was quiet in the coffeehouse, the twenty-seven-year-old Hamil-

Aaron Burr, son of the president of Princeton College, teamed with Hamilton on numerous court cases. Later, however, Hamilton feared he would undermine the Union. (Oil on canvas, probably by Vanderlyn, 1802; Chase Manhattan Archive)

ton rose to his feet and warned his audience that if they did not move swiftly, Livingston's proposal might soon become law; somehow, he said, the silver-tongued chancellor had bewitched the rural majority into believing that his bank was "the true philosopher's stone that would turn all their rocks and trees into gold." The truth of the matter was, of course, that such an institution closely resembled the notorious "land banks" of colonial days. In times of panic and financial crisis such banks—with only one-third of their capital subscribed in specie—lacked the liquidity to redeem their outstanding bills. And they certainly lacked the resources to help their credit-worthy but temporarily hard-pressed customers through the immediate crisis.

It is likely Hamilton also pointed out that, due to their close ties to the legislature, such land banks historically had often become highly politicized institutions, denying financial assistance to opponents while granting abundant favors—frequently in the form of hugely inflated property appraisals—to supporters. In the decades prior to the Revolution, noted Hamilton, such cronyism among its Royalist managers had caused the paper of the New York land bank to trade at 60 percent of its face value, while the notes of land banks in Massachusetts and North Carolina depreciated to one-fifth and one-tenth of their face values, respectively. Doubtless, some of the merchants present in the coffeehouse that night must have wondered if Livingston and his friends intended to use this land bank, as had the Royalists before them, as a great engine for the restoration of the landed aristocracy to a position of preeminence in the affairs of the state.

The best way for the merchants to finesse Chancellor Livingston's *land* bank, declared Hamilton, was for them to swiftly counter with a proposal of their own for "a Bank on liberal principles, the stock to consist of specie only." This *money* bank would be capable of initiating loans secured, not by mortgages on land, but by the short-term promissory notes that merchants and traders used in their day-to-day commercial transactions.

Alexander Hamilton undertook to draft the new commercial bank's constitution. The former firebrand McDougall—now mellowed by time and service as a major general under Washington—was elected leader of this rival venture. Perhaps, also, the assembled merchants hoped that McDougall's presence might still command some influence with his old mentor, Governor George Clinton. The capital stock of the institution, to be known as the Bank of New York, would be made up of a thousand $500 shares, for a total of $500,000.

Three weeks later, more than half the necessary subscriptions had been placed, and a board of directors was elected. The board then chose the boisterous McDougall president of the bank and William Seton, a Loyalist Scot who had remained in New York during the British occupation, became cashier.

On June 9, 1784, the Bank of New York opened its doors at the premises of the Walton House at 159 Queen's Street. The bank was an immediate success. While it did make loans on real estate, its primary business was the "discounting" of commercial paper at 6 percent. This meant, for example, that a storekeeper in Albany could order $1,000 worth of imported china dishes from a merchant in New York on April 15; the storekeeper would enclose with his order a written promise to pay the merchant the full $1,000 upon the safe delivery of the dishes on May 15. Without the facilities of a commercial bank, the merchant would have to dispatch the dishes and tie up his capital for the thirty days until May 15, before presenting the storekeeper's note for collection. With the Bank of New York in business, the merchant could ask its cashier, Mr. Seton, to "discount" the storekeeper's note the moment it arrived on April 15; if Seton knew the storekeeper to be a man of probity and substance then he would accept his promise to pay $1,000 one month hence, on May 15, while also presenting the merchant with a sum of $995 in cash now, on April 15. True, the merchant had not collected his full $1,000. But he had received the major part of it, which

could now be used—if he so wished—to place an order for another bulk shipment of china dishes from Paris or London.

While assuming the task of collecting the $1,000 from the storekeeper, the bank had earned $5 interest (or one half of one percent) for loaning almost $1,000 to the merchant for a month. If the loan were made for a year the interest on $1,000 would come to $60, or 6 percent.

Neither $5 nor $60 seems like much of a return but, as was customary in that day, the Bank of New York might issue up to $1.5 million worth of bank notes backed by the security of its capital of $500,000. Thus it was possible, if all its resources were put to work, for the bank to generate an income of $90,000 per year, or a gross return of 18 percent on the capital invested by its stockholders. In the process of discounting commercial paper, two additional advantages also accrued to the bank. First, a minor benefit, the bank was not receiving its $5 interest for lending $1,000 but for lending $995; and that interest was paid up front, at the moment the merchant received his payment.

The other advantage was more substantial. The merchant could, if he wished, take the $995 and place it in his office strongbox. However, it was far more likely that he would choose to leave most of those bank notes in his account at the Bank of New York while he prepared to purchase a whole new shipment of china dishes from the manufacturers in Europe. Though the notes deposited in that account belonged, technically, to the merchant, the bank could make use of their presence in its vault, within certain constraints, to engage in additional commercial ventures.

While Livingston's land bank proposal never reached the floor of the assembly, the unchartered and unincorporated Bank of New York did well from the day its doors opened. After only six months of operation it declared a dividend of 7 percent for its stockholders. Such a notable success, however, did nothing to improve relations between Hamilton and the haughty Robert Livingston, who began referring to his rival as an "adventurer . . . not native to this soil." Livingston also spoke scathingly of him as "a merchant's clerk from the West Indies," a reference to the fact that Hamilton had—at age 12!—once worked in a countinghouse on the Caribbean island of Nevis.

The Bank of New York sought, in vain, to obtain a charter of its own from the state legislature in 1785. Some of this failure was undoubtedly due to the envy of the Livingston clan. Much of it, however, arose as a result of a growing rift among the victors of the Revolution concerning the course that their new nation should steer. The Federalists, led by Hamilton and many like-minded patricians in other states, sought the creation of a country that enjoyed social order and a strong economy at home, while commanding respect abroad. In contrast the Republicans, led by Jefferson and Clinton, sought to create an agrarian Arcadia of small landowners who could work their farms and govern themselves without fear of interruption by a distant, imperial authority. A commercial bank, these Republicans believed, was a device employed by European monarchs to impose order upon their people and acquire, by a process of legerdemain, the fruits of their labors for the royal purse.

Many of the inhabitants of Jefferson's Arcadia were semiliterate. They dwelt in a world where Eve still lay with Adam in the Garden of Eden, a world in which mechanical clocks, steam power and Newton's laws of planetary motion were viewed with suspicion. In such a setting the theories of Professor Adam Smith, who spoke of abstractions like limited liability, negotiable instruments and free trade, were beyond human comprehension. And Smith's pronouncements about the utility of paper promises that amounted to three, four and five times the promiser's ability to pay were deemed to be both meaningless, and wrong. The best minds in the land had trouble appreciating the point of creating such a pyramid of credit. Indeed, notes the financial historian Bray Hammond, "to John Adams, as honest and intelligent a man as there was in the States, such a thing seemed a monstrous cheat. To Thomas Jefferson it was a swindle."

Governor George Clinton and his following of pioneer farmers, storekeepers and mechanics agreed. A chartered bank, while making three or four times more promises than it could keep, had the legal authority to take away a man's land if he broke so much as a single promise to that bank. Such a one-sided arrangement was unfair and contrary to nature. In short, any bank remained "a monstrosity, an artificial creature endowed with powers not

possessed by human beings." A bank, these agrarian republicans believed, was incompatible with the principles of true democracy. Yet without a bank the New York merchant could not deliver the order of china plates to Albany, and the local wheat factor would have trouble delivering the farmer's harvest to the warehouses of New York.

"For the most part, the interests of the Jeffersonians lay in the land, of the Hamiltonians in the cities," states Herbert Agar in his magisterial treatise *The Price of Union*. "An economy of factories and shipping lines and commercial paper needs the support of government more than an economy of land and horses and crossroads blacksmith shops. The former wants a strong government to enforce contracts; the latter prefers a weak government which will let it alone."

The people who worked with the horses and the land and lived at the crossroads knew that it was impossible to enforce a contract with Nature. Wheat did not ripen on a specified day, like a promissory note. Time may be money to the banker and the big-city merchant, but to the farmer it was ineluctably tied to the vagaries of the weather and the slow and frequently erratic passage of the seasons. "Were we directed from Washington," wrote

Thomas Jefferson, "when to sow, & when to reap, we should soon want bread."

The conflicting philosophies of Hamilton and Jefferson were to imperil the passage of the new Constitution in 1788 and they were, for better or worse, to plunge the institution of banking into the center of the the political cauldron and keep it there for centuries to come. While most other states approved the new Constitution, New Yorkers remained locked in acrimonious debate through the spring and summer of 1788. New York City and several federalist counties in the south threatened to secede. Even then, Governor Clinton yielded his grudging support only when he was assured that certain amendments (later known as the Bill of Rights) would receive swift passage. Two years later, after the dust had settled, the directors of the Bank of New York again sought a charter and were again rebuffed by the Clintonians in the legislature.

In 1791 Hamilton, now Washington's first Secretary of the Treasury, persuaded Congress to approve a twenty-year charter for the Bank of the United States. The new national bank would have a capitalization of $10 million and it would cunningly help the government bind the new Union together by assuming all legitimate debts incurred by the individual states during the Revolutionary War. While the bank's head office was to be in Philadelphia, plans were already underway for the opening of branches in other major cities, including New York.

The sudden appearance of Hamilton's financial juggernaut caused Governor Clinton to revise his strategy, if not his attitude, toward local banks. To prevent the federal bank from dominating the state's economy the legislature now granted a charter to the Bank of New York. At the time of its incorporation in 1791 the bank declared its total assets in specie to be $1.3 million plus £95,000 sterling. Indeed, the bank had by now become so prosperous that it paid its faithful cashier William Seton an impressive annual salary of $3,000.

By the early 1790s the newly settled lands in the upstate counties began to produce record quantities of lumber, grain, and corn. To facilitate trade along the Hudson, and to further dissipate the power of Hamilton's bank, Governor Clinton approved the charter of the Bank of Albany (capital: $260,000) in 1792, and the Bank of Columbia (capital: $130,000) at Hudson, New York, in 1793. These, however, quickly showed themselves to be Federalist in their political attitudes and their loan policies. Then Clinton and his supporters took a memorable step. Instead of fighting a rearguard action against the encroachments of Federalist power, they decided to turn, and attack the problem head on; if the state of New York has to have banks, they reasoned, then let them be *our* banks!

In the summer of 1798 the city of New York had suffered an epidemic of yellow fever that eventually carried off more than a thousand souls. The cause of the fever was thought to be the contaminated water that came up to the street pumps in many of city's poorer districts. It was decided to incorpo-

rate a new institution with a capitalization of $2 million, called the Manhattan Company, which would undertake to bring "pure and wholesome water" into the city by means of wooden pipes. Many citizens of substance, both Federalist and Republican, got behind the project. Aaron Burr, who had served as Clinton's attorney general for a while before defeating old Philip Schuyler in a run for the U.S. Senate, would steer the new venture through the Albany legislature.

After its charter in 1799, the Manhattan Company did, in fact, dig a number of wells in Lispenard Meadows, and one of the newfangled steam engines was employed to pump substantial quantities of clear water into the city. But the company also decided there was a future in the banking business and promptly opened an office for that purpose at 40 Wall Street. When the directors of the Bank of New York protested that this was a flagrant infringement of the Manhattan Company's charter, Burr smoothly referred them to Section 8 in the water company's by-laws stipulating that it might use its "surplus capital as may belong or accrue to the said company in the purchase of public or other stock or in any other monied transactions" not inconsistent with the laws of the land. Burr was subsequently accused of putting a fast one over on the Federalists, many of whom had voted for the bill. But that would not seem to be the case. Alexander Hamilton himself had read, and apparently approved, the original proposal. His brother-in-law, John B. Church, was associated with the venture, as was Gulian Verplanck, a former president of the Bank of New York. When a Senate committee had raised a

The dynamic polymath Elkanah Watson opened the New-York State Bank at 69 State Street in Albany. This institution played a leading role in financing the Erie Canal. Hooker's original portico (see next page) has been incorporated into the flagship office of the Fleet Bank of Upstate New York. (Oil on canvas by Ezra Ames, 1810; Albany Institute of History and Art)

question about Section 8, Burr had breezily explained that the directors "might have a bank, an East India Company, or anything else that they deemed profitable."

The Manhattan Company's banking activities, while remaining controversial, did alter the balance of business and politics in the state. According to one observer, the city's two established banks, "governed by *federal* gentlemen, were employed in a great measure as *political engines*. A close system of exclusion against those who differed from them on political subjects was adopted and pursued. There were but few active and useful Republicans that could obtain from those banks discount accommodations." The incorporation of the Manhattan Company, he argued, "corrected the evil. All parties are now accommodated."

Now the Republicans had a political engine of their own. And in 1800

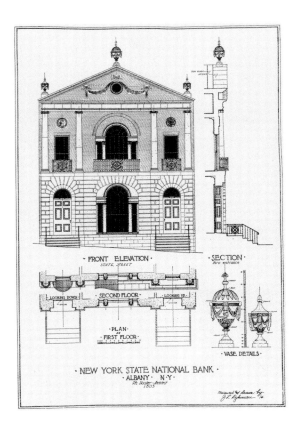

FRONT ELEVATION
STATE STREET

SECTION
thru entrance

LOOKING DOWN   SECOND FLOOR   LOOKING UP

PLAN
AT
FIRST FLOOR

VASE DETAILS

· NEW YORK STATE NATIONAL BANK ·
· ALBANY · N·Y·

Aaron Burr took matters a step further by using the bank's resources to buy land and thereby enfranchise many laborers in the city of New York. His loyal "martlings," as he called them, helped carry the state for Jefferson and to propel Burr, after some controversy, into the vice presidency. Two years later, when the new bank came under the direct control of the Clinton and Livingston families, it was discovered that Burr had run up a debt to the bank of $112,400.

In 1803 Hamilton attempted to organize a fourth bank, the Merchants Bank, in New York City. However, the agrarians in the state legislature had now learned that, while all banks might be pernicious monstrosities, some banks were clearly more pernicious than others. The legislators proceeded to deny Hamilton's request, while chartering—under the leadership of the dynamic polymath Elkanah Watson—a brand new Republican bank of their own, to be called the New-York State Bank of Albany, with its offices at 69 State Street. This institution, later known as the State Bank of Albany, was to become the "oldest bank in the United States continuously occupying the same location." In 1972, with its original portico preserved as a centerpiece of a new sixteen-story structure, the bank was to become the flagship institution of the Fleet Bank of upstate New York.

In 1804, one year after the bank's charter, Albany's Republican legislators were eager to prevent the Merchants and any other Federalist institution from operating without a state charter, as had the Bank of New York twenty

Richmond Hill, Aaron Burr's palatial mansion in Greenwich Village, inspired high living and equally high expenditures. (Citibank Archive)

years earlier. They therefore passed a "restraining law" that forbade any *association* of persons without a bank charter from "receiving deposites [*sic*], or discounting notes or bills." As will be seen, this did not prevent *individuals*, under common law, from doing a banking business on their own.

The incorporation of the Manhattan Company and the suppression of the Merchants probably put the seal on the rift between Hamilton and Burr. Twenty years earlier, in the first days of peace, the two brilliant young lawyers had seemed to many like Damon and Pythias. Though never formal partners, they worked as a legal team on numerous occasions. Hamilton's fees were impressive, but Burr's were often extraordinary; on occasion he would receive $2,000 or more for a single case. Even then, Burr's expenses often outstripped his income. He entertained lavishly at his mansion Richmond Hill which, together with its extensive lawns, occupied an entire block on what is now MacDougal Street in Greenwich Village. He also plunged heavily in real estate. Burr was accustomed to borrowing substantial sums from his richer clients, and on occasion—a telling revelation of character—he became querulous when they refused to renew their loans.

Sometimes Alexander Hamilton found himself serving as Burr's personal attorney in the latter's convoluted attempts to remain solvent. Once the slapdash Aaron accused "Sandy" of mislaying a document. "I distinctly recollect," replied Hamilton icily "that . . . Winship's mortgage was returned

Sketch of a raffish, middle-aged Burr who, undismayed by debts and political defeats, continued to claim that the ideas of English radical William Godwin had the power to liberate society and "unshackle the mind" from conventional values. (Citibank Archive)

to you." Relations cannot have improved when Burr decided to run against Philip Schuyler, Hamilton's father-in-law, for the U.S. Senate.

By today's standards, the final falling out came over a seemingly trivial incident. In 1804 Hamilton, perhaps still smarting over the Manhattan Bank and the Merchants Bank fiascos, quietly employed all the influence in his power to prevent Burr's election to the governorship of New York. He'd had the dubious privilege of witnessing Burr's maneuverings over money and women from a ringside seat. And he knew Burr to be a political opportunist who greatly admired the English radical William Godkin. "If we have an embryo-Caesar in the United States," Hamilton noted, "'tis Burr."

Even if the embryo-Caesar were not seizing power in Washington he might, if elected governor, abet New England's half-formed plan to secede from the federal Union. Hamilton's quiet campaign worked, and Burr lost the election. But he became suspicious of Hamilton's role when he came across a letter addressed to Philip Schuyler from a certain Dr. Cooper, saying that Alexander Hamilton "looked upon Burr as a dangerous man, and one who ought not to be trusted with the reins of government." Cooper archly concluded his note by saying that he could, if called upon, "detail you a still more despicable opinion which General Hamilton has expressed of Mr. Burr."

When this letter subsequently found its way into the columns of the *Albany Register*, Burr wrote to Hamilton demanding the "acknowledgement or denial of the use of any expression which would warrant the assertions of Dr. Cooper." Hamilton replied that it was impossible to confirm or deny the

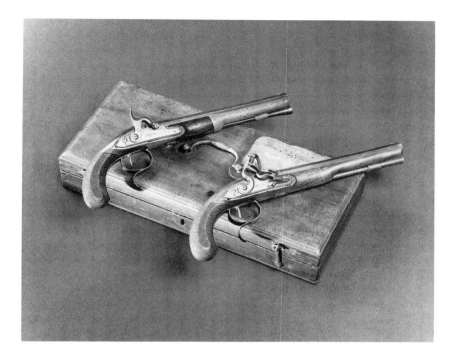

utterance of an expression that was so vaguely defined. He then inexplicably concluded his letter with the words, "I can only regret the circumstances and must abide the consequences." Under the eighteenth century's archaic code of honor this was the lethal phrase used by gentlemen who wished to challenge an opponent to a duel. Burr wrote again for clarification. Hamilton offered a statement saying his conversation with Dr. Cooper had turned purely on political topics, and did not relate to Burr's "private character." Burr deemed this proposal unacceptable and a meeting, with loaded pistols at ten paces, was arranged for the dawn of July 11 on the cliffs of Weehawken, New Jersey.

In retrospect it is amazing that these two middle-aged men—former friends and both profoundly learned in the law—could not have figured a way out of this fatal encounter if it had pleased either of them to do so. Unlike Burr, who had just lost a bruising campaign for governor, Hamilton had everything to live for. He had seven children, the youngest a toddler aged 2. Even more perplexing was the fact that the Hamiltons' son Philip had died just three years earlier in a similar "political" duel fought on the same stretch of the Weehawken shore. At the time the bereaved father had pronounced himself thoroughly opposed to the practice of dueling. So why did Hamilton, in responding to Burr's original inquiry about his "despicable opinion," gratuitously conclude his note with the time-honored challenge of the duelist?

It is unlikely that the true motivations of the participants will ever be known. But certain facts pertaining to the pistols have lent a sinister cast to the whole encounter. The weapons were provided by John B. Church,

In the fatal encounter on the shore at Weehawken, New Jersey, Burr (facing away) fired first, mortally wounding Hamilton, who died in great pain thirty-one hours later. (Chase Manhattan Archive)

Hamilton's brother-in-law. Made in London by the famous firm of Wogdon, these were the same pistols that failed young Philip Hamilton in his own lethal exchange three years previously. How then, one wonders, could the elder Hamilton even bring himself to touch—let alone stake his life upon—the weapons that had killed his son?

The answer to this question was revealed in 1974 when the Chase Manhattan Bank, the present owner of the pistols, requested a master gunsmith in Italy to replicate the weapons for display in the U.S. bicentennial celebrations. When the gunsmith dismantled them he found that they were equipped with a secret hair-trigger mechanism. If Hamilton pushed the trigger forward before pulling it back, the pressure required to discharge the weapon would be reduced from ten pounds to one-half pound, thereby markedly improving the weapon's aim. Thus Hamilton's opponent, though he held an identical weapon in his hand, would find himself at a significant disadvantage. Was this, then, the reason for Hamilton's strange eagerness to challenge Burr? It wouldn't be a fair fight, exactly. But it would *seem* fair. And there wasn't too much risk. All he had to do was to draw a swift bead on Burr and fire, thereby ridding America of its embryo-Caesar forever.

When finally squared off against his opponent at Weehawken, Hamilton found that he could not see too well in the morning sunlight and decided to wear his spectacles. On the given command Burr beat Hamilton to the punch, and fired first. Struck just above the right hip, Hamilton collapsed. His own shot is said to have gone wide, into a nearby tree. Burr moved forward as if to assist his fallen opponent but was pulled back by his seconds. The mortally wounded Hamilton was then carried gently down to the boat that would carry him back across the Hudson. Burr clambered across the rocks in a renewed attempt to speak to Hamilton, but was again restrained by members of his party. The former Secretary of the Treasury was taken to the home of William Bayard in Greenwich Village where, after suffering great pain, he died thirty-one hours later.

The news became public when a handwritten notice was pinned to the door of the Tontine Coffee-House. Popular feeling ran strongly against Burr, who left his mansion at Richmond Hill and took a rowboat over to Perth Amboy and thence overland to St. Simons Island, off the coast of Georgia, where he is said to have spent the rest of the summer in hiding. Later he was accused of leading a conspiracy to detach several southern territories from the Union. Burr lived for thirty-two more years "suspected of plotting treason, enduring penurious exile, returning to lasting disrepute."

The founding of the Manhattan Company and the death of Hamilton were events that foreshadowed the end of the Federalist party, and many of the ideas for which it stood. Though it had once viewed itself as the champion of business enterprise, the party realized that it could no longer dominate nor even control the economic forces that now began to break loose in the land. A new kind of economy, a new kind of business leader and a new kind of bank, with a management that had a distinct outlook of its own, now began to emerge. It is true that a remnant of the old Federalist party "was to linger on, monied and ineffective, while its young men flocked incongruously into Mr. Jefferson's Republican ranks and later into General Andrew Jackson's Democratic ones." Such young men, noted Bray Hammond, would make it possible for these two popular leaders "to clear the way for a new, larger, and more powerful class of money-makers than could have existed before enterprise became democratic."

3

The Great Projector

ONE MORNING late in the fall of 1807 a young jurist named Joshua Forman strode out of his frame house in the little village of Onondaga Hollow, kissed his wife Margaret good-bye, and mounted his horse for the long ride down to the statehouse in Albany. Judge Forman, aged thirty, could hardly be viewed as a typical hard-scrabble pioneer; he was, in the quaint phrase of the day, a "Projector," someone with an uncanny knack for conceiving and promoting startling new ideas in the field of commerce and industry.

Forman graduated from Union College in Schenectady in the late 1790s, before studying law in New York in the offices of the celebrated attorney Miles Hopkins. While there he met "under romantic circumstances" a young lady named Margaret Alexander, the daughter of a Scottish member of Parliament. Joshua and Margaret were married a few months later. But the Formans did not choose to settle in Manhattan, nor in any of its neighboring communities. Instead, the star-struck couple answered the call of the wilderness by voyaging up the Hudson River and then hauling their household possessions 120 miles west through the forest to the picturesque little village of Onondaga Hollow, situated in what is now Syracuse, New York. Through the uncleared forest, just one mile to the south, lay the ancestral lands of the Onondaga Indian nation.

Joshua Forman was a persuasive and resourceful attorney and his law practice, mostly concerned with land sales, prospered. First he was elected to the position of judge in Onondaga County, and then to the post of assembly-

The Great Projector
58

man in the state legislature. Now, in the fall of 1807, he was on his way to Albany. As he rode along the Old Genesee Road across Oneida County and down to the banks of the Mohawk River, he encountered another assembly-man, Judge Benjamin Wright, also bound for Albany. Before entering the law Wright had served as a land surveyor and an engineer. As the two legislators rode along the river bank and observed the resplendent autumn foliage, it is probable that they discussed what the future might hold for the sparsely populated lands that they had been chosen to represent in the state assembly. It is also probable that Forman told Wright about the rich saline deposits near his home, and how he had devised a way of obtaining pure salt by a mysterious process he called "solar evaporation."

By the time they had crossed the river again at Schenectady, and ridden on down to Albany, Forman and Wright had become friends. They arranged to share a room in a boardinghouse near the statehouse. The city, with its population of 8,000 and its new capitol being built on the hill above the Hudson, was already "a place of extensive business." While the legislature was in session, the city's inns and taverns were always crowded with an assemblage of office seekers, land speculators, influence peddlers, cardsharps, and religious visionaries eager to found a new Jerusalem somewhere in the wilderness off to the west. As the legislative session wore on, however, both Forman and Wright wearied of this tipsy carnival; eventually, in an effort to

Even in the early 1800s Albany, viewed here from across the Hudson, was a city crowded with "office seekers, land specu-lators, influence peddlers, card sharps and religious visionaries, eager to found a new Jerusalem somewhere in the wilder-ness off to the west." (Lithograph by De-roy from Milbert's Hudson River Views. Wallach Division, New York Public Li-brary)

FACING PAGE: Joshua Forman: "To hear him express an opinion was to be con-vinced." (Oil on canvas, artist unknown; Onondaga Historical Association)

The Great Projector

make the long winter nights a trifle more elevating, they decided to subscribe to a periodical called *Ree's Cyclopaedia*.

One evening, while reading the sixth issue of the magazine, Forman became excited over an article entitled "Canal." It was about the waterways of Great Britain. The point that particularly impressed him was that the English, under the observant eye of the visiting Benjamin Franklin, had discovered that instead of selecting river passages and attempting to render them navigable to barge traffic, it was cheaper to build canals, so to speak, from the ground up. "Rivers are ungovernable things, especially in hilly countries," Franklin had noted. "Canals are quiet, and very manageable."

After reading the piece several times, Forman observed to Judge Wright that, in view of President Jefferson's recent decision to spend the surplus funds in the Treasury on internal improvements, perhaps "something ought to be done to prevent the people of Pennsylvania from drawing away the trade of our state." Then Forman declared that he was "in favor of building a barge canal all the way from Albany to Lake Erie."

Judge Wright, who had once worked under the great English canal engineer William Weston, told his friend that "it would be folly" to build the last 150 miles parallel to "the good sloop navigation" offered by Lake Ontario. Forman countered that "the rich country through which it would pass would, of itself, support a canal." After a long, wrangling debate Forman somehow convinced Wright that such a project was feasible. Shortly thereafter the two men submitted a resolution to the assembly. Many legislators viewed Forman's proposal as a "wild and visionary project" but they voted for it anyway.

While survey parties sought to determine the best route for the waterway, Joshua Forman journeyed down to Washington to seek an interview with Mr. Jefferson. Part of his proposal, of course, was not new. Since the summer of 1783 when George Clinton and General Washington had ridden up the Mohawk River valley together, there had been talk of a canal that might link the Atlantic ocean to the waters of the Great Lakes. But Forman took the thought a huge leap further by suggesting a direct inland link to Buffalo and the wheat fields of the west. Indeed, if the canal were built it would sharply diminish Pennsylvania's incentive to construct a waterway from Erie, Pennsylvania, down to the upper reaches of the Allegheny. The economics of his proposal, Forman believed, were so sound that all it needed was the services of a determined and persuasive Projector.

Joshua Forman was nothing if not determined and persuasive. A contemporary portrait shows him to be a tall man with dark wavy hair and a large nose. The down-turned corners of the mouth carried with them a strong hint of humor, while the eyebrows seemed poised to flick up, at any moment, in ironic surprise. One acquaintance noted the power of Forman's "most winning smile"; at the same time "his manners were elegant, his demeanor dignified, and his conversational power of the rarest kind." Another observer noted that Forman's "voice was musical, and whenever he talked he had an audience." The master politician Thurlow Weed, no special friend of the assemblyman from Onondaga County, once declared that "to hear Judge Forman express an opinion was to be convinced."

On arriving in Washington, even then a city of rhetoricians, Judge Forman had to bring all his powers into play. After surmounting numerous obstacles, he finally obtained an appointment to see the president. Mr. Jefferson, himself the originator of many ingenious projects, listened to Forman with close interest. When the presentation was over, the president looked at the assemblyman from New York and said, "You talk of making a canal of 350 miles through the wilderness—it is little short of madness to think of it in this day." Jefferson seemed to sense Forman's disappointment, for he hurried on to say that the Erie Canal was still "a fine project, and might be executed a century hence." Perhaps Jefferson also divined that the federal government was well out of a venture that would, inevitably, pit the commercial interests of two major states against one another.

The assemblyman's response was respectful but firm. "The State of New York," he briskly informed the president, "would never rest until it was accomplished."

When he returned to Albany, Forman realized that most people were skeptical of New York's ability to raise the required $6 or $7 million on its own. But he kept on talking, and persuading. Among Forman's many converts was DeWitt Clinton, then mayor of New York who, after two treks through the western counties, became an enthusiastic supporter. The War of 1812 halted all internal improvements, but Forman never missed an opportunity on or off the floor of the assembly to point out how much stronger Fort Niagara, recently captured and now occupied by the British, might have been if it had been served by an inland canal. To haul a medium-sized cannon by wagon over the rocky turnpikes to Buffalo cost the state $1,600, or four times the value of the weapon. Barges, Forman rightly claimed, could have transported whole batteries of cannons at three times the speed, and one-tenth the cost.

But, even when the war was over, where was the money to come from?

Back in 1808, Jefferson had warned Joshua Forman that one hundred years might go by before sufficient funds materialized. And if 1808 was bad, then 1817 was worse. The country was submerged under war debts. In 1817 the state of New York had a total paid in banking capital of barely $15 million. Floating a loan of $7 million would be the financial equivalent in 1990 of having the state raise—without federal help—a sum of more than $200 billion.

But the size of the investment was not the worst problem confronting the canal's projectors. In New York most of the inherited wealth of the old Federalist families was now being sopped up in the purchase of stock in the second Bank of the United States, chartered the previous year. Foreign money markets did not look any better. The Dutch seemed cool, despite— or perhaps because of!—their expertise in canal construction. And the British, often a ready source of capital in the past, were surly. They'd fought the Americans twice now in the space of thirty years. And they were per-

The newfangled steamboat Clermont *prepares to dock at Cornwall-on-the-Hudson circa 1810; such ingenious mechanical innovations did much to break Britain's stranglehold over the budding American economy. (Gouache by Edward L. Henry; Stokes Collection, New York Public Library)*

turbed by the way the embargoes of 1812 had served to stimulate American manufacturing. Indeed, now that the war was over they were making it an article of policy to dump cheap textiles on to the hapless Americans. "It is worth while," Henry Brougham told the House of Commons, "to incur a loss on the first exportation in order, by a glut, to stifle in the cradle those rising manufactures in the United States which the war has forced into existence contrary to the natural course of things."

The natural course of things, in the mercantilist view espoused by Brougham and many of his fellow countrymen, was that America should continue to work out its destiny as an economic colony of Great Britain. Helping the colonists of New York find $6 million or $7 million for their precious canal would be quite nonsensical.

The haughty Brougham, of course, lacked some rather important information. He had not seen Robert Fulton's little steamboat, the *Clermont*, puffing up and down the Hudson River. He did not know that emigrating English mill workers, relying on memory alone, had successfully re-created the basic mechanisms of Arkwright's loom and Hargreaves's spinning jenny on American soil. And nor, at that time, was Brougham familiar with either the eloquence of Joshua Forman or the the growing power of a shadowy political combination that would soon come to be known as the Albany Regency.

Assembled and led by an urbane attorney from Kinderhook named Martin van Buren, the Regency was unlike most political machines. It was courtly, sagacious and efficient. For the most part, commented Thurlow Weed, one of the Regency's more notable opponents, "they were men of great ability, great industry, indomitable courage and strict personal integrity." Though the

Regency was generally viewed as "largely a bankers' affair," it included in its upper ranks a surprising number of newspaper editors and publishers. William Marcy, a minor hero of the War of 1812, was from Troy, where he edited the *Northern Budget*; he subsequently became governor of New York and U.S. Secretary of State. His father-in-law, Benjamin Knower, was president of the Mechanics' & Farmers' Bank of Albany. Major Azariah Flagg, another veteran of 1812, owned the *Plattsburg Republican* and became a leader in the assembly, and then served as state comptroller and supervisor of banking. Edwin Crosswell, editor of the *Albany Argus*, generally acted as the Regency's public spokesman. Silas Wright, an attorney from Canton, did not own a newspaper. But after a stint as state comptroller he would become U.S. senator and subsequently governor of New York.

The legislature finally approved construction of the canal in April 1817. But even then the Regency's leaders were mindful that the project was still an unknown quantity to most of the investing public. By their calculations it would cost about $21,000, on average, to construct one mile of the projected waterway. The best strategy, they decided, lay in starting modestly and then building step by step on each small success so that the culminating impression was one of competence and credit-worthiness. When potential investors had 10 or 20 miles of completed canal bed to view, their confidence would increase commensurately.

Of course, no bank or consortium of banks had the resources to provide direct financing. But two Albany banks, both with strong connections to the Regency, agreed to act as "loan contractors" on an initial issue of $200,000 in canal stock. They were the New-York State Bank and the Mechanics' & Farmers' Bank, whose charters required that the state own 40 percent and 10 percent of their stock, respectively. The canal stock, the bulk of it in $100 certificates, would pay an annual interest of 6 percent until the stock certificates' redemption twenty years hence, in July 1837. Toll revenues would be the primary source of repayment, but until the time when the canal opened for traffic interest payments would be assured by the creation of a special Erie Canal Fund, to be financed by duties from the auction of lands, and a state tax of 12.5 cents on every bushel of salt produced in parts of the state, like Onondaga County, that would benefit from the construction of a canal. In the twenty years to redemption, these salt taxes would contribute more than $2 million to the Canal Fund; as an appropriate *quid pro quo* the persuasive Joshua Forman arranged for a special spur of the canal to run north up to the salt springs at Salina.

Contrary to the schemes of Henry Brougham and his fellow imperialists,

the first stock issue of $200,000 sold smoothly; indeed, the largest single block of stock, worth $74,000, was taken up by two enterprising British insurance companies. An issue of a similar size a few months later listed no major foreign purchasers, and the bulk of it was acquired not by those of great inherited wealth but by enterprising individuals with "substantial, but not great, savings." Of this second issue, the biggest single purchaser would be the Bank for Savings in New York, recently founded to encourage thrift "among the laboring classes." This bank was limited by charter to investments in state and federal loans, and by the end of 1821 it held nearly 30 percent of all outstanding canal stock.

These, and many of the twenty-two subsequent issues of canal stock, were brokered through the State and the Mechanics banks of Albany. In return for paying a small premium on each issue—and this was a typical Regency touch—the state would in return pay, where possible, all contracts and wages in the paper currency of the Albany banks, thereby increasing both the volume and the credibility of their circulation. In another Regency flourish, the Manhattan Bank became the general transfer agent for all canal stock.

Construction moved ahead at a great pace. A major economic depression overtook both Europe and the United States in 1819. The price of wheat, a critical export for New York, fell from $2.72 to 68 cents a bushel. In the ensuing uncertainty, canal stock became increasingly popular with major domestic and foreign investors; indeed, some were so eager to obtain it they were prepared to pay a premium of $4.50 or more for each $100 certificate. With the additional capital the canal commissioners accelerated their construction schedule, and in November of 1825 DeWitt Clinton rode the whole length of the waterway from Buffalo to New York in his gubernatorial barge, and in an event that came to be known as "the wedding of the waters," ceremoniously poured a keg of Lake Erie water into the ocean near Sandy Hook.

The balladeers of the day commemorated the opening of the canal, reserving a few jabs for the skeptics, and for the Henry Broughams all over Europe.

> 'Tis, that Genius has triumph'd—and Science prevail'd
> Tho' Prejudice flouted, and Envy assail'd
> It is, that the vassals of Europe may see
> The progress of mind, in a land that is free.

The completed canal was both an engineering and a financial feat. In its first year of operation 13,000 boats passed between Buffalo and Albany, yielding tolls of more than half a million dollars. The boats never stopped coming, night and day. "Having taken your position at one of the numerous bridges," noted one observer, "it is an impressive sight to gaze up and down the canal. In either direction, so far as the eye can see, long lines of boats can be observed. By night their flickering head lamps give the impression of swarms of fireflies."

The impact of the toll revenues—$121.5 million by 1882, when they ceased—was to transform the demographic and the commercial map of the entire state. The canal commissioners were legally bound to invest these revenues in a prudent and productive fashion, and the booming communities of the so-called canal counties, and their banks, were leading beneficiaries of this requirement (see back endpaper).

The deposits made by the Canal Fund would be paid out in wages, and then, as the great wheel of prosperity turned, redeposited by merchants and farmers and mechanics who had provided the constructors of the canal with their goods and services. All of these depositors might then apply for loans to further expand their businesses. When construction was completed and the canals opened, the banks would likely provide safekeeping for the toll revenues before their dispatch to Albany.

The wheel of prosperity continued to spin. With the sharply lowered costs of transportation, the farmers might now seek further loans to get more acres under cultivation. Then, the additional produce would, when transported to market, further increase toll revenues . . .

Once it became clear that the canal could redeem its stock on schedule, the company used additional income to build a maze of ancillary waterways

that ran north to Carthage in Jefferson County and southwest to Olean in Cattaraugus County. One of the first, and shortest, feeder canals completed was the spur that ran up from the village of Syracuse to the salt springs at Salina. In 1832 Henry Wells established the Bank of Salina with a capital of $150,000. For many years this bank was deemed to be one of the most prosperous in the region. Wells later went on to found, with C. D. Fargo, the Wells Fargo Express Co. Later still, he became the prime mover in the founding of Wells College in Aurora, New York.

The little community of Newtown (which in 1828 changed its name to Elmira) on the Chemung River didn't even wait until the Erie was complete before it began to agitate for a connecting canal. In 1823 its leading citizens and legislators pushed for a 23-mile-long waterway that would enable all traffic on the Chemung to proceed to Watkins on the southern end of Lake Seneca. Then, after a 35-mile voyage down the lake, the barges—some under sail, some towed by the new steam tugs—could enter the main channel of the Erie at Geneva.

The Canal Commissioners and the legislature, however, did not approve the project until 1829, after the Albany Regency realized that such a waterway, with an additional 10-mile "feeder" running west from Horseheads to what is now Corning, would pull into New York a large portion of the production of the Blossburg coalfields in Pennsylvania.

Horse-drawn barge comes around a bend in the Erie Canal at rural Pittsford, near Rochester. (Watercolor by George Harvey, 1840; New York State Historical Association, Cooperstown)

The Great Projector

With an appropriation of $300,000 the forked canal was completed in 1832. Business in Elmira and the nearby regions immediately boomed and the frontier community demanded, and obtained with unusual promptness, a charter for the Chemung Canal Bank in 1833. The bank's authorized capital of $200,000 was oversubscribed by a factor of seven, with many of the pledges coming from residents of Pennsylvania. Thomas Olcott, cashier of the Mechanics' & Farmers' Bank in Albany and one of the leading operatives in the Regency, collected the payments on the Chemung's stock subscriptions. But, ever-mindful of the state's traditional economic rivalry with Pennsylvania, he insisted that all major purchasers of the bank's stock be residents of New York.

Not all canal communities, however, were able to arouse the Regency's interest so readily. Perhaps, after the canal had gone through, the attentions of the commissioners were focused elsewhere. The community of Little Falls, sitting astride the deepest lock on the whole Erie system, applied for a bank charter in 1831, but was denied. The log rolling began. Only after recruiting most of the leading citizens of the region, and placing severe pressure upon the legislature, did the Herkimer County Bank of Little Falls finally receive its charter in 1833. Significantly, one of the most influential assemblymen in the Regency, Abijah Mann, was subsequently invited to become a member of the bank's board of directors.

The growing trade of New York also attracted another kind of banker. In 1800 Alexander Brown, an auctioneer from County Antrim in Ireland, had emigrated to Baltimore and opened a warehouse for linen. Soon he became well established in the banking business and his sons opened branches in Philadelphia and Liverpool, England. His fourth son, James, had been dispatched to New York in 1825 to open a new office called Brown Brothers & Co. The bank prospered in the complex and highly competitive trade of exporting cotton, wheat and tobacco and importing textiles and manufactured goods from Europe. Besides acquiring major tracts of prime Manhattan real estate, the House of Brown also operated a growing fleet of sailing clippers, and helped finance the introduction of steam-powered packets on the North Atlantic run.

The commissioners of the Canal Fund were quick to grasp the economic impact of their operations. "The magnitude of the Canal Fund is now such as to have an important influence over the banking concerns of the State," they noted. Deposits from the Fund in "nearly all institutions, particularly in the country, directly or indirectly participate in the use of the capital which it affords." Obviously, a demand that these funds be repatriated to Albany or sent to the Manhattan Bank in the city could have a severe impact on the community that had grown up around the canal. Indeed, the commissioners suspected that the presence of the canal deposits might have tempted some of the smaller banks to overextend themselves. "The circulation of the last year," they reported, "is more than could have been sustained without the aid of that Fund, and more perhaps than prudent operators should have hazarded upon such a reliance." What would happen to the community and what

Jacob Barker, a flamboyant entrepreneur who operated his unchartered Exchange Bank on Wall Street in defiance of state regulations. Though he was not a lawyer, Barker annihilated a succession of state prosecutors in court. (Engraving; author's collection)

would happen to the Fund's deposits if such a bank failed? Indeed, what would happen to the whole financial structure of the state if it were subjected to a panic like that of 1819?

And there were other, more fundamental, problems. Many of the state's medium-sized banks had been chartered between 1815 and 1825 in what later came to be known as the Era of Stock Notes. (Included among them was the Commercial Bank of Albany, founded in 1825; nearly one and a half centuries later this bank was to fuse with the First Trust & Deposit Co. of Syracuse to form the cornerstone of Key Bank of New York.) During the construction of the canal, observed Azariah Flagg, a leading member of the Regency who subsequently became state comptroller, "a very loose system prevailed in regard to the incorporation of banks in the state."

Honest bank managements often lacked experience. They were frequently baffled by the arcane and sometimes convoluted "theorizings" in the financial literature of the day. The problems engendered by printing and circulating their own currency were especially perplexing. What was a sound ratio between capital and currency? Four to one? Three to one? Two to one? How was the ratio affected by the "quality" of the capital paid in? Did sizable deposits strengthen a bank, or did they render it more vulnerable in a time of panic? What proportion of specie should one prudently have on hand to guard against such an event?

Not all bank managements, however, were honest. Many of the charters issued in the Era of Stock Notes permitted a new bank to commence operations with only 12 percent of its capital paid in. Some banks had an even more tenuous relationship with their designated capital. On occasion, notes Flagg, "individuals who were more desirous of borrowing money than of lending it, would make arrangements to procure 12 per cent of the nominal capital, in order to get the control of the bank, and after retaining the specie for a few weeks, would return it to its real owners." The new owners of a bank would then substitute their own promissory notes for the absent specie. As a last line of defense such fly-by-night operators sometimes kept several barrels of broken glass, topped with a few gold coins, in the vaults to "prove" that the vanished specie was still on hand.

One popular abuse, often practiced by quite respectable managements, was to charge double the legal maximum of 6 percent interest on a loan by requiring the borrowers to leave "one half of the sum with the banks until the note is due, thereby receiving usurious interest." Another loophole was to be found in the Restraining Law of 1804. While it forbade *associations* from doing business without a charter, it had not prevented *individuals* from lending money, and from issuing bills of credit. Many tavern keepers, metal smiths and merchants had gone into business for themselves and had circulated notes for as low as 12½ and even 6¼ cents among their communities. The popularity of these fractional notes was increased by the fact that gold and silver coins were often scarce, and banks seldom printed currency in denominations below the $10 bill.

The most flamboyant of the individual bankers was undoubtedly Jacob Barker, a merchant shipowner from Nantucket who settled in Manhattan and opened the unchartered Exchange Bank on Wall Street. Barker, born in 1779, was a bumptious, big-hearted man who counted Thomas Jefferson and Andrew Jackson among his personal acquaintances. Barker helped found Tammany Hall and was involved in at least one duel with the president of a rival bank. On stormy days, when many pilots were apprehensive about the heavy seas beyond the Verrazano Narrows, Barker would sail out to his incoming ships and personally bring them into New York harbor.

The legislature questioned Barker's right to operate a bank, and brought suit against him. Barker, acting as his own attorney, thoroughly confused the court and obtained a dismissal. His chief argument was that any man, under common law, had a right to make loans and issue as many promissory notes as he chose. Employing a number of stratagems, Barker subsequently acquired the Bank of Washington & Warren in Hudson Falls, but this collapsed in 1825. Though he had no formal education in the law, Jacob Barker once again defended himself against charges of fraud and conspiracy. And, once again, his ingenious and often humorous argumentation so confused the judge, prosecutor and jury that the matter went to a second and then a third, indecisive trial. Though the government's attorneys always seemed to be on the losing side in their confrontations with Barker, Governor and later President Martin van Buren retained an abiding affection for the rumpled entrepreneur. "A great banker in New York," he wrote of Barker, "and everywhere and in every situation an extraordinary man and always my personal friend."

Operation of the state's more conventional banks was not made any easier by the legislature's decision to charter more than seventy insurance companies and so-called lombards, savings associations permitted to loan money on deposits. By 1828 these organizations had an authorized capital of more than $30 million. Yet, according to a confidential report written by James Buchanan, the British consul in New York, no more than 10 percent of this was paid in. Unlike banks, these companies did not have the power to issue currency notes. Some of them, noted Buchanan dryly in his report to the British government, "issued bonds in the nature of negotiable securities, which has proved ruinous." One lombard, set up in 1825 with a paid-in capital of only $30,000, proceeded to issue bonds to the amount of $1 million; it failed the following year.

For a while the new, popular and highly aggressive brand of capitalism that gathered momentum with the construction of the Erie Canal defied explanation. A number of European economists who visited New York in the 1820s were appalled by the people's brash new spirit of enterprise, and by a financial system that seemed ever awash in "fictitious" capital, bankrupted corporations and unrelenting peculation.

However, as James Buchanan pointed out in one of his confidential reports sent back to London, something unusual was happening in the state of New York, a territory that was itself half the size of the entire British Isles. By giving banks the power to print money, he wrote, the New York legislature had "sought to draw forth the energies of the people." By and large this seemingly haphazard experiment in the creation of whole new currencies was proving to be a great success. It had certainly unlocked a productive capability that "in the history of nations affords no parallel."

There had been numerous setbacks, of course, "and though much capital had been lost, and many individuals ruined, yet the general state of the people is improved." Bridges, though sometimes shaky, were built. Turn-pikes, though often clogged with mud, were thrust through the wilderness. Steamboats, though frequently equipped with explosive boilers, were launched. The interests of the people and the economy were served.

And should a bridge collapse, or should that boiler explode, then an indomitable spirit took hold. A stronger bridge, and a bigger boat with a better boiler, would soon be built.

The nature of this special spirit intrigued Buchanan. It seemed to form the glue that held these querulous, ever-competitive people together. It was the force that—most of the time—prevented that house of cards, built on a foundation of fictitious capital, from falling in upon itself. The extraordinary success of the New Yorkers, Buchanan bluntly noted, was a "reproach to British rule" in the territories to the north. The proof of this judgment, he

Country and City Banks of New York, 1828

COUNTRY BANKS.

Bank.	Notes discounted and loans.	Capital paid in.	Notes.	Deposits.	Specie.	Balance due from banks.
(1) Jefferson County Bank	$109,343	$74,000	$94,545	$18,921	$14,113	$66,012
(2) Bank of Utica	1,198,799	500,000	607,046	176,041	25,500	83,541
(3) Bank of Geneva	489,522	300,000	372,654	128,248	30,745	319,602
(4) Ontario Bank	1,118,987	500,000	500,944	267,776	28,937	186,064
(5) Farmers' Bank	618,433	278,000	153,397	79,686	11,660	-----------
(6) Bank of Troy	948,660	352,000	326,379	96,394	10,533	-----------
(7) Mohawk Bank	273,080	165,000	78,128	83,893	12,941	16,947
(8) Bank of Auburn	228,393	143,928	264,630	49,470	30,455	200,909
(9) Middle District Bank	567,807	397,485	293,750	45,288	15,684	155,656
(10) Catskill Bank	414,747	110,000	274,510	80,940	7,965	39,900
(11) Central Bank	217,749	86,000	171,527	16,208	18,096	58,493
Total	6,185,520	2,906,413	3,137,510	1,042,865	206,629	1,127,124

CITY BANKS.

Bank.	Notes discounted and loans.	Capital paid in.	Notes.	Deposits.	Specie.	Balance due from banks.
(1) Mechanics and Farmers' Bank, Albany	$1,017,962	$312,000	$325,000	$396,774	$26,000	$170,053
(2) Bank of Albany	484,077	240,000	100,700	151,018	30,261	-----------
(3) New York State Bank, Albany	791,814	369,600	178,002	359,707	30,976	94,202
(4) City Bank, New York City	1,267,033	1,000,000	244,904	219,215	66,806	47,711
(5) Union Bank, New York City	1,252,840	1,000,000	200,320	222,068	45,754	113,890
(6) Bank of America, New York City	2,328,074	2,031,200	221,884	332,238	184,610	206,480
(7) Mechanics' Bank, New York City	2,848,898	2,000,000	607,105	755,794	199,114	432,356
(8) Merchants' Bank, New York City	2,083,298	1,463,000	574,325	625,992	222,396	308,779
(9) Tradesmen's Bank, New York City	743,454	363,160	198,140	248,046	33,357	54,428
(10) New York Bank, New York City	2,904,991	1,973,200	540,955	796,912	99,978	349,641
(11) Phoenix Bank, New York City	980,026	500,000	337,288	340,324	79,078	175,108
Total	16,702,467	11,252,160	3,528,623	4,448,088	1,018,330	1,952,648

wrote, "is to be found by crossing the St. Lawrence from any part of the state of New-York, into Canada," where the economy still lay under the cautious hand of London. Such a journey, noted Buchanan, would afford the traveler "an opportunity of comparing the enterprize, energy, and industry of one country, with the lassitude, torpidity, and indolence which prevail in the other." Such a judgment may sound harsh. But coming from one of their own, it may have finally convinced the British government that their mercantilist dreams had almost no chance of taking root in North America.

While Governor Van Buren undoubtedly agreed with Buchanan, he had no taste for gratuitous disasters. In 1828, as the toll revenues continued to flow in, he experienced a growing unease about the ultimate soundness of the state's banking system. "The solvency of the banks," he declared, "and the consequent stability of their paper is their principal, and almost only point in which the people have much interest." The governor then called upon Joshua

Forman, the ingenious Projector, to make a detailed examination of the state's forty-odd banks and present his ideas, together with legislative recommendations, as to how the banks could be restrained from speculative excesses while, at the same time, continuing to provide the capital resources needed to sustain "the increasing commerce of New-York, and the new field of business opened along the line of the canals."

Forman accepted the governor's invitation with alacrity. One of the first things he discovered on studying the annual summaries submitted to the legislature was that the city banks and the country banks were engaged in two fundamentally different kinds of business (see the table for summary of the condition of eleven country and eleven city banks in January 1829). The city banks, it was clear, "depended upon their paid up capital and their deposits for the ability to discount and loan rather than upon their credit in the form of bank notes." For them, notes in circulation amounted to less than one-third of their capital. In contrast, currency notes of country banks exceeded capital and amounted, on average, to three times the amount of deposits; for the country banks "every note discounted made a new emission of currency."

Of course, not all banks were average. The condition of the Catskill Bank (established 1813) must have caused Joshua Forman to raise an eyebrow. Though it only had paid-in capital of $110,000, it had $275,000 worth of notes in circulation and, in the event of panic, only $7,965 worth of specie "on hand" to redeem them. When the currency notes were added to the $81,000 in deposits, the Catskill had a specie/note-deposit ratio of about 1 to 44. The ratio of the average country bank was 1 to 19, while city banks ran a ratio of about 1 to 8.

In the previous decade seven banks, with a *nominal* capitalization of more than $2 million, had collapsed. Some of them, Forman acknowledged, had been founded by well-meaning men "only to be bought in by knaves, who, after circulating three or four times the amount of paper they paid for them, could withdraw what capital there was, and leave the public to bear the loss."

Forman's apprehensions were further heightened by the increasingly raucous debate about the future of the second Bank of the United States; if its charter were repealed in 1836, as the Jacksonian Democrats advocated, then the financial responsibilities of the country would fall entirely upon the banks of the separate states. How, he must have wondered, could banks in the state of New York be strengthened so that they could safely ride out the severest financial storms?

Forman's insights into the significance of multiplicate currencies, and his grasp of the connections between price levels and the balance of trade were far ahead of his time. The amount of currency in circulation, he informed the New York legislature, must be "kept in just proportion to the necessities of business." If banks issued too many bills and were too generous with their loans, then, said Forman, "the first effect is to raise the price of commodities." As a result those goods can no longer be exported with profit and "thus the specie in the country is sent abroad to pay debts and buy merchandize." After a while the sales of those who produce goods "come to a stand" and at this point the "circulation, ever moving as the atmosphere, not being kept out by the necessities of business, flows in upon the banks." Then due to the decline of business, the banks are forced to press their debtors, who in all likelihood include the producers of goods; these, in turn, are forced to sell their goods at greatly reduced prices. At this point, said Forman, "a sharp exportation takes place; the specie drain is stopped . . . prices rise to their proper level, and the sun of prosperity again beams upon the country."

The key questions, of course, for anyone attempting to understand—and perhaps tame—the swings of the economy were these: What, exactly, constituted a "just proportion" of circulating currency? What, exactly, constituted a "proper level" of prices?

Implicit in Forman's analysis is the thought that these numerical entities were not constants but variables that would, if all went well, fluctuate according to "the necessities of business." Those fluctuations, however, would be required to take place within a set of clearly defined limits. What, then were those limits, and how could they be determined?

The charter of the Bank of New York, with which Alexander Hamilton had been closely associated, permitted liabilities (excluding deposits) to expand to three times the value of specie capital. Later Hamilton allowed the first Bank of the United States—backed, admittedly, by the credit of the federal government—to operate with liabilities worth up to five times specie capital. And Adam Smith himself had suggested that a bank could safely circulate promises-to-pay equal to five times the amount of specie in the vault.

How were such ratios derived? Had they been deduced, logically, by the application of a complex mathematical formula that somehow took all the variables into account? Or had the ratios simply been "discovered" by a grim process of trial and error? Banks with one set of ratios survived and prospered while others, with a different set of ratios, inexplicably failed.

As he pondered these questions, Forman began to grasp a more general point. No bank existed in a vacuum. It swam in a sea of customers and potential customers. All banks swam in such a sea and it was clear that the decisions made by the directors of one bank were affected, for better or worse, by the decisions of all the directors in all the other banks. Examining banks in isolation made no sense; it was the behavior of the entire system, working as an organic whole, that was significant. In the wake of the *Empress of China*'s extraordinary voyage to the Orient in 1784, Joshua Forman had made a point of studying the commercial history of China, and he concluded that the situation of the state banks resembled that of the Hong merchants in Canton, where "a number of men, each acting separately, have by the grant of government the exclusive right of trading with foreigners and are all made liable for the debts of each other in case of failure." In the same fashion, Forman argued, that "since banks profited from the public's use of their notes as money, they ought to guarantee that the public suffer no loss from that use."

To this end Forman recommended that each bank chartered in the state

must open its books to inspection by the representatives of three newly appointed banking commissioners. If a particular bank should still fail to redeem, then its outstanding currency would be bought up by a Bank Safety Fund. This fund would derive its capital from the state banks themselves, each of which would contribute annually, for a period of six years, a sum equal to one-half of one percent of its capital. Thus, if the banks of New York had a combined capital of $10 million, then they would accumulate an insurance fund of $300,000, plus interest, over a period of six years.

Another critical feature in the new legislation was that all banks must ensure that their capital was fully paid up. Also, the value of the bills printed and circulated as money by each bank must not be permitted to exceed an amount equal to "twice its capital stock then paid in and actually possessed." On such terms a country institution like the Catskill Bank would be required to reduce its circulation of $275,000 or increase its capital of $110,000. The bill also decreed that a bank's loans and discounts outstanding must never equal more than two and one half times that capital. Once again, on these terms the Catskill Bank would have to reduce its loans and discounts from its current $415,000 by $140,000 to a total of no more than $275,000.

By the standards of the day, these reserve ratios were exceptionally stringent. The new state law attempted to compensate the banks for this tough new regimen by undertaking not to charter too many banks, by exempting banks from taxes, and by permitting the banks to charge 7 percent instead of the customary 6 percent interest on loans to customers. Forman submitted his Safety Fund plan to Van Buren in January of 1829. The governor liked

Typical one-dollar bill, issued under the auspices of the state Comptroller upon "the pledge of public stocks," by the Saint Nicholas Bank of New-York. (Martin Gengerke, Stack's Rare Coins, New York)

the idea, as did his special advisor on banking, Thomas Olcott, the cashier of the Mechanics' & Farmers' Bank.

Somewhere in the committee stage, however, Forman's proposals were amended—in all likelihood by Abijah Mann—to insure not only the circulating *currency* of the banks, but also the *deposits* of their customers. As Professor Richard Sylla, the co-author of *The Evolution of the American Economy*, notes, the new requirement "foreshadowed bank deposit insurance, one of the most significant innovations of twentieth century American banking." But it also imposed a huge new burden upon the Fund, with no commensurate increase in resources. Indeed, the new requirement effected a radical change in both the philosophical and the financial scope of the law. While the change undoubtedly increased popular confidence in the system, it also made some depositors less discriminating about their choice of bank. At the same time, bank officers, knowing that their depositors' interests were secure, might be tempted to become more cavalier in their attitudes toward financial risk. Azariah Flagg argues, none too convincingly, that depositors were more "competent to judge" the soundness of a bank than note-holders, a group that included, in his view, the "more ignorant part of the community."

Predictably, Forman's plan encountered "fierce opposition" in the legislature, much of it from the banks in the city of New York who, since they had the greatest capital, would be making the largest contribution to the Safety Fund. The Jefferson County Bank in Watertown, with its paid-in capital of $74,000, would pay a mere $370 each year, but the Merchants Bank of New York would have to make an annual contribution of $7,315. If that were not enough, the big city banks did not see why their paper currency, which generally traded at par, should be "leveled" with that of the upstate banks, whose paper was currently traded well below par.

The Albany Regency, however, held the whip hand. Of the forty banks in the state, the charters of no fewer than thirty-one would be up for renewal in the next four years; if they refused to recharter now under the conditions set

by the Safety Fund Act, the Regency informed them, then they need not expect to recharter under the old conditions at some time in the future. All thirty-one institutions found this argument persuasive, and agreed to come in under the new regulations.

Bray Hammond, the eminent financial historian, notes that in its broadest context the Safety Fund's "prime importance was its embodiment of Joshua Forman's intelligent understanding that banks constitute a system, being peculiarly sensitive to one another's operations, and not a mere aggregate of free agents." The concept of the Safety Fund quickly spread to other states, including Vermont (1831), Indiana (1834) and Michigan (1836).

Judge Forman continued to be an active projector until the end. He returned to Syracuse for a while and perfected his salt-making plant. He built a gristmill and arranged to drain the marshes around Onondaga Lake, which he found "to be the cause of much sickness." Perhaps he hoped to obtain a position in the large and prosperous Bank of Salina, founded in 1832. Forman had pioneered much of the technology for the salt business, and the bank had, after all, been established under the principles of his Safety Fund. However, Henry Wells saw fit to appoint Nathan Munro the bank's first president, and Ashbel Kellogg became its first cashier. Contemporary documents speak of Forman's being denied a position for which he had "high expectations."

Judge Forman subsequently acquired an interest in a copper mine, and

Syracuse in 1851. Shortly before his death Joshua Forman, the Great Projector, returned to the city, where he was hailed at a huge banquet as "the Founder of the Town." (Tinted lithograph by D. W. Moody, 1852; Stokes Collection, New York Public Library)

then moved away to Rutherfordton, North Carolina, where he bought a large tract of land and "established a newspaper, printing press, and stage-line, and was considered for a time the most enterprising man in that part of the State." Shortly before his death in 1848 he made his last visit to Syracuse, where he was hailed at a huge banquet of dignitaries as the "Founder of the Town." In the years ahead, however, the Great Projector's two most memorable ventures—the Erie Canal and the creation of a banking system that acknowledged its responsibility to the society in which it operated—would have an impact that extended far beyond the borders of New York and, indeed, beyond the borders of the nation.

4

The New Breed

IN MANY WAYS Erastus Corning typified the brash new breed of entrepreneurs that were to take over and dominate the financial life of nineteenth-century America. In true Horatio Alger fashion, Corning began his business career at the age of 13 when he went to work as a stockboy in a hardware store situated on the waterfront of Troy, New York. From this meager start to the time of his death in 1872, Corning assembled and then became the first president of the New York Central Railroad, founded one of the most influential banks in the state of New York, and amassed a personal fortune of $8 million. Besides serving in Congress and as mayor of Albany, Corning's foundries and mills provided much of the material for the armored battleships—including the ironclad Monitor—of the Civil War. He was also engaged in numerous land speculations and helped establish the prosperous city that now bears his name in western New York.

The challenge of developing the potential of the lands to the west called for a new kind of commercial outlook, and a new kind of bank. Under the Federalists society had been cemented into a multilayered hierarchy. The semifeudal Rensselaers and Livingstons stood with their great estates at the top, and the semiliterate immigrants, many brought from Ireland and Germany to dig the Erie Canal, labored and died like animals at the bottom. But the gathering momentum of the economy changed the nature of the social equation. "The United States in the 1830s and 1840s," noted Arthur

The New Breed

Schlesinger, Jr., in *The Cycles of American History,* "entered the period of takeoff into self-sustaining growth."

Almost overnight, a social structure based upon the primacy of horse-power and human muscle became irrelevant. No longer was it either necessary or productive to set man over man in an elaborate pyramid of coercion and control. The new challenges now pitted man—his strength greatly augmented by his knowledge of steam power and hydraulics—directly against Nature. When it came to blasting a new lock into the side of the Niagara escarpment, or moving a thousand tons of wheat down the Hudson overnight, the hierarchy counted for almost nothing; indeed, its efforts to assert its faltering authority frequently became an impediment to progress.

In the state of New York the first crack in the old order came with the meeting, in the fall of 1821, of the convention to revise the state constitution. The debate was long and convoluted. The conservatives culled the annals of ancient Greece for numerous horrifying examples of popular democracy run amok. However, the Albany Regency, under the watchful eye of Martin van Buren, led the convention to the conclusion that the ownership of property should no longer be a qualification for male suffrage. Henceforth, the right to vote would be extended to all white men who'd paid their taxes and were over the age of 21. These newly enfranchised citizens joined with their brethren across the country to style themselves Republican Democrats, or simply Democrats. They found their champion in Andrew Jackson, who contended that the government of a truly democratic country must be more powerful than any particular class or concentration of wealth within it. In 1824 these new voters helped Jackson gain a plurality of electoral votes. In 1828 they made him president.

From the first, it seemed as if the conservative nightmare had become reality. "It was like the inundation of northern barbarians into Rome," wrote one aristocrat of Jackson's inauguration in Washington, as crowds of celebrating farm laborers, backwoodsmen, soldiers and housewives surged past the guards into the White House; once in the executive mansion the visitors elbowed the official guests aside and roamed through the rooms as if they were their own. When waiters attempted to bring out refreshments, the people surged forward, knocking the food to the floor. Many patricians referred to the new regime as "the reign of King Mob."

But Jackson's supporters saw it differently. "It was a proud day for the people," wrote a newspaper editor named Amos Kendall, "General Jackson is *their own* president." Much of Old Hickory's popular appeal lay in the fact that, unlike previous presidents, he was a self-made man. His career, unfolding amid the freedom and the fierce competition of the Tennessee border, epitomized the frontier belief that any individual might rise to greatness.

Privilege and entrenched wealth were anathema, the new Democrats believed. They were suspicious of all chartered corporations, and banks were viewed with an especially baleful eye. The litany of complaint was familiar. A bank's charter gave it the right to install itself in a particular community and no rival, under penalty of law, was permitted to encroach upon its

FACING PAGE: *Erastus Corning, pioneer of synergy, had an uncanny ability to make all the parts of diverse enterprises—banks, railroads, foundries— mesh into a larger whole. (Oil on canvas by C. L. Elliott, 1864; Albany Institute of History and Art)*

The New Breed

domain. While ordinary folks worked hard for money, the bank had the right to print up just about as much as it wanted. And in a bad season that bank had the power to take away the land a family had worked for two or three generations. Such privileges and immunities were undemocratic. They were "always for the benefit of wealth," wrote one pamphleteer. "These immunities are never bestowed on the poor." Anything, declared the new Democrats, that could be done to diminish or eradicate such privilege was beneficial.

In the state of New York such sentiments held a powerful appeal for the ordinary laborer who hoped one day for a farm of his own. They appealed to those who worked in the scores of small factories that had grown up beside the falls of the Mohawk, the Seneca and the Genesee. They greatly appealed to settlers in the western counties, many of whom felt themselves to be in thrall to the land development companies. And they also appealed to the thirteen-year-old Erastus Corning as he swept the floors, cleaned the lamps and stocked the shelves of Heartt & Smith's hardware and iron store on the waterfront of Troy.

Like many of the great entrepreneurs, Corning did not have the benefit of much formal education. Nor was he blessed with good health; due to a crippling accident in infancy, Corning could not walk without the assistance of crutches. But, as if to make up for such misfortune, he had handsome visage, a plausible address and a quick mind that, while attentive to detail, had an uncanny ability to make all the parts of any business enterprise mesh neatly into a larger whole.

Young Erastus was a capitalist from the beginning. After he had finished purveying nails and frying pans from the shelves of the hardware store, he would endeavor to interest the store's customers in his own goods, which he had taken on consignment. They might include everything from political pamphlets to the fresh lemons he would purchase by the box from the steamboat captains coming up the Hudson from New York. At the age of 19, Corning moved across the river to work at John Spencer & Co., a major wholesaler of hardware, in Albany. A little later he used his savings of $500, and a business loan, to buy first a junior and then a controlling partnership in the company. With the acquisition he also gained title to a small foundry that stamped out iron nails, a product of special significance in a pioneer society. Corning, always eager to cut out the middle man, was shortly dealing directly with merchants in England for their manufactured products and their high quality rolled iron.

Many of his wholesale customers ran general stores in the new communities opening up along the projected route of the canal. Though compelled to hobble about on crutches, Corning made numerous visits to the west to take orders and collect unpaid debts. Since a greater part of this wholesale business was handled on credit, the experience, with its occasional loss, gave him a shrewd ability to assess human character and the likelihood that a particular customer would, or would not, keep his promises. It also gave him firsthand insight into the potential of western New York and the economic impact of the canal when it was completed. After 1819, when he married Harriet

The first train ride on the Mohawk and Hudson, 1831. The 14-mile railroad enabled travelers to bypass the first eight locks of the Erie Canal. (Oil on canvas by E. L. Henry; Albany Institute of History and Art)

Weld, the daughter of another hardware dealer, Corning came to serve on numerous civic committees in Albany. In 1828, at the age of 33, he was elected to the position of alderman. Soon he began to develop ties with the state legislature and the men of the Albany Regency. Three years later Corning became interested in the operations of the Mohawk & Hudson, the first railroad ever built in the state. Its 14 miles of track, running from Albany to Schenectady, enabled a passenger coming up the Hudson from New York to take a shortcut past the first eight locks of the Erie Canal before boarding a boat, thereby telescoping a long day's travel into half an hour. While most merchants and businessmen focused their attention on the possibilities brought about by the canal, Corning became fascinated by the potential of the railroad. Not only did the locomotive travel ten times faster than the barge, but its tracks could be laid through terrain where no canal could go. And perhaps even more to the point, it was built of iron, a product in ample supply at Erastus Corning's own foundries along the Hudson. In the fall of 1831 Corning purchased some stock in the Mohawk & Hudson. Two years later he was elected a director of the company and proposed the creation of a new railroad which, like the M & H, would further circumvent the laborious haul of the canal boats up the Mohawk. The track of the proposed railroad would run the 80-odd miles from Utica to Schenectady on the bed of the old Mohawk Turnpike, along the river's northern shore.

The venture, with its capitalization of $2 million, would become a classic demonstration of Erastus Corning's entrepreneurial skill. He knew that this railroad could not, like the Mohawk & Hudson, be dismissed as a convenient adjunct to the operations of the canal; its construction posed a direct challenge to the economic validity of the whole idea of transporting cargoes and passengers by water. It was also clear to him that such a project would cause intense dismay to the individuals and to the financial institutions, like the New York State Bank, that had invested their time and treasure in the construction of the Erie. He therefore made sure that the new railroad's subscription books would be opened in both New York City and in communities not directly served by the canal. Demand for the new stock was brisk. Within the space of a few days the railroad's 20,000 shares, with a par value of $100, were oversubscribed by a multiple of seven.

Such enthusiasm enabled Corning to proceed with an ingenious plan for both financing and retaining control of the railroad at minimal cost to himself. Only those subscribers willing to pledge their proxies to Corning and his associates would be permitted actually to purchase the stock they had requested. Having used his proxies to ensure his election to the presidency of the company, Corning then applied the Regency touch by declaring that he would accept "not a cent in salary, asking only that he have the privilege of supplying all the rails, running gear, tools and other iron and steel articles used by the railroad, his profits on the same being his only recompense."

The economics of early railroad construction are intriguing. Like the canal, every mile of the railroad cost about $20,000 to lay, and equip. Each mile of single track also required about 100 tons of rail and 100 tons of rolling stock, thereby requiring Corning's foundries and machine shops to supply, without competitive bid, a total of 16,000 tons of iron and steel. This figure doubled when the board of directors voted to lay two tracks side by side. Corning, however, was aware that it would be difficult, if not impossible, to finance these huge purchases out of capital funds. Such issues of stock, like those of most internal improvement projects, were generally purchased piecemeal, over a substantial period of time. Indeed, many stockholders customarily paid for the last third of their subscriptions with dividends accrued after the project was complete. How, then, was Corning to acquire the necessary financing for his huge purchases of iron track and rolling stock?

Though he had been a director of the New-York State Bank since 1826, neither that bank nor any other of the established Albany institutions were enthusiastic about helping the U & S get started. The only way to accomplish his objective, decided Corning, was to start his own bank.

Once again, Corning kept his hand firmly on the tiller. Nothing would be left to chance. Subscription books for the $500,000 capital stock of the Albany City Bank opened in June 1834, and two days later were oversubscribed by $600,000. Again, Corning seems to have assured his election as president by insisting that the bank's shares be sold, where possible, to those willing to pledge their proxies to him. His long-established relationship with the leading members of the Regency, and his mercantile connections throughout Albany and the western counties made the City Bank an immediate success. Though authorized to issue up to $1 million of its own currency, City Bank "preferred deposit credit to circulating notes" for the bulk of its transactions with customers.

Under the commercial law of the day it was not forbidden for a bank to make substantial loans to its officers, and it is clear that Corning took full advantage of this privilege. Even then, in January 1835, with only $160,000

received in payments on the railroad's stock certificates, Corning found it necessary to seek a loan of $100,000. He came to an understanding with John Jacob Astor, a fellow director of the Mohawk & Hudson: Astor agreed to lend Corning $100,000 in return for a pledge of 1,500 shares of the Utica & Schenectady's stock. Eighteen months later the tracks of the U & S were complete. Additional subscription calls had by then pushed the paid-in capital to $1.5 million. Early dividends were retained by the company to offset final subscription calls.

Corning, aware of the commercial potential of railroading, took care to establish cordial relations with banks in small but growing communities across the state. Not only did he demonstrate his optimism by purchasing substantial blocks of stock in such institutions as the Madison County Bank of Cazenovia (where he invested $5,000), the Broome County Bank of Binghamton ($3,675) and the Buffalo Bank ($6,250). He also saw to it that the City Bank became the chief "corresponding agent" for all Albany banks in the redemption of notes issued by even the most distant country banks. Ballston Spa Bank was an early correspondent. If Corning sensed a particular out-of-town bank was likely to get an unusually heavy call on its circulating paper, he would endeavor, where possible, to give it some advance warning of the event.

Nicholas Biddle, a facile and well-con-nected young Philadelphian, became president of the Bank of the United States in 1823. When he opened addi-tional branches in Utica and Buffalo, many New Yorkers believed he intended to engross the profits of the Erie Canal. (Engraving; Library of Congress)

Such services were especially important at a time when the struggle over the rechartering of the second Bank of the United States had thrown the finances of the entire nation into turmoil. On the termination of the first Bank's charter in 1811, the federal government deposited some $23 million in ninety-four strategically placed state-chartered banks across the country. To fill the vacuum in New York the legislature approved twenty-three new state charters, with an authorized capitalization of $17.3 million in the years between 1811 and 1818. Not all the charters were taken up, but two promi-nent new institutions established in 1812 were the City Bank (capitalization: $2 million)—one of the precursors of today's Citibank—and the Bank of America ($6 million), whose capital was largely subscribed by many former stockholders of the lapsed Bank of the United States.

Beyond the borders of the state, however, matters had not worked out so well. Many of the government's "pet banks," particularly those in the western states, used their federal deposits to expand their paper currency and make speculative investments in real estate. When the second Bank of the United States received its charter in 1816, it immediately demanded the return of these deposits. Many banks, however, were unable to comply. In an effort to pry the bullion loose, the Bank of the United States proceeded to accumulate large quantities of state bank paper and present it to the parent banks for redemption in gold.

Such demands drove banks to contract loans, foreclose mortgages, and in many cases file for bankruptcy. Their difficulties also did much to precipitate the crash and recession of 1819. To ordinary families, who were forced to surrender the farms they had carved out of the wilderness, it seemed as if the new federal bank was a monster, determined to gobble up all the property in the land. In 1823 Nicholas Biddle, a facile and well-connected young Philadelphian, became the bank's president. Though shrewd enough to avoid the mistakes that had exacerbated the recession of 1819, he kept the pressure on the surviving state banks, often causing their paper money to fluctuate wildly in value. Indeed, so volatile had the nation's currencies become by 1828 that Andrew Jackson, in his inaugural address, warned Biddle's bank that it might be disbanded if it failed to establish "a uniform and sound currency."

Resentment ran particularly high among the bankers of New York, many of whom believed that the Bank of the United States, with its decision to open new branches in Buffalo and Utica, sought to clamp a financial stranglehold on trade along the Erie Canal. All three branches discounted commercial paper at 6 percent, making it impossible for state banks to do business at the 7 percent authorized under the Safety Fund Law. In the city of New York bankers were particularly irked to see, each year, some $12 to $15 million worth of federal tariffs on cargoes landed on their own docks deposited not in their own vaults, but in the local branch of the Bank of the United States. When not using them to undercut their discounting operations, the city branch would dispatch these funds to the bank's head office, located in Philadelphia, a city deemed by many to be New York's preeminent rival. Often New York's banks refused to grant loans for fear that their paper might "come into possession of the federal Bank" and be returned to them, accompanied by a peremptory demand for redemption in specie.

Biddle and his assistants replied, with considerable justification, that the central bank was merely discharging its duty to keep the state banks' currency bills at par, and to ensure that merchants and other businessmen could discount their paper at a fair and productive rate. In the wrong hands, however, such powers were clearly open to abuse and the Jacksonians were concerned that the bank could easily become, in Vice President Van Buren's words, "the great pioneer of constitutional encroachments."

In hope of resolving some of these conflicts, Jackson sought to decentralize the federal bank in a way that would permit it to serve the needs of ordinary people in the different regions of the country. Such an institution ought not to work so obviously for its own interest—as the present bank seemed to be doing—in the vague hope that its example would somehow translate into an acceptable policy for the nation as a whole. Any new institution would somehow have to walk the line between the fierce and often highly politicized demands of the present and the vital, but still unarticulated, needs of the future. Today versus tomorrow, the actual versus the potential. Though Jackson and his aides had the assistance of James Hamilton, the gifted son of the first secretary of the treasury, it seemed impossible to devise an institution capable of striking the delicate balance between such conflicting, and often paradoxical, requirements.

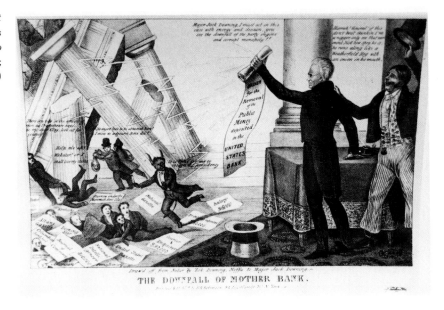

THE DOWNFALL OF MOTHER BANK.

Biddle sought to divert the Jacksonians from restructuring the bank by offering to take over the national debt—then about $50 million—in return for a recharter of the bank four years ahead of time. Henry Clay of Kentucky thought the idea could be used as a campaign issue against Jackson, and pushed it through both houses of Congress. Not surprisingly, however, the president began to harbor serious doubts about the neutrality of the bank in politics. It was known that many congressmen, government officials, and influential newspapers had received low-interest loans and other special services from the bank. On the basis of such evidence, Jackson denounced the existing bank as a "hydra of corruption, dangerous to our liberties every-where." His attorney general, Roger Taney, prepared a veto message that charged the bank with making "the rich richer and the potent more power-ful." Jackson now turned the tables on Clay by making this veto the founda-tion of his campaign for reelection in 1832. When the electoral votes were counted, Jackson—with Van Buren as his running mate—had 217 votes to Clay's 49.

The bank's charter, however, still had four years to run. The president now ordered all future federal deposits to be channeled into state banks. Biddle responded by tightening credit, thereby throwing the country into a contrived recession. Loans to state banks were called in, and acceptance of their paper money was further limited so that westerners and southerners could neither purchase manufactures nor move their crops to market. In seven months the dying bank squashed $18 million of credit out of the state banks. "Nothing but the evidence of suffering abroad," Biddle blandly told an assistant, would bring about recharter.

Yet Jackson was adamant. To one group of New York merchants who petitioned him for help he replied, "Go to the Monster, go to Nicholas Biddle. I will never charter the United States Bank." The New Yorkers, alas,

did not get much sympathy from the equally determined Mr. Biddle. "All the other banks and all the merchants may break," was his chilling response, "but the Bank of the United States shall not break." The recession deepened.

"Money has become very scarce," noted Robert White, the chief cashier of the Manhattan Company, in the summer of 1833. "There is no export or demand for specie from abroad. The branch [of the federal bank] here draws specie from the banks weekly. Yesterday the state banks were called upon for $200,000 . . . " By flexing its muscles in this fashion the federal bank may have cowed a few people, but the state banks and most ordinary citizens were outraged by the arrogance of such a policy. In the state of New York help came from an unexpected quarter. The Erie Canal Fund had some $2.8 million on deposit in thirty-six banks throughout the state, including $400,000 in Albany and half a million in the vaults of the New York city banks. It had planned to withdraw more than $1 million of this to make an early redemption of outstanding canal stock. The moment he divined Biddle's true strategy Azariah Flagg, the state comptroller, "abruptly abandoned the purchase of all stock and resumed lending to banks."

By the spring of 1834, New Yorkers had become so irked by the lack of credit that they began to push hard for a state-based issue of currency. Biddle

opposed this vehemently, thereby eliminating any lingering doubt in the public's mind that he was the true author of the recession. In a second miscalculation Biddle reversed his policy of constriction and unleashed a wave of credit upon the nation, further emphasizing his responsibility for the recession. Though their final victory was sweet, Jackson and Van Buren knew that they had not solved the underlying problem of how, precisely, to structure the nation's financial system. Many ideas were floating in the air, including the establishment of a network of subtreasuries, but none seemed to meet the situation's complex, and often contradictory, requirements.

To the victor belong the spoils. As the affairs of the Bank of the United States wound down, the number of banks chartered in New York State rose from fifty-eight with a capitalization of $20 million in 1832 to ninety with a capitalization of $32.5 million in 1836; deposits in New York's larger banks had more than doubled, from $5 million in 1834 to more than $11 million.

The success of the Erie Canal had inspired a national mania for bridges, canals, railroads and steamboat companies. This mania was coupled to a parallel frenzy of speculation over the new lands that would be opened up by such internal improvements. Between 1834 and 1836 sales of public lands nationwide increased from $4.5 million to $39.5 million. Purchases, however, were often made in dubious bank paper. Newly enriched Americans used their paper profits to purchase European manufactures and then, as if to return the compliment, many Europeans joined the speculation in American land.

As a rule, the banks of New York fared well. Since Seneca Lake had proven to be such a productive tributary of the canal, the Regency was persuaded to look favorably on the establishment of a bank at the southern end of Lake Cayuga, and the Tompkins County Bank of Ithaca (capital $250,000) received a charter. Its first president was Hermon Camp, a successful merchant who had come as a boy from Owego. The year 1836 also saw the chartering of the Bank of Attica and the Rochester City Bank, which were later incorporated, respectively, into the Marine Midland Bank and the Lincoln Rochester Trust Company. The existence of the Safety Fund gave the paper currency of the New York banks a special acceptability throughout the territories to the west. The annual profit of the state's banks, expressed as a percentage of return on capital, soared from 12 percent in 1834 to more than 24 percent in 1836.

Erastus Corning and the Albany City bank rode the rising crest of prosperity with aplomb. The Utica & Schenectady railroad made its first run in the fall of 1836, and Corning was already investing in and promoting new companies that would take his passengers and freight even farther west. Much of the iron for their tracks and rolling stock came from the Albany Iron Works and other foundries of his along the banks of the Hudson. Because new railroads and the communities that grew up beside them needed land, Corning had become a major stockholder in the American Land Company. By 1836 this consortium had acquired 130,000 acres of public lands in nine states and territories; these included 10,000 acres in Ohio and 25,000 in Michigan, where Corning had hopes of gaining control of the troubled Michigan Central Railroad.

But the danger signals were already flashing. In July 1836 an American merchant resident in London wondered, "How all the goods shipped in the last six months and still shipping are to be paid for, I cannot tell." British businessmen, he wrote, "think you are all quite wild in America" and that "half of the Americans at least are going to fail." In the space of six months the Bank of England's specie reserves fell from £7.4 to £4.2 million. Concerned, the British central bank increased its rediscount rate from 4 percent to 4.5 percent and then to 5 percent.

Though he would not have cared to admit it, President Jackson agreed with the Bank of England that speculation in America had gotten out of hand. In July 1836 he issued his famous Specie Circular that henceforth required all purchases of federal land to be made in gold or silver. This decision was shortly followed by the news that a bad harvest in America was likely to produce a sharp increase in wheat prices. For a while matters hung in balance. Then, early in March 1837, the merchant house of Herman Briggs & Co. in New Orleans could not sell its cotton at a high enough price to cover the cost of its extensive purchases, and it failed. A rash of similar failures occurred in New Orleans and then in New York.

The larger banks in the city of New York were particularly concerned about the increasingly strident European demands for payment in specie. In April a committee of bankers and merchants, headed by the former secretary of the treasury Albert Gallatin, traveled to Albany to seek a loan of "four or five millions from the State" to ease the pressure on their hard currency. Once again, Azariah Flagg and the commissioners of the Canal Fund rose to the occasion. While Comptroller Flagg refused to lend the bankers hard cash, he did suggest, in a move to allay European apprehensions, that $3.3

million of the state's canal stock could be distributed to the city's eight major banks in proportion to their capital. The stock, noted Flagg, had a value that was "at least equal, if not superior to, the par of gold and silver." The banks would, in turn, sell their certificates only to the merchants and importers facing legitimate demands for hard currency from foreign creditors. Alas, while the finishing touches were still being put upon these plans, a run on the New York banks brought about the collapse of the New-York Dry Dock Company Bank. When it locked its doors an outraged crowd assembled. Only an eloquent plea for order by the mayor prevented the mob from breaking in.

Poorer citizens were particularly perturbed by the crash, and for a while it seemed that the city's three principal savings banks might go under. The Bank for Savings, one of the first substantial investors in the Erie Canal, was "jammed with depositors crying, 'Pay, pay,' women were nearly pressed to death, and the stoutest men could scarcely sustain themselves."

On May 10 most New York banks, along with major institutions in other states, suspended specie payments. Even then, Comptroller Flagg indicated to the banks that they could rely on the state's continuing support "when the banks were ready to resume specie payments." This event would not take place for a year and in the meantime even the richest New Yorkers felt the pinch. "The immense fortunes which we heard so much about in the days of speculation," lamented the investment banker Philip Hone, "have melted away like the snows before an April sun. No man can calculate to escape ruin but he who owes no money . . ."

Across the Atlantic the confidence of European investors in American securities was badly shaken by the sudden, almost cavalier, suspension of specie payments. Many British manufacturers had shipped huge quantities of manufactures and saw no clear prospect of being paid in acceptable currency. William & Jas. Brown, the representative of Brown Brothers & Co. in Liverpool, reported that it "was loaded up with bills on exports to America that had not been paid for." Though now assisted in England by the talents of a brilliant young partner, Joseph Shipley of Wilmington, Delaware, there was every indication that the firm was on the brink of collapse; in all likelihood the American branches would be pulled under, too. But the imminent demise of the House of Brown did not sit well with the Bank of England, which had often been helped by the Browns on its sterling dollar exchanges; it had also been advised by them on "the troublesome effects of the recent alteration in the American bimetallic currency system." In an unprecedented move the British central bank stepped forward and agreed to extend almost £2 million in credit to the American firm.

Back in the United States the crash and the ensuing depression produced the failure of eleven Safety Fund banks. The three largest institutions were Buffalo banks, with total assets of more than $3 million. In one way or another all eleven seem to have fallen prey to the speculative fever of the mid-1830s, when banks were generating, on average, net revenues of more than 24 percent on invested capital. Embezzlement by employees, many of

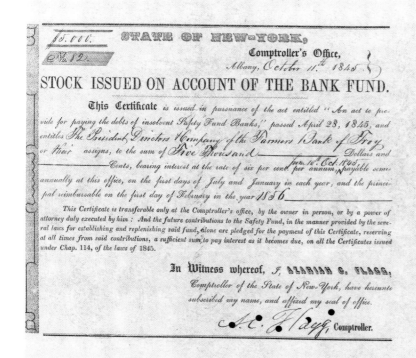

whom found themselves overextended as the result of some speculative venture, played a major role in the collapse, as did bank officers lending to themselves or to close friends on insufficient collateral. Boards of directors, in almost every case, were too passive. Many of the failed banks sought to revive their fortunes by issuing currency beyond their legal limits. In the future, the comptroller's office would insist on holding the engraved plates after printing. The eleven failures, which had paid a mere $86,000 into the Safety Fund, were to cost the fund a total of $2.5 million. All but a million of this sum was recovered by the sale of assets, and additional contributions by the surviving banks. If the law had been framed as Joshua Forman originally urged to merely ensure currency notes, and not deposits, then the fund could have more or less covered its obligations. As it was, however, it had to cover the remaining costs by the $1 million issue of 6 percent state bonds.

The crash, of course, also caused serious political turbulence. For several years now the Loco-Focos, a splinter group of New York's Democrats, had been attempting to push the Jacksonian revolution one step further. Now that the Bank of the United States was out of the way, perhaps the privileges and the legislative log rolling that enveloped the chartering of state banks should also be eliminated. The Loco-Focos were particularly irked by the banks' unique authority to print money and grant credit to their influential friends. No paper currency should be circulated, they said, if it was not matched dollar for dollar by specie held in that bank's vaults. The group—composed primarily of mechanics, urban laborers and a leavening of social reformers—had acquired its odd name when opponents cut off the gas lights at one of its caucuses. The assembly, undeterred, continued its meeting by the light of patent matches called loco-focos.

"One of the major impulses behind the anticharter doctrine," James Sharp notes in *The Jacksonians versus the Banks*, "was an intense egalitarianism. As corporations had been used to limit the power of the king in the past, many felt that charters were being used in the nineteenth century to limit the sovereignty of the people." The Loco-Focos were joined in their dislike of the log rolling over new charters by the fanatical "levelers" of the Antimason party.

But there was also significant criticism of the chartering procedure from the Whigs on the right. To Millard Fillmore, an attorney from Cayuga County who would serve as state comptroller before entering the White House, the chartering process in New York was notorious and "became so shameless and corrupt that it could be endured no longer." Even the otherwise imperturbable British consul James Buchanan seemed startled by the wholesale bribery and manipulation involved. When the City Bank of New York was chartered in 1812, it was required to pay a "bonus" of $120,000 to the common school fund of the state, and a further "bonus" of $50,000 to the state itself. In addition, the price of incorporation included making a loan of $500,000 to the state. The Bank of America, chartered in the same year, had been required to pay various bonuses and loans amounting to $200,000. Nine years later, matters had become even worse when the North River Bank only obtained its charter "on condition of lending to certain persons (having political influence,) $100,000 under pretense of enabling them to reclaim marshes . . . the Bank to hold the land so to be improved, as security for repayment." This Faustian bargain, however, fell through when the bank's directors shrewdly indicated their preference for "paying Sixty Thousand Dollars, rather than lend 100,000 Dollars, to the proprietors of the marshes." Such flagrant attempts at extortion could not help but provoke a feeling of "popular revulsion" against the established chartering process.

Yet when the Loco-Focos approached the New York legislature in January 1837 with a proposal to eliminate both the extortion, and the privileges, of individual charters by making banking open to all, they were dismissed with the breezy rejoinder that, come what may, New York "had the best banking system in the world." Now, with the suspension of specie payments, that proud boast aroused both amusement and contempt. Governor William Marcy, a conventional Jacksonian Democrat and a boyhood friend of Erastus Corning, feared that the Loco-Focos might bolt the ticket and throw the next election to the conservative Whigs. He therefore took up their cause and pushed the so-called free banking law through the legislature in March 1838.

In the view of the financial historian Bray Hammond this legislation was "the most important event in American banking history" because, more than any other measure, it established "a distinctively American system of banking." Instead of forcing each prospective charter to run a legislative gauntlet of champion log rollers, the new measure stood as a kind of generic banking bill, decreeing that any group of citizens meeting certain clearly stated conditions was "free" to establish a bank. The act required new banks to do the following:

1. Have paid-up capital of at least $100,000;
2. Secure any issue of paper currency by pledging an equal value of approved government stocks into the care of the state comptroller, who would then present the bank with the authorized amount of notes, registered and countersigned. If a bank failed to redeem its notes the state comptroller would sell the securities on the open market, and pay off the note holders;
3. Maintain a specie reserve equal in value to 12.5 percent of the paper currency in circulation;
4. Designate the place and term of its existence;
5. Ensure that officers and directors were not held personally liable for the bank's obligations.

Existing banks would continue to operate under the terms of their present charters, thereby instituting two parallel systems of regulation. Though New York banks would not resume specie payments until May 1838, the new law was popular, with 184 charters being issued during the first twenty months after passage. Many of the smaller communities throughout the state acquired their first bank in this period. The experience of Ballston Spa, 4 miles west of Saratoga Lake on the Schenectady & Saratoga Railroad, was typical of many upstate communities in the era before free-chartering. The village, and many citizens in neighboring villages, first applied for a bank charter in 1813, only to be rebuffed without explanation. The village applied for a bank again in 1823, with similar results. In 1838, under the leadership of the thirty-one-year-old merchant James Cook, the community applied under the new law and opened for business immediately with a capitalization of $100,000. Cook, the son of a prominent judge, became the bank's first president, a position in which he served for eighteen years. During that time he held many elected state offices, including that of senator; he became state comptroller in 1854 and served as state superintendent of banks from 1856 to 1861.

The year of 1839 alone launched such diversely located institutions as the Allegany County Bank of Angelica, the Bank of Dansville, the Mohawk Valley Bank of Mohawk and the Bank of Corning. Unlike the Safety Fund banks, whose charters generally ran to 20 years, many founders of free banks chose to run their charters out to 100 years. Some even asked for 1,000 years and one fanciful soul asked that his bank's life-span be extended to 4,050 years!

Magnificent dreams, however, were not enough. Due to inexperience, undercapitalization, and depressed economic conditions following the panic and crash of 1837, one in four of the "free" banks failed in the first three years of operation. However, several hardy and well-managed institutions pulled through and have survived to the present day. They include the Bank of Vernon, which opened in 1839 with a capital of $100,000. The community stands some 20 miles west of Utica, on the old turnpike road to Syracuse; one of the sons of the bank's first president, John Knox of Knoxboro, later became comptroller of the currency in Washington. The Delaware Bank of Delhi was also established under a free charter in 1839.

But the free-charter system was by no means free from risk. Noteholders of the banks that failed did not always get their money back since the comptroller's forced sale of government securities sometimes yielded as little as 70 cents on the dollar. Also, some problems arose between the new banks and the Safety Fund banks, particularly on the discounting of each other's paper. Most of the older institutions, including the Bank of New York and other major city banks, converted to the free bank system on the expiration of their charters.

The crucial significance of such a law, declared Hammond, was that it "surrendered to democracy and to *laisser faire* a business hitherto set apart in general estimation and by special laws privileged and restricted." It also formed a model that would inspire the passage of similar laws by other state legislatures and, eventually, by the Congress with its creation of the National Banking Act of 1864.

But New York's free banking act also paved the way for subtler and more far-reaching innovations in the business of banking. By requiring a specie reserve of 12.5 percent, it foreshadowed the principle "then barely emerging into notice, that control [of bank credit] should be sought through the medium of required reserves."

At the same time, the act also contained the seed of an even more provocative thought: gold and other cumbersome metals might not, after all, represent the ultimate measure of economic value. New York's legislation, says Hammond, "took the bold step of resting the value of money on political authority; and opened the way to the relegation of gold to a mystical arcanum where the State is absolute and the individual never enters to touch the precious stuff."

Through the 1840s things went well for Erastus Corning. He was now in the prime of life. Though Harriet and he had suffered tragedy—only two of the Cornings' five sons lived to maturity—the atmosphere in the old house at 102 State Street lightened measurably when they adopted the four daughters of Harriet's scapegrace brother, Thomas. The Albany City Bank, with only $300,000 in currency outstanding, had weathered the crash of 1837 without serious stress.

Though the depression dragged on into the middle 1840s, the chartering of the free banks created a strong demand for the government securities that

the banks were now required to deposit with the comptroller. Erastus Corning and his Albany City Bank frequently acted as underwriters or "loan contractors" for major issues of New York state stock. So solid were canal revenues that the general public was often prepared to pay a premium of 8, 12, or even 15 percent percent above par for the twenty-year five-percents. As a rule an approved loan contractor like the Albany City would acquire the stock from the Canal Fund at par—or if the bank was feeling competitive, for one or two points above—and then split the premium with a major retail broker like Prime Ward King & Co. of New York City. In a typical offering with which Corning was associated, $300,000 worth of Chenango Canal stock was acquired at par and resold by the bank at a 3 percent premium to Prime Ward, who resold to its retail customers at an 8 percent premium, for a commission of 5 percent. In this particular transaction, a sum of $50,000 was paid down, with the remainder of the stock handed over in weekly installments of $50,000. Thus, after deduction of brokerage fees, the Albany bank received a sum of $8,250 while Prime Ward, the retailer, received some $15,000 less brokerage fees. Later, Corning helped form a syndicate of Albany banks to underwrite the sale of major issues of New York state stock.

Corning's Utica & Schenectady Railroad was becoming very prosperous. Feeder lines were built westward from Utica to Syracuse, via Rome, and from Syracuse to Auburn, and then to Rochester. By 1850 the U & S was generating some $600,000 a year in profit, on total revenues of more than $1 million.

Advertisements proclaimed that it was possible to ride "express" by railroad

The spread of railroad track across the state transformed the economy of many communities. In an effort to increase efficiency, the presidents of seven major railroads met in Rochester in the early 1850s (see contemporary sky view, above) to consolidate into the New York Central, which would operate under the chairmanship of Erastus Corning. (Tinted lithograph by D. W. Moody, 1853; Stokes Collection, New York Public Library)

The New Breed

from Albany to Buffalo in fourteen hours. However, one passenger who bought a ticket complained that it took him thirty-eight hours to complete the odyssey over a patchwork of seven different tracks. He and his fellow travelers spent much of their time parked, like a herd of cattle, in sidings without food, water, or heat. Since there was no official timetable the passengers did not dare to stretch their legs for fear that the locomotive might lurch back into motion at any moment.

Corning decided something must be done. The presidents of the railroads involved were summoned to a meeting in Rochester in the hope that they might be able to hammer out a common policy on schedules, fares and the handling of immigrant travel. Better still, declared Corning, why not merge the railroads and bring a total of 540 miles of track under single management? After lengthy negotiations the other railroads agreed to exchange each $100 share of their companies' stock for a $100 share in an umbrella organization under the presidency of Erastus Corning. The new giant would be known as the New York Central Railroad, and its capitalization of $23 million would make it the largest corporation in the world of American finance.

Just as the Erie Canal had provided a catalyst for the growth of numerous small villages along its route, so now the new network of railroads brought a dramatic expansion and prosperity to scores of communities along the tracks. Sometimes banks even seemed to move with the traffic. The Palmyra Bank of Wayne County opened in 1843, then it moved 10 miles down the road to Newark and then on another 6 miles to Lyons, where it became the Palmyra Bank of Lyons, with a capitalization of $52,000. Further east the connection between railroad construction and the establishment of banks was clearly demonstrated in Madison County. When the Syracuse & Utica Railroad first sought a right of way for its track in 1848, a landowner and speculator named Sands Higginbotham granted the request on one condition: all trains must make a scheduled stop of at least ten minutes' duration in the little hamlet of Oneida. That way, reasoned Higginbotham, the visitors could see the sights of Oneida and refresh themselves at his nearby restaurant. After the railroad opened in 1849, Higginbotham's restaurant and land business picked up markedly. Two years later he and his son Niles opened the Oneida Valley Bank, with a capital of $105,000, in a wing of his residence; the building, now the home of the Madison County Historical Society, still stands.

For most of these developing communities the establishment of a bank represented both a commercial and a social milestone. It became a concrete symbol of common effort, proof that a cluster of houses and stores situated next to a railroad line or at some unnamed bend in the river was more than just a waypoint on the road to somewhere else; the presence of a bank, like that of a church, indicated that a community had a life of its own, and a future. For James Gibbons, a noted banker in Manhattan in the 1850s who was also a shrewd commentator on human affairs, the foundation of a bank in a small community represented the difference between barbarism and civilization. Before the arrival of a bank, declared Gibbons, the traveler to the villages of upstate New York could not help but be struck by "the lack of energy, the rudeness of life and character, and the almost savage features of the common people." A few years later, after the establishment of a bank, a visitor could return to discover that "a new life has been infused into everything; even the countenances of the people are softened; and a less brutal and more intelligent spirit beams from their eyes."

Off to the west the savage features of the people were softened when the Marine Bank of Buffalo began operations under the presidency of George Palmer in 1850. A great portion of the $170,000 capital stock was put up by James Wadsworth, a director of the Attica & Hornellsville Railroad. And in the remotest southwestern corner of the state a more intelligent spirit had a chance to beam from the eyes of the inhabitants when the Jamestown Bank (capital: $98,000) was founded in 1853. Later, while serving as a brigadier general in command of New York volunteers, Wadsworth was wounded in the Battle of the Wilderness; he subsequently died in a Confederate hospital.

Sometimes the process of civilization, like a good wine, took time to mature. In 1821, two years before the completion of the Champlain Canal, an assemblyman from Warren County named William McDonald obtained approval for the construction of a 10-mile-long "feeder canal" around the rapids of the upper Hudson at Glens Falls. The feeder opened up the immense lumber resources and the limestone and black marble quarries along the higher reaches of the river. Glens Falls was incorporated as a village, with a population of 1,300, in 1839, but it did not open its first bank until 1851, with the founding of the Glens Falls Bank (capital: $100,000). Two years later, for reasons that are not wholly clear, Assemblyman McDonald and the leading lumberman of the region, Augustus Sherman, broke away from the first bank to establish the Commercial Bank of Glens Falls, with a capitalization of $136,000.

A similar development took place among the people of the Chenango Valley. In 1833 the people of the valley counties pushed Albany into approving construction of a 97-mile canal connecting Binghamton (and the waters of the Susquehanna) directly to the Mohawk at Utica. Large quantities of Pennsylvania coal were brought up through the waterway after 1846 to provide steam power for the new textile mills in Utica. In the following decade communities like Waverly and Owego along the southern tier river system became prosperous enough to open banks. The Bank of Tioga, established in Owego in 1856, would become the cornerstone of today's Owego National Bank, with total assets of $38 million.

Though the new feeder canal up to the Mohawk system never paid for itself, a number of communities along its route prospered. In that same year, 1856, the Bank of Norwich, with a capital of $125,000, opened its doors. One of its leading customers was a local farmer named Gail Borden, who patented a process for producing evaporated milk in the same year the bank opened.

The counties on the east bank of the Hudson saw the foundation of the Bank of Rhinebeck (capital: $25,000), the Union Bank of Kinderhook (capi-

The spirit of tranquillity engendered by the appearance of canal, railroad, and bank is captured in this evening scene of Clinton Square, Syracuse, circa 1870. (Oil on canvas by Johann M. Culverhouse, 1871; Onondaga Historical Association)

tal: $125,000) and the Bank of Commerce of Putnam County (a bank owned by an individual, W. Kelley, with an estimated capital of about $100,000), all in 1853. The Bank of Coxsackie (capital: $120,000) also opened its doors on the far side of the Hudson in the same year, and the Stissing Bank (capital: $72,000) made its appearance in Pine Plains in 1858.

In the life of each of these small communities the founding of a financial institution, even one so small that its office was situated on the first floor of a residence, formed a critical step on the high road to prosperity. "A *bank* has been the starting point of this new career," noted James Gibbons. "The mill-dam has been built across the little streams of capital, and the social machinery is brought into play. After it is organized, a bank gathers capital by *saving*. It presents the first idea of economy and increase to thousands of people."

5

The Great Leap Forward

THE YEARS between the election of Jackson in 1828 and the election of Lincoln in 1860 saw the transformation of the United States from an agrarian backwater into a flourishing industrial power. This was America's Great Leap Forward, the economic miracle that scores of nations in the century ahead would—with mixed success—attempt to emulate. In the opinion of Professor Page Smith, these three critical decades embraced "the most remarkable era in American history, or even, it might be argued, in the history of the world."

It was, by any measure, an era of remarkable achievement. Buoyed up by the discovery of gold at Sutter's Fort and thoughts of manifest destiny, Americans annexed Texas, California, and much of the territory in between to increase the geographic area of their country by half as much again. During the same period the arrival of 8 million immigrants, many thrust from their homes by the revolutions of 1848 in Europe and the potato famine in Ireland, helped the population to triple, to a total of more than 30 million. Between 1840 and 1860 agricultural output doubled and the production of manufactures increased nearly fivefold, to equal two-thirds that of Britain. The laid track of the railroads jumped from a few miles to more than 30,000 miles by 1860. Exports came to register an annual worth of $280 million— two-thirds of which passed over the wharves of "mast-hemmed Manhattan"— while imports amounted to $368 million.

But the great leap forward was also a great leap into the unknown. There

By 1860 almost two-thirds of the nation's international trade passed over the wharves of "mast-hemmed Manhattan" resulting in busy scenes like that portrayed above by J. W. Hill in 1853. (Aquatint engraving by Himely and Mottram, after oil on canvas by J. W. Hill, 1853; Mariners Museum, Newport News, Virginia)

was no master plan, and no guide to warn of financial pitfalls ahead. By annihilating rather than amending the power of the Bank of the United States, the Jacksonians had sentenced the state-chartered banks of America to carry the burden alone; in the words of Bray Hammond, they had condemned thousands of inexperienced and woefully undercapitalized banks to roam "at large in the jungle of *laisser faire*."

Together with several of the more progressive states, New York had sought to strengthen its banks with a thin veneer of regulation. But such regulations were for the most part prescriptive, static lists of Do's and Don'ts incapable of providing the leadership and the day-to-day guidance the system needed if it were to perform as a coherent whole. There is no question that a modified Bank of the United States, shorn of Nicholas Biddle's political manipulations, could have moved American banks forward when economic expansion was called for and restrained them when the liabilities ventured on the excessive. But without a central bank of their own, New York's financial institutions found themselves increasingly tied to the vagaries of the British economy and, ultimately, to the policies of the Bank of England. The lion's share of American imports and exports came to be financed by credits from British banks, which generally ran from four to eighteen months in duration. In addition, much of America's trade with other nations—particularly those with which it held an unfavorable balance of payments—was also financed by Britain. At each stage of the long chain of credit by which goods were moved from grower to manufacturer and from manufacturer to consumer, little or no money changed hands. Instead, the holder of the goods, be he merchant, jobber or retailer, would, on delivery, receive a note promising to pay cash at some future date. "Commerce, in its broadest sense, is carried on by promissory notes," complained James Gibbons, an eminent New York banker, in 1858. "The multiplication of this form of credit is beyond all control. It leads every department of trade from pins and needles up to cargoes of grain and cotton. It represents ships, railroads, manufactories, public and private contracts."

The sugar that reached the wharves of New York from Havana, noted Gibbons, "has two or three sets of notes predicated on it before the first hogshead is discharged from the vessel; and it continues to accumulate notes as it passes through the hands of the refiner to those of the grocer." The terms of repayment along the chain of paper frequently outran the utility of the products upon which they were based. For the Cuban sugar cane, even "after it had been swallowed in confections, its notes were still floating, unliquidated, in the market." That market, as a whole, "carries millions of notes for what is already consumed, and millions more for what is not yet sprouted in the furrow."

A great proportion of this paper, coming and going, ran through the ledgers of banks like Brown Brothers & Co. in New York. Since James Brown opened an office in New York in 1825, the bank's capital had increased by some 16 percent a year so that by 1856 the partnership had a total capital of $7.5 million, which surpassed that of most of the banks in Manhattan and made Brown Brothers & Co. significantly larger and more influential than the famous House of Baring in London.

While international banking firms like Barings, the early Morgan firm and Brown Brothers sought to handle the complex transactions of the state's massive export and import trade, the precise nature of those services was not easily understood or appreciated. Due to its efficiency and its determination to stand by its word, Brown Brothers had attracted a major portion of the southern cotton trade to New York. In a typical transaction Brown might make out a "bill of exchange" (somewhat like a cashier's check that had international acceptability after a specified date) to a cotton merchant like Toulmin Hazard & Co. of New Orleans, for $10,000 payable sixty days after it was received. This constituted an advance payment on 100 tons (or 224,000 pounds) of baled cotton to be shipped from New Orleans to Liverpool, England, where it would be sold at auction. In 1855 the price of cotton in New Orleans was about 8.4 cents a pound, and that same cotton could be sold by Brown, Shipley in Liverpool for 5.6 English pennies a pound, or a total of £5,227. Brown would then convert this, at the rate of $4.80 to the pound sterling, into $25,088 in New York, deduct the advance payment of $10,000 and its 6 percent commission of $1,505, and send a bill of exchange for the remaining $13,583 to Toulmin Hazard in New Orleans. The cotton merchants would then make a final payment of some $8,816 to the plantation owners who sold them the original consignment of cotton.

This final settlement left Toulmin Hazard with $4,767 as payment for

" Come, gentlemen, don't wander too far from the subject before the Board. The question is, whether Mr. Thrush's note is good enough to be discounted."

their services and for their assumption of all speculative risk. It is likely, however, that a merchant such as Hazard's would invite the plantation owners—universally known for their willingness to gamble—to join with them in sharing those risks in return for a proportionate share of the profits. Of course, in a lean year the baled cotton might sell in Liverpool at a reduced price; in 1851, for instance, the Liverpool price of baled cotton was 12 percent lower than the price paid for it on the docks of New Orleans, thereby causing a loss for both grower and merchant.

The cost of transporting the cotton across the Atlantic and insuring it generally ran about one American penny a pound. Brown Brothers, which owned a fleet of sail and steam vessels, would often provide such shipping. But when it was provided by another line its commission was reduced commensurately. Though frequently invited to become principals in the cotton and tobacco trades Brown's preferred, as a matter of policy, to take their modest but assured commission and leave the speculation to the planters.

Brown's also did a substantial business in the granting of "letters of credit"—not unlike a modern traveler's check—for those doing business abroad. As time went by it also became a major dealer in currency exchange, typically converting dollars to pounds for American importers in the spring and summer months, and pounds to dollars in the fall and winter months when American wheat, cotton and tobacco merchants were exporting their crops to England. In 1854 the house of Brown transacted $42 million worth of business in foreign currency exchange; the firm customarily charged a commission of one-half of one percent on such transactions. In unsettled times, however, currency exchange became a highly speculative business. But even then the Brown brothers held their own. Like their Presbyterian father from County Antrim, they knew "when to go in, how long to stay, and when to get out."

Knowing when to get in and when to get out also presented a challenge to the land-bound banks of New York as they sifted through their own pyramids of financial paper. James Gibbons, author and bank president, gave his readers some fascinating insights into the daily decisions that might confront a major institution in Manhattan just before the outbreak of the Civil War. The decision to accept or reject a promissory note for discount was critical if the prosperity of a bank was to be maintained. On two "discount days" each week—usually Tuesday and Friday—the bank's entire board of directors met in the institution's boardroom between 9 and 10:30 in the morning to determine which paper to accept and which to reject; this activity, said Gibbons, constituted the board's "principal business." On discount day in a major bank the applicants "placing their paper on offer" generally numbered between seventy-five and one hundred, and the funds disbursed to successful applicants would amount to between $400,000 and $500,000.

When a board meeting was called to order, the chief cashier read through the "offering book" and the directors either approved or rejected the applications for credit. The task was somewhat simplified by the fact that most of the regular customers had an established line of credit, generally set at between two and three times the amount they held on deposit. If the application was within the limit and no adverse rumors had been heard about the applicant's business, the request would be approved. If the applicant backed his request with especially substantial resources then in the quaint phrases of the day, his note might be adjudged "fire proof" or "as good as wheat."

If a difference of opinion arose among the members of the board as to the worthiness of an applicant then a discussion, either pointed or rambling, might ensue. What was known of the applicant's personal habits? Was he a strong family man? Had the stress of business driven him to drink a little too much brandy? What, had someone seen him in a gambling den or in one of the bawdy houses about the city? "To a person outside the door," said Gibbons, "it would seem as if the members were engaged in a general wrangle."

In other cases the board might vote to reject or "let 'em slide" because an applicant's credit was "a notch too low." Or, even if an applicant's credit was sound the board might vote "too long," indicating that the commercial paper supporting the applicant showed he would not be paid by his own debtors in sufficient time to liquidate the note. Great geographic distances and poor communications were an ever-present concern for the board. If an applicant's supporting promissory notes came from Halifax or even Mexico, they might be acceptable. But one director warned that a note written in California should be viewed with suspicion. "Too far off," he sagely declared. "T'other side of the world."

On a typical discount day the board might complete its deliberations by half past ten. The applications, with their supporting paper, were then handed to the bank's discount clerk, who would respond to each customer anxiously approaching the cage. The letter A (for Accepted) marked against a

A tight day at the Discount Desk.

man's name in the ledger enabled the clerk to answer "either by an affirmative nod, or the monosyllable 'done'." The letter R (for Refused) in the ledger indicated that the applicant's offering has been rejected, and the envelope of papers was returned to him. Some disappointed applicants took their medicine quietly, while others might scowl and demand to know why they'd been turned down.

"What is the reason for that, sir?"

"Market tightened up, sir," the discount clerk might reply with a touch of diplomacy. "Deposits down. Offerings very heavy."

With its twice-weekly meetings such a board of directors might authorize the disbursement of between $3 million and $4 million a month in short-term loans on promissory notes held by merchants, jobbers and retailers. By keeping its loans short the bank was able to skim the waves. If the level of business activity declined or expanded then the bank's discount operations could readily be trimmed to fit the new set of circumstances. Either way, the funds for the new loans were derived primarily from the repayment, or "liquidation," of similar loans made to customers two and three months previously and now come due.

If one of those previous applicants could not repay the $15,000 he owed— perhaps he was a merchant and two of his ships had been delayed by bad weather—then the bank's ability to make new loans was impaired. The merchant might ask the bank to "accommodate" him by renewing his loan until his ships made port. But in Gibbons's day the whole matter of "accommodation paper," of renewing any loan, was a particularly vexing and controversial one. When describing the deliberations of the board on discount day, Gibbons noted that "for the hundreth time, perhaps, then comes up a discussion as to what constitutes accommodation paper, and the impropriety of banks discounting it on any terms." If the board denied the merchant then it might well drive him into bankruptcy and, after a substantial lapse of time,

A Veteran Specie Clerk.

collect only a a few nickels on the dollar. Alternatively, if the board renewed, it might be throwing good money after bad. More, it might be setting a poor precedent; if a customer's loan was renewed once, then he would expect it to be renewed again, and yet again. The customers, so the thinking went, would cease to review their financial options carefully. And soon the bank was no longer skimming the waves of commerce. Instead, it would begin to sink under a load of long-term "accommodations."

Most banks in the city had three tellers, each with distinct duties that differ markedly from the duties of the teller today. The first, or paying teller, stood immediately below the cashier in rank. He was responsible for the vault and for paying out all coin and paper currency to customers. The second, or deposit teller, accepted and registered all incoming coin, bank bills, checks and other documents representing money. Finally, there was the third, or note teller, who received money for promissory notes as they fell due. He, too, kept a register—colloquially referred to as "the tickler"—to remind the bank and its customers when their notes would be coming due.

The tellers were assisted in their tasks by a number of clerks and bookkeepers. In the opinion of Gibbons, however, the most impressive figure of all to work in the bank was the porter. This Dickensian character was responsible for the bank's physical security; he unlocked the bank in the morning and locked it up at night. But he also had the additional duties of counting all the coin in and out of the vault and delivering bags of specie and securities to the receiving tellers of all the other banks in the city. His satchel of valuables, with its thick leather shoulder strap, was carried under his left arm, leaving his right hand free to administer a drubbing to any who might seek to interfere with his appointed rounds.

The nature of his tasks required that the porter be burly, shrewd, and unimpeachably honest. For the most part such men were savvy and streetwise and could spot a forger or a confidence man in the lobby at a glance. Often the porter's deliveries of specie and documents to competing institutions provided the president of his own bank with critical intelligence on the state of the marketplace. Despite their "diligent habits and faithful service," declared Gibbons, such stalwarts frequently suffered from a "cross-grained disposition." But Gibbons remained unabashed in his admiration for the porters. In the previous quarter century, he noted, there had been but one instance of dishonesty found among them. And though they were generally drawn from a class having "a want of cultivation in early life," he believed that one-fifth of all the banks then in the city would be "improved by transposition of office between the Porter and the President or Cashier."

Between 1834 and 1854 the number of banks in the state of New York increased from 78 with a total capital of $27.6 million to 334 with a total capital of $83.7 million. In 1843, after some early failures among the free-charter banks, the power of oversight was transferred from the bank commissioners to the state comptroller. At the same time, the comptroller was made the custodian of all the engraved plates used in the printing of new notes, thereby putting a damper on "fraudulent and excessive" issues of bank currency. Due to the surge in the number of new banks, however, the legislature finally decided to set up an independent banking department with its own superintendent in 1851. The first superintendent, D. B. St. John, and his deputy, Edward Hand, received salaries of $2,500 and $1,500, respectively. To assist them were ten clerks and "registers" whose primary task seemed to be the signing and authentication of currency.

St. John's first annual report showed that banking was a volatile business to be in. While twelve existing banks, most of them in small communities like Ellenburgh, Granville and Ashford, indicated their intention to close, a total of twenty-six new banking associations and eleven banks owned by individuals deposited securities required by law, and commenced business. The new associations included the Hanover Bank and the Irving Bank of New York, and the Merchants' Bank of Syracuse. Accounting figures are sketchy, but free-charter banks throughout the state had, on average, a capital of $176,800 and a circulation of $39,700. Three years later the upstate banks had become substantially more prosperous, with an average capital of $236,000 and $88,400 circulation.

Such was the surge of business in the 1850s that the number of banks in the city of New York increased from twenty-four to sixty. The presence of the newcomers created congestion. Then, as yet more institutions opened, mat-

Confusion was inevitable; the Old Fashion of Settlement on Friday. (Sketch by Herrick; author's collection)

ters became so chaotic that leading banks had to devise radical new ways of transacting business.

Under the established system every bank at the end of each working day totaled up what it owed, or was owed, by every one of the fifty-nine other banks. Then the porter of each bank, carrying his leather satchel and a book of entry, marched through the streets of Manhattan to square accounts with every other bank. This set sixty porters in motion at the same time. The scene was often one of confusion. "The porters crossed and recrossed each other's footsteps constantly; they often met in companies of five or six at the same counter, and retarded each other; and they were fortunate to reach their respective banks at the end of one or two hours."

As the number of banks increased to sixty, the number of individual daily transactions between porters and banks increased geometrically from 625 to 3,600. Disparities and petty confusions were inevitable. Each Friday, after completing their rounds, all sixty porters made a point of meeting on the steps of a Wall Street bank. Then, in what came to be known as the Porters' Exchange, they had a final collective reckoning as to who actually owed what to whom. In October 1853 the banks of the city carried this idea of an exchange one step further and set up what they called the Clearing House Association. Under this new arrangement each bank sent two men, a specie clerk and a settling clerk, to meet in a large room on the fourth floor of the Bank of New York building at Wall and William streets. At ten o'clock each morning the settling clerks would sit in order on the inside of a large hollow table. The specie clerks, each holding a tray with packets of checks due from each bank, stood in a ring on the outer rim of the table.

On a given signal the specie clerks then presented the appropriate packet and a receipt list to the settling clerk sitting in front of him. The settling clerk

Making the Exchange in Six Minutes, at the Clearing House.

took the checks and signed the receipt list. Then the whole line of specie clerks, carrying trays and receipt books, advanced one step like "a military company in lock-step." The parade continued until each specie clerk arrived back at his starting point with an empty tray and a receipt book full of signatures. Unlike the old system, which took hours and placed large sums of specie at hazard in the streets of Manhattan, the Clearing House generally completed all transactions between banks in the space of six minutes.

So far no cash had changed hands. But by one o'clock all the net debtor banks had to bring in the amount they owed in cash to the Clearing House, and at 1:30 P.M. all net creditor banks sent clerks to collect the cash due them. Each day some $30 million to $40 million worth of countervailing obligations were presented, and squared, with the systematic redistribution of more than $1 million in specie. Since $1 million worth of gold coins weighed about three tons, the Clearing House soon arranged for the Bank of America to establish a specie depository. When a member bank made a deposit of coin it would receive paper receipts in $1,000, $5,000 and $10,000 denominations. Subsequently, instead of wheeling carts of specie through the streets, member banks simply traded endorsed depository receipts back and forth between one another.

Even more important than the increase in safety and efficiency, the Clearing House created a new sense of mutual dependence. A mismanaged bank could quickly infect all the other banks in the Clearing House with its problems; thus each member bank was required to submit every week a sworn statement of account. If the statements presented a confused or disquieting pattern of business, then the Clearing House Committee had the power to make a rigorous examination of the bank. Depending on the nature of the problem, the offending bank might be helped back on to its feet or expelled

CLEARING HOUSE PROOF.

March 20th, 1857.

Clearing House proof. (Table data from James S. Gibbons, Banks, p. 310; author's collection)

No.	BANKS.	Balances due to Clearing House.	BANKS Dr.	BANKS Cr.	Balances due to Banks.	
1	Bank of New York.....	....	780 070 76	842 539 19	62 468 43	1
2	Manhattan Company....	....	1 198 412 96	1 377 768 55	179 355 59	2
3	Merchants'.............	....	8 484 091 94	8 782 778 77	248 686 83	3
4	Mechanics'.............	179 476 86	1 592 992 22	1 413 515 86	.....	4
5	Union................	12 929 43	2 818 023 77	2 800 094 34	.....	5
6	Bank of America.......	285 304 33	2 600 723 68	2 315 419 30	.....	6
7	Phenix................	....	1 115 098 42	1 133 515 85	18 416 93	7
8	City.................	85 502 19	580 666 56	545 164 37	.....	8
9	North River...........	....	172 720 94	196 283 59	23 562 65	9
10	Tradesmen's...........	....	104 139 78	107 791 84	3 652 11	10
11	Fulton................	....	241 717 85	254 445 12	12 727 27	11
12	Chemical..............	....	197 007 27	197 816 47	809 20	12
13	Merchants' Exchange...	....	410 632 22	526 873 22	116 241	13
14	National..............	89 217 96	452 994 22	418 776 26	.....	14
15	Butchers' & Drovers'..	....	129 719 75	131 771 66	2 051 91	15
16	Mechanics' & Traders'.	11 587 23	41 182 48	29 595 25	.....	16
17	Greenwich.............	....	85 404 ..	87 882 56	2 478 56	17
18	Leather Manufacturers'.	....	991 464 07	1 053 650 08	62 186 01	18
19	Seventh Ward..........	....	180 572 87	243 770 ..	63 197 63	19
20	Bk. of the State of N. Y.	....	3 893 899 27	4 035 962 93	142 063 66	20
21	American Exchange.....	....	3 076 473 27	3 109 168 27	32 695 ..	21
22	Mech. Banking Assoc'n.	....	247 589 06	254 257 05	6 667 99	22
23	Bank of Commerce.....	294 626 99	3 272 050 33	2 977 423 34	.....	23
24	Bowery................	....	72 330 36	77 006 08	4 675 72	24
25	Broadway..............	4 858 02	218 402 41	213 549 39	.....	25
26	Ocean................	....	334 539 77	358 516 63	23 976 86	26
27	Mercantile............	....	446 973 09	579 107 92	132 134 83	27
28	Pacific...............	1 951 43	92 845 83	90 894 40	.....	28
29	Bank of the Republic..	164 525 52	2 352 505 08	2 187 979 51	.....	29
30	Chatham...............	....	79 367 82	80 167 13	799 31	30
31	People's..............	....	94 507 05	96 111 76	1 604 71	31
32	Bank of North America..	....	686 922 86	724 620 78	37 697 92	32
33	Hanover...............	....	352 352 64	420 800 52	68 447 88	33
34	Irving................	....	117 442 73	115 237 48	.....	34
35	Metropolitan..........	2 205 25	1 760 562 96	1 663 260 05	.....	35
36	Citizens'.............	97 302 91				36
38	Grocers'..............	....	88 984 55	101 304 17	12 319 62	38
40	Nassau................	17 019 11	112 690 88	112 692 55	1 ...	40
41	East River............	....	331 872 15	314 853 04	.....	41
42	Market................	8 451 80	52 996 92	57 828 88	4 831 96	42
43	Saint Nicholas........	....	207 143 25	198 691 45	.....	43
44	Shoe and Leather......	108 597 02	295 366 85	345 923 39	50 556 54	44
45	Corn Exchange.........	2 498 35	366 901 55	268 304 53	.....	45
47	Continental...........	63 020 44	1 038 328 69	1 085 825 84	.....	47
48	Bank of Commonwealth	50 721 86	1 390 188 88	1 327 163 39	.....	48
49	Oriental..............	....	847 108 34	796 886 48	.....	49
50	Marine................	....	38 782 03	40 745 32	013 29	50
52	Atlantic..............	21 788 70	390 693 54	368 904 84	.....	52
53	Importers' & Traders'.	47 889 89	247 581 91	199 992 02	.....	53
54	Park..................	....	810 624 45	860 601 47	49 977 02	54
55	Artisans'.............	....	579 850 08	658 471 74	73 621 66	55
		1444 419 79	40 515 703 66	40 515 703 66	1444 419 79	

from the Clearing House. Fear of such a fate kept most city banks on the straight and narrow. Indeed, so successful was the clearinghouse concept that similar institutions were established in Boston in 1856 and in Philadelphia in 1858. In 1913 the principle would eventually become the model for the check-clearing process operated by the Federal Reserve System.

It was not long before the New York Clearing House idea was tested in another, more exacting fashion. On August 24, 1857, the Ohio Life Insur-

Wall Street on Suspension Day. Oct. 14, 1857.

ance & Trust Co. failed. The trust had borrowed heavily from several New York banks, many of which also panicked and immediately stopped discounting commercial paper, even for the most reliable of their customers; this caused several trading houses to close. The market was already soft due to the decline in wheat sales on the termination of the Crimean War. It received two further blows when it was learned that much of Ohio Life's capital had been embezzled by its own executives, and that a ship on the way from California with $2 million in gold had been lost at sea. Gibbons's great paper pyramid of promises then began to implode. By the end of September, banks in Pennsylvania, Maryland, and Virginia had suspended specie payments. A run on New York City banks began, and most of them suspended on October 14. The Chemical Bank, which earned the sobriquet "Old Bullion" in the panic of 1837, continued to redeem its own paper in gold. After two days the public became convinced that Chemical meant what it said so that the *Commercial Advertiser* was able to report that "there is little or no pressure on them to-day for redemption, and they are receiving a large addition to their deposits" from those who previously kept their accounts at other institutions. Between October 3 and December 5, 1857, the Chemical's deposits increased from $992,000 to $1,620,000.

Much of the problem in 1857, according to James Gibbons, arose from the tunnel vision of individual banks. Some institutions took advantage of the confusion by attempting to squeeze and then crush their rivals. The officers of many banks "fell back, each to his separate place to 'fortify' his institution," contrary to the best interests of the community. One bank came close to failing altogether after the discovery of a $70,000 embezzlement by its paying teller, but eventually all institutions were carried through the crisis by the Clearing House, enabling specie payments to be resumed in December. To guard against future trouble, member banks resolved to keep specie on hand equal to 20 percent of deposits. The whole experience, however, led Gibbons to question the morality of many bankers who placed competitive advantage over the interest of the community at large. And it caused him to wonder about the "true office of gold in commerce." The metal, he decided, was "not an indispensable pledge for the soundness of paper money" if the issue of that paper were strictly circumscribed by law, as in New York. In this double negative could be found the seeds of the greenback and the fiat money that William Cornwell would so heartily deplore nearly four decades later.

6

The Thousand Dollar Breakfast

WITH THE ATTACK on Fort Sumter in April 1861, the banks of the northern states found themselves thrust into a world unhinged; every financial precept which they had built and operated upon in the past now appeared to be invalid or open to serious question. At the time of the assault President Lincoln had occupied the White House for little more than a month. After some consideration he chose Salmon P. Chase, a senator from Ohio who had unsuccessfully challenged him for the Republican party nomination, to serve as his Secretary of the Treasury.

Chase was undoubtedly one of Lincoln's more controversial appointments. A lawyer by training, he was a great hulking fellow with sharp wits and a determination to get things done. Such qualities might have served the North well on the battlefield, but they were to prove less effective in the paper wars now about to be waged along the bleak corridors of Washington. In such a setting the new Treasury chief quickly became known for his domineering manner and a turn of phrase that often bordered upon the sarcastic. Perhaps even more troubling was the fact that Chase had no direct experience of high finance. And there was little time to learn. As he moved into his office, the new secretary was alarmed to discover that his immediate predecessor in the Buchanan administration had ceased to collect customs revenues and, in consequence, the total funds available in the Treasury's vaults amounted to a mere $1.7 million.

One of Chase's first acts was to summon the representatives of the leading

banks of Boston, Philadelphia and New York to meet with him in April 1861. At that time New York's banks held $92.0 million (close to a third of the nation's total) in deposits, and $49.7 million (70 percent of total) in gold and silver coin. Sharp differences of opinion quickly surfaced. The banks agreed to loan Chase $150 million in three installments, the last to be paid four months hence. In return they would receive $150 million in 7.3 percent three-year Treasury notes, which they would endeavor to sell to the public. Since the banks of the three cities collectively held only $63.1 million in specie they intended to hold the proceeds on the sale of the notes in specially constituted federal accounts. Then, when the government wished to make a disbursement for food, military uniforms or military pay, it could simply write a check against those federal accounts, which the banks would then pay in their own currency.

Salmon Chase, however, had grown up a Jacksonian Democrat and he had a westerner's mistrust of banks and "soft" money. The Treasury, he declared, would not leave the loans on deposit in the banks. And he did not want paper money. He wanted hard cash, to be paid directly into the Treasury. In reply, the assembled bankers pointed out that it was impossible to deliver on such a request, since their own reserves amounted to less than half the amount Chase demanded. Many expected the government to finance the war not by borrowing, but by means of a broad program of taxation. Furthermore, the bankers said, their ability to pay specie for the 7.3 percent notes would be undermined if Chase proceeded with his plan to issue an additional $50 million in demand notes, redeemable at any time in specie.

This argumentative response led Chase to conclude that the big city banks were willfully obstructing the government's policies. Either that or, he surmised, the pampered existence of the bankers had rendered them intellectually unable to grasp the severity of the crisis. "I was obliged to be very firm," he subsequently said. The ensuing exchange of pleasantries led

Chase to question whether the nation's financial system, as presently constituted, was capable of sustaining a major military effort. In his concluding remarks the secretary expressed his hope that the banks would give him their support. "If not," he told them sternly, he would "go back to Washington and issue notes for circulation; for, gentlemen, the war must go on until the rebellion is put down, if we have to put out paper until it takes a thousand dollars to buy a breakfast."

With the Union army's defeat at the battle of Bull Run in July, the prospects of an early victory for the North became significantly dimmer. As Confederate forces skirmished along the banks of the Potomac, the representatives of the major city banks requested a second meeting with the Secretary of the Treasury. This time it was held in Chase's Washington office. The group was joined by Senator John Sherman of Ohio, younger brother of the famous general and himself a future Secretary of the Treasury. As the sounds of Confederate artillery rattled the windows, the bankers presented demands that seemed to be out of touch with reality. They asked the government to (a) legalize the suspension of specie payment, (b) "carry on the war upon the basis of the paper money of the banks" while (c) issuing no paper money of its own. Senator Sherman could not believe his ears. The Union was fighting for its life. Young men on both sides were dying by the hundreds for every week that passed. The North would shortly have 500,000 men under arms, a decision that would eventually cost the government nearly $2 million a day.

Thousand Dollar Breakfast

The departure of New York's 7th Infantry Regiment for the front. (Oil on canvas by Thomas Nast; New-York Historical Society)

In such a crisis Sherman and Chase were baffled by the bankers' seeming inability to come up with anything more than the same financial plan they had "substantially adopted in the War of 1812."

After the leading bankers from Philadelphia, Boston and New York had completed their presentation, Sherman looked around the ring of faces. "That was the scheme presented to us by very intelligent gentlemen engaged in the banking business. They were honest and earnest," conceded Sherman, but the plan "appeared to me as pretentious and even ludicrous."

This second interview further soured Salmon Chase's attitude toward the banks. It was now apparent to him that appeals to reason, and to common patriotism, were ineffective. In Chase's view it was time to start cracking eggs for the thousand dollar breakfast. He decided that the cabinet, with the assistance of Congress, had no choice but to force the financial system into delivering the resources needed to win the war.

For a while, it is true, the New York banks attempted to cooperate with Chase. But when the secretary, due to the exigencies of the battlefield, found it necessary to issue \$33.5 million worth of the demand notes, the banks were caught in an even tighter squeeze. Their gold and silver reserves quickly fell from \$49.7 to \$29.4 million by December 1861, and they suspended specie payments. Banks throughout the North quickly followed suit.

Treasury Secretary Chase admitted later that he had to inflate the currency with $400 million worth of greenbacks (see contemporary sketch of Chase's Patent Greenback Mill hard at work) before the five-twenty bonds "could be floated easily at par." (Library of Congress)

Less than two months after suspension, Congress approved the issue of another $100 million worth of notes which, together with the original $50 million, would now be accounted legal tender for all public and private debts. But these notes would no longer be redeemable on demand. They were quickly dubbed "greenbacks." At the same time Congress also authorized the issue of $500 million worth of 6 percent bonds. These in turn came to be known as "five-twenties" because, though the government was compelled to discharge its obligation in twenty years, it nevertheless reserved the right to recall these bonds for refinancing after only five years. Their interest would be paid in specie.

To the dismay of commercial banks there was no stipulation on when the greenback would be retired, and no pledge against further issue. However, it should be noted that the greenbacks could not yet be classified as bona fide "fiat" money, that is, money that derived its acceptability not from any right to convert it into coin but from the general credit of the government issuing it. Until July 1, 1863, it was still possible to convert greenbacks into five-twenty bonds, whose interest would be paid in specie. Only after that deadline passed could legal-tender notes be classified as genuine fiat money.

Further issues of greenbacks, totaling in all some $300 million, would be made before the end of hostilities. At first the five-twenty bonds sold slowly, but Chase appointed a resourceful and imaginative Philadelphia banker named Jay Cooke to serve as chief agent for the merchandising of bonds in return for a commission of three-eighths of one percent of all sales. Cooke was a banker's banker. He was described by a contemporary as "slender, light-haired, blue-eyed, fair-complexioned, and of radiant countenance" and a man who could handle the most complex banking business like a "smoothly flowing stream of noiseless water." By using patriotic—not to say Orwell-ian—promotional stunts ("Our National Debt is a National Blessing"), Cooke worked through numerous subagents, including many banks in the state of New York, to sell well over a billion dollars worth of government bonds. Though there was some talk of "profiteering" at the time, Cooke is said to have personally netted a mere $220,000 from his ingenious cam-paigns.

In contrast to the bond drives, most of New York's banks viewed Secretary Chase's mammoth issue of the greenbacks with alarm; to many they seemed little better than a forced loan from the people to the federal government. As if this were not enough, many bankers were also perturbed by Chase's seemingly underhanded scheme to sell a further $1 billion worth of federal bonds. The secretary, they asserted, had intentionally inflated the currency in an attempt to force the more affluent members of the public into purchas-ing the five-twenties. And Chase did not deny the charge. Later he was to observe—with some complacency—that it "required the printing and paying out of $400 million of greenbacks before the five-twenty 6 percent bonds could be floated easily at par."

Despite these strong-arm tactics, Chase was not without his supporters, particularly among the more forward-looking men in the New York banking community. Preeminent among these was John Thompson, publisher of *Thompson's Bank Note Reporter* and one of the founders of the First National Bank in 1863. Thompson had such an admiration for Chase that, on starting another bank in 1877, he was to name it after the secretary.

During the war years First National's head teller, a burly youth with a steel-trap mind named George Baker, also made a strong impression on Secretary Chase. Soon Chase was consulting Baker as to the optimal terms obtainable in future government bond issues. Later, at Chase's request, he made several visits to Washington, where he was introduced to President Lincoln, Senator Sherman and several members of the war cabinet.

The widening rift between the government and the established financial institutions and the mounting loss of life on the battlefield made Chase ever more determined to bring the nation's banking operations under a single roof. For months, however, he had difficulty formulating a plan that would have a serious chance of passing Congress. Then a well-researched article appeared in *Hunt's Merchants' Magazine* advocating the establishment of a national paper currency. This would, wrote the author, be a federal version of the free-banking system currently in force in the state of New York. Each bank, in return for a pledge of federal securities, would be permitted to issue a like amount of the federal government's currency bills. For each dollar denomination—be it $5, $20, or $100—the bills would be identical except for the fact that, like those of New York, they would be overstamped on one side with the issuing bank's name. Such a currency would breed a sense of confidence. Its dozen or so denominations would be well printed and easily recognized. All notes would be readily acceptable at par throughout the country. Banks accepting a deposit, and citizens about to close a deal, would

John Jay Knox

no longer have to sift through 3,000 legally issued state bills—and a similar number of forged look-alikes—to ensure they were not being cheated. Finally, it conferred an element of elasticity upon the currency; in times of general crisis it could, in theory at least, be temporarily expanded to provide a measure of additional liquidity.

The author of this article was a young financier named John Jay Knox. A few months later another of his articles appeared in *Merchants' Magazine*, this time describing how a national banking system could be established. Secretary Chase was intrigued and invited young Knox to come by his office for a chat. It seemed that Knox, who would one day become comptroller of the currency, had a firsthand knowledge of banking in the state of New York. He had been born in Oneida County, where his father was the president of the Bank of Vernon. After graduating from Hamilton College, Knox had worked for two years in his father's bank. Then he moved on to the Burnett Bank of Syracuse before becoming the cashier of the Susquehanna Valley Bank in Binghamton, New York.

Secretary Chase was so impressed with Knox that he persuaded him to accept a clerkship in his office. Using many of Knox's ideas Chase presented a National Currency bill to Congress late in 1862. The bill passed the House in February 1863. But the vote was close. In the Senate, John Sherman of Ohio delivered a powerful speech in which he pointed to Article I, Section 10, of the U.S. Constitution, which stipulated, among other things, that "No State shall . . . emit bills of credit." Therefore, thundered Sherman, the emissions of paper currency so dear to the hearts of the state-chartered banks were, in fact, unconstitutional. Even with such powerful arguments, however, the bill barely passed the Senate, with a vote of 23 to 21. This act,

One-hundred-dollar note issued by the Leather Manufacturers National Bank of New York in 1865. Under the overarching rubric of National Currency it carries the words "This Note is secured by Bonds of the United States deposited with the U.S. Treasurer at Washington." (Martin Gengerke, Stack's Rare Coins, New York)

together with its companion legislation, the National Bank Act of 1864, was to establish "the dominant American banking and currency system for the next fifty years."

Under the new laws any state bank with a capitalization of at least $100,000 properly paid up could take up a federal charter, providing two-thirds of its stockholders approved. A lower capital was permitted in communities with fewer than 6,000 inhabitants. To obtain a supply of the new national bank notes the bank must place not less than $30,000 worth of Treasury bonds with an official called the comptroller of the currency, who then presented the bank with a supply of notes worth up to 90 percent of the bonds deposited. Each bank would be rigorously examined at least once a year, or more often if necessary. All banks were required to maintain reserves of specie and greenbacks that must amount to at least 15 percent of deposits. Leading financial centers—such as Philadelphia, New York, and Boston—were to be designated "central reserve cities" while other other major centers of business were termed simply "reserve cities." As rural banks and those in small towns joined the system they were required to maintain reserves equal to 15 percent of deposits; of this 15 percent, three-fifths, or 9 percent, could be deposited for interest in national banks situated in designated reserve cities. In like fashion the national banks in reserve cities were required to maintain reserves equal to 25 percent of their total deposits, and of these, up to one-half could be held in the national banks of the central reserve cities.

In the country as a whole the idea of incorporating banks under a national charter had a mixed reception. On June 20, 1863, Charter No. 1 was issued to the First National Bank of Philadelphia, a creation of the financier Jay Cooke. Within five months, 134 of the new national banks had been chartered. Of these 38 were in Ohio, 20 in Pennsylvania, and only 16 in the state of New York. Of the new national banks approximately one-half were conversions; the remainder were started from scratch, and the difficulties of creating an entirely new institution in an entirely new system were typified in the experiences of the First National of New York.

John Thompson, an irascible man with spectacles and a spadelike white beard, had been the president of a bank in Manhattan before it was wiped out in the panic of 1857. Thompson knew banking inside out; it was his life. But as the economy recovered he became increasingly aware that his failure made it difficult—if not impossible—for him to serve as the principal officer of any new institution. For several years he supported himself, and his family, by publishing his authoritative *Bank Note Reporter*, whose weekly circulation eventually amounted to 125,000. With the introduction of the new, uniform federal currency, he now realized, the *Reporter* might lose some of its appeal. Perhaps he could use a small stratagem to get back into full-time banking. By now his sons Samuel and Frederick were in their mid-twenties, old enough to serve as the president and vice president of a new federally chartered institution that he, the discredited father, would in fact manage.

When the charter of the First National Bank of New York was approved, the Thompsons promptly dispatched a wire to Albany asking a young government clerk named George F. Baker to serve as the bank's head teller. With some misgivings the twenty-three-year-old clerk, who entertained dreams of becoming a "commercial agent" in the schooner trade between the exotic atolls of the Sandwich Islands, accepted the Thompsons' offer. The adventurous youth, alas, would never make it to the South Pacific. But over the next half-century he would change the face of American banking and transform the infant First National into one of the paramount financial institutions of the nation.

Born in Troy, New York, in 1840, Baker was the son of an assemblyman and newspaper editor who later served as a personal assistant to Secretary of

State William Seward and to New York's Governor Myron Clark. Young George got his first job at the age of sixteen as a clerk in the New York State Banking Department. His swift but precise enumerations (he once accurately numbered three hundred state bank notes in the space of thirty-six minutes), his good humor and his sound judgment soon made him chief clerk of his section. Baker also had a quick eye for forged notes, a gift that made him a valued authority for the editor of *The Bank Note Reporter*. When Baker accepted the Thompsons' invitation they offered to hold some of the new bank's $200,000 capital stock in his name. After carefully thinking over the offer, however, the young man boldly took his life savings of $3,000 and purchased thirty shares outright. By the mid-1920s Baker would own 22,000 shares of First National, valued at $170 million. Harvard University would subsequently receive some $6 million of this for the endowment of the world's first graduate school of business administration. Baker named many of the school's halls—Hamilton, Gallatin, Chase, Sherman, Mellon—after Secretaries of the Treasury whose work and character he particularly admired.

Like many of the other new banks with federal charters, the early years of the First National were not easy. The long-established institutions in New York viewed the newcomers with suspicion; some even may have seen the

First National as a financial spy planted in their midst by the great ogre Chase back in Washington. Snubs were commonplace. The New York Clearing House repeatedly rejected the First National's application for membership. And often the city's larger banks would only clear checks written on the First at a discount. The U.S. Treasury, sensing that the bank was becoming a scapegoat for its own tough-minded policies, designated the First National as a leading agent for the sale of government securities. After that matters improved, and the First was allowed to join the clearinghouse in 1865. And, contrary to expectations, the Thompsons' *Bank Note Reporter* continued to flourish. In 1887, after a merger and several evolutions in editorial format, the respected publication would change its name to its present title, *The American Banker*.

Back in Washington, not everyone was enthusiastic about the rash of national banks that were being founded from scratch. The primary intention of Hugh McCullogh, the first comptroller of the currency (and former president of the well-run State Bank of Indiana) was not to *create* a whole new set of institutions but to *induce* the existing state-chartered banks to enlist in the national system. This plan, however, seemed to falter. By November 1863 the number of New York banks to seek a national charter had increased to 100, but of the total 584 banks now in the national system only some 300 had been previously established under state charter. Many, like the First National Bank situated in the small hamlet of Candor, in Tioga County, were started from scratch. This bank, when merged with the Farmers & Merchants Bank of nearby Spencer, would subsequently form the foundation stone of today's Tioga State Bank (total assets: $80 million).

Congress eventually decided to force the issue, and in March 1865 it limited circulation of state currencies by imposing a tax of between 2 and 10 percent on every state bank note issued or used in any subsequent financial transaction. The dam broke. At the end of 1866 a total of 1,663 banks nationwide, with a total capitalization of $417 million, had entered the national system. In the state of New York, 243 banks, with a capital of $115.7 million and a circulation of $60.6 million, had adopted national charters. There were, however, significant disparities in the kinds of business practiced by the big city banks and the smaller upstate banks (see table).

The conversions included old Mr. Knox's bank up in Vernon, New York, population 300. The bank had $100,000 in capital, $102,000 in deposits, and a total of $78,000 of the new federal banks notes in circulation. Knox's inventive son John Jay, author of the articles that helped shape the federal banking system, made a fast rise through the ranks of the U.S. Treasury. After going to San Francisco to examine the branch of the U.S. Mint, he moved on to New Orleans, where he "discovered a defalcation of $1,100,000 in the office of the Assistant Treasurer of the United States." In 1867 the younger Knox was appointed deputy comptroller of the currency. Five years later he was appointed comptroller by President Grant, a position he held until 1884, when he became president of the National Bank of the Republic in New York, with paid-up capital of $2 million.

TABLE
The First National Banks
State by State

States and Territories.	Organized.	Closing or closed.	In operation.	Capital paid in.	Bonds deposited.	Circulation issued.
Maine	61		61	$9,085,000 00	$8,396,250	$7,451,820
New Hampshire	39		39	4,715,118 07	4,727,000	4,121,253
Vermont	39		39	6,310,012 50	6,411,000	5,676,800
Rhode Island	62		62	20,364,800 00	14,144,600	12,369,850
Massachusetts	208	1	207	79,932,000 00	61,270,300	56,740,570
Connecticut	83	1	82	24,584,220 00	19,471,500	17,177,450
New York	313	5	308	116,267,941 00	75,970,400	67,135,485
New Jersey	54		54	11,233,350 00	10,324,150	9,030,745
Pennsylvania	203	2	201	49,200,765 00	43,324,350	38,099,640
Maryland	32		32	12,590,262 50	10,052,750	8,745,450
Delaware	11		11	1,428,185 00	1,348,200	1,179,300
District of Columbia	6	1	5	1,550,000 00	1,442,000	1,276,500
Virginia	20		20	2,500,000 00	2,397,300	2,044,900
West Virginia	15		15	2,216,400 00	2,236,750	1,980,650
Ohio	136	1	135	21,804,700 00	20,771,900	18,375,230
Indiana	72	1	71	12,867,000 00	12,400,850	10,888,280
Illinois	82		82	11,570,000 00	10,818,400	9,448,415
Michigan	43	1	42	4,985,010 00	4,313,600	3,778,900
Wisconsin	37		37	2,935,000 00	2,818,750	2,512,750
Iowa	46	1	45	3,697,000 00	3,680,150	3,204,395
Minnesota	15		15	1,660,000 00	1,682,200	1,484,000
Kansas	4		4	325,000 00	332,000	269,000
Missouri	17	2	15	4,079,000 00	2,903,100	2,712,490
Kentucky	15		15	2,840,000 00	2,615,000	2,311,270
Tennessee	10		10	1,700,000 00	1,306,200	1,096,790
Louisiana	3		3	1,800,000 00	853,000	727,000
Nebraska	3		3	200,000 00	180,000	150,000
Colorado	3		3	350,000 00	131,000	59,500
Mississippi	2		2	150,000 00	75,000	65,500
Georgia	9		9	1,700,000 00	1,305,500	1,124,000
North Carolina	5		5	370,750 00	309,000	228,600
South Carolina	2		2	$500,000 00	$140,000	$126,000
Arkansas	2		2	200,000 00	200,000	179,500
Alabama	3		3	500,000 00	304,000	262,500
Utah	1		1	150,000 00	50,000	41,970
Oregon	1		1	100,000 00	100,000	88,500
Texas	4		4	548,700 00	403,500	337,750
Nevada and Montana	2		2	235,000 00	195,000	166,000
	1,663	16	1,647	417,245,154 07	332,467,700	292,674,753

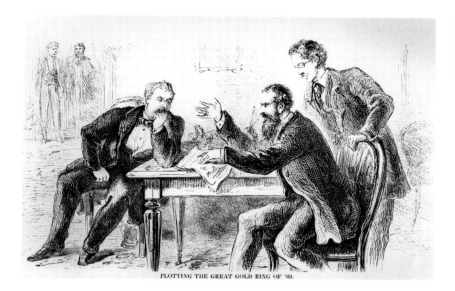

PLOTTING THE GREAT GOLD RING OF '69.

Perhaps the greatest threat to the new banking system, and indeed the entire economy, lay in the fact that specie payments had not yet been resumed. At one point toward the end of the war the value of the greenback had dropped to below 40 cents on the gold dollar. The gap between the value of domestic paper currency and the value of gold continued to fluctuate over a broad range, a situation that had an unsettling effect on the nation's international trade. The gap also rendered the system vulnerable to exploitation by unscrupulous speculators. In 1863 young Pierpont Morgan and an associate named Edward Ketchum had briefly imposed a lock upon the price of gold. After buying bullion quietly for some time they startled speculators and gold dealers alike by allegedly shipping $2.3 million worth of bullion to England. The price of gold shot up. Morgan, however, had placed only $1.2 million on the boat. He and Ketchum sold the remainder at inflated prices for a profit of $132,000.

Then six years later Jay Gould, the leading partner in a brokerage house named Smith, Gould, Martin & Co., and Jim Fisk, a circus promoter who had smuggled cotton through Union lines in the Civil War, set out to acquire enough bullion to be able to dictate the price of gold. Classic financial predators like Vanderbilt and Daniel Drew of the Erie Railroad seemed to be no match for the sly and wholly amoral machinations of the youthful Gould and Fisk, aged 33 and 35. "His touch is death," said Daniel Drew when, after a Byzantine struggle involving millions of dollars in watered stock, Gould forced Drew to relinquish control of the Erie Railroad.

As a first step in their plan Gould and Fisk put up $500,000 for the purchase of the Tenth National Bank of New York situated on Wall Street. This institution had assets of $10 million, including no less than $6.5 million in cash and legal tender notes; during their raid the conspirators would make great use of the cash, and the cashier's checks, of this bank. These funds, together with those in the treasury of the Erie Railroad, would form Fisk and Gould's war chest. On the morning of August 20, 1869, the price of gold coin was equal to $132 of the new paper currency. Fisk and Gould began to buy gold anonymously, through more than a dozen independent brokers, in the Stock Exchange's designated Gold Room. By September 20 gold was up to $137.25 and two days later it jumped from $137.5 to close at $141. Big merchant houses and many financial institutions who used gold in the import-export trade found the rise both ruinous and inexplicable. For banks like Brown Brothers & Co. such fluctuations rendered even short-term arrangements on foreign exchange highly volatile.

As Fisk and Gould sought to "bull" the price of gold higher and higher, the merchants and the established bankers struggled to pull it back down by throwing more and more of their own gold on to the market. But still the prices went up. The bears appealed to George Boutwell, the Secretary of the Treasury. In the normal way of things, Boutwell might be expected to release sufficient quantities of Treasury bullion to get the price down and restore equilibrium. However, in September 1869 things were not normal; by means of bribes and many other subterfuges, Fisk and Gould had convinced President Grant and a number of his associates that the Treasury should remain "neutral" and permit the price of gold to "determine its own level."

When the bears had sold most of their own gold they sought to protect their position by borrowing yet more gold, and pushing it back on to the market. Under the arcane rules that governed activity in the pit, a trader could borrow gold if he secured it with a pledge of paper dollars and a written promise, or call, to return the gold on the demand of the lender. As the price went from $145 to $147, a chest containing $1 million of gold borrowed at $1,450,000 would now cost $1,470,000—or an additional $20,000—to replace. Fearful that further price increases would make their previous borrowings impossible to return, the bears were drawn back into the market in an unending upward spiral of borrow-and-sell, borrow-and-sell. Though many of them did not know it at the time, the bears were, in fact, being driven to borrow this additional gold from their tormentors, the bulls. From their secret command post in an office building across the street, Fisk and Gould gleefully maintained the pressure.

James Brown, now seventy-eight years old and walking with a cane, visited the Gold Room on a couple of occasions. He was accompanied by a young broker-bodyguard from Brown Brothers & Co. named Kruger. The septuagenarian decided that matters had gone quite far enough. The wild fluctuations in price were making a shambles of the foreign exchange market. In addition, the withdrawal of large quantities of gold from Manhattan banks had thrust the stock market into a panic, and the price of commodities such as wheat and cotton had slumped badly. If the bulls were permitted to corner the market they could, indeed, strangle the economy by pushing the price of gold to $180 or perhaps even $200. Something must be done.

Brown, who had been alive when George Washington was president, had seen his share of crises. He knew that breaking the Gold Ring was not just a question of resources; as in all such duels, the willpower and the mentality of

a protagonist often made the difference between victory and disaster. Brown and his partners had strong suspicions as to the identity of their opponents. And, as the price went remorselessly upward, Brown sensed the bulls were seeking a confrontation, a *mano a mano* showdown, in which they would demonstrate their domination over the bears. As the price continued to rise, dollar by dollar, the bears were clearly in over their heads. But the bulls were vulnerable, too. What if, after purchasing all that gold at $150, the price fell back to $135? Sooner or later, Brown knew, the bulls would overreach themselves, and then he would call their bluff.

When the market closed on Thursday, September 23, it seemed that the bulls had finally trampled the bears. The price of gold had roared up to $144.25, more than three dollars higher than its closing price on the previous day. Sales for the single day amounted to $325 million, more than five times the usual daily total. The Tenth National Bank alone had certified more than $25 million in checks for the Gold Ring, which now held "calls" worth more than $100 million. This meant that it would now make a cool $1 million every time the price of gold increased by a single dollar. And it also meant that the Ring had the legal right to demand immediate delivery of $100 million in gold certificates and coin—this was, absurdly, nearly seven times more than the amount of bullion and specie available in the vaults of the New York banks. Fisk and Gould spent a riotous night celebrating in their offices situated above the Grand Opera House, which they owned, on Eighth Avenue at West Twenty-third.

On the morning of Friday, September 24, gold started at $145 and quickly jumped to $150. James Brown, bow-legged and moon-faced, his eyes shining behind rimless spectacles, was angry; but he was also determined to play his cards right. He stepped up to the rail at the center of the Gold Room and signaled his desire to sell $500,000 of gold at $150. Done. The gold was bought by Albert Speyers, one of Fisk's foremost brokers. An hour later Fisk, determined to squeeze the bears, had pushed the price to $155 and James

Brown offered to sell another $500,000 worth of gold. Done, to Speyers again. The game of cat-and-mouse continued. Fisk, now intending to crush the bears, ordered the diminutive Speyers to push the price to $160.

"One hundred sixty for any part of five millions," called out Speyers, and then repeated the call. The entire Gold Room fell silent. "Terror became depicted on every countenance," wrote a reporter who was sitting in the gallery. "Cool, sober men looked at one another, and noted the ashy paleness that spread over all."

Nobody bid. Nobody moved. The Gold Ring had its dominant corner, and now it could charge for gold whatever price it chose. Even those who had no financial interest in the proceedings "were seized with the infection of fear, and were conscious of a great evil approaching." In a victory dance to underscore the annihilation of the bears, Speyers continued to push the price up.

"One-sixty-one for any part of five millions?" he called, only to be greeted by silence. No takers.

"One-sixty-two for any part of five millions?" Silence.

Now. This was the moment. James Brown, aged 78, lifted his head.

"Sold one million at one-sixty-two," called out Brown in a clear, firm voice. Speyers and Brown stared at each other wordlessly across the trading pit. Done, said Speyers finally, with a sharp intake of breath. The broker seemed shaken, as if undecided what to do next. Then, in a lower voice he called out, "One hundred sixty-one for any part of five millions." Immediately, like the lash of a whip, came the reply.

"Sold, one million at one-sixty-one," said Brown. The tide was turning.

"One-sixty for five millions," called Speyers, in full retreat.

"Sold five million at one-sixty," barked Brown, eyes glittering.

Suddenly brokers all over the floor were seeking to sell. The retreat turned into a rout. In minutes gold crashed from $160 to $140, bounced back to $150 and then crashed again to $133. The unfortunate Albert Speyers seemed to have lost his wits. He scrambled around the room "like a goblin rather than a man," said one observer, "with dim eyes and face as pale as ashes." At the same time other brokers seemed to have recovered their judgment, and while they bought and sold for $140 or even $135 only a few feet away Speyers, ignored by the rest of the traders, continued to scream out offers to buy at $160.

The nerve and the controlled anger of James Brown, backed by more than half a century's experience in international banking, had broken the Gold Ring. The victory was confirmed minutes later when the Treasury announced its decision to sell $4 million worth of gold on the open market.

When the dust settled the investigations began. Daniel Butterfield, in charge of the U.S. Subtreasury in New York, and President Grant's brother-in-law, Abel Corbin, were deeply implicated in the plot. The House Banking Committee was under the chairmanship of an active young congressman from Ohio named James Garfield. Many of his potential witnesses, it seemed, had left on "extended tours" of Europe. But Albert Speyers was around to give his inside account of the Gold Ring's manipulations and old James Brown appeared to boast "if the bull had been as strong as twenty elephants I would have tackled him." While Gould was solemn and relatively straightforward, Jim Fisk had the Banking Committee "convulsed with laughter." According to one member "he talked with great rapidity and illustrated his utterances with grotesque actions, and interlarded them with copious interjections and profanity."

Garfield was quick to realize that the whole idea of a "corner" in gold would have been impossible if the value of the greenback had not been divorced from that of gold. The Civil War, and Salmon Chase's determination to put the nation on the path to a thousand dollar breakfast, set the premise upon which the Gold Ring operated. Garfield also noted that their testimony to the contrary, the manipulations of Fisk and Gould were no joke. The gold crash devastated the American economy. In the last week of September 1869 the value of all stocks traded on the New York exchange dropped by $100 million, and in the following year trading continued at half its normal rate.

Fisk and Gould were effectively protected from much of the federal probe by judges beholden to Tammany Hall. In addition, the mountain of paper documenting the final crazed transactions in the Gold Room proved to be beyond comprehension to even the most experienced investigators. Both men stayed out of jail and continued to control the operations of the Erie Railroad for a while longer. After much high-living Fisk was shot and killed in 1872 on the stairs of the Grand Central Hotel by one of the boyfriends of Josie Mansfield, Fisk's former live-in girlfriend. His partner Gould went on to assemble a fortune of more than $70 million—worth more than $1 billion today—with strong holdings in railroads, telegraph companies and big-city streetcar systems. He and his wife Helen, however, were repeatedly snubbed by the Astors and the Vanderbilts and, though he owned a magnificent steam yacht, the New York Yacht Club denied Gould's application for membership. On the day after Gould's death from natural causes in 1892, the New York Stock Exchange experienced a sharp rally.

7

"Why, Senator,
That's an Inspiration"

ON THE NIGHT of Saturday, October 19, 1907, a train pulled out of the station at Richmond, Virginia, hauling two railroad cars that contained the opulent and very private sleeping and dining accommodations of J. Pierpont Morgan, Sr. The legendary financier, now in his seventy-first year, had arrived in Richmond only a few days earlier to attend the triennial convention of the Episcopal Church. He was accompanied by three Anglican bishops and their wives. Since handing over the day-to-day operations of the Morgan bank to his younger partners, Pierpont had become increasingly caught up in obscurantist debates concerning the liturgies and canonical procedures of his church.

The Morgan party planned to leave Richmond on Sunday, at the conclusion of the convention. But something strange was going on in New York. A growing number of telegrams had been delivered to the sumptuous office aboard the railroad cars as they lay parked on a nearby siding. On occasion the telegrams would be handed to Mr. Morgan while the company sat at lunch, or dinner. After reading the dispatch the financier would put the palms of both hands on the table and stare fixedly ahead, lost in thought. The telegrams continued to arrive. Finally, on the day before the party was due to leave Richmond, Morgan turned to Bishop William Lawrence and said: "They are in trouble in New York; they do not know what to do, and I don't know what to do, but I am going back."

For sometime now there had been hints that the economy was not doing well. The previous year Morgan had a nasty encounter with President Theodore Roosevelt at the Gridiron Club in Washington. After inveighing against the "malefactors of great wealth" on Wall Street and the depredations of the great cartels in railroads, oil, tobacco, sugar and steel, Roosevelt declared that "changes must be made." Then the president, holding the notes of his unfinished speech in his left hand, abruptly stepped down from the podium and marched over to where Morgan sat. "And if you don't let us do this," thundered Roosevelt, shaking his fist in the financier's face, "those who will come after us will rise and bring you to ruin." For several seconds the gathering sat in shocked silence as the world's most influential financier and the president of the United States glared at one another like two angry schoolboys. Morgan's eventual response was terse; when Roosevelt went on his next African safari, he declared, he trusted that the first lion he encountered would not hesitate "to do its duty."

The wrathful encounter was witnessed by many newspapermen. The general public did not know what to make of it, but over the next few months some $3 billion in cash was drawn from banks and trust companies. In New York the city began to have trouble selling its bonds, and a streetcar conglomerate went bankrupt. Even more disquieting was the collapse of the Knickerbocker Trust Co., which had made unsound loans to Charles W. Morse, a high-stakes speculator in copper and shipping. When, over a period of six months, the prices of copper declined from 26 to 12 cents a pound, Morse and the Knickerbocker Trust found themselves in serious difficulties.

For many years now the so-called trusts had been something of an anomaly on the New York banking scene. Under federal law national banks were forbidden to provide trust services, or operate a department capable of handling wills and investing in securities for estates and well-endowed individuals. Over a period of time such tasks were undertaken by independent, state-chartered trusts. Though these trusts were not permitted to issue their own currency notes they could provide mortgages, make loans and take deposits in the same way as commercial banks. At first the trusts had served as a useful adjunct to banks, but their far more relaxed regulatory requirements soon led them to compete aggressively with commercial banks for depositors. While national banks were required to maintain cash reserves equal to at least 25 percent of demand deposits, many trusts were able to maintain reserves of 15 percent and often less. As a result the trusts had more resources available, and they were able to use them to engage in highly speculative ventures; often these included high-risk investments in the stock market and the lending of margin loans or "call" money to brokerage houses.

Morse's financial setback in the international copper market precipitated a sharp run on the Knickerbocker Trust and two associated institutions, the Lincoln Trust Co. and the Trust Company of America, with its head office on Wall Street. Soon apprehensive depositors sought to withdraw their deposits from even the healthy trusts. The stock market slumped and speculators, desperately seeking to cover their positions, drove the interest on call money

up to more than 15 percent per month! As he pored over his telegrams J. P. Morgan concluded that the contagion might soon spread to commercial banks.

The trouble must be contained, and extirpated. The palatial railroad cars, with their lavish carpeting and antique furniture, thundered north through the night. There was a brief stop in Washington during which Morgan sat on the rear observation platform and smoked one of his specially rolled cigars, often described as "cannon-like" by his financial associates. Then the train started again and the galley, under the noted restaurateur Louis Sherry, produced an elegant late supper for Morgan's personal party and the three Episcopal prelates and their wives. Next morning, as the train approached New York, the passengers enjoyed a breakfast of hot coffee and freshly baked rolls.

After seeing the churchmen into their cabs, Morgan proceeded to his famous library of priceless artifacts at 29 East 36th Street. There, away from the ears and eyes of the press, he discussed the crisis with an inner circle of associates that included the hawk-faced James Stillman, president of the National City, and George F. Baker, president of First National. This meeting was also attended by two younger men, Thomas Lamont, the thirty-six-year-old secretary of Bankers Trust, and the forthright and charming Harry P. Davison, aged 40, then a vice president at Baker's First National.

The Knickerbocker Trust Co. in midtown Manhattan was under siege. Should relief forces be dispatched? Or was the institution beyond saving?

What kind of financial rampart could be erected to prevent it from drawing other, more healthy, institutions into Morse's widening circle of failure. All those present knew prompt action was essential. But first the rescue committee under Morgan, Baker and Stillman had to have an accurate and unbiased accounting of the financial facts.

The group turned to Harry Davison; he as much as anyone had ready access to a pool of able, trustworthy talent. Four years earlier Davison had proposed the creation of a "pet" trust that, because its stock was jointly held by the most prominent commercial banks, would not attempt to appropriate the banks' regular customers, and their deposits. The Bankers Trust, as it came to be called, was an immediate success. Its board of directors included many of the city's up-and-coming commercial bankers, and it was this close-knit group that Davison now called upon to make lightning examinations of the beleaguered trusts.

Davison's teams worked night and day evaluating the condition of more than a dozen institutions. As they perused a thousand ledgers and sifted through mountains of fiduciary paper, the examiners lived off a diet of sandwiches and coffee. Often, in the small hours, visitors might encounter them spread-eagled on the carpet or curled up in a corner, taking a brief nap before resuming their investigations. One of the team leaders was Benjamin Strong, aged 34, the assistant secretary of Bankers Trust. Late one evening, after completing one exhausting examination, Strong was sent home to Greenwich, Connecticut. But he was to get no rest. "At about two o'clock in the morning," he subsequently recalled, "my telephone rang and I was asked by someone speaking for Harry to motor in from Greenwich immediately, to assemble the committee which had been working with me the day before and start at once an examination of the Trust Company of America."

The debonair Davison set up his headquarters in the Belmont Hotel and was generally viewed by his youthful followers as "the commanding general over the forces in the field." Born in Troy, Pennsylvania, Davison had first worked at the small, genteel Astor Bank. But within a few years his energy, his imagination, and his ability to cut to the heart of any financial problem had earned him a vice presidency at the First National Bank. Under the bold yet conservative leadership of George Baker, now aged 67, the institution had become immensely profitable as a "wholesale" bank by offering its services primarily to other financial institutions and to such giant corporations as U.S. Steel, the Northern Pacific Railroad and the Ford Motor Company.

Besides his banking skills, Harry Davison also possessed an impish charm, and he knew how to put both the shyest and the most cantankerous people at ease. He once suggested that the fearsome J. P. Morgan, thirty years his senior, "hop on a steamer and go to Europe." The great financier was both irked and amused by his junior's importunity. "No, Davison," replied Morgan, endeavoring to suppress a smile, "*you* hop on a steamer and go to Europe. I'll follow later, if you think the situation warrants." When diplomatic functions and fashionable garden parties got too stiff-necked for com-

fort, Davison might wander over to the orchestra and borrow the first instrument that came to hand and begin to serenade his fellow guests. "Whether it were a violin or a 'cello, flute or French horn," recalled one eyewitness, "he would always be able, after a little experimenting, to draw from it the melody that he was searching for." Soon the rest of the orchestra picked up on Davison's lead, and the champagne corks would begin to pop.

Now, in the financial crisis of 1907, Davison drove his examiners night and day. But he also sought to keep their spirits up by appearing among them at any hour to talk, and to crack a joke or two. He would listen to all reports with great attentiveness and, in the flick of an eye, spot a flaw or a loophole amid the reams of accumulating data. If anyone produced a bright new idea as to how a difficulty could be resolved, Davison's face would light up and he would say, "Why, that's an inspiration." Often the stickiest problems arose with the officers of the trust under investigation. With their reputations and the future of their institution at stake, these executives might by turns display resentment, fear, arrogance and, all too frequently, ignorance of how their own business worked. Davison took it all in stride. "It was in dealing with the human equation that Harry's supreme talent was shown," wrote Strong. "He reconciled differences of view, calmed the uneasy and the anxious; he inspired the timid, sometimes disciplined the cowardly, but with it all his courage never flagged, his industry was unceasing and his good temper never failed him."

The Morgan bank arranged for a loan of $10 million, but the slump in the stock market and the worsening of business conditions in general, including the collapse of the giant Tennessee Coal and Iron Co., made it clear that the weaker trusts could not survive without an infusion of at least $25 million. The crisis came to a head on Saturday, November 2. Morgan invited all the trust company presidents to meet with him in his legendary library. When they arrived the aged financier found it ominous that most of the presidents were strangers to one another and had to be introduced. Few of the plans proposed by the embattled presidents seemed either imaginative or workable. Sometime after midnight Morgan sent word into the library that his bank and its associated institutions had many other obligations, and that the trusts would have to use their collective resources to rescue themselves.

Though they had been urged to join on many occasions, the trusts were not members of the New York Clearing House. Now, said Morgan, they must begin to think of collective security. The healthy institutions must step forward and assist their brethren who, like the Trust Co. of America, were experiencing trouble meeting short-term obligations. This statement, reported Ben Strong, "filled the trust company heads with consternation." There was even more consternation when the bankers discovered that Morgan had locked them into the library, and tucked the key into his vest pocket. Surrounded by ancient tapestries and glass cabinets filled with illuminated manuscripts, the assembled presidents pondered. They were, alas, unable to derive much inspiration from the artistic masterpieces on display around them. After much cogitation and some desultory chatter, no new thoughts were forthcoming. The trust men, decided Strong, seemed incapable of taking any kind of concerted action.

The hours ticked by and still they were at a loss. Finally Morgan unlocked the door and reentered the library at about four o'clock in the morning. He carried with him a piece of paper that showed, on the basis of Davison's examinations, how much each trust might safely subscribe to produce a common relief fund of $25 million.

"There you are, gentlemen," growled Morgan, as he laid the document on the table with a flourish.

Nobody moved. According to Thomas Lamont, who was present, the "bankers shifted from one foot to another, but no one stepped forward. Mr. Morgan waited a few moments. Then he put his hand on the shoulder of his friend, Edward King (president of the Union Trust Co.), and gently urged him forward. 'There's the place, King,' he said kindly, but firmly, 'and here's the pen,' placing a handsome gold pen in Mr. King's fingers. Mr. King signed. The ice was broken. They all signed."

PUCK

MERGER

BILLION DOLLAR BANK

THE CENTRAL BANK.

Why Should Uncle Sam Establish One, When Uncle Pierpont Is Already on the Job?

As the depression deepened in the wake of the 1907 panic, the public came to view Morgan less as savior and more as grasping villain. (Sketch in Puck *by Frank Nankivelt, 1910; Pierpont Morgan Library)*

The Bankers' Panic, as it came to be called, was over. But the economic scars—and the public outrage!—remained. For a while J. P. Morgan was viewed by the people as a hero. But even the most conservative observers began to think that the fist-shaking Theodore Roosevelt might have been right. After all, what kind of a financial system was it that depended for its survival upon the good offices and the dominant personality of a single individual? How many more midnight train rides could the great J. P. Morgan be expected to make? And who, after he had gone, would have the moral stature to lock future miscreants into a single room and keep them there until they settled their differences?

Since the end of the Civil War the crashes and the panics had, like immense oceanic rollers, continued to strike with monotonous regularity. On September 8, 1873, the New York Warehouse & Security Co., an investment house particularly involved in railroad financing, failed. Ten days later Jay Cooke & Co. of Philadelphia, which had been deeply involved in the financing of the Northern Pacific Railroad, also collapsed. Panic ensued, and it became clear that many major railroads had overbuilt, sending lines into territories with scant population and no natural resources. Also, the outbreak of the Franco-Prussian war in 1870, with its aftermath of civil chaos and economic depression, had rendered Europeans increasingly wary of making investments in the United States.

At the First National the crisis hit with particular severity. Under the presidency of John Thompson's son Samuel the bank had recently "bought some big drafts on London for the government through Jay Cooke, who failed a few days later." As the panic gathered momentum, Samuel Thompson became fearful and suggested the bank be liquidated and its assets distributed among shareholders immediately, before matters became worse. George Baker, by now the First National's chief cashier, disagreed. The bank, in which he had invested his entire life savings, should stay in business. "In times of distress," he argued, "loan to good customers, don't hoard." The bank, he maintained, should "pay every claim presented as long as the money lasts."

But to Sam Thompson such a policy seemed suicidal. He was for selling up, and getting out. The confrontation in the president's office, surrounded as it was by lines of distraught depositors, became increasingly tense.

"Sam, if you are so anxious to get out," Baker finally declared, "I'll buy your stock myself."

Thompson was skeptical. "With what?" he asked, a mixture of exasperation and despair in his voice. Then his younger brother Fred Thompson spoke up. "You might as well know where I stand. George controls this bank. He has 652 shares and I have 2,000. I vote them with George."

The Thompson brothers would not be on speaking terms for years to come. In the wake of this sulphurous exchange Samuel submitted his resignation as president to George in return for a written promise from Baker that he would purchase, at some date to be decided, Samuel's and old John Thompson's shares for about two times their par value. It took four years for Baker to complete his side of the bargain. In 1877 he became president of First National, and John Thompson, now aged 75, and his son Samuel went forth with $600,000 in hand to establish a successful new bank called the

Chase National (capitalization: $300,000), with offices at 117 Broadway, just a few yards up from those of the First National.

Most New York banks, however, were not so lucky. Indeed, if it did nothing else, the crisis of 1873 underscored the structural inadequacies of the system set up under the National Bank Act in 1864. When panic struck, many individual banks froze in their tracks, like rabbits in the glare of oncoming headlights. Central reserve city banks often refused to release the deposits of reserve city banks, which in turn froze the deposits of the local banks in their region. Outside the major clearinghouse cities no plan or mechanism existed for the pooling of resources. It was every man for himself and in such a climate each bank, surrounded by angry depositors, was compelled to fight—and often die—alone.

In an effort to ease the pressure the New York Clearing House authorized the issue of $10 million worth of gold certificates that could be issued to member banks on the pledge of sound but illiquid paper. Further liquidity came when the U.S. Treasury agreed to buy $12 million worth of bonds

In the summer of 1908 the president of the New York Clearing House bluntly told the state's bankers, assembled for their annual convention at the Frontenac Hotel, situated on an island in the St. Lawrence River, that "this country is handicapped by an inferior banking system." (Watercolor by William DeM. Rolland)

"Why, Senator, That's an Inspiration"

Senator Nelson W. Aldrich manifested the zeal of a new convert.
(Photo; Library of Congress)

from national banks, thereby providing them with a like sum of national bank notes to put into circulation.

The ensuing depression was long, and severe. In the years that followed, the economy—and the country as a whole—was wracked by the increasingly strident dispute over hard and soft money; the battle culminated in the crash of 1893. Now, a mere fourteen years later, came the Bankers' Panic. "One might almost have begun to think that the American people had become completely hardened to their currency troubles," commented Thomas Lamont, who later became the senior partner at J. P. Morgan & Co. "But the sudden and shocking money panic of 1907, with banks failing all over the land, aroused the country, as no similar trouble had ever done before, to the urgent necessity of revising its currency system. It had become obvious how stupid a thing it was, for a nation of the size and resources of the United States, to undergo these recurring spasms when countries of Europe, with far less resources, were able, by means of a more scientific currency mechanism, largely to avoid such cataclysms."

These sentiments were echoed on the mighty St. Lawrence when the New York State Bankers Association held its annual meeting at Frontenac Island in early July. Here Alexander Gilbert, president of the New York Clearing House Association, told the assembled bankers that the American people "are beginning to understand that, in competition with the nations of the old world for the trade of the world, this country is handicapped by an inferior banking system." Gilbert went on to criticize the bond-secured currency amid applause from the bankers. "A Central Bank," he bluntly declared, "is what this country needs."

This time Congress needed no goading. America deserved a system that was as good, if not better, than those of Europe. In August 1908 it set up the National Monetary Commission under the chairmanship of Senator Nelson Aldrich of Rhode Island. In appearance Aldrich, aged 67, looked just the man to accomplish a major overhaul of the nation's financial structure. The sharp, penetrating eyes of a prosecutor stared out from under an expansive forehead while a bristling white mustache, pointing sharply downward, lent a pessimistic cast to his features. But in fact Aldrich seems to have entertained an ambivalent attitude toward the whole idea of change. He was a Republican from Rhode Island, a successful merchant who had married a woman of considerable wealth; then the Aldrichs' daughter had gone on to marry the son of John D. Rockefeller.

The senator himself was a firm supporter of the bond-based currency that had been in place since 1864. And, like J. P. Morgan, he believed that the present banking system was basically sound. According to Barton Hepburn, president of the Chase National Bank and the senator's intimate friend, it was Aldrich's secret intention to "sidetrack" any major attempts at reform.

On the recommendation of Mr. Morgan, Senator Aldrich invited Harry Davison, by now a Morgan partner, to join the National Monetary Commission as a representative of the nation's practical banking interests. The senator asked Frank A. Vanderlip, a vice president and future president of National City Bank, to join the Commission. And to the surprise of many, Aldrich also invited Paul M. Warburg to join his inner circle of advisors. Warburg was an outspoken and somewhat controversial German banker who had only recently arrived in New York to serve as a partner in Kuhn, Loeb & Co. The new immigrant, however, was not unduly awed by the great titans of Wall Street. Indeed, he was so perturbed by what he believed to be the appalling deficiencies of the American banking system that he published, in short order, a number of newspaper and magazine articles outlining his views as to how they should be rectified.

Many American bankers, including National City's James Stillman, viewed Warburg as a presumptuous upstart, just off the boat. But the émigré, who still spoke with a heavy German accent, quickly won over Stillman and many other skeptics when one of his articles, entitled "A Plan for a Modified Central Bank," appeared at the height of the 1907 panic. These insights, together with Warburg's encyclopedic knowledge of international banking practice, ensured his appointment. Aldrich's inner advisory group was completed when a young Harvard economic statistician named A. Piatt Andrew agreed to serve as special assistant to the chairman.

After granting numerous interviews to American newspapers, Aldrich and his party sailed from New York on August 4, 1908, aboard the German liner *Kronprinzessin Cecelie*. The Commission was warmly welcomed by the

Paul M. Warburg, who had recently emigrated to the United States, was not awed by the titans of Wall Street. (AP/Wide World Photos)

leaders of both the commercial and the central banks of Europe. After all, making the American financial structure more stable could only improve the efficiency and soundness of their own institutions, so they "threw their books open for complete inspection, and they gave a large amount of their time to the visiting Americans." The Commission began by submitting written questionnaires to private and government bankers in London, Paris, Berlin, Zurich and Vienna. Then, after collating the responses, the subcommittee planned to travel to each country in turn for a series of face-to-face hearings and interviews. It was in these hearings that Davison displayed a forensic gift for asking the pointed question that cut right to the heart of the issue under discussion.

One of the key concerns of the visiting Commission was the distinction, in practical terms, between a bond-based currency like that in the United States and the assets-based currencies of Europe. At this time the quantity of American currency in circulation was fixed by law. The only way to expand it was for American banks, collectively, to buy more government bonds, exchange them for national bank notes, and then push those notes into circulation. The central banks of Europe, in contrast, could increase liquidity by the simple expedient of accepting and "rediscounting" a greater quantity of commercial paper that working banks had already discounted for their customers.

The European method was virtually self-regulating. A central bank would accept a commercial bank's endorsed promise to pay 30, 60, or 90 days in

the *future* and then, after deducting a nominal interest in advance, pay that bank *today* in the currency notes of the realm. The central bank was, in fact, providing a mechanism for the conversion to cash of sound, short-term loans at a moment's notice, thereby eliminating most of the seasonal illiquidities that plagued farmers, manufacturers and banks in the normal run of business. This rediscounting process also gave the central bank an element of day-to-day control over the level of credit in the economy. If the tempo of business activity began to overheat and verge on the speculative, then the central bank could gently increase the interest rate charged at its rediscount window. At the higher rate corporations, and their bankers, would think twice before contracting additional business. If, on the other hand, business was slackening the central bank could, in effect, pump more credit into the system by lowering its rediscount rate.

Under such a system, the Europeans maintained, it would no longer be necessary for the House of Morgan to provide New York banks with midnight loans of $10 million or $25 million; all those banks had to do was to take their outstanding commercial paper and transform it—at will—to cash at the discount window of a central bank.

Through the autumn of 1908 the Commission sat through long hearings at the Bank of England and La Banque de France. At first Aldrich was skeptical. Such systems might be fine for medium-sized nations with a long tradition of disinterested public service. But the United States, with its populist traditions and its huge geographic diversity, would never accept such centralized authority. In America officials were not appointed for faithful service to the crown but for their party affiliation; since they might be turned out of office at the next election, many would inevitably be tempted—like Nicholas Biddle—to place the interests of party and faction above the interests of the country.

"Why, Senator, That's an Inspiration"

Who, then, in America could be trusted to formulate, and then execute, the policies of a central banking authority in a disinterested fashion? And who would determine the rediscount rate and decide on purely economic grounds when it should go up or down? Such questions played upon the worst fears of the Americans. Could they expect to see a reincarnation of Mr. Biddle, astride a new hydra-headed monster, spurring the country into yet another artificial depression? Or, at the opposite end of the spectrum, perhaps such crucial authority could fall into the hands of a demagogue who believed the nation's banks were crucifying mankind upon a cross of gold?

Such fears served to keep Senator Aldrich tied to the concept of a bond-based currency. But the accumulated testimony began to have its effect. Early in January 1909 the Commission staff left Paris for extensive hearings in Berlin. In the middle of a long discussion with the directors of the Reichsbank, Aldrich had a revelation. True, the American bond-based currency had its advantages. But he suddenly found himself acknowledging that an assets-based currency, with its semiautomatic mechanism for controlling the money supply, had even greater advantages. The exchange was recorded by the Commission's stenographer.

> *Question* (probably Davison):   Your cash reserve was very close to the line of your limitation?
> *Answer* (Dr. Von Lumm, Director of the Reichsbank):   It was about 41.3 percent.
> Q: Was that exceptional, or had it at any time been lower?
> A: That is a very great exception indeed. It has only been lower at one time, namely, the end of 1906, when it was 40.3 percent.
> Q: What would happen if it went to 32 percent?
> A: We should have to go on discounting bills. We should simply have to do it. We could not stop it. If we did it would bring about the greatest panic that we ever experienced.
> Q: What steps do you take to increase your gold reserves or to protect it?
> A [after an aside about foreign bills of exchange]: . . . We increased the rate of discount. We consider that this measure is the only effective one.
> Q: How high was the rate at that time?
> A: 7.5 percent.
> Q: If this increase had not been sufficient, you would further have increased the rate?
> A: Yes.

Aldrich's conversion was sudden, and complete. It was clear that Dr. Von Lumm would go to any length to avert a panic, even if it entailed a massive reduction in reserves. And the idea of an adjustable rediscount rate was particularly intriguing: here was the scalpel that, when wielded by a steady hand, might expunge all prospect of future panics. The American senator was transformed overnight from a foot-dragging conservative bent on side-tracking reform into an ardent advocate of a central bank that would have far more authority than anything envisaged by Vanderlip and Warburg.

It has been suggested that Harry Davison long favored an assets-based

currency and had played an amiable but somewhat Machiavellian role in Aldrich's conversion, jollying him through the interminable hearings and asking the questions that precisely illuminated the points he wished the able but often dogmatic senator to grasp. Many interpretations are possible. But it is very unlikely that Davison, with his easy-going ways, had a preconceived agenda. According to Thomas Lamont, the future senior partner of J. P. Morgan & Co., his friend Harry "had never been a profound student of the Continental banking systems." But he was a quick study. On boarding ship Davison—when not enlivening the nights with instruments borrowed from the *Kronprinzessin Cecelie*'s orchestra—undertook a course of serious reading. By the time the vessel docked in Southampton he had acquired "an excellent working knowledge of the main points that the Commission was to explore."

While still in England Davison probably realized that the notion of basing currency on commercial assets was worth serious consideration. After that, all it took was some perspicacious questioning, and a little time, before Davison was able to turn to the newly converted Aldrich, beam him a big smile, and say, "Why, Senator, that's an inspiration."

On their return to the States, Aldrich and several other Commission members experienced difficulty in combining their insights into a single coherent piece of legislation. Pressures were intense. Despite their experiences in the Bankers' Panic of 1907, many of the oldest and most respected bankers in the state of New York—including such potentates as George F. Baker—were still militantly opposed to banking law reforms. "They understood the old, the haphazard system," wrote Frank Vanderlip, who would shortly become president of National City Bank. "Consequently, they were

"Why, Senator, That's an Inspiration"

disposed to reprove younger men, who wanted to change, by reminding them that the existing national banking system had served the nation through the years of expansion after the 'sixties."

The newly converted Senator Aldrich was, however, determined to press on. While the overall direction of the legislation seemed clear, multiple and sometimes contradictory versions of each section, and even each subsection, began to proliferate in the files of the Monetary Commission. In addition, Aldrich found himself "harassed by the daily grind of his parliamentary duties."

The only effective way out of the impasse, decided Davison, was to assemble all the leading framers in a single place, far beyond the reach of the telephone and the log-rolling eloquence of the rainmakers who even then infested the halls of Congress. Old Mr. Morgan and James Stillman were members of the Jekyl Island Club, situated on a privately owned sandspit off the coast of Georgia. A national magazine had recently noted that it was "the richest, the most exclusive, the most inaccessible" club in the world. Stillman, with his penchant for the clandestine, approved the idea, and it was arranged for Aldrich, Warburg, Vanderlip, Davison, Benjamin Strong and Professor Andrew (by now serving as an Assistant Secretary at the U.S. Treasury) to travel down to Georgia on November 11, 1910. The Jekyl Island Club had not yet opened for the winter season so, apart from a few servants, they would have the place to themselves.

The financiers made their departure from New York amid conditions of utmost secrecy. Each was instructed to pose as a duck hunter and make his way, under cover of darkness, to the railroad terminal at Hoboken where they would find Senator Aldrich's private car parked on a siding. "We were told to leave our last names behind us," recalled Frank Vanderlip, who had recently become president of City National Bank. "We were told, further, that we should avoid dining together on the night of our departure. We were instructed to come one at a time and as unobtrusively as possible to the railroad terminal." Davison and Vanderlip got into the conspiratorial swing of things by giving each other the code names of Wilbur and Orville, after the pioneering aviators.

In the ten days that followed, the six men, aided by Aldrich's secretary Mr. Shelton, hammered out a clear draft of a bill containing most of the terms and the specific language that would eventually become the backbone of the Federal Reserve Act of 1913. The discussions began at dawn when Davison and Strong noisily clumped out of the clubhouse—often amid invective from those still abed—"to get a horseback ride or a swim before breakfast." The talk, sometimes philosophical and sometimes down-to-earth, ran through lunch and supper and seldom concluded before midnight. It continued right through Thanksgiving dinner, at which Southern country ham and "wild turkey with oyster stuffing" were served. Frank Vanderlip, a distinguished graduate of the University of Chicago, later reported that these wide-ranging, nonstop debates stimulated his mental faculties to "the highest pitch of intellectual awareness that I have ever experienced. It was entirely thrilling."

At first, many general discussions deteriorated into arguments between two individuals over minutiae. Vanderlip got matters back on track by offering a tip he'd learned from the chairman of a major railroad. The only "proper way to conduct a conference," declared the railroad tycoon, was to "set down those things about which we are agreed; then, one by one, we can take up those things about which we seem to disagree."

The list of commonly accepted points got the discussions off to a strong start. But then Aldrich, Warburg, and to a lesser extent Strong found themselves expressing serious differences of opinion on (1) how many regional banks should be authorized, (2) should the rediscount rate be set locally or systemwide, (3) how long should that rediscounted paper be permitted to run—30, 60, 90 or 180 days?—and (4) which individuals should serve on the various boards, and how would they be selected? Sometimes the talk drifted away on to such arcane topics as the significance of "syndicate operations" and "the doctrine of real bills." With the enthusiasm of a recent convert Senator Aldrich continued to push hard for a central bank on the European model, with a dominant head office in the capital and satellite branches in commercial centers ready to execute its policies, whatever they may be. However, Warburg, who had worked for years in Hamburg under such a system, suspected that Aldrich's proposal would raise the Jacksonian hackles of every Democrat in Congress. In an effort to get a passable bill he proceeded to argue vehemently for a confederation of semiautonomous branches, each attuned to the needs of its region.

As tempers, inevitably, began to flare Davison was always ready to step in with a jest, or a question that would cause the debaters to see the issue from a new, and often enlightening, perspective. "A keen intellect and unusual will power," wrote Paul Warburg of Davison, "blended with these lighter strains, made him a rare leader of men. Not that he exacted subordination; he led in most cases, I believe, because men enjoyed following him."

Now all the Jekyl Island party had to do was to sell their proposals to Congress, businessmen, bankers and the public at large. Many of these groups proved suspicious even after Aldrich traveled to New Orleans in 1911 to assure the American Bankers Association that the suggested system was "not a bank, but a *cooperative union* of all the banks of the country. . . . It is, in effect, an extension, an *evolution of the clearing house plan modified* to meet the needs and requirements of an entire people." An election was approaching and the Aldrich Bill, as it was called, languished in committee.

When, in 1912, the Democrats under Woodrow Wilson gained the White House and majorities in both houses of Congress, one of their first priorities was reform of the banking system. Representative Carter Glass, a newspaper publisher from Lynchburg, Virginia, became chairman of the House Banking & Currency Committee. Much of Glass's attitude toward big bankers had, it seemed, been crystallized by an incident that occurred nearly fifty years before. Glass, then a boy of seven, had been walking barefoot along a forest trail in the hills above his hometown when he heard the sound of hoofbeats rapidly approaching from behind. Before the lad could climb a tree or bolt into the bushes a troop of cavalry, clad in dusty dark blue, galloped toward him. They were the first Union soldiers he had ever seen.

No fewer than eighteen of young Carter's uncles and cousins had lain down their lives in defense of the Confederacy. And in the closing phases of the war it had become common knowledge throughout Virginia that these hard-bitten Yankees took pleasure in burning the homes of women recently widowed by war, and in slicing the ears off little boys.

The Union officer raised a gloved hand and brought the column to a halt. Then he stared down into the small face, which appeared to be contorted by an unholy mix of awe, disdain, and mortal fear. The officer did not, however, draw his saber in preparation for slicing ears. Instead he simply chuckled and said, "Hi, sonny. Where are you bound for?" The petrified Carter stuttered that he was headed back to his house in Lynchburg. Without more ado the lieutenant lent down, scooped up the lad, and carried him on his saddle for several miles toward home. Young Carter Glass "never forgot that ride, but it was all too rough and bouncing and breathless to remember clearly in detail. The officer seemed jovial and high-spirited, and he might have liked him, only—'damn Yankee!' "

Now, after surviving a cutthroat half-century of journalism and politics in Virginia, Representative Carter Glass no longer experienced mortal dread. But many in Washington believed the diminutive, hot-tempered legislator continued to view damn Yankees—and their seemingly all-powerful financial institutions—with a perplexing mixture of awe, and disdain. Like many former newspapermen, Glass was brutally frank about the nature of the problems as he saw them. "The Siamese twins of disorder were an inelastic currency and a fictitious reserve system," he declared of the banking debacle in 1907. "The sum total of the idle bank funds of the nation was congested at the money centers for purely speculative purposes." In his view those Yankee money centers, and the ones in Chicago and San Francisco, should never be in a position to pull such a stunt ever again.

After extensive hearings the Glass-Owen Bill was presented for debate with the wording of three different texts printed up in parallel columns. One of these, sponsored by the conservative Democrat, Senator Gilbert Hitchcock, was almost identical to the Aldrich Bill. The discussion, particularly in the Senate, was prolonged, detailed and frequently vehement. The tenor of the debate was not improved by the recent inquiry of the House Banking & Currency Committee under its previous chairman, Representative Arsene P. Pujo of Louisiana. A celebrated trial lawyer from New York named Samuel Untermyer had grilled J. P. Morgan, Sr., George Baker, James Stillman and many other Wall Street bankers about their interlocking directorships and their seeming control over the nation's financial affairs.

Now, despite its misgivings about the power of the so-called Money Trust, the Congress by and large accepted the wording and the sense of the Jekyl Island version of the new banking bill. However, Wilson and Carter Glass did insist on some substantive modifications. The final version voted into law contained thirty articles, many of them concerned with minor matters of procedure. The basic provisions called for the creation of twelve district reserve banks that would each (1) have a board of nine directors, (2) be permitted to issue Federal Reserve notes if they were secured by commercial paper and a reserve of 40 percent in gold, (3) be permitted to rediscount ninety-day commercial paper, and (4) maintain a reserve of lawful money of 35 percent against deposits. This was, all parties agreed, intended to create a system capable of functioning like a city clearinghouse, writ very large.

The precise number of district reserve banks had been hotly debated in Congress. Some pushed for as few as four, others for as many as forty-eight, one in every state. If there were too few, the arguments went, then they would be liable to fall under the control of a single political entity or faction; if too many, the nation's reserves would be so dispersed as to be of little effective help in times of serious trouble. In the end, a round dozen was selected on the ground that any financial institution subject to adversity would be within a single night's train ride of a reserve bank. Then the president of the stricken bank "could gather the 30, 60 and 90 day commercial paper he wanted cashed, take the train for the city where the Federal reserve bank is situate [sic], and be able to wire that he had cashed sufficient securities to meet the demands of all depositors."

The 7,400 national banks were required to be a part of the Reserve System, and the 19,000 state banks were encouraged to join if they chose. All banks that processed their checks at face value (par) could use the System's check-clearing facilities without charge. Member banks, however,

had to maintain reserves of between 12 percent (for country banks) and 18 percent (for central reserve city banks) against demand deposits. At the same time the Federal Reserve Board—made up of the Secretary of the Treasury, the comptroller of the currency, and five presidential appointees—retained the right to alter reserve requirements and the right to review and ultimately determine rediscount rates within the system. The board later undertook the task of coordinating the district banks' purchases and sales of government securities (open market operations).

President Wilson invited Paul Warburg to serve on the Federal Reserve Board while, after considerable persuasion by Warburg and Harry Davison, Benjamin Strong agreed to become the first governor of the New York district bank. The tall, crag-faced Strong was forty-one years old and accustomed to expressing himself freely; he would shortly describe American bankers as little better than "an unorganized mob." Strong was also frank in his criticisms of the Federal Reserve Act. It was a mistake, he said, for the government to lend its credit to the new Federal Reserve notes. And he found the system too disjointed to be an effective central bank.

The Federal Reserve System opened to mixed reviews. "For those who do not believe in socialism," the American Bankers Association had warned its members, "it is very hard to accept and ratify this proposed action on the part of government." Horace White, the noted expert on banking and currency problems, remarked that "this is the system of the Imperial Bank of Germany with the difference that the latter is less liable to change of personnel of the bank directorate."

Though the architects of the system had hoped the stronger state banks could be enticed to join, in the system's first three years of existence only 53 of the 10,000 institutions eligible actually took out a federal charter. To many it seemed that the government itself, when it failed to transfer its deposits from the subtreasuries, had questions about the the system's viability. Even Senator Aldrich, now 73 and ailing, began to harbor doubts about his own brainchild. He feared that the Federal Reserve Board, with its presidentially selected membership, would act as a "political machine rather than as a force in financial circles." It would, he predicted, "be unable to assist a bank or community in time of trouble."

However, the response from abroad was encouraging. An official of the Deutschebank declared that "the American Act is one of the greatest undertakings that has ever been attempted in the realm of banking, surpassing the English reform of Sir Robert Peel in 1844." The noted British economist Morton Frewen was even more enthusiastic. "A new day has dawned," he noted. "This Act is a bigger thing, by all odds, for the world's trade than the Panama Canal." For their part the bankers of New York adopted a position of guarded optimism at the NYSBA annual meeting. In his presidential address delivered at the Griswold Hotel on Eastern Point, Connecticut, Robert H. Treman, head of the Tompkins County National Bank, declared: "Whatever the individual opinion of the bill may be it is, taken as a whole, a good bill which should receive the hearty support of every banker until practice discovers defects which should be corrected. Certainly until then it should be faithfully supported."

In the months ahead, as the armies of Europe braced for war, it became clear that America's new banking system would need all the faith and all the support it could get.

8

The Shadow War

THE LOT of a bank examiner is seldom a happy one. In the years that preceded the outbreak of war in Europe it had become particularly doleful. Indeed, most of New York's financial institutions viewed the representatives of the state's Department of Banking as a tactless and often vindictive species of financial police who thrust their way into the offices of a bank "for the sole purpose of disturbing everybody and upsetting everything, and sending somebody to the Penitentiary."

With 740 state-chartered financial institutions (total assets: of $3.9 billion) to supervise, the department was heavily overburdened; on average, each state examiner was responsible for eighteen institutions, each one of which had to be visited two, three, or even four times a year. Perhaps the pressures of the job could best be explained in the semihumorous words of W. P. Milburn, a state examiner who eventually went on to become an assistant secretary of the U.S. Treasury. In 1910 the average examiner, declared Milburn,

does not see his family oftener than once a week. He gets home late Saturday afternoon and leaves early Monday morning or perhaps Sunday afternoon. He examines two, three, four or five banks a week, working until late at night in the bank, and then working later writing up his report. He eats what he can get or goes without eating; he sleeps where he can and when, and he rides on passenger trains or jitneys when he can, and at other times on freight trains, getting his only sleep perhaps lying on a bunk in the way car. He gets up early in the morning, drinks a cup of something called coffee, and eats what was

once an egg, and goes to the bank. He is greeted with a loud groan and a general scowl from the President down to the messenger. He feels he is in a hostile atmosphere from the time he goes into the bank to the time he leaves it. Anything he wants he has to ask for two or three times—he can often get but scant information from the clerks and officers in regard to the loans and he feels instinctively that he is not getting all the facts and, under those conditions, if he is occasionally cranky or does not consider the condition of the bank exactly the same as the officers do, he is, as I have said, perhaps excusable.

In the first weeks of 1914 Governor Martin Glynn and the leaders of the New York senate decided that the Department of Banking must expand its mission from that of cranky and often obstructive watchdog to one of active leadership in the financial community. First, a new superintendent must be chosen who, unlike many of the yeoman bureaucrats that preceded him, was capable of welding the state's vast and sometimes contradictory patchwork of banking law—much of it enacted piecemeal back in the 1830s and 1840s—into a coherent body of regulation attuned to the requirements of the new Federal Reserve Act. The new candidate must have the social poise to reason with—and, if necessary, talk back to—federal officials and the old school ties in the big banks. Also, with war clouds hanging over Europe, the new superintendent must have the ingenuity and the qualities of leadership to somehow figure out a way of harnessing the state's "immense banking power" to halt and then reverse the depression that had gripped the rural regions of New York for three decades.

After a prolonged search, and an increase of the superintendent's salary

from $6,000 to $10,000 a year, Governor Glynn and the senate found their man in the person of Eugene Lamb Richards, a fifty-one-year-old trial lawyer in Manhattan. At this time the Department of Banking was situated in Albany's old State Hall, an elegantly columned building just off Capitol Park. Shortly after assuming office on March 27, 1914, the tall athletic Richards met with his staff of clerical assistants and forty-six full-time examiners in the hall's spacious rotunda. To many of those present Richards was already a figure of legendary renown. The son of a professor of mathematics at Yale, he had quickly established a reputation for brains and leadership on attending that university. Besides winning the prestigious Bristol Scholarship for excellence in math and classics and the Townsend Prize for oratory, young Richards was chosen to captain the football team in 1884; in this role he had devised an audacious set of offensive plays that resulted in a 52 to 0 victory over Harvard. The Crimson's humiliation was so complete that its faculty voted to ban football from its campus altogether, and no game was played between the two universities the following year.

This determination to push matters to a successful conclusion, no matter where the chips might fall, was to become Richards's trademark in the years ahead. After a spell as a trial attorney in Manhattan, he became a deputy attorney general of New York, where he prosecuted a number of fraudulent fire insurance companies and defended the mayor of New York from a series of savage legal and journalistic attacks by William Randolph Hearst, who claimed he had been bilked of victory in the city elections of 1906.

After explaining the new salary scales to his staff, Richards indicated that he would attempt to dissipate the hit-and-run flavor of the present examination system by recruiting dozens of commercial accountants to work as part-time examiners, at the per diem rate of "$8 and railroad fare." Richards also hoped to stimulate a more sympathetic attitude among bankers by explaining the examiner's side of the story at public forums around the state.

"The Banking Department ought to be called the Department of Public

Confidence," Richards subsequently told a group of bankers on Long Island. "I shall not only require unceasing vigilance and activity in my Department, but I need your daily cooperation and support. I am determined, so far as it in me lies, to do all in my power to clean up the waifs, strays and frauds in the community; and I am convinced that I can do it if such men as are here will stand up and hold up my hands."

Richards knew that he would need every bit of help he could get from the banking community if he was to pull the state's rural regions out of their prolonged economic slump. The task would not be easy. Over the last three decades more than 30,000 farms and 2.5 million acres of fertile land had been abandoned. Many families had forsaken the land for work in the factories that were springing up around major cities like Binghamton and Rochester. Those that remained behind were subjected to a life of back-breaking penury not unlike that endured by their great-grandparents in frontier days. In consequence the problems now facing the small and medium-sized banks of New York were, Richards noted, "startling, if not appalling."

By prairie standards the New York farm, with an average area of 104 acres, was both small and inefficient. Even in 1914 few farmhouses had running water, and only one in a hundred had an indoor privy. Most rural residences had no electricity, no school bus and no mail delivery by the U.S. Post Office. As a result of such meager services whole communities in rural counties such as Jefferson, Essex, Lewis, Steuben and Allegany vanished from the tax rolls, and often from the map itself.

Unable to purchase the necessary steam- and gasoline-powered machinery, most farmers continued to till the land by horse-drawn plow. In many of the more remote communities wheat was still threshed by hand. A traveler in Delaware County during those years reports seeing on numerous occasions "three or four lithe figures beating out the grain with their flails in some sheltered nook, or some grassy lane lined with cedars." In return for such herculean labors a single man on an upstate farm received about seven cents an hour, plus room and board. A married man, with bed and board out, received ten cents an hour, or six dollars a week for work that generally consisted of six ten-hour days. It was therefore not surprising that "few young people of the state deliberately chose the occupation of hired farm laborer as a life's vocation. For them the glamor of the urban community with its more attractive economic opportunities was always a mecca."

With the relatively fixed demand the value of upstate land fluctuated with the changing prices of the crops produced; even in times of relative stability rural banks felt compelled to charge farmers interest at a rate of one, and perhaps two, percentage points above that of their more urban customers. Many banks were also reluctant to furnish long-term assistance, either through a loan or the refinancing of a mortgage, that would have enabled even the more prosperous farms to acquire modern machinery.

One of Superintendent Richards's first moves was to set up an organization that he called a Land Bank. Though its name would have given Alexander Hamilton and many colonial New Yorkers pause, the Land Bank was

basically a vehicle for the equitable distribution of mortgage funds to even the most remote regions of the state. Thus a commercial bank or a savings and loan association in a prosperous part of the state could use its idle funds to purchase Land Bank bonds, yielding between 4 and 5 percent interest, free of state tax. The Land Bank would then lend these funds out at interest to banks in remote rural regions so that "sections where farms are now being abandoned may be again more fully populated and the whole state profit from the development of those sections."

To be eligible for this service the rural bank or savings institution had to purchase Land Bank bonds equal in value to at least 5 percent of the total sum borrowed, and pledge as security mortgages to the bank worth 125 percent of the amount borrowed. Thus, to put $100,000 into new mortgages, the rural institutions had to purchase $5,000 worth of bonds and pledge as collateral $125,000 worth of existing mortgages. No country resident's mortgage could be for more than $4,000 or run longer than eleven years.

Richards's Land Bank proved to be an even more spectacular success than his victory over Harvard. Many of the state's major banks expressed enthusiasm for the project and, as a public service, the officers of the Guaranty Trust Co. volunteered their help in the task of getting the Bank established. Thousands of farmers and small householders across the state promptly took advantage of the Land Bank's service to retain title to their property. And once again, it was clear that New York had broken new ground in the field of banking. "Numerous enquiries have been received from other states," Richards told the *New York Times* in December 1914. The new bank, he said, might become a model for all states "and possibly for a still greater institution of national scope." In fact, the New York Land Bank was to serve as the prototype for the Federal Farm Loan Bank that would be approved by

William G. McAdoo, who supervised construction of the first railroad tunnel under the Hudson, was known for his brains and his can-do attitude. Here, he inaugurates new transatlantic radio link. (AP/Wide World Photos)

Congress in July 1916. In 1938, a quarter century after its founding, much of the experience generated in the Land Bank's operations·would be used for the formation of Fannie Mae, the Federal National Mortgage Association.

Richards had barely got the Land Bank up and running when war broke out in Europe. On June 28, 1914, a Serbian nationalist shot and killed Archduke Franz Ferdinand at a military review in Sarajevo. Ferdinand was the heir to the throne of the Austro-Hungarian Empire. Outraged, the empire declared war on Serbia exactly one month later. In an implosion of interlocking treaties the czar of Russia then ordered general mobilization, Germany declared war on both Russia and France, and Britain, in accordance with its previous commitments, declared war on Germany.

In the ensuing financial chaos the New York Stock Exchange suspended trading; it would remain closed for five months. Two days later, early on Sunday, August 2, Secretary of the Treasury William McAdoo was informed over the telephone by Mr. Woodward, president of the Hanover National Bank, that the New York Clearing House feared that an extraordinarily heavy run would take place when banks opened the following morning.

McAdoo, a tall hook-nosed man known for his brains and his "can-do" attitude (as president of the Hudson & Manhattan Railroad he had built the first tunnel under the Hudson River), was immersed in the task of recovering American citizens stranded in Europe by the unexpected outbreak of hostilities. In the panic even the most fashionable hotels and travel agencies refused to accept American traveler's checks and, in some instances, U.S. dollar bills. After arranging for the dispatch to Europe of the cruiser USS *Tennessee* bearing $1.5 million in gold coin, McAdoo left for New York on the Congressional Limited Express.

The Shadow War

That evening he and Comptroller of the Currency Skelton Williams met a select group of bankers in a conference room at New York's Vanderbilt Hotel. The group included J. P. Morgan, Jr. (whose father had died the previous year), Frank Vanderlip, Harry Davison, A. J. Hemphill of Guaranty Trust, Barton Hepburn of Chase National, Edward Sheldon of the United States Trust Co. and Eugene Richards.

The new superintendent was at ease with this group. He spoke their language. Indeed, it is likely that many of the men present came up to slap him on the back. According to a recent story on page one of the *New York Times*, a fire that began late at night in a defective electrical connection had burned Mr. and Mrs. Richards' elegant mansion on Staten Island's north shore to the ground. Richards sounded the alarm and evacuated the building, only to learn that three "panic stricken" housemaids were trapped up on the third floor. Despite the infernolike heat Richards reentered the burning house, ascended the back stairs and, by exercise of great strength, half-dragged and half-carried the three women back down through the flames and smoke to safety.

The men in the Hotel Vanderbilt, however, had an even bigger crisis on their minds. The financiers wrestled until well after midnight with the question of how, without the help of the still unformed Reserve System, the international money crisis might best be averted. A major source of contention lay in whether the Treasury would, in fact, release the entire $154

The Shadow War

million it said it had available in emergency currency. Finally, Secretary McAdoo cleared his throat and announced that he would issue currency to all national banks with circulating notes to the maximum permissible under the Aldrich-Vreeland Act of 1908.

But Frank Vanderlip then declared that this measure would not help his bank. "The National City, as you know," he said, "has no banknotes in circulation." McAdoo replied: "And I suppose you need emergency currency as much as anybody."

"We certainly do," said Vanderlip with emphasis. "Probably more than anybody else. We have more country correspondents than any other New York bank." Superintendent Richards followed Vanderlip, with a question about the standing of banks with state charters. After much discussion, the secretary informed the assembled bankers that he would return to Washington immediately and seek to have the law amended by Congress. The proposed changes in the law, passed within twenty-four hours of McAdoo's return, permitted banks to receive currency worth up to 125 percent of their capital and surplus, regardless of their bills in circulation. And, by way of response to Eugene Richards's question, state-chartered banks and trust companies would be granted the same privilege if they "signified their intention" of joining the embryonic Federal Reserve System.

As the international crisis deepened many bankers argued that the launch of the Federal Reserve System should be postponed, at least until gold ceased to sell at a premium. But McAdoo and President Wilson believed that the severity of the European crisis required that the system be set up immediately, whatever the ensuing difficulties. When Benjamin Strong, normally a most decisive man, raised a number of questions with McAdoo about vault space, procurement and personnel the Secretary of the Treasury, with a hint of exasperation, thrust a copy of the Federal Reserve Act into his hands and ordered him to "buy a few chairs and pine-top tables . . . hire some clerks and stenographers, paint 'Federal Reserve Bank of New York' on your office door, and open up."

McAdoo wanted the bank open by November 16 but Strong was unable to find even barely adequate office space until November 4, when he took a three-year lease on an old bank building at 62 Cedar Street, two blocks up from Wall Street. By opening day Strong had assembled a staff of seven officers, only three of whom were permanent, and eighty-five clerks, most of whom had been borrowed from the Manhattan Bank and his own Bankers Trust. Vault space was still a problem and he arranged to make temporary use of the vaults of the New York Clearing House and the U.S. Subtreasury.

Most Americans were stunned by the speed and the ferocity of Kaiser Wilhelm's attack. In less than a month of fighting, Germany's gray-clad legions had forced their way into the outskirts of Paris and brought some of the most beautiful buildings in the world within range of their massive siege guns, much as they had done in the war of 1870. Matters were even worse on the banks of the Vistula, 1,000 miles to the east, where the German and Austrian

An Orthodox priest conducts divine services in a primitive Russian field hospital during the battle of Tannenberg. (Bettmann Archive)

forces blocked and then annihilated several huge but disorganized Russian armies at the battles of Tannenberg and the Masurian Lakes. In these bloody encounters the czar's infantry proved itself to be courageous but "hardly trained; many were even without rifles, and had to snatch them from the hands of their dead comrades."

As the German offensive ground its way across Europe, President Wilson issued a Proclamation of Neutrality that called upon all U.S. citizens to be "impartial in thought as well as in action." The president hoped to prevent the country from being sucked into the widening European bloodbath and, even more to the point, he hoped to preserve peace among America's patchwork of ethnic groups, many of whom maintained a passionate adherence to one or the other of the warring nations. The proclamation was well intentioned. And it worked for a time. When the House of Morgan sought to obtain a loan of $100 million for the beleaguered government of France, Secretary of State William Jennings Bryan sternly warned the bank that such financial assistance to belligerents on *either* side would be viewed as "the worst of contraband" and "inconsistent with the true spirit of neutrality."

Meanwhile, up in Albany, Superintendent Richards was grappling with numerous crises of his own. In addition to their ordinary examinations of state banks, his staff was now called upon to investigate all foreign-owned institutions doing business within the borders of New York. In the next year his teams, most of them working out of the old State Hall, completed no fewer than 338 "special investigations." Of the twenty-three foreign banks registered in the first year of European hostilities, most had their head offices in Canada, Britain or other English-speaking countries. A German bank, Deutsch Brothers, suspended its North American operations in 1914. When the investigations were completed the only remaining institution that could in any way be connected to the Central Powers was the Bohemia Joint Stock

Bank, headquartered in Prague, Bohemia; its New York branch was at 1389 Second Avenue in Manhattan's Germantown district.

The superintendent's next mission carried with it a strong hint of the cloak, and the dagger. Through the years numerous European steamship companies and travel agents had established offices in New York. Besides dealing in international currency these operations, contrary to state law, were also providing their customers with banking services. Many were unaware that such activities were illegal. But careful study by Richards's examiners also revealed that several German shipping lines were permitting their businesses to be used as a cover for foreign agents who, besides engaging in industrial espionage, also sought to manipulate America's political processes for their own ends.

A leading participant in these practices was a tall, heavy-set Prussian named Dr. Heinrich Albert. Shortly after his arrival in the fall of 1914, Albert had opened a suite of offices in the Hamburg-American Line's building at 45 Broadway. The doctor's appearance and brusque manner did little to inspire trust. Like the sinister villains portrayed in adventure yarns of the then-popular American novelist E. Phillips Oppenheim, Albert displayed several livid dueling scars upon his cheeks, and spoke with an accent so guttural that it was necessary for him to communicate even the most elementary idea to the natives in a bull-like roar.

At first Albert was viewed by the Banking Department's top investigators as a harmless, if somewhat bizarre, representative of German commercial interests. But after a while the doctor began to draw attention to himself by striding into some of the city's larger banks where, after imperiously summoning the cashier, he would produce a battered suitcase filled with

Deutschmarks and demand that they be promptly converted into U.S. dollars. These visits became increasingly frequent, and the transactions often involved amounts of $25,000 and more.

Richards's men handed the Albert case over to the Secret Service in the U.S. Treasury Department. After careful surveillance, which included the cracking of enciphered messages to and from a German-operated radio station at Sayville on Long Island, the authorities discovered that Dr. Albert was, in fact, Berlin's chief undercover operative in the United States. Since Germany and the United States were not at war, Albert could not be arrested. But the Secret Service eventually found a way of putting an end to his activities. In the summer of 1915 Dr. Albert and a number of associates traveled uptown on a subway train. As they were about to disembark, Secret Service Agent Frank Burke stepped out of the crowd and deftly relieved the doctor of his bulging attaché case. The contents of this case were on Treasury Secretary McAdoo's desk within twenty-four hours; Albert's papers provided detailed documentation of the Reich's attempts to foment factory strikes, bribe legislators and acquire American patent rights in the hope of blocking construction of certain aircraft. A selection of these papers was subsequently leaked by McAdoo to the New York *World*.

In all, it transpired, the Kaiser's agents planned to spend close to $27 million on a variety of projects designed to keep America neutral. At the same time, they hoped to destabilize the government of Mexico and stir up trouble in the U.S. for France, Britain and other Allied nations. "The publication of the Albert papers," George Viereck, editor of the militantly pro-Kaiser newspaper *The Fatherland*, subsequently noted, "was a German tragedy. . . . The inner workings of the propaganda machine were laid bare."

New Yorkers as a whole did not take long to attune themselves to the wartime economy. President Wilson's proclamations notwithstanding, the commercial instinct of Americans proved as irrepressible as it had been in the days of George III. The ban on stock trading was among the first of Wilson's edicts to be challenged, and then circumvented. First half a dozen, and then a score, of stockbrokers gathered each morning on the curb of New Street in downtown Manhattan. Here they traded back and forth among themselves the stock of major corporations. It was not long before a hundred brokers were buying and selling bootlegged shares in this "outlaw market." Street traffic often came to a halt in the turmoil as traders vied to place their bids.

Soon some of the more active brokers began to distribute typewritten sheets at the end of each day, listing closing prices of major stocks. A number of trust departments in New York banks, fearful that the value of their holdings might be undermined, panicked. A few—apparently oblivious of the First Amendment—threatened to sue any newspaper that dared print the renegade lists. As always, such threats backfired and even the papers that had previously ignored the lists now made a point of printing them. To the banks' surprise, however, the news from the curb was not all bad. After a brief period of disruption, the prices of most major stocks leveled out at about 10 percent below their prewar range.

President Wilson's other attempts to impose neutrality in thought and deed quickly ran into trouble. As the war in Europe descended into a bloody stalemate, military doctrine on both sides of the conflict maintained that the road to victory lay in the conscription of ever bigger armies, and the application of ever more force. On October 15, 1914, as the Allied demand for food, clothing and munitions soared, Wilson's government reversed itself abruptly and approved the granting of credit for nonmilitary purchases made in the United States. This was the first step onto a long and slippery slope that would eventually pull the United States into war. Even the ban on munitions ceased to be absolute. While no *credit* could be granted for their purchase, a foreign power might acquire them if *full payment* were made in gold bullion or high-grade government securities.

These new arrangements, however, did not resolve the massive supply problems of France and England. As they placed their orders for foodstuffs, the price of wheat rose from 85 cents to $1.10 and then to $1.67 a bushel by February 1915. This was good news for the American farmer. But, to their annoyance, the French and the British often found themselves bidding against one another for American commodities, thereby pushing prices ever higher. Sometimes, in the case of the British, different departments of the same government found themselves competing against one another for contracts in wheat, mules and shoe leather.

As such conflicts became more acute, J. P. Morgan & Co. perceived an opportunity. In November 1914 the bank arranged for Henry Davison to "hop on a steamer" with Sir George Paish, leader of a special mission from the British Treasury, as he prepared to return from New York to London. Despite the menace of German U-boats, Davison's lighthearted spirit rendered the voyage congenial. No doubt Harry reached into the orchestra from time to time and tried his hand with a variety of instruments. Soon, the Treasury men found themselves wondering out loud why their country did not appoint the Morgan bank to serve as its agent in New York, with the authority to coordinate all purchases in the United States. Why, Sir George, that's an inspiration! And, while we're on the subject, perhaps the Morgan bank, in an effort to keep Allied currencies buoyant, might consider underwriting a massive bond issue with the American public? Egad, another inspiration!

After installing himself at Claridge's, the fashionable London hotel, Davison made the rounds of Whitehall. He spoke to Lord Kitchener, the Secretary of War, whom he had met a few years earlier on a hunting trip up the Nile. Within a month the persuasive Morgan partner was lunching with Prime Minister Herbert Asquith and attending meetings of the British war cabinet.

The British were impressed with Davison's down-to-earth manner and his determination to get things done. Soon, they voted to make the Morgan

In an effort to justify the attack in the eyes of world opinion, this German propaganda picture of the sinking Lusitania falsely depicts two gun turrets on the liner's foredeck. (Bettmann Archive)

bank their chief bargaining agent for the purchase of supplies in the United States. A similar arrangement was worked out for France through Herman Harjes, Morgan's representative in Paris. For these services Morgan would take back a commission of 1 percent, a service which would eventually produce a windfall of some $30 million for the bank.

All the combatant nations knew that continued supplies from North America were critical to the Allied cause. The British Royal Navy had orders to keep transatlantic trade routes open, whatever the cost. At the same time, it sought to place a tight blockade upon Europe's Central Powers. Germany, of course, resisted such a policy. By way of retaliation it began to wage submarine warfare, first against Allied shipping and soon after against any neutral shipping that endeavored to trade with the Allies. At each click of the ratchet, Germany brought itself ever closer to open conflict with the United States.

In the mind of the American public, as in the court of world opinion, it soon became clear that there was a significant moral disparity to be found in these opposing mercantile strategies. While the Royal Navy was able to execute its policy of *arresting* ships and impounding cargoes with little or no bloodshed, the German submarine policy generally entailed the *sinking* of ships and the killing of large numbers of noncombatants, many of whom were children. The Allies, with the help of clever propagandists, were able to exploit this moral disparity to great effect.

In January 1915 an American freighter loaded with wheat for Britain was bombarded and sunk by a German warship in the South Atlantic. Four months later, the Cunard liner *Lusitania* was torpedoed and sunk by a German submarine off the coast of Ireland, with the loss of 123 American lives. Among the Americans who perished were the great theatrical impresario Charles Frohman, the millionaire sportsman A. G. Vanderbilt, and Elbert Hubbard, the Sage of East Aurora, whose presence had so often graced the dinner table of William Cornwell, the founder of the New York State Bankers Association. Hubbard was now himself a banker of some

renown; after establishing the Roycroft Community, he had, with Cornwell's advice, gone on to establish the prosperous and successful Roycroft Bank in 1904. Prior to the *Lusitania's* departure from New York, Hubbard told reporters that he hoped to interview the Kaiser while in Europe. After the torpedo from the U-20 struck, he and his wife Alice made no attempt to clamber into the overcrowded lifeboats. Instead, they made their way to a quiet corner of the upper deck, and were last sighted holding hands as the *Lusitania* finally keeled over, and sank.

In response to vehement American protests the German government pointed out—correctly—that the liner was secretly carrying several hundred tons of American-made munitions to England. But the deliberate sinking, with a total loss of 1,195 lives, did more than anything to crystallize public opinion in America. Before the incident the New York *Journal of Commerce* had referred to the British blockade as "a reversion to barbarism." After the sinking of the *Lusitania* it stridently demanded that the blockade be extended to all neutral nations on the continent of Europe.

By the fall of 1915 the treasuries of both France and Britain were almost empty. When the Allied governments asked the Morgan bank to underwrite a bond issue of $500 million there was little objection from official Washington. Yet the Morgan venture was to become not only the largest but also the most controversial bond issue ever made. Not to be outdone, the government in Berlin—also strapped for funds—determined to stage a rival bond drive in the United States. To the consternation of Woodrow Wilson, who was campaigning for reelection, the dueling bond drives were to polarize voter opinion more sharply than any issue since the Civil War. Indeed, it would

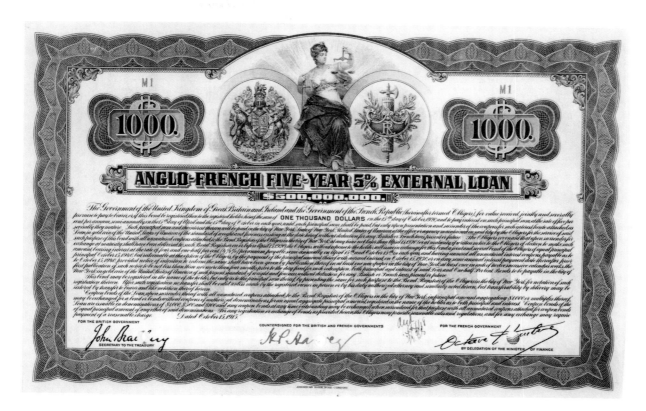

The Government of the United Kingdom of Great Britain and Ireland and the Government of the French Republic (hereinafter termed Obligors), for value received, jointly and severally promise to pay to bearer, or if this bond be registered to the registered holder being the owner of **ONE THOUSAND DOLLARS** on the 15th day of October 1920 and to pay interest on such principal sum at the rate of five per cent per annum, semi-annually on the 15th day of April and the 15th day of October in each year, until such principal sum shall be paid, but only upon presentation and surrender of the corporate and annexed bonds attached as severally they mature. Such principal sum and the annexed thereon will be paid in the City of New York, State of New York, United States of America at the office of agency maintained as sent City by the Obligors for the service of said Loan or, failing the United States of America, at the standard of weight and fineness existing at the date hereof without deduction for any British or French taxes, present or future...

ANGLO-FRENCH FIVE-YEAR 5% EXTERNAL LOAN

$500,000,000.

FOR THE BRITISH GOVERNMENT
John Bradbury
SECRETARY TO THE TREASURY

COUNTERSIGNED FOR THE BRITISH AND FRENCH GOVERNMENTS

FOR THE FRENCH GOVERNMENT
Octave Homberg
BY DELEGATION OF THE MINISTER OF FINANCE

not be so sharply divided again for another half century, in the later years of the Vietnam war.

Both bond issues were in trouble from the beginning. The Allies had initially proposed an issue of $1 billion, but this was halved by Morgan. One in ten Americans was of German descent. While most were neutral in outlook Dr. Charles Hexamer, president of the National German-American Alliance, argued that the Allied bonds were no more than a stratagem to ensnare American business, and eventually the American people, into aggressive support of the Allied cause.

Such charges were not without foundation. To ensure that as many citizens as possible could participate, Morgan's arranged for the Anglo-French bond certificates to range in size from coupon bonds of $100 to registered bonds of $50,000. A total of 289 syndicate managers, of which 45 were in New York state, were to receive the 5 percent bonds at the price of $96.25 for resale to the public at $98. In five years the bonds would be convertible into 4.5 percent British and French 15–25-year treasury bonds.

In the wake of the Pujo hearings, many ordinary American citizens were convinced that such terms would simply enable the Morgan bank, as the alleged ringleader of the "Wall Street Money Trust" to extract millions in commissions from the Allies in the time of extremity. Sharp criticism also emanated from the investment community itself. Although the funds from the Anglo-French bonds had to be spent in the United States, and only then for nonmilitary purchases, Henry Goldman of Goldman, Sachs refused to

Anglo-French five-year 5% $1,000 bond; not until the Vietnam war, half a century later, would public opinion be so sharply divided. (J. P. Morgan & Co. Inc.: Photo by Sarah Wells)

The Shadow War

help Morgan underwrite the issue. Kuhn, Loeb, another house with strong European affiliations, indicated that it would participate only if the French and British promised they would not use any of the materials purchased to aid the anti-Semitic autocracy in Russia. The *Wall Street Journal* tried, in vain, to put the whole matter in perspective. Those who opposed the loan, it argued, were wrong because their position "assumes that we are lending money for war. We are not. We are financing American trade."

Soon brokerage houses with strong German connections, like Zimmerman & Forshay at 9 and 11 Wall Street, began to advertise a rival issue of 1,000 Mark German Imperial Government 5 percent bonds for $210, or 16 points below par, in American currency. The worst fears of the cynics seemed to be confirmed when, on the morning of September 25, 1915, just as the final terms of sale were set, the French armies attacked the German lines on a 20-mile front in Champagne. The British launched a parallel attack 100 miles to the north, through the coalfields of Loos. Were these offensives, many wondered, timed to coincide with the launching of the bonds?

The first headlines from the front were euphoric. The Syracuse *Post-Standard* hailed its readers in headlines two inches tall:

FRENCH ADVANCE TWO AND A HALF MILES.
TWENTY THOUSAND GERMAN PRISONERS TAKEN.
BREAKTHROUGH EXPECTED.

The news, with its hints of imminent victory, undoubtedly boosted initial subscriptions to the Allied bonds. Then the dispatches turned sour, and it seemed that the Kaiser's generals were also aware of the significance of the Allied offensive. In the bitterest fighting of the war, the advance was eventually halted at the second line of German trenches. In ten days of attacks and counterattacks the trench line moved only a few hundred yards forward, at the cost of 140,000 German and 240,000 Allied lives. There would, after all, be no breakthrough and no easy victory. As the ghastly struggle continued in the mud along the Somme, it reinforced the worst fears of many Americans about any kind of entanglement with foreign governments.

The stalemate on the battlefield seemed, if anything, to intensify the struggles between the Anglo-French and the Imperial German bonds in the New York market. As some 1,600 financial institutions—mostly banks—opened their subscription books across the country, many communities with a substantial number of German-American customers, such as Buffalo and the city of New York, attempted to blunt criticism by running advertisements side by side that invited investors to purchase the Allied and German bonds. The *Wall Street Journal* carried ads of similar size on alternating days.

In the battle of the bonds both sides claimed victory. Dr. Karl Helfferich, secretary of Germany's Imperial Treasury, declared in Berlin that he had successfully raised a loan of $3 billion dollars. In the same speech he also pointed out that Germany was more efficient at the task of making war; while England spent $25 million dollars a day, Germany devoted only $15 million a day to its war effort. By early October the Anglo-American loan was said to be oversubscribed by $300 million; the largest subscription was said to be $35 million, while John and William Rockefeller were rumored to have bought close to $20 million between them.

In its negotiations the Morgan bank had arranged for banks selling Allied bonds to keep the funds on deposit, interest free, until they were needed to pay for the purchase of supplies. The other big winners, of course, were companies like Ford Motor Co., Bethlehem Steel and DuPont, which were now able to sign major contracts with the Allies. Soon the activity on the reopened stock market became so intense that, as one financial publication noted, "million and a half share days are becoming an almost daily occurrence." The price of Baldwin Locomotive rose from $40 to $154 a share in 1915, and that of Bethlehem Steel went from $46 to $700 a share by November 1916. In many major brokerage houses cots were being installed in offices and "meals are being served on desks, so great is the rush of business."

The total amount of bank clearances increased from $9.9 billion a month at the outbreak of war to $20 billion by December 1915, and to $27 billion a month by the end of 1916. The only discouraging note came from an editor of the *Bankers Magazine* who wondered, with sad prescience, if it was not "becoming apparent that these loans may have the effect of an indefinite prolongation of the War?"

Indeed, by the spring of 1916 it seemed clear that the leading nations of Europe were bent upon a course of mutual annihilation. In France a total of 158 Allied divisions prepared for an even more bloody assault on the 117 German divisions entrenched behind the tributaries of the muddy, slow-moving Somme. In Galicia the Russian armies were in disarray. At sea, the Royal Navy tightened its blockade, and German submarines increased their assaults on merchant and passenger vessels alike. In the United States explosions at factories engaged in war production were attributed to sabotage. German spies, real and imagined, seemed to be everywhere.

In an incident typical of the shadow war now being fought along the eastern seaboard, Frank Vanderlip, president of the National City Bank, was visited in his office by two men, an American agent and a well-tanned Englishman who looked like a naval officer but claimed, with a breezy smile, to occupy some obscure post in the British Treasury. The visitors casually suggested that Vanderlip might want to place one of National City's clerks under surveillance. A few days later the bank's own security men discovered that the clerk was making copies of shipping manifests used to document commercial paper on cargoes in the North Atlantic trade. Then, when the clerk thought the coast was clear, he would place the lists in a small container and toss them out the window to a German courier standing in the street below.

The final step on America's road to war came in January 1917, with Germany's declaration of unlimited submarine warfare and the decoding by British naval intelligence of the so-called Zimmermann telegram. In this note to the Mexican government Kaiser Wilhelm's foreign minister pledged Germany's help in recovering its historic territories of Texas, New Mexico and Arizona if Mexico would, in turn, support Germany in any war against the United States. Two months later, Congress declared war on Germany. The shadow war, where every American decision seemed at least two steps removed from reality, was over.

The United States now moved with great expedition. First and foremost, it needed money. Three weeks after the declaration of war the U.S. Treasury opened its first drive when $2 billion worth of Liberty Bonds were offered at 3.5 percent interest to the American public. In planning this first great drive, Treasury Secretary McAdoo made a point of studying Salmon Chase's fund-raising strategies in the Civil War, and decided that to be successful a campaign "had to capitalize upon the emotion of the people" in a way that "sweeps them along on a powerful stream of romanticism." McAdoo did his job so well that this first bond issue was oversubscribed by more than one half.

The stream of national romanticism engaged the passions of the soberest businessmen. Charles G. Dawes, a prominent Chicago banker and a former comptroller of the currency, agreed to become national chairman of the loan drives. When an aide suggested to Dawes that the 4 percent interest planned for the second Liberty Bond might not be attractive enough to sell the entire issue of $3.8 billion, the banker became angry. If anybody "declines to subscribe for that reason," he solemnly told the aide, then "knock him down."

In total, the national bond drives would eventually generate a sum of $20.8 billion; all of this was sold tax exempt at par, with interest rates that successively rose from 3.5 percent to 4.75 percent. For the ordinary people everywhere the willingness to buy Liberty Bonds became a stern test of patriotism. Even the smaller communities like that of Jefferson County, with

Treasury Secretary McAdoo sought to "capitalize upon the emotion of the people" in the relentless drive to sell U.S. Liberty Bonds. The emotions of Hatred and Fear are harnessed in the poster at left, while an appeal to Pity and the Spirit of Sacrifice is put to work, at right. (Bettmann Archive)

only 80,000 citizens, began each drive with an impressive parade that included military bands and marching troops. Sixty-second speeches on patriotic themes were made in factories and offices by "one-minute men," while every wall was adorned with stirring posters exhorting citizens to slay the Hun and stop his jackboots from trampling upon the American heartland.

Nothing was left to chance. Team leaders were appointed in every village and township and raised a total of $25 million. Banks in such sparsely populated regions generally assigned a clerk full or part time to loan business. Regular customers were offered easy credit so that they could make even greater purchases than they could have otherwise afforded. Thus, a $100 bond might be acquired for as little as $5, the remainder to be paid on stipulated dates.

In the state's larger cities the bond drives assumed the proportions of a major spectacle. The experience of the city of Buffalo was typical. Here Myron S. Hall, president of the Buffalo Trust Co., headed all five loan drives to sell, in total, $249.9 million worth of bonds. In their patriotic zeal banks frequently violated their confidential relationship with customers. Myron Hall himself headed up a group entitled the "Not Enough Committee." It was made up of the "junior officers of the banks who each day reviewed all subscriptions of $1,000 or more to determine whether or not the same were adequate."

And Buffalo, it was said, could never have sold its quota of war bonds without the efforts of the Special Subscriptions Committee, under the chairmanship of Harry T. Ramsdell, president of the Manufacturers and Traders National Bank. The committee's function, noted the official report, "was to readjust the perspective of men who would ordinarily subscribe for $10,000 of bonds, but who by the liberal use of credit could subscribe for $50,000." Yet another group was assigned the task of "readjusting the perspective" of those capable, by a glance at their bank accounts, of subscribing to $100,000 or more in war bonds. Some German-Americans, suspected of hanging on to their cash, were strong-armed into buying Liberty Bonds "by the threat to publish the list of subscribers to German war bonds."

As more than nine million men between the ages of 21 and 31 registered for the draft, special boards for the production of shipping, aircraft, food, and munitions quickly opened in Washington. Soon all the citizens of New York not in uniform were beset by a barrage of special days; besides being required by the state food administrator to observe "wheatless Mondays" and "meatless Tuesdays" they were also called upon to endure "gasless Sundays" and "lightless nights."

The state was also caught up in some of the more absurd manifestations of patriotism. To speak German in a public place might well bring arrest, and the public frequently objected to entertainers with German names and to the performance of works by Wagner and Beethoven. Sauerkraut became "liberty cabbage," frankfurters were dubbed "liberty pups" and, in the rising wave of prejudice, the German American Bank of Buffalo found it necessary to change its name to the Liberty Bank. In the city of New York the German

Exchange Bank became the Commercial Exchange Bank and the Germania Bank was hastily renamed the Commonwealth Bank.

Back in Albany, Superintendent of Banks Eugene Richards was able to report that by early 1917 New York had "witnessed the most wonderful expansion in the business and commerce of the State which history records." Much abandoned farmland had come under the plough again, and real estate dealers specializing in rural properties were reporting farm acreage selling at a premium throughout central New York. In the summer of 1916 Congress had capitalized on Richards's idea of a state land bank and created twelve federal Farm Loan Banks, whose resources of $60 million would be used to provide cheap mortgage money for farmers across the country. The average price of wheat in New York had now climbed to $2.20 a bushel, and the wages of farm workers had nearly doubled. The revival in agriculture was reflected in the prosperity of New York's state-chartered banks and trust companies, whose total resources increased from $2.9 billion to $3.6 billion, a jump of some 24 percent in a single year. Deposits in New York's 380 savings banks and cooperative loan associations had come ahead by a similar amount.

On the international scene, Americans were making their presence felt. On Independence Day 1917, General John Pershing led a parade of 14,500 troops through wildly cheering crowds in Paris. Three months later—as 20,000 women marched down Broadway in a suffrage parade—the dough-boys fought in their first action in a battle near Luneville, France. The shadow war had finally become real war. In the year that followed, all enemy aliens in the United States were forced to register, President Wilson enumerated his Fourteen Points to Congress, an airletter was flown nonstop from Chicago to New York in just under thirteen hours, and all Broadway theaters were ordered closed to conserve coal.

In their annual convention at Atlantic City's Hotel Traymore in June 1918, the members of the New York State Bankers Association felt confident enough of victory to open their proceedings with a touch of humor. Immediately after the invocation, J. H. Herzog of Albany rose to his feet to observe that the association had survived for twenty-five years without a gavel to maintain any semblance of order among its members.

"Some of us country bankers, away from home, might get frisky and cut up, and the Chairman has not the proper emblem of authority to call us to order. I therefore take great pleasure in presenting this gavel, with the hope that it will be used at many meetings of our Association." The bankers, unabashed by Herzog's hint of their unruliness, greeted his presentation with loud applause.

In his presidential address, John H. Gregory, head of the Central Bank of Rochester, told the assembled members that while the nation had, as yet, "no realization of the meaning of war," the American people "have simply worked with an energy and growing efficiency heretofore unknown, and are now producing at a rate undreamed of, and on a scale of magnitude that staggers the imagination." He went on to tell the bankers that New York state had invested a total of $2.58 billion in the first three issues of Liberty Bonds. "In other words," said Gregory, "with one-tenth of the population of the country, New York State subscribed over one-quarter of these bonds. Truly are we the Empire State."

Early that fall more than a million American servicemen successfully overcame the German army's last great stand in the Meuse-Argonne region of France. On November 9, Kaiser Wilhelm II abdicated his throne and fled to Holland. Two days later the Armistice between the warring nations was signed in a railroad car set in the forest of Compiegne.

9

Havana-on-the-Hudson

JUST THREE WEEKS after the signing of the Armistice, 100,000 New Yorkers gathered at the foot of West 14th Street to welcome the ocean greyhound *Mauretania*—now painted dark gray and "covered with weird streaks of camouflage paint"—as she brought home the first contingent of soldiers from the American Expeditionary Force in Europe. The 4,500 troops who hung on the *Mauretania*'s rails included many wounded men and the aviators of twenty-three air squadrons, their number sadly depleted by recent aerial battles over France. As the *Mauretania* neared the dock the returning heroes seemed to have only one thought on their minds: "Has New York gone dry yet?"

The replies may have been drowned out by the boom of dockside bands as they thumped out "When Johnny Comes Marching Home," and "Home, Sweet Home." The crowd sang along as the soldiers marched down several special gangways decorated with red-white-and-blue bunting. Man and woman, veteran and civilian, were delighted to see one another again after such a long and arduous separation. Indeed, the feeling became so intense that Mayor Whalen telegraphed the War Department for permission to hold a giant welcoming parade that very afternoon.

As the frantic celebrations ran their course, however, the joy of reunion was tempered by the realization that a kind of chasm had opened up between the Americans who had marched off to war, and those who had remained at home. As more troops returned this moral fissure would eventually cut across

Ocean greyhound Mauretania, *decked out in camouflage to avoid German U-boats, brought the first Doughboys home to West 14th Street in 1918.*
(Brown Brothers Photo)

the entire population. "The world I found on landing in New York bore no resemblance whatever to that I had left behind," noted the celebrated war correspondent Oswald Garrison Villard. "It was then, and for years thereafter, like a different planet."

There was certainly a brittle new confidence in the air. Hadn't America won the war, and saved the world for democracy? And wasn't her industrial might now second to none? In the four years since the European war began the United States had transformed herself from a debtor nation into the world's greatest creditor nation; by 1918 she had unquestionably become "the arbiter of the world's financial fortunes."

In the first three years of the conflict, America had increased its total gold stock by 55 percent, from $1.8 to $2.8 billion. Moreover, the establishment of the Federal Reserve System had itself resulted in the creation of an additional "super-structure of credit." In all, the Federal Reserve's total holdings of bullion more than tripled, from $203 million to $754 million worth of gold. And national banks had been measurably fortified when an additional $150 million dollars worth of gold entered their vaults; this, in the estimate of some, gave them the power to increase loans *twelvefold* upon the total then outstanding.

But the stateside Americans carried their new attitude toward the world far beyond a healthy whoop of victory. To Garrison Villard and his fellow veterans it seemed that Americans who had stayed home had discovered—despite the absence of any real hardship or any real danger—a new kind of "patriotism" rooted in ignorance, and in fear. It was, wrote Villard, as if many of these sedentary patriots had transferred the focus of their "war hate" from the defeated Germans to real, or imagined, enemies at home.

The tendency to discover a terrifying new set of ghouls under the bed was further exacerbated by the apparent success of the Bolshevik revolution in

Russia. When a bomb exploded outside the Morgan bank at 23 Wall Street, killing thirty bystanders, it seemed to confirm the fear that America itself was under siege. Every New York tenement, it was presumed, now harbored a nest of red-eyed anarchists, just waiting for the chance to ignite another fuse. Soon those in authority came to view any criticism of America's "capitalist system"—no matter how inconsequential—with suspicion. In Albany a joint committee under the chairmanship of Senator Clayton Lusk set out to investigate all "enemies of government." The thoughts and habits of schoolteachers, with their special closeness to the young, were subjected to particular scrutiny. The New York legislature also challenged the seating of five assemblymen said to be associated with a socialist splinter group. Despite an eloquent speech by Governor Al Smith arguing that all had a right to be heard, no matter how disagreeable their utterances, the Assembly kept its doors firmly locked.

On the national scene a former Quaker named Mitchell Palmer became President Wilson's attorney general and initiated a witch hunt that was, in the view of those who lived through it, "far more violent and destructive

A huge anarchist bomb exploded outside the Morgan bank in September 1920, killing thirty bystanders. (AP/Wide World Photos)

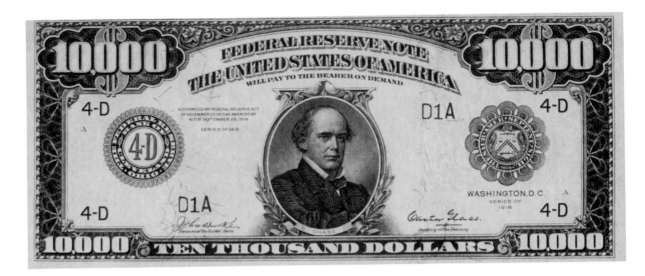

FEDERAL RESERVE NOTE
THE UNITED STATES OF AMERICA
WILL PAY TO THE BEARER ON DEMAND

10,000   10,000

4-D   D1A   4-D

4-D   D1A   WASHINGTON, D.C.   4-D
SERIES OF 1918

10,000   TEN THOUSAND DOLLARS   10,000

Salmon Chase's visage appeared again on the new $10,000 Federal Reserve Notes of 1918. The easing of federal regulation now precipitated a "striking expansion of American foreign banking machinery." The Fed itself soon established its own foreign branch in Havana, Cuba. (National Numismatic Collection, Smithsonian Institution)

than McCarthyism after the Second World War." Sixty thousand recent immigrants from Europe were declared by Palmer to be "organized agitators of the Trotzky doctrine." A mid-European accent was enough to bring arrest, and the new attorney general solemnly dedicated his department to the task of "sweeping the nation clean of such alien filth." With chilling effect Palmer often used the traditional Quaker "thee" and "thou" instead of the more conventional "you" when grilling suspected troublemakers. While Washington attempted to build its case for mass deportation, a resurgent and almost untrammeled Ku Klux Klan launched a series of pogroms against Jews, Catholics and blacks. On another front the Women's Temperance Union, mightily strengthened by the acquisition of the vote, waged a campaign to close up every saloon and ginmill in America.

It was against this stark backdrop that the nation's leading bankers began to ponder how America's huge increase in financial resources, most of it concentrated in New York, could most profitably be put to work. Benjamin Strong, at the Federal Reserve Bank of New York, and Frank Vanderlip, president of National City, urged support for a massive program of reconstruction in Europe. But the new patriotism was thrusting a broad cross section of the population, including many of the nation's leading bankers, into an isolationist mood.

A Europe too quickly restored to prosperity, they feared, might provide untoward competition in the decades ahead. And, they argued, America's former allies should at least *attempt* to pay off their war debt before obtaining further credit. Included in this school was James A. "Jamie" Stillman, who had become chairman of National City on the death of his father in 1918. Unwilling to resolve or to contest the growing divergence in policy, Frank Vanderlip resigned shortly thereafter. But the question of how, precisely, to deploy America's extraordinary new financial power remained.

On the domestic front, any serious attempt to expand was blocked by New York's restrictive laws on branch banking. Abroad, most countries in Western

Havana-on-the-Hudson

National City Bank's elegantly sculpted offices in St. Petersburg, Russia, were closed, along with many other traditional "diplomatic" branches, in a postwar drive for new business overseas. (Citibank Archive)

Europe were overloaded with bitterness and debt. Russia was in the throes of revolution. And parts of China were once again sinking into anarchy. In face of such global instability New York's major banking institutions began to seek out serious investment possibilities closer to home, in Central America and the Caribbean. Their task was greatly helped by the provisions of the Federal Reserve Act that had removed many legal obstacles in the chartering of overseas branches, thereby permitting "a striking expansion of American foreign banking machinery."

Foreign branches of commercial banks would henceforth cease to serve as little more than a diplomatic "presence" in another nation's capital. Now the banks began to go overseas with the intention of doing business and making money. This aggressive expansion of banking machinery would, in turn, compel top managements to think in global terms. Many large and medium-sized New York banks closed or rusticated their branches in London, Paris, St. Petersburg and Vladivostok while opening brand new branches in such exotic cities as Canton, Shanghai, Caracas, Singapore, Mexico City and Yokohama, Japan. For the majority, however, the most alluring prospects seemed to lie closer to home, upon the volatile and surpassingly beautiful island of Cuba.

Since its liberation from Spanish rule in 1898, the fertile soil of this subtropical paradise, often referred to as the "Pearl of the Antilles," had yielded up an unprecedented cornucopia of tobacco, sugar cane and coffee. Herds of cattle waxed fat upon the lush upland pastures of the Isla de Pinos. And beneath the plains of Camaguey and the thickly wooded hills of the Sierra Maestra lay a trove of precious metals that included copper, manganese, nickel and chromium. But for years the island's sugar crop had provided by far the sweetest—and the most risky—return on investment. In the two decades following 1894 the price of Cuban sugar on the world market had increased from 3.4 cents a pound, to 5, and then to 10 cents a pound. During the Great War it had, for a few dizzy moments, topped 70 cents a pound.

Back in 1905 J. P. Morgan & Co had established the Trust Co. of Cuba in Havana. Twelve years later Chase National led a group of thirty-four commercial banks to found a branch of the American Foreign Banking Corp. in the Cuban capital. Similarly, Guaranty Trust, working in conjunction with Brown Brothers, set up the Banco Mercantil Americano de Cuba.

But of all the New York banks, young Jamie Stillman's giant National City made far and away the biggest commitment. As was its custom, National City moved cautiously at first, quietly acquiring control of the Banco de la

Heavy machinery in centrales like this could produce one pound of sugar by grinding only ten pounds of cane. (Citibank Archive)

Habana. Then, after the new Cuban peso was made virtually interchangeable with the U.S. dollar in 1914, it quickly established a chain of twenty-three of its own branches in the capital and in other major cities around the island. Working through these branches the bank financed the construction of numerous large, highly efficient sugar-cane mills that came to be known as *centrales*. Such mills had to grind a large quantity of sugar cane to remain efficient, and National City and other New York banks began to finance the construction of railroads to haul cane from plantations 80 or 100 miles distant from the *central*.

The industry, already profitable, became yet more productive with new grinding and refining technologies that involved "vacuum panning" and the use of huge centrifuges to separate and crystallize the sugar from the cane juice. Now it was necessary to grind only ten pounds of cane to produce one pound of sugar. By the end of the war sugar was fetching more than 20 cents a pound, and National City, along with Guaranty Trust and Chase, had established "a hundred million dollar acceptance pool" in Havana to help get the sugar crop efficiently to market.

The surge of overseas activity introduced a new generation of able young New Yorkers to the rewards, and the subtly coded urbanities, of international finance. For men like James H. Durrell and Roger S. Farnham, reared in the straight-arrow tradition of the Ivy League, the exotic sights and sounds of life in Havana presented the starkest of contrasts to the sedate existence they had known among the snowdrifts of suburban Buffalo and White Plains.

In Cuba the sun almost always shone. Even in December the nights were warm and filled with the sinuous rhythms of the tango and flamenco. While Prohibition held the American homeland in its joyless grip, any one of Havana's 1,300 *cantinas* could provide the visiting pilgrim with a daiquiri or an ice-cold bottle of pilsner for the price of two American nickels. The new arrivals quickly discovered that it was one thing to evaluate the credit worthiness of a fellow countryman, and something else again to assess the reliability of an individual whose customs, language and mode of thought were rooted in an entirely different culture. As time passed the New Yorkers began to absorb, along with the sunshine and the daiquiris, some of the buccaneering outlook of those who had plundered the Spanish Main in centuries gone by. This swashbuckling style of management would eventually be reflected back across the Gulf Stream and become embedded, with fateful consequences, in the executive culture of some of New York's largest financial institutions.

During the immediate postwar years the venture into Cuban sugar proved immensely profitable, and that period subsequently became known as "The Dance of the Millions." Such was the influx of money from New York and Texas that Cuban plantation owners, who had already borrowed from one bank all they needed to harvest their crop, were begged by rival bank managers to borrow more. This, noted one American observer, "was the prevailing spirit of the banking business carried on in Cuba. Wall Street beamed upon it. This was not an irrigation by fertilizing streams of American capital. It was a cloudburst of bank credit which struck Cuba."

During Cuba's Dance of the Millions the focus of expatriot life became the Sevilla Hotel, situated on the eastern side of Havana's Prado. It is said that this elegant yet raffish establishment, then owned by a flamboyant Canadian entrepreneur named Jack Bowman, subsequently provided the inspiration for "Rick's Place" in the movie *Casablanca*. "The atmosphere of the Sevilla," noted one world-weary traveler at the time, "has something of the sophisticated *chic* of the Ritz, and something also of the cosmopolitan smartness of the Hotel de Paris at Monte Carlo." When not trying their luck at the roulette tables or dancing away the night under the stars up on the hotel's celebrated roof garden, nine stories above the Prado, most of the Sevilla's patrons seem to have devoted their energies to hatching romantic and commercial plots in the hotel's downstairs bar, with its long mahogany counter and its stone terrace, illuminated at night by a score of flaming tapers. Included among its habitués were "worldly-wise men and women, and bronzed travellers of the never-never lands; of monocled men and beautifully dressed women of fashion." Besides Cuba's somewhat debilitated plantation society and several Spanish grandees "seeking an improvement in their circumstances," the Sevilla also played host to individuals like the highborn English rum-runner, James Barbican. A hero of Vimy Ridge and the Somme, the tall sardonic Barbican and his associates periodically visited Havana to bank the earnings of their syndicate and to arrange for further consignments of Cuban rum.

The Sevilla was also the rendezvous of several American engineers with a taste for hardship and high adventure. These "stern-faced pioneers of the jungle," many of whom helped construct the Panama Canal, had a special affinity for the men from Guaranty Trust and National City; it was they who took the plans and blueprints approved in the tranquillity of the banks' head offices in New York, and transformed them into a modern sugar mill, a deep-water harbor or a 1,000-foot bridge. Such men knew how to drain a swamp, fight off malaria and "tame two hundred miles of snake-infested jungle with twin rails of steel."

Brown Brothers, Chase, Morgan and Guaranty Trust were all deeply involved in the development of Cuba. With "strong Head Office encouragement" National City also plunged heavily. By the middle of 1920 it held nearly one-fifth of the outstanding bank loans in Cuba. Cooler heads sensed the peril. But Jamie Stillman had, it seemed, become intoxicated by the easy ways of the Sevilla and the sound of the northeast tradewind rustling through the palms on the Malecon at night. Or perhaps he had become distracted by the highly publicized divorce proceedings against his beautiful but athletic young wife Fifi. In any event, National City's new leader let the bank increase its Cuban holdings eightfold for a total investment of $79 million, an amount equal to nearly 80 percent of the bank's outstanding capital.

Back in the United States the businesslike minds at the Federal Reserve Board, eager to "sterilize" the postwar economy from the "taint of inflation," increased their rediscount rate to 6 percent on ninety-day commercial paper and on agricultural paper maturing within six months. On June 1, 1920, the Reserve banks of New York, Chicago and Minneapolis went a step further and lifted their rediscount rate again, this time to 7 percent. These measures, when coupled with a bountiful European harvest, caused the price of American farm products to collapse. By fall, No. 1 Northern Wheat fell from $3.15 to $1.46 cents a bushel, and the price of a 100-pound barrel of beef dropped from $9.13 to $5.58.

Predictably, the Federal Reserve's heavy-handed efforts to sterilize the economy had a devastating effect upon the operations of the New York banks in Havana, where the price of sugar dropped from 22 cents to 10 cents and then drifted to 1.3 cents a pound. While no branch of an American bank failed, substantial sums had to be rushed from New York to the Cuban capital. The crisis, however, precipitated a run on Cuba's native-owned banks, and by the spring of 1921 eighteen had collapsed, with a total of $130 million still owed to depositors. With the failure of the Banco Nacional and the Banco Español, New York's National City became the leading financial institution in Cuba, and in the months that followed it was repeatedly called upon to shoulder the additional task of functioning as that island nation's central bank. National City's new dominance, however, was obtained at crippling cost. The head office of National City now had some $34 million tied up in the bale-out of its Cuban branches. In addition, as the Cuban economy disintegrated and even the most substantial native entrepreneurs defaulted, National City became the reluctant heir to hundreds of miles of railroad track, a dozen locomotives, scores of railroad cars, several hundred thousand acres of plantation land, sixty sugar mills, and oversight of a small army of starving, disaffected *campesinos*. For every American banker such unsought obligations represented the stuff of nightmares. Indeed, the debacle brought the bank close to ruin as it suffered "the worst setback in National City's long history."

In May 1921 Jamie Stillman resigned. In his place a financier with vast landholdings in West Texas named Eric P. Swenson was appointed chairman of the bank. Swenson, a gentleman of the old school who insisted on wearing

white spats to the office, was chosen for his reputation of "total rectitude" and for his cool judgment under pressure. Later, after a brief search, a brusque, decisive National City executive named Charles E. Mitchell was invited to become president. Though an untried force Mitchell, then aged 42, was to become in the years ahead the symbol of all the strengths—and many of the excesses—of American banking. As the Roaring Twenties began to gather momentum, his freebooting style, reminiscent of the high rollers in Havana's glitziest casinos, was to blaze the trail for a new breed of stock-market speculator. Eventually his unquenchable optimism—ever bullish even in the face of disaster—inspired a financial attitude that came to be known throughout the United States as "Mitchellism."

The son of an affluent Boston wholesale merchant, Mitchell had graduated from Amherst in 1899. After working as assistant to the president of the Trust Co. of America in New York, he had founded his own investment firm and in 1916 became the head of National City's underwriting subsidiary. From the start, the new president of National City set a blistering pace for both his subordinates and his competitors. Mitchell, declared one observer, "was a physical marvel. He seemed to live without sleep yet never tired. Virility, in sparks, leaped from him." He played vigorous games of tennis and golf. He rode horseback and loved to race his pals in high-powered sports cars out to their respective summer homes situated on the further reaches of Long Island.

Despite his dashing profile and Gatsby-like preoccupations, Mitchell was capable of serious thought. "I have a high regard for him," noted Ben Strong, no flatterer of persons, in a confidential memo to one of his subordinates at

the Federal Reserve Bank of New York. "He is probably one of the ablest of our bankers." In truth the founder and leading exponent of Mitchellism radiated confidence. His gaze was steady. And his judgments on the markets, delivered *basso profundo*, carried a finality that brooked no discussion. A few skeptics may have detected a whiff of dogma in these pronouncements, but most of his listeners were convinced, and National City quickly became the largest distributor of securities in the nation.

On assuming the presidency of National City, Mitchell promptly tightened and shortened the organization's straggling chain of command by forcing the resignation of all but one of the bank's middle managers. Early in 1922 he led a delegation of fellow bankers in two chartered "flying boats" from Key West to Havana. After a tête-à-tête with President Zayas—one president to another—Mitchell ventured into the interior. The ensuing tour of stagnant and nearly bankrupt sugar plantations, abandoned mills and defunct refineries had a profound effect upon the Americans. For the next eight days the party trekked by train and mule cart through the back country. Not only was Mitchell bewitched by the surpassing beauty of the land and the natural gaiety of the people; everywhere he appeared he was greeted as a godlike figure, the great economic savior who had the magical power to get the mills turning again.

On his return to Havana, Mitchell, now more pitchman than banker, told the people what they wanted to hear. He informed President Zayas and a luncheon of two hundred Cuban businessmen that if their country could "put her house in order" and balance her budget then a loan of $50 million would be forthcoming from New York. On the surface, Mitchell's offer was generous. But its long-term effect was to pull the Pearl of the Antilles further

Havana-on-the-Hudson

on to the long, slippery slope to economic colonization. Within a year the U.S. Federal Reserve System would open its first overseas branch in downtown Havana, and soon the American community would find itself viewing rigged elections with equanimity and supporting increasingly oppressive regimes simply because they were "friendly" to business. The same story would, in the years to come, be reenacted all over Central America.

Back in the United States, farmers were again in trouble. As the market price of wheat, corn and beef collapsed, the per capita income of those who lived on the land fell from $193 to $119, an amount equal to less than one-third of that received by urban dwellers. In New York the impact of the new privation was cushioned by the state land bank and a branch of the new federal land bank in Springfield, Massachusetts, which sought to eliminate the rate differential between urban and rural borrowing. In 1923 further relief was provided by a network of federal "intermediate credit banks" that helped bring both stability and liquidity to rural financing by offering to rediscount loans made to farmers by commercial banks.

However, the true emancipation of those who worked on the land—and, indeed, the great multitude of ordinary New Yorkers—came from an unexpected quarter. And it cut right across class lines. Between 1915 and 1930 the number of gasoline-powered vehicles on the roads of New York increased tenfold, from 255,000 to 2,330,000. Even white-bearded Charles Adsit, a Signer of the Call and octogenarian cofounder of the New York State Bankers Association, put aside his pony trap and took to careering around Steuben County in the exercise of a new sport he chose to call "automobiling."

Like the completion of the Erie Canal in 1825 and the establishment of the interconnecting railroad system in the 1850s, the mass acceptance of the automobile precipitated a major revolution in the way business in general, and banking in particular, was done in the state of New York. The impact of this new quantum leap in transportation was, of course, most profound in rural areas. Prior to the Great War, most of the farmer's operating capital

Welthea Marsh took over the First National Bank of Groton, New York, on the death of her husband and became the first woman bank president in the nation. Though shrewd and efficient, she deemed it prudent to sign all correspondence W. M. Marsh "lest any man doubt the reliability of a bank run by a woman." (First National Bank of Groton)

came from the bank in the nearby village. Much of this capital would be secured either on the farmer's signature or by liens upon his growing crops and livestock. For his living expenses between harvests, the farmer traditionally expected to purchase food, clothing and other necessities on credit at the general store. Rather than tie up assets the store manager then frequently obtained a loan at the village bank by pledging his accounts receivable.

These traditional purchasing patterns were modified in the years before the war by the emergence of mail-order houses like Sears Roebuck and Montgomery Ward, which could deliver the most exotic items in their catalog to the most remote communities in the state. Such orders not only diminished the role of the local store; they also cut into the business of the local bank, since most mail-order houses arranged for their financing at one or more of the big regional institutions.

The small community bank's natural market was further circumscribed by the fact that instead of shopping at the village store, or through the catalog, it was now easy for the farmer and his wife to hop into their flivver and drive to a nearby town, or even all the way to the county seat, for their weekly purchases. The old general stores either closed or, in the larger communities, were taken over by chains like the Atlantic & Pacific Tea Co., most of which did their financial business with the big regional banks. Small banks were also hit hard. The Groton Carriage Co. in Tompkins County, one of the best-known manufacturers of horse-drawn vehicles in the county, "suffered the devastating effects of the motorized automobile" and had to pledge all its remaining assets to the First National Bank of Groton (established 1865; current assets: $41 million) to cover a debt of $60,000. At that time the bank was operating under the direction of Welthea Marsh who, on the death of her husband, had become the first woman bank president in the history of the state, and perhaps the nation. Though both shrewd and efficient, Mrs. Marsh veiled her identity by signing all notes and correspondence W. M. Marsh, "lest any man doubt the reliability of a bank run by a woman."

Unlike agriculture, the industrial sector of the economy remained buoyant throughout the postwar era. The growing dominance of American industry was further strengthened by the fact that, despite the recovery of European agriculture, France, Germany and Britain were eager to acquire American manufactures. This, together with the enhanced capital base and the pent-up domestic demand of the war years, combined to launch the U.S. economy into the Roaring Twenties and one of greatest expansionary drives in economic history. From its low of 63.9 in August 1921, the Dow Jones Industrial average would increase sixfold, to a high of 382.2 in the summer of 1929. Many believed that, with the Federal Reserve System in place, crises like the Panic of 1907 could never occur again.

In this "New Era," as it was often called, many forces combined to form a great tide of genuine prosperity. Much of this stemmed from the discovery and exploitation of the mass purchasing potential of the so-called "working poor." Advertising wizards like Bruce Barton and James Webb Young, armed with the new insights of popular psychology, managed to "create" demand for everyday products that ranged from washing machines and off-the-hanger suits to canned foods, cheap cosmetics and basic medical items like aspirin.

Few men, making $20 a week in a foundry, could afford to buy a $20 suit or a $25 washing machine outright. But the development of installment credit, with small weekly or monthly repayments of principal and interest, enabled both manufacturers and financial institutions to develop this new "consumer" market. While most commercial banks were at first reluctant to make such loans, numerous industrial loan companies (often referred to as Morris Plan banks after their originator, a corporate lawyer from Tarboro, North Carolina, named Arthur Morris) were prepared to lend relatively small sums secured by a chattel mortgage on the product purchased.

In 1927 John Sinnott and Michael Wald established the Morris Plan Bank of Utica with an initial capital of $75,000. Like a thrift the bank could have savings but no checking accounts. Nine years later, the bank had proven so successful that it obtained a commercial charter; it is today known as Bank of Utica, with total assets of more than $250 million.

As the decade progressed many commercial banks began to offer installment loans for big-ticket items like farm machinery and automobiles. Installment financing had the effect of both broadening markets and reducing prices. The triumphs of the Ford Motor Co. stood as an economic paradigm

Cloche-hatted heartthrob Suzette Dewey leads fashion among the younger set as she prepares to mount her well-equipped Ford roadster. (Library of Congress)

for the era. Between 1908 and 1927 the company sold fifteen million units of the Model T, a peppy two-seat runabout often referred to as a "tin lizzy," while reducing the retail price of each car from $825 to $260. By 1928 more than 15 percent, or $6 billion a year, of all goods sold were purchased on installment credit.

The Great Bull Market was also propelled forward by less benign forces. As the Dow doubled, and doubled again, it seemed that stock prices could only increase. Bearish speculators, figuring that it was finally time for a "correction," were repeatedly squeezed out. Soon there were no bears left. Even tycoons like old George Baker, whose success had been built on relentless hard-eyed skepticism, seemed to climb on the bandwagon. As improbable advance followed improbable advance, the number of American "paper" millionaires exceeded 10,000. Talk of the stock market replaced the weather as a fitting topic of conversation between strangers waiting for a train. What's Steel doing? Four points up? And Eastman Kodak's at $116? Amazing!

Soon the appetite for risk and the go-for-broke ethos of "Mitchellism" caused a new generation of Americans to challenge their elders and betters. For the younger set whalebone corsets, string quartets and chaperones were out. Tennis, double-breasted jackets, bobbed hair, Gillette safety razors, the turkey trot and hip flasks were in. Despite Prohibition, even the staider families of upstate Rochester and Syracuse established an arm's-length con-

nection with the neighborhood bootlegger. Indeed, the afternoon "cocktail" party became quite fashionable. Here, glass in hand, frenzied youth could discuss the Babe's backswing or Al Jolson's performance in *The Jazz Singer*, Hollywood's first talking movie. The cigarette, set in an outrageously elongated holder, became a wand of sophistication. But all who wielded it must be prepared to discuss, with brittle familiarity, the psychiatric teachings of the newly discovered sage, Dr. Sigmund Freud.

Yet even the most urbane cocktail banter always seemed to return to the single, all-engrossing topic: How was the market doing? New York Central up five points? You don't say! RCA, the glamor offering of the radio decade, quadrupled its value in a single year. In the atmosphere of euphoria previous financial disasters, including the fiasco in Cuba, became little more than a bad memory. The presence of the Federal Reserve System, with its branches spread like a great safety net across the land, made the recurrence of such nightmares seem not only illogical but impossible. Yet to many older folk, more set in their ways, it appeared that New York had been suddenly transformed into one vast libidinous drunken casino, Havana-on-the-Hudson.

The news for banks in the state of New York, however, was not all good. The growing profitability of leading manufacturers like Ford Motor and General Electric made them less dependent upon banks for their working capital. Indeed, the more successful manufacturers discovered that they could acquire capital for expansion not by borrowing but by floating a new issue of securities on the ever-buoyant stock market. In consequence, many commercial banks found themselves turning—as they would, again, half a century later—to the booming real estate market in their efforts to reap an adequate return on resources. Another lucrative, but increasingly risky source of revenues for the banks was the call loan market.

At the beginning of the decade brokerages might lend a customer half the amount he needed to purchase a block of RCA or U.S. Steel stock. But as market prices moved ever upward, brokers began to lend clients 80 and even 90 percent of the purchase price. As advance piled upon advance securities dealers, and the banks that lent to them, came to believe that the system was foolproof. Call loans were generally made for a period of twenty-four hours for an interest rate that generally ran between 6 and 12 percent per annum. At the end of each working day such loans could be called in, or renegotiated on mutually agreeable terms. If the market price of the security should experience a momentary dip, then the broker—who had physical possession of the stock—would tell the customer to "put up more margin." If the customer did not, or could not, comply, then the broker acquired title to the stock and could protect himself against any loss by selling the securities on the open market. Better still, he might postpone the sale until the stock's price—as it inevitably must—further appreciated in the market's next up-ward surge.

The big-city banks were not alone in offering such lucrative services. Even the smallest commercial banks of upstate New York seem to have been swept up in the same speculative fervor, and in the massive downside risks, that beset their big-city brethren. In the six years from 1923 to 1929 the 750-odd commercial banks outside the city of New York embarked upon a period of "phenomenal expansion." Their total resources increased by some 50 per-cent, from $2.12 billion to $3.20 billion. The changing nature of the banking business was underscored by the fact that commercial loans and investments increased only by some 20 percent over this period, while loans on real estate jumped by some 150 percent. Those loans for which securities were pledged as collateral increased by $500 million, a jump of 125 percent over a six-year period.

As the diagram of its financial profile suggests, the *typical* upstate bank did not hesitate to lend substantial sums directly to its customers for use in the stock market. In the six years following 1923 the bank's investments and commercial loans remained more or less constant, its loans secured by real

FINANCIAL PROFILE OF TYPICAL
UPSTATE NEW YORK BANK, 1923-1929

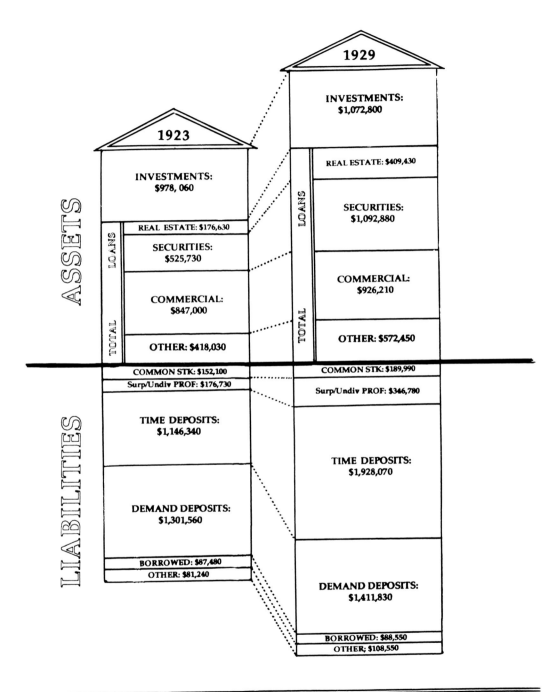

1929

INVESTMENTS:
$1,072,800

REAL ESTATE: $409,430

SECURITIES:
$1,092,880

COMMERCIAL:
$926,210

OTHER: $572,450

1923

INVESTMENTS:
$978, 060

REAL ESTATE: $176,630

SECURITIES:
$525,730

COMMERCIAL:
$847,000

OTHER: $418,030

ASSETS

LOANS

TOTAL

LIABILITIES

COMMON STK: $152,100

Surp/Undiv PROF: $176,730

TIME DEPOSITS:
$1,146,340

DEMAND DEPOSITS:
$1,301,560

BORROWED: $87,480

OTHER: $81,240

COMMON STK: $189,990

Surp/Undiv PROF: $346,780

TIME DEPOSITS:
$1,928,070

DEMAND DEPOSITS:
$1,411,830

BORROWED: $88,550

OTHER: $108,550

TOTAL NUMBER of BANKS:	**719 BANKS**	**786 BANKS**
TOTAL ASSETS of TYPICAL BANK	**$2,945,450**	**$4,073,770**

estate increased from $177,000 to some $409,000, and loans secured by the pledge of stock more than doubled to $1,093,000.

The marked increase in the profitability of banking inspired many banks to embark upon aggressive campaigns of acquisition and merger. In the city of New York alone no fewer than fifty mergers took place between 1926 and 1929. By 1927 the process of agglomeration had created seventeen "super-banks." Some of these giant institutions then coalesced, in turn, to produce five "mega-banks" under the leadership of Guaranty Trust, Hanover National, the old Bank of America, Chase National and its arch-rival, National City. The last of these, with Charles Mitchell now firmly entrenched as chairman, led the merger drive by acquiring both the Farmer's Loan & Trust Co and the Corn Exchange Bank Trust Co. This meant that National City now controlled more than two hundred branches and, with total assets of $2.3 billion, was far and away the largest bank in America.

FACING PAGE: *Profile of typical upstate bank, before The Crash. (Chart created by J.T.W. Hubbard)*

Havana-on-the-Hudson

The frenzy in stock-market speculation was further stimulated in the mid-1920s by the creation of scores of so-called "investment trusts." Many had an impressive title and an impressive lineage. Dillon, Read & Co. founded the United States and Foreign Securities Trust in 1924, while J. P. Morgan & Co. managed the United Corporation. Operating somewhat like closed-end mutual funds, the more speculative trusts would buy securities for their stockholders through one or more brokerages on 90 percent margin. Sometimes they established a controlling interest in a second trust which might, in its turn, purchase control of a third trust. Goldman, Sachs founded the Trading Corporation with a capitalization of $100 million; this entity then moved on to launch the Shenandoah Corporation (capital: $103 million), which in its turn gave birth to the Blue Ridge Corporation ($142 million). Such multiple leverage was leveraged yet again by the fact that many of the trust's initial investors had also purchased their shares on margin, thereby piling margin upon margin in a massively unstable inverted pyramid of credit.

The general euphoria seemed to unhinge the judgment of even Benjamin Strong, the market's chief watchdog. In the summer of 1927 Strong met secretly with Montagu Norman, the governor of the Bank of England, at the Long Island estate of Mrs. Ruth Pratt, the Standard Oil heiress. In an attempt to keep the world economy buoyant, Strong undertook to "give a little *coup de whiskey* to the stock-market" by reducing the New York Fed's rediscount rate from 4 percent to 3.5 percent. In the opinion of many economists today this was a disastrous move; at a time when the Fed should have been reining in the economy, it provided the already overheated market with a further stimulus. In 1928, when he still might have grasped and corrected his mistake, Strong fell mortally ill; he went into surgery for an abscess and died one week later, at the age of 55.

Strong's little *coup de whiskey* thrust the market into its final spasm of speculation. The bulls now seemed to enter into a state of hypnotic intensity. As with all closed systems of belief, anyone who expressed even a shred of skepticism about the continued upward climb of the stock prices was turned upon and publicly berated. When Roy Young, the new chairman of the Federal Reserve Board, spoke out against "excessive speculation" early in 1929, he was openly ridiculed by Charles Mitchell, the arch bull himself. The nation's investors, argued the chairman of National City, must not be denied. If the Fed attempted to curb lending, declared Mitchell, then his bank would nullify the policy by making a sum of $25 million available to traders. "We feel," he told Young, "that we have an obligation which is paramount to any Federal Reserve warning, or anything else, to avert any dangerous crisis in the money market."

The circle was complete. In Mitchell's view the banks ought to commit a major portion of their resources just to keep the speculative flames burning ever higher. Mitchell's threat was all the more startling since he himself had recently become a director of the Federal Reserve, the institution he was now attacking. Young, who lacked Strong's savvy and his commanding presence,

did not see fit to challenge the founder of Mitchellism. But the peppery Carter Glass, now aged 71 and a senator from Virginia, was made of sterner stuff. He had helped establish the Federal Reserve System and, as secretary of the Treasury under Wilson, he had shepherded it through its formative years; he was not about to see his handiwork demolished by a gang of greedy Wall Street bankers, or "Yankee croakers," as he was wont to call them. "He avows his superior obligation to a frantic stockmarket over against the obligation of his oath as a director of the New York Federal Reserve Bank," declared Senator Glass of Mitchell in acid tones. "The bank should ask for (his) immediate resignation."

Battle had been joined. The bulls, clearly in preponderance, rushed in to assist Mitchell in his attack on the Fed. One eloquent pit bull was an economics professor from Princeton named Joseph Lawrence. After branding Young's warning "a punitive excursion against the stock market . . . in contravention of every principle of justice," Professor Lawrence suggested, among other things, that the Wall Street banks "abandon the Federal Reserve System altogether."

On October 15, 1929, Charles Mitchell completed a month-long tour of European financial centers. He radiated confidence. After boarding the passenger liner *Majestic* for the voyage back across the North Atlantic, he told a press conference that, in his opinion, "the markets are generally now in a healthy condition." The bears, and those in the Federal Reserve System who would meddle with the way stock-market business is transacted were, as usual, just plain wrong. Stock prices would inevitably continue to rise. And American business would, with equal inevitability, continue to expand. "I cannot see anything," the chairman of the nation's biggest bank confidently declared, "to check that continued expansion."

One week later, on October 23, all appeared to be right with the world as the *Majestic* docked in lower Manhattan. Eddie Cantor was opening in *Whoopee* down on 8th Street East. Wanamaker's had a men's fashion sale with $75 three-piece suits knocked down to $42. Herbert Hoover, aboard the presidential barge, was leading a leisurely parade of vessels down the Ohio River for the opening of a new section of inland waterway. The Great Bull market and the Minotaur-cult of Mitchellism had the momentum—or so it seemed—to roar and snort its way through another decade of prosperity. The only disquieting note on the morning of October 23 was set by a young adventurer named Urban F. Diteman, from Billings, Montana. After fueling his Barling monoplane with 165 gallons of gasoline at an airfield near St. Johns, Newfoundland, Diteman announced his intention of becoming the second man to ever complete a solo flight across the North Atlantic. A few minutes later he took off and headed eastward into a misty, sunlit morning. He was never seen again.

10

The Great Depression

AT ABOUT 11 o'clock on the morning of Thursday, October 24, 1929, pedestrians on Wall Street detected a "weird roar" emanating from within the New York Stock Exchange. True, trading had been erratic on the preceding day. But now it seemed that the entire market had gone into a free fall, with no bottom in sight. Henry Pomares, who would one day become comptroller of the Empire National Bank in Middletown, New York, was at that time a twenty-two-year-old clerk on a monthly salary of $170 in the cashier's cage at the brokerage house of Dominick & Dominick.

"Of course, none of us understood at the time what was happening," he recalled more than half a century later. "I was working with fifty or sixty other fellows in the wire-mesh security cage recording the details—quantity, par value, certificate numbers, ownership—of each batch of securities as they were pushed through the window by messengers. No matter how fast we worked we couldn't keep up; there was just an avalanche of paper coming into the cage."

On a regular day the clerks would finish up at about 4 P.M., in time for the securities to be placed in the time-lock vault downstairs, before it closed at 5 P.M. However, on Black Thursday, when the vault closed the clerks were still surrounded by stack upon stack of securities that had yet to be registered. "It was a rule that the stock certificates could not be left in the cage overnight," noted Pomares. "So we continued to register the stocks on the official 'blotters' until about 11:30 P.M. Then we packed them all into boxes and

carried them down to the U.S. Post Office on Church Street, which stayed
open 'til midnight, and sent them by Registered Mail back to ourselves; that
way the securities were safe, and we had the stamped receipt to prove it."

There was no clear-cut reason for the sudden drop in prices. During the
previous week stocks had fluctuated, up and down, in accordance with
previous patterns. But the volume seemed heavier and on a number of
occasions the ticker began to drag twenty, and sometimes thirty, minutes
behind the price at which stocks were actually trading on the floor of the
exchange. This sense of uncertainty was further exacerbated by a severe ice
storm that had torn down telegraph poles throughout Illinois and Ohio and
caused a general disruption of communications through much of the Middle
West. That evening, it seemed, many anxious investors decided that now
was the moment to "get out" before the nervous contagion spread any further.

The Great Depression

VOLUME

10:30	3,259,800
12:00	8,378,200
1:30	12,652,000
2:10	13,838,000
TOTAL	16,410,000

TAPE   LATE

10:15	5 MIN
2:50	88 ..
3:00	135

10-29-29

Black Thursday was followed, five days later, by Black Tuesday. As the volume of shares traded soared past 14 million, the stock-market ticker fell more than two hours behind, further heightening public panic. (Museum of American Financial History; photo work by Joshua Nefsky)

As the market opened on Thursday, October 24, it seemed that almost every stockholder in America wanted to sell. Yet none was eager to buy and, amid very heavy volume, stock prices seemed to march over a cliff. While such popular stocks as Montgomery Ward fell from $84 to $33, General Electric toppled to less than half its original price of $368 and RCA plunged from $92 to $29. By 12:30 P.M. such was the bedlam on the floor of the exchange that officials ordered the visitors' gallery cleared. One of the spectators shooed out was a rising British journalist-politician named Winston S. Churchill.

As the ticker fell one hour, and then two hours behind, a sense of panic began to infect the mind of the financial world. To many it seemed that the work of an entire decade had been washed away in the space of a single day. The *New York Times* estimated the paper loss at more than $4 billion. Amid scenes of mounting disorder, a group of New York's most prominent financiers met in the offices of J. P. Morgan & Co. Their number included Albert Wiggin, chairman of Chase National; William Potter, chairman of

Guaranty Trust; Seward Prosser of Bankers Trust and Charles Mitchell of National City. Under the chairmanship of Thomas Lamont, the senior partner of Morgan's, the group resolved to pool their resources in an effort to slow and, if possible, reverse the terrible slide. At 1:30 P.M. Richard Whitney, brother of a Morgan partner and acting president of NYSE, strode on to the trading floor and began to use the pool's funds to place orders of 10,000 shares on more than a dozen of the nation's leading stocks.

For a while the pool, with assets conservatively estimated at $40 million, slowed the rout. But the word was out. Many of the out-of-town banks, including those in upstate New York, sought to withdraw their funds from the call market, where they had been earning 10 percent interest. For most it was not an easy decision. As prices fell, and the call money market dried up, thousands of investors, buying on margin, were angry to learn the next day that their entire portfolios had been liquidated by their brokers without warning.

Hollis Harrington, who later became chairman of the State Bank of Albany, was a twenty-one-year-old clerk in the loan department of the bank when the crash came. "We had three teller windows to serve customers with call loans," he recalls. "By then many of them were playing the market on a 90 percent margin—that is to say, an individual would be able to secure a loan of $9,000 by pledging certificates of stock that had a market value of $10,000." It was the job of Harrington and a couple of other clerks to sit behind the tellers and pull the 'collateral card' from the file for each customer as he approached the window. Then, using the morning newspaper to obtain the previous day's closing stock prices, the clerks would total the current value of the customer's portfolio, and then hand the card on to the teller. "If the market value of the stock had fallen," says Harrington, "then the customer would be told that he must either increase his collateral or see the bank sell off some, or all, of the stock in his portfolio."

In the last week of October 1929, recalls Harrington, "the market was falling so fast that, instead of once daily, the collateral cards had to be re-evaluated three or four times a day." The bank had no stock ticker in its office, and the radio upstairs in the president's office gave only the most fragmentary information. In consequence, gangs of clerks and messengers from every bank in the city staked out the offices of the Albany *Times-Union* to grab the latest editions off the press and return, hot foot, to their desks behind the tellers' cages. With salaries of only $25 a week, few clerks could afford to invest anything in the market. But it was agonizing for them to watch the effect of tumbling stock prices upon the customers, many of whom were very wealthy men. "Borrowers were devastated," notes Harrington, "and many financially ruined."

The new investment trusts, with their top-heavy pyramids of credit, swiftly learned that the multiplier effect of "leverage" also worked with brutal effi-cacy on the downside. The ensuing sell-off was enough to halt and then sweep away any countervailing efforts by the Morgan-led pool. Now even the largest and most sober-minded bankers lost their nerve, and five days later, on October 29, Black Thursday was followed by Black Tuesday. With numer-ous "after-shock" tremors, the market continued to deteriorate through the remaining months of the year. By November 13, the *New York Times* industrial average had fallen from 442.77 to 223.58. In the collapse, blue chips were hit as hard as speculative stocks. The split price of RCA fell from $92-3/8 to $22-3/4 and General Electric toppled from $368 to $173 a share. In all, the value of securities had suffered a paper loss of close to $30 billion.

The sharp drop in the value of real estate pushed the Bank of the United States, founded by the Russian-born Joseph Marcus in 1913, to the brink of disaster. The bank, which held a state charter, had total assets of $315 million, but much of this was locked up in the construction of major real estate projects, including the construction of the San Remo apartment build-ing on Central Park West. A visit by state examiners revealed the bank had further weakened its capital position by lending an untoward sum to its various financial affiliates. Such irregularities caused a merger with three other banks to fall through; the bank experienced a major run by depositors and was closed by state order. Later the founder's son, Bernard Marcus, was sentenced to prison on the charge of fraudulent banking practice.

Only eight months prior to the stock-market crash, Herbert Hoover, hailed by his admirers as "a Great Engineer and a Great Humanitarian," had been inaugurated as president of the United States. Hoover was also an accomplished administrator and businessman, and he believed that the only viable solution to the deepening depression was to induce both federal and state governments to reduce spending and balance their budgets.

It took Congress and the new president many months to realize that such an approach was too simplistic. It assumed that the U.S. economy was a machine that could be tuned—and tinkered with—in isolation. They failed to understand that for many years now it had formed an integral part of a far bigger organism that included the economies of the world's industrial and many preindustrial nations.

The Hawley-Smoot Act—often erroneously referred to as "Smoot-Hawley"—passed in the summer of 1930, was intended to protect American products from foreign competition by raising import tariffs on average from 33 percent to 40 percent, the highest rates in American history. However, the new measure served only to deepen the depression. In the months ahead both exports and imports faded to a trickle. Many European nations were forced off the gold standard. In the ensuing inflation, their currencies were no longer deemed acceptable either as war reparations or as repayment of war loans. In the squeeze, hundreds of millions of dollars of European obligations were repudiated and several Austrian and German banks came close to failing. This in turn severely weakened numerous New York institutions holding European bank bonds.

Often, sound banks were imperiled by the difficulties of less well-managed institutions in the same community. When the Ontario County Trust Co. in Canandaigua was forced to close in October 1931, it precipitated an aggressive run on the Canandaigua National Bank & Trust Co. just a few blocks farther up the street. But George W. Hamlin, Canandaigua National's president, had anticipated such a crisis. So that the local people would not be aware that he was leaving town in that "excitable and rumor-filled environment," Hamlin did not go to the town's railroad station. Instead, he loaded a suitcase of documents into the back of his auto and drove to the neighboring town of Clifton Springs, where he boarded the train for New York. After arranging for help from the Federal Reserve, he returned by the same route. A few days later, as nervous depositors crowded the bank's lobby, Hamlin was able to quiet much of the panic by stacking $1 million "in plain view" behind the bars of a teller's cage.

Sometimes a healthy, well-managed bank felt compelled, for the sake of the community, to take over the responsibilities of a troubled institution. Just before the stock-market crash Stephen Medbury, president of the First National Bank of Ballston Spa (total assets: $2 million), broke into the locked desk of a teller and discovered that he had, among other things, embezzled $115,000 by manipulating certificates of deposit at their time of renewal. When word got out, the bank, already overburdened by portfolio losses in both Russian and German bonds, could not meet its customers' demand for cash.

In October 1931 the well-managed Ballston Spa National Bank (assets then $3 million) took over the First National and assured all its customers that their business would be taken care of without interruption. The smaller bank's "interest accounts, passbooks and certificate of deposit transactions would be honored" and its depositors' checks would be accepted and processed until new checks could be printed; even Christmas Club accounts

would be continued without disruption. As a sign of the hard times, the liquidated bank's magnificent three-story stone office building, which had cost $30,000 to erect, went on the block for a mere $2,500.

In an effort to control the damage, President Hoover placed a one-year moratorium on payment of reparations. But in the fall of 1931 Britain, the United States' closest ally, was forced to abandon the gold standard. In New York the Federal Reserve Bank was in a quandary. In the wake of the stock-market collapse it had attempted to restore equilibrium by expanding credit. In November 1929 it reduced its rediscount rate from 5 percent to 4.5 percent. By the following June this was further cut to 2.5 percent and then to 1.5 percent in May 1931. At the same time the Federal Reserve Board in Washington attempted to stimulate the private sector of the economy by quadrupling its open-market purchases of government securities. Such strategies, however, had little short-term effect. As business activity slowed and went into active decline, unemployment leapt upward from 8.7 percent in 1930, to 16 percent in 1931 and then up to 24 percent—or one worker in four—in 1932.

The human cost of the deepening crisis has been vividly chronicled in photography, literature and film. Over the next few months more than a million Americans would take to "riding the rods" in their desperate search for work. If there was no work in this town, the reasoning went, then there might be something down the line, in the next county or the next state but one. Alas, on arrival such travelers rarely found employment of any kind. Instead they discovered, in the words of one participant, "more closed banks and stores, cold factory stacks, bigger and better bread lines." Wolcott J. Humphrey, Jr., now chairman of the Wyoming County Bank of Warsaw, New York (established 1851, current assets $192 million), vividly recalls seeing, at the age of 8, "long lines of desperate, out-of-work men camped along the Buffalo Rochester & Pittsburgh's right-of-way on Warsaw's East Hill." Later, a soup kitchen was set up for the men outside the county jail.

Shanty towns, or "Hoovervilles" as they were called, grew up on the edge of every major community; even Central Park in New York City played host to a sprawling township of shacks made of packing cases and tar paper. Families who were slightly better off loaded their possessions onto trucks, farm wagons and tin lizzies and simply hit the road for California or Oregon, just as many West Coast families headed East in search of work.

In the years that immediately followed the crash, the blind, unceasing search for the basic necessities of life sent "fear-stricken men, women and children, whole families, fleeing in every direction, as if pursued by un-known foes." One prominent government official who traveled across the country by train from New York to Los Angeles in 1932 reported that he had "looked into the faces" of thousands of adult Americans, many of them elderly. They had, he noted, "the frightened look of lost children." The threadbare clothes, the tattered baggage and the hopeless stares of this multi-tude transmitted a single, poignant message: "We're caught up . . . in some-thing we don't understand."

In truth, the economic calamity that had beset the country seemed to defy explanation. Many inhabitants of New York City were hungry, while potatoes rotted in the fields of Long Island because, at the price of 24 cents a bushel, farmers could not afford to dig them out. In upstate counties the apple harvest fell to the ground untasted. Then an industry spokesman had the idea of giving the unemployed a bag of fresh apples on consignment, and soon the streets of New York were filled with some six thousand men and women, many quite well dressed, selling their wares at a nickel apiece. On a lean day, when no buyers could be found, the apple sellers were often forced to consume their own stock.

In their efforts to bring the economy back to life, the president and Congress created a sometimes helpful, and sometimes obstructive, patchwork quilt of quasi-government agencies. In October 1931 most major New York banks participated in the establishment of the National Credit Corporation. The NCC required the more affluent banks to pool $500 million of their own funds to rediscount commercial paper that had been rejected by the

Federal Reserve. This service, it was hoped, would enable distressed commercial banks to improve their liquidity. But, like the Fed, the NCC's credit requirements were extremely rigid, and it accepted a mere $150 million of bank paper.

Four months later Congress established the Reconstruction Finance Corporation, which was empowered to inject $3.3 billion into the financial base of the economy by making secured loans to troubled banks, insurance companies, railroads and numerous other public utilities. At the same time Hoover advocated legislation that would reform the nation's banking structure. His proposals included recommendations to place all commercial banks in the Federal Reserve System, to separate commercial banking from stock market operations, to create a system of mortgage discount banks, and to permit national banks to engage in statewide branch banking. But Congress, after much agitation by small banks across the country, defeated the measure.

Congress did, however, establish the Home Loan Bank System to rediscount first mortgages on homes for savings banks, building and loan associations, and insurance companies. At the same time, the Federal Land Banks, in existence since 1916, were given a further $125 million of capital, and an Agricultural Credit Corporation was set up to make short-term loans to farmers.

The banking community shared the economists' puzzlement concerning the true cause of the nation's difficulties. Charles Mitchell, by now chairman of National City, was summoned to Washington on numerous occasions to help Congress understand how the country had gotten into this crisis. At first various committees seemed to view the nattily attired Mitchell with respect, as if he were "the leading prophet of the New Era." But as the economic crisis deepened, the questions flung at the man to whom *Time* magazine

now referred as "the rampant bull" became increasingly hostile. Had National City and other brokerages sold bonds, foreign and domestic, that they knew to be insecure? Senator Carter Glass, Mitchell's historic antagonist, demanded to know if National City had peddled Anaconda Copper at $100 a share in the summer and fall of 1929, knowing full well that its prospects were speculative enough for its price to drop, within the space of a month, to $4 a share? And what of the stock-purchasing pools favored by many banks? Glass contended that they, as much as anything, had "devastated the economy."

The questions hit closer to home in February 1933 under the cross-examination of the Senate Banking Committee's counsel, Ferdinand Pecora. Why had National City provided a special fund for its officers—but not its ordinary employees—to cover their losses incurred by their purchases of National City stock? How was it that Mitchell had been rewarded with compensation of more than $1 million in 1929, a year in which the price of National City stock had fallen from $500 to $212 a share? Why had he not paid one cent in income tax? And why had Mitchell sold 18,000 shares of National City stock to his wife? Mitchell replied that he had subsequently repurchased the stock, and that the move had been made "to establish a tax loss" of $2,870,000.

Such stratagems were a little too sharp for National City's board of directors, and Mitchell resigned his chairmanship of the bank early in 1933. A few days later he was personally arrested by an aggressive young U.S. assistant district attorney named Thomas Dewey, and charged with tax evasion. To the surprise of many in the courtroom, Mitchell was acquitted on all criminal charges but was later compelled to pay $1.1 million in taxes and interest after losing a civil action brought by government attorneys. Mitchell subsequently became head of the Wall Street brokerage Blyth & Co.

One month after Mitchell's arrest Albert Wiggin, chairman of the Chase National Bank, was charged with even more serious offenses. Subsequent court proceedings showed that Wiggin, described as a "reserved, rather scholarly" man, had operated two secret Canadian companies named after his daughters Shermar and Murlyn. Not only had these outfits generated huge profits by operating a stock-trading pool in Sinclair Consolidated Oil; it later transpired that they had also played the lead role in a bear raid on the stock of Wiggin's own bank. In all, the reserved, rather scholarly Wiggin personally netted more than $4 million by shorting Chase's stock between September and November 1929.

Such revelations of criminality in high places besmirched the reputation of the entire financial community. "The title of banker, formerly regarded as a mark of esteem in the United States, is now almost a term of opprobrium" declared a writer in the *American Mercury* magazine, who went on to speculate that "we may even see the day when to be called a son-of-a-banker will be regarded as justifiable ground for the commission of assault and mayhem."

The incidents also had a decisive impact on the provisions of the Glass-Steagall bill, now before Congress. Indeed, when Winthrop Aldrich succeeded Wiggin as chairman of Chase National, he declared himself heartily in favor of President Hoover's proposal to divorce the bank from its securities affiliate; the temptation to commingle the two kinds of business was, in his view, just too great. And, Aldrich boldly opined, other commercial banks should do likewise. But, with the passage of years, most mainstream economists now tend to downplay the role of banks' securities activities as a primary cause of the crisis. Indeed, in recent times the Federal Reserve Board, upheld by the courts, has authorized companies that own banks to also own securities firms, with appropriate safeguards—or "firewalls" as they are often termed—against abuses.

As the Senate Banking Committee groped for answers, the banking industry was now beset by yet another crisis. In November 1932 a two-term governor of New York named Franklin Roosevelt had challenged, and defeated, Herbert Hoover in an election for the presidency of the United States. The fifty-year-old descendant of Isaac Roosevelt, one of the founders of the Bank of New York, was not only a Democrat. He was also known to have devoted much of his time in Albany to concocting, and then field testing, a number of "socialistic"—some said revolutionary—programs like unemployment insurance, old-age insurance, regulation of public utilities, minimum-wage/maximum-hours work laws, and a plan for the "stricter regulation of the banks and the use of other people's money."

Many affluent citizens took fright. Some members of Roosevelt's "brain trust," it was rumored, intended to take the country off the gold standard and to inflate the face value of paper currency by as much as 49 percent. In the four-month hiatus between Roosevelt's election and his inauguration on March 4, 1933, well-to-do people began to sell their stocks and bonds, demanding that their banks pay them not in paper but in gold dollars. As Inauguration Day approached, the tempo of withdrawal increased. Some hoarded their gold in private safes. Others secreted it abroad, and not a few of the very rich converted their fortunes into gold bars which they then shipped to London and locked in the vaults of the Bank of England.

In all, gold holdings of Federal Reserve banks fell by $209 million. Could the banking system, many wondered, survive such a massive outflow of bullion? Would the larger banks retrench, causing many of the nation's smaller institutions to fail? Fearful that they might lose their deposits, many less wealthy citizens also began to withdraw their funds. Unable to send them to the Bank of England, they commenced to stuff them under their rugs and into their mattresses. But the effect was the same. As the panic gained momentum, more than $800 million worth of paper currency was withdrawn in the early months of 1933. By Inauguration Day nine states across the Union had placed limits on further withdrawals. New York's leading banks came under increasing pressure, much of it from their correspondent institutions located out of state. The New York Clearing House somewhat peevishly declared that the "unthinking attempt of the public to convert over $40 billion of bank deposits into currency at one time is on its face impossible."

Finally, after an all-night session with banking authorities, Governor Herbert Lehman of New York agreed to declare a two-day suspension of banking throughout New York State. The order went out at 4:30 A.M. on Saturday, March 4. This "bank holiday," as it was called, required that all banks in the state remain closed until the start of business on the morning of Wednesday, March 8.

The unexpected order aroused some confusion and not a little consternation among New York's upstate banks, many of which took a special pride in their conservative policies and ongoing financial strength. The experience of the First National Bank of Glens Falls was typical. The bank did not receive the telegram from the Federal Reserve Bank of New York until 9:30 A.M. Saturday, after customers were already lined up and doing business inside the bank. The order put the bank's president, Maurice Hoopes, in a quandary. The First National's legal counsel, after studying the telegram, declared that the bank had a right to remain open. "But in checking with banks in neighboring cities, including Albany, they found that the Governor's proclamation was generally accepted as mandatory." Reluctantly the Glens Falls bank swallowed its pride and decided to close.

Upon his inauguration, Roosevelt immediately declared a nationwide moratorium on all banking activity. No institution would be permitted to reopen until Monday, March 13. And to do so they must first have been examined and given a license to resume operations. If the bank was a member of the national reserve system the license must be approved by the Secretary of the Treasury (working through the Federal Reserve Bank), and if it held a state charter but was not a member of the federal system it must be examined and

approved by the various state superintendents. In the meantime, commercial banks would be permitted to cash payroll checks, provide access to safe deposit boxes, and allow limited withdrawals of deposits "for the relief of distress."

Across the country licenses were granted to 12,817 banks and withheld from 2,487 banks. Of the latter, 1,070 institutions (with total deposits of $890 million) were placed in receivership while 1,417 were placed not in the hands of a liquidator but in those of a new kind of official called a "conservator," who was appointed to ensure that the interests of the bank's depositors were protected and that the institution's affairs were managed as effectively as possible.

The Emergency Banking Act of 1933 was, of course, a temporary measure to halt the panic. It gave the president the power to control all dealings in foreign exchange, silver and gold. If the hoarders of gold did not return their holdings of bullion and coins to the government promptly, their names would be released to the newspapers. On Friday, March 10, more than 4,000 plutocrats, many carrying heavy canvas bags, lined up outside the Federal Reserve Bank of New York and redeposited some $20 million worth of bullion and coin.

Five weeks later, on April 19, 1933, Roosevelt and his brain trusters earned the undying enmity of these most affluent of Americans by abandoning the gold standard. The predictions had been true. The paper dollars the plutocrats received over the counter were, by Christmas, equal in value to no more than 60 percent of the bullion and gold coin they had faithfully lugged into the Federal Reserve Bank. While Hoover, like Grover Cleveland, had staked his presidency on retaining the gold standard, the new administration believed that this willful inflation—they referred to it as "reflation"—served two important purposes: it invigorated the economy by boosting domestic price levels, and it also rendered American products markedly more competitive in trade with those of other nations.

In addition, the emergency act also enabled national banks to bolster their working capital by permitting them to sell, upon approval of the comptroller of the currency, nonassessable preferred stock to the Reconstruction Finance Corp (RFC). Under the New York constitution, state-chartered banks were expressly forbidden to issue such stock, but Superintendent of Banks Joseph Broderick and his staff holed up in the state office building in downtown Manhattan and worked around the clock on legislation that would permit them to participate in the program. In the next two years New York's national and state-chartered banks would receive a total of no less than $95 million in recapitalization from the RFC.

In the first "Hundred Days" the Roosevelt administration enacted into law a whole alphabet soup of regulatory bodies that were to form the backbone of the promised "New Deal." The Congress passed the Federal Emergency Relief Act, designed to coordinate, through the Federal Emergency Relief Administration (FERA), all state and federal relief; the Agricultural Adjustment Act, designed to raise and stabilize agricultural prices; the Tennessee Valley Authority Act, the first comprehensive federal venture into the generation of electrical power. The legislative fever carried well into the middle of June as the Congress passed the Home Owners' Refinancing Act, designed to refinance home mortgages through the Home Owners' Loan Corporation; the National Industrial Recovery Act (NIRA), designed to cut unemployment and improve labor relations through the National Recovery Administration (NRA) and the Public Works Administration (PWA); and the Farm Credit Act was passed to consolidate all rural credit agencies under the Farm Credit Administration.

One of the *least* original pieces of new legislation was the Glass-Steagall Banking Reform Act, which embodied most of the recommendations, including the separation of investment and commercial banking, made by Herbert Hoover more than a year before. The new act was passed June 16, 1933, and contained thirty-four sections, of which the most important provisions were (1) the raising of the minimum capital requirement of any national bank to $50,000; (2) the separation of stock investment activities from normal commercial bank operations; (3) the prohibition of interest payments on demand deposits in national banks; (4) the creation of a permanent open market operations committee, with one member drawn from each Reserve bank (on a rotational basis); and (5) the establishment of the Federal Deposit Insurance Corporation (FDIC) whose function "it shall be to purchase, hold, and liquidate . . . the assets of national banks which have been closed by action of the Comptroller of the Currency or by vote of their directors . . . and to insure, as hereafter provided, the deposits of all banks which are entitled to the benefits of insurance." A total of $150 million of the FDIC's stock would be subscribed by the U.S. Treasury, and the rest would be contributed by participating banks to the amount of .05 percent of the deposits to be insured.

Basically the concept of the FDIC represented a continentwide version of New York's Safety Fund, first proposed by Joshua Forman in 1829. And, like the old Safety Fund, many of the stronger banks covered were opposed to its establishment. The September 1933 issue of the *Journal* of the American Bankers Association sought to unsettle its readers with these apocalyptic, and quite erroneous, observations about deposit insurance: "It runs counter to all past experiences in states which have tried guaranty, always with disastrous results. It forces sound banks to make good the losses and mistakes of poorly managed banks. It possesses a certain specious appeal to a public insufficiently familiar with banks' operations. The plan is dangerous not only to banking, but to the entire country." Indeed, the ABA was so perturbed that it actually offered a prize of $50 for the best 150-word essay on the theme, "Guaranty of Deposits: How can this Threat to Sound Banking be Met?"

The bankers of New York, however, were far more sanguine. "If we review the situation calmly," George V. McLaughlin (president, Brooklyn Trust Co.) told the New York State Bankers Association in his presidential address, "we must reach the conclusion that the problems that came as the result of the depression were too big and difficult for us to handle, and that Government penetration into business came as a result of our own appeals."

Many critics of deposit insurance had declared that it would stimulate a sense of irresponsibility in bank managements. But, at least during the early years, it had the effect of liberating small and medium-sized banks from the thrall of government regulation. Several, including the Bank of Holland, New York (established 1893, current assets $20 million), pulled out of the Federal Reserve system altogether. "After FDIC, we just had no use for it," declared president Harold Hawes, a frontier-style financier who, at the age of 91, is now the most senior bank CEO in the nation. Once, rather than surrender any portion of the bank's resources, he heaved two would-be robbers down a flight of steps and then locked them in a basement. "We're very conservative around here, and keep all our business within ten miles of the village," said Hawes. Such hard-nosed strategies had made Hawes's institution one of the most profitable small community banks in the country, with an average annual return on assets of 2.71 percent.

In the state of New York, with its long banking tradition and its comparatively stringent regulations, the survival rate for commercial banks was markedly better than the national average. In Manhattan, of course, the big money market banks opened without difficulty. But in the period between 1929 and 1933 the number of banks in the rest of state had declined from 786 to 679, a loss of 107 to merger and liquidation (see diagram).

The three prime causes of collapse, the accumulated data of examiners reveal, were likely to be (1) poor management, (2) internal fraud and (3) depreciation of assets. The first cause promptly eliminated banks like the Ontario County Trust Co. of Canandaigua with its unwarranted "security

FINANCIAL PROFILE OF TYPICAL
UPSTATE NEW YORK BANK, 1923-1933

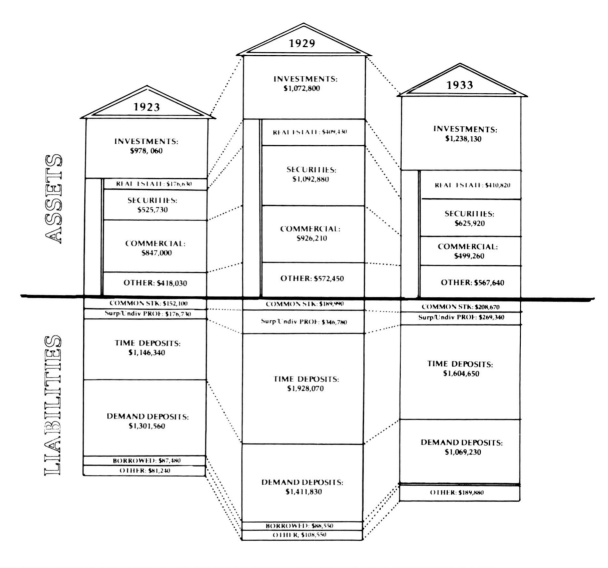

	1923	1929	1933
TOTAL NUMBER of BANKS:	719 BANKS	786 BANKS	679 BANKS
TOTAL ASSETS of TYPICAL BANK	$2,945,450	$4,073,770	$3,341,770

Diagram of financial profile of typical upstate New York bank, 1923–1929–1933. (Chart created by J. T. W. Hubbard)

The Great Depression
214

speculation." The second cause swiftly brought about the demise of such institutions as the Bank of the United States in New York and First National of Ballston Spa, with its fraudulent teller. But in the case of depreciation of assets—the most common cause of liquidation during the Depression years—it was as if troubled institutions had been sentenced to suffer death by strangulation. For months, and sometimes for years on end, "problem" banks were compelled to inhabit a twilight realm in which they did not know whether they would live or die. In such equivocal circumstances some managements just gave up the struggle and went into liquidation. Others, due in large part to the dedication of officers, directors and stockholders, just refused to give up the ghost.

Though examiners would later soften their assessments with such concepts as "prudent investment value" and "normal appraised value," in the immediate aftermath of the crash they insisted on applying old-style depreciation schedules. Often their rigid judgments alone were sufficient to precipitate a crisis. In the wake of one needlessly brutal examination, the Bank of Castile in Wyoming County (established 1869, current assets $116 million) was, according to cochairman James Van Arsdale III, "forced to sell much of its bond portfolio at 50 percent or less of maturing value." The bank recovered, but it was a close call. The Orange County Trust Co. (established 1892, current assets $101 million) dealt with a similar request from regulators by making a successful call upon the bank's stockholders to double the amount of their investment.

The most dramatic campaign of all was, in all likelihood, fought by the First Trust & Deposit Co. of Syracuse. Indeed, the bank's epic fight for survival under the leadership of Albert B. Merrill became an inspiration to similarly beleaguered bankers throughout the state of New York. As the struggle progressed, even the *Wall Street Journal* would, from time to time, arch an eyebrow in wonderment that the coolheaded yet unspectacular Merrill had, against all odds, somehow managed to shepherd his institution through yet another crisis.

Fortitude in face of adversity, no matter how overwhelming, was a lesson that Merrill had learned long before he could read and write. Born in 1888 on a farm among the rolling hills of Fabius, a small community a few miles to the southeast of Syracuse, young Merrill grew up milking the cows and walking behind his father's plow. In the long summer evenings, after the chores were done, Albert and his brothers would sit on the porch and listen to their grandfather's stories of how he and their grandmother had come west in a wagon from Massachusetts in the 1840s and grappled with snowstorms, wolves, and predatory neighbors in their efforts to build a log cabin and "pioneer" much of the valley that now lay below them in the twilight.

At the Fabius village school young Albert—his friends called him "Ab"—learned to be a precise speller and became exceptionally quick with numbers. He also heard the oft-repeated story of Quintus Fabius Maximus, the Roman general after whom the village had been named. More than 2,000 years ago the mighty armies of Hannibal, accompanied by a great herd of armor-plated elephants, had crossed the Alps into Italy. The only force between them and the conquest of Rome was the diminutive army of Fabius, who, rather than risk his soldiers in a frontal assault, chose to wear down Hannibal's invaders in a long-drawn guerrilla campaign of diversion, surprise attack and sudden withdrawal. Through the years ahead such lessons were not lost on Ab Merrill. After obtaining work as an office boy in Syracuse, he was hired in 1913 to work as a bookkeeper at the old Trust & Deposit Co. Merrill's ability with numbers, his steadfast character and his vision of the bank's potential gained him swift promotion. In 1927, at the age of 38, he was appointed to the presidency of First Trust, which at that time had 41,000 depositors, total assets of $65 million, and six offices spread around the city of Syracuse.

Throughout the 1920s Merrill had become increasingly impressed by the expansive ideas and the swashbuckling style of Charles E. Mitchell and the National City, his "billion dollar bank." Perhaps, thought Merrill, the strategies of "Mitchellism" could be applied—in a lesser key, of course—to make First Trust the principal source of financial services throughout central New York. "Some years ago banks with $100 million assets were scarce," Merrill told a meeting of the American Institute of Banking shortly after his appointment as First Trust's president. "Today we mind that banks have assets of a billion dollars and in another twenty-five years we may have banks with assets of probably five billion dollars."

At first things had gone well for Merrill and First Trust. In the spring 1929 the bank merged, by a mutual exchange of stock, with two medium-sized commercial institutions—the Third National (assets: $5.4 million) and the Liberty National (assets: $5.6 million)—in the city of Syracuse. In another, especially audacious move, Merrill also extended First Trust's reach into neighboring communities by creating the First Securities Corp., a wholly-owned subsidiary specially created to engage in the "purchase and sales of bank shares and in other ways control affiliated banking institutions." First Securities swiftly circumvented the antiquated regulations against local branching by acquiring substantial blocks of stock in seven banks situated in outlying communities. These included the State Bank of Parish, the Cazenovia National Bank, the Liverpool Bank, the Fayetteville Commercial Bank and the Baldwinsville State Bank.

As he gave tentative approval to this expanding financial consortium, the state superintendent of banks asked Merrill to consider an additional merger with the far larger City Bank (assets: $42.7 million). The Department of Banking was concerned because, in the words of Henry W. Schramm, author of *The Dynamic Years* and a former First Trust executive, "City had overextended itself in granting mortgage loans and was in deep trouble." Elmer Eshelman, the president of City, was "a nice guy, but he couldn't say no." After a careful audit, Merrill agreed to the proposal. With total assets of $118.3 million, he believed, the new combination should be able to handle any softness in City's loan portfolio. And, of course, the move brought Merrill materially closer to his dream of making his bank the financial powerhouse of central New York.

First Trust, however, barely had time to assemble all its constituent parts before it came under attack from every point of the compass. When the state examiners visited the bank in February 1930, they found an ominous amount of "doubtful and slow loans" and a substantial quantity of "securities of doubtful value" in the bank's portfolio. Matters deteriorated quickly from there. On closer analysis Ab Merrill discovered that throughout the go-go years of the 1920s his merger partner, City Bank, had frequently taken on "mortgages that Syracuse Savings and Onondaga Savings, the two main line savings institutions in the community, had turned down." City, recalls a retired vice president of First Trust, had also "offered mortgages to any of their own customers who wanted one, with perhaps not the best credit checks. Additionally, they had acquired a lot of bad commercial loans."

As if this were not enough, the bank now began to receive increasingly desperate demands from its outlying affiliates for loans of $18,000 and $25,000 and then for $50,000 for "strengthening their liquidity" and for "protecting them from almost certain bankruptcy and safeguarding the deposits of thousands of Upstate residents." By the middle of 1931 matters were at a crisis point. The Fayetteville Commercial Bank, situated 10 miles to the east, demanded a loan of $25,000, only to demand a further $20,000 four months later. Meanwhile, the problem-plagued Baldwinsville State Bank on the northwest side of town was sapping First Trust's resources at almost double the rate of the Fayetteville bank. As the economy slowed further, President Merrill struggled to cut costs. Branches were consolidated, and closed. About one-third of the bank's staff, some 130 individuals, was laid off.

First Trust, like many institutions across the state, was advised by the superintendent to discontinue stockholder dividends. Interest payments on savings accounts were reduced to 2 percent, and then to 1.5 percent. In the spring of 1932 the bank applied to the Reconstruction Finance Corporation for a loan of $13 million, to be secured with much of the bank's questionable paper. As the recession bit deeper this request was increased by a further $5 million, for a total of $18 million. When the RFC—still under the Hoover administration—granted the loan it was for a mere $7 million.

The strain was beginning to take its toll. First Trust and its affiliates were now "carrying" more than 1,300 nonperforming home and farm mortgages on their books. Indeed, since the crash most banks in upstate New York had lived out their existence under a similar cliff of overvalued paper. A home purchased for $5,000 with the bank taking back a ten-year mortgage of $3,500, might typically be valued at $2,500 by 1933. Thus, in the great spiral of deflation, the bank's mortgage would now be "secured" by a property worth a mere 70 percent of the mortgage's face value. In many cases the owner of the house may have lost his job and be delinquent in both his mortgage and his property tax payments. In such a situation the bank's traditional remedies were ineffective. Foreclosure would not only put the family out of their home and on to public relief; it would also inflict upon the bank a net loss of $1,000, and perhaps a great deal more when back taxes had been satisfied. Thus most banks, for both business and humanitarian reasons, were loath to exercise the privilege of foreclosure. Instead, to the occasional ire of the regulators, they continued to carry such mortgages.

Ab Merrill's great dream of making First Trust the financial hub of central New York seemed to be disintegrating rapidly. Several friends in the business community advised him that perhaps it would be best to "just let the bank go into liquidation," and put his energies into some more fruitful line of work. But that was to reckon without Merrill's peculiar cast of character. To some he was just plain stubborn but others, like William Tolley, chancellor of Syracuse University, described him as "lion-hearted." Of average height, bespectacled, and, at the age of 43 almost completely bald, Merrill may not have projected the traditional "presence" of a great leader. But among his special gifts was a cool temperament and a probing intelligence that enabled him to see and grasp all sides of an issue. Such insights made him a formidable negotiator when dealing with regulatory officials. And it also enabled him to produce unusual solutions to seemingly intractable problems. In his struggle to save First Trust he never used apocalyptic words like *crisis* and *disaster* to describe the bank's condition. Instead he simply spoke of it as "being in a hole" as if it were a hay wagon that had somehow got one of its wheels stuck in the mud. On several occasions he wandered down the corridor to comptroller Mark Hanlon's office long after closing time and presented him with a manila folder. "Mark, work up some figures on this," he'd say. "It's one way we might be able to get the bank out of this hole."

Merrill's level-headed competence became a byword among the embattled
bankers of New York State. In 1931, as the financial crisis deepened, they
elected him vice president of the New York State Bankers Association. He
was invited to become the NYSBA's president in the following year, but, due
to the First Trust's ongoing struggle for survival, Merrill reluctantly declined
the honor.

After passage of the Glass-Steagall Act of 1933, Merrill hatched a new
strategy. Like his mentor, Quintus Fabius, he realized that playing for time—
and the chance of a brighter day—lay at the heart of any effective defensive
effort. Perhaps, for the time being, the First Trust should swallow its pride.
Instead of being a large, weak bank it might be better off riding out the storm
as a smaller, more secure institution. First, Merrill took the bank's paper
promises to repay the RFC's $7 million loan, and exchanged them for $7
million worth of the bank's interest-bearing debentures, created by the board
of directors especially for this purpose. Thus, by the stroke of a pen, Merrill
had transformed the role of government in First Trust's affairs from that of
fuss-budget creditor to full-fledged partner. With his base secure, Merrill
then reduced the par value of the bank's capital stock from $20 to $6 a share,
thereby reducing the official worth of the bank's capital from $5.4 million to
$1.6 million. He then used the freed-up funds to pay down and write off
many of the bank's most dubious assets.

Merrill's resourcefulness, and his "unfailing friendliness," aroused the
sympathy of many government regulators. Once, on Merrill's suggestion,
Alex Cowie, the First Trust's attorney, dropped by the office of Jesse Jones,
the new head of the RFC in Washington. "I just wanted to stop by and thank
you for what your agency has done for First Trust," declared Cowie. At first
Jones seemed startled. Then he grinned with delight. "In all my years in
politics," he replied, "that's the first time anyone has taken time to come by
and thank me."

For a while, as the economy began to recover in the mid-1930s, matters
went well for New York's troubled banks. The recent introduction of deposit
insurance renewed the confidence of ordinary citizens and brought a sharp
increase in their deposits. This, in turn, enabled the bank to make mortgage

loans on properties with realistic assessments. At First Trust, the staff also used these new resources to develop an active business in Morris Plan-type installment loans on automobiles and household appliances.

Ever eager to get back into the black, First Trust paid off $400,000 worth of debentures held by the RFC late in the summer of 1935. Two years later, by the end of 1937, the bank had bought back the remainder of the debentures. Ab and Rena Merrill celebrated by joining the members of the New York State Bankers Association for their annual meeting, most of which would take place on the sunlit decks of the S.S. *Washington* as she steamed down to the island of Bermuda. The cruise went well, and in his presidential address Raymond Ball, head of the Lincoln-Alliance Bank & Trust Co. of Rochester, proposed that "this cruise be recorded as the first *annual* cruise of the New York State Bankers Association." According to the minutes, his suggestion was greeted with loud applause.

The party, however, was premature. Just as the economy had begun to get moving again, the government sharply curtailed spending by the Public Works Administration—which Republicans frequently assailed as a boondoggle—and reined in the RFC's ability to lend to business. Such retractions of credit, however, quickly thrust the economy back into what later came to be called "a sharp recession within a depression." Industrial production, according to the Federal Reserve, fell by one-third nationwide. In New York some banks weathered the storm easily, but in the more fragile upstate economy many banks again came under great pressure. In Warsaw, New York, Wolcott Humphrey, now chairman of the the family's Wyoming County Bank and Financial Institutions Inc., with total assets of more than $500 million, recalls how times were so tough in the fall of 1937 that his mother had to sell her parents' home and open a rooming house for paid boarders near the local school. In Syracuse the Franklin Car Co., a prime manufacturer, went out of business and the city's clearinghouse declared that interest rates on special deposits would have to be reduced, once again, to 1.5 percent.

Over at First Trust matters again became critical as its affiliate, the Fayetteville Commercial Bank, was forced into receivership, and another affiliate, the State Bank of Baldwinsville, complained of serious liquidity problems. Costs, which had already been cut to the bone, were cut again. At about this time Niver Wynkoop, a future president of the bank, was summoned to Merrill's office and offered a promotion. No raise, however, would come with the new responsibilities. "But I wouldn't be too disappointed," said Merrill with grim humor. "All the other officers will be taking a 10 percent cut."

Lesser men might well have quit and washed their hands of the whole mess. But after seven years of unrelenting struggle to save First Trust, Ab Merrill was not about to let go. Instead, he sat down and devised a new, wholly unorthodox plan for pulling First Trust out of the hole. It was, Merrill decided, time to play his trump card. First Trust was in its present fix, he told federal and state regulators, because it had been a good corporate citizen and acceded to the state superintendent's request to purchase the troubled City Bank back in 1929. Despite his best efforts, the plan had not worked. Now it was time for the regulatory authorities to put First Trust & Deposit back on its feet.

While the regulators were sympathetic, they pointed out that the law forbade such a move. At this point Merrill quietly pointed to an obscure new regulation stating that the FDIC could, in certain circumstances, advance funds to help consolidate a merger between two troubled institutions. True, replied the regulators, but with whom would the First Trust merge? Simple, replied Merrill. First Trust would merge with one of its own affiliates, the State Bank of Baldwinsville.

At first, the suggestion that First Trust should receive massive assistance to merge with a bank it already controlled seemed more than a little irregular. But then, under the urging of William R. White, the state's new superintendent, the federal officials agreed to take Merrill's ingenious new proposal under advisement. The months ahead found First Trust's employees working harder than ever, despite their recent pay cut. They came to the office at 8 A.M. and often worked through until midnight. One summer morning, Comptroller Mark Hanlon recalls, he left the bank at 4 A.M., just as the birds were beginning to chirp. Four hours later, after a nap, a shave and a shower he was back at his desk, wading through a new pile of manila folders.

After much deliberation the FDIC announced, in March 1940, that it would pay $23.6 million for the First Trust's substandard assets. At the same time the RFC would purchase an additional $5.5 million of the bank's preferred stock. Even the *Wall Street Journal* was full of praise. "It is understood that the Syracuse reorganization is the most important step in a program which the FDIC had developed to weed out the few remaining weak spots in the New York State banking picture," it declared. "The Syracuse bank is understood to involve more government money than any of the other remaining problem banks." Ab Merrill's fight to save his bank was finally over. The First Trust's valiant struggle to survive had been admired, and frequently emulated, by numerous smaller institutions around the state. In all, the long march to victory had taken eleven years, a period more than *three* times as long as the time endured by Quintus Fabius Maximus and his men in their successful campaign to wear down, and eventually destroy, the invading hordes of Hannibal.

11

Lollipops and Free Parking

WHEN HE FIRST HEARD that the Japanese had bombed Pearl Harbor, Arthur Roth was standing in the dining room of his home on Harvard Avenue, in Rockville Center, Long Island. "I was laying the table for lunch," recalls Roth, who was then cashier of the struggling Franklin Square National Bank in the heart of Nassau County. "I heard the first bulletin on our old RCA cabinet radio, which had been playing light music next door in the living room. The newscaster spoke the words in such a dispassionate way, and yet in those few seconds I realized that our entire world had turned upside down."

The outspoken, iconoclastic Roth knew something about revolutions. In the seven years since he had become cashier of the Franklin Square at the age of 29, he had gone far toward turning the world of New York retail banking upside down. Conventional banking, he believed, was no more than "a gentleman's game, played according to rules that made as much sense in the 1940s as the court etiquette of Louis XIV." And now, with the coming of war, Roth hoped to hasten the demolition of what he referred to as the banking profession's remaining "traditions, taboos, shibboleths, veiled by conventions, protocols, and other kinds of mumbo jumbo all knotted up with an Old School Tie."

Founded in 1926 with a mere $68,000 in capital, the Franklin Square National Bank somehow managed to muddle its way through the early years of the Depression. In those days the community was little more than a

village, with a historic inn called Kalb's, on the old Hempstead-Farmingdale turnpike. The trains never stopped there, for it had no railroad station. On several occasions the bank had been threatened with the prospect of closure by an exasperated comptroller of the currency. But when Arthur Roth was hired away from the Manufacturers Trust Co. in 1934 to serve as Franklin Square's cashier, things became very businesslike. A tall raw-boned clerk with a roosterlike glint in his eye, Roth was already known around the Manufacturers for his incisive time-and-motion studies, and his ability to crack the most complex financial problem down into its contingent parts. On his arrival the new cashier sat down and made a detailed analysis of the banking legislation recently promulgated in Washington. As his notes and cross-references accumulated in the margins of the documents, young Arthur realized that the new laws could become a gold mine to any bank that had the imagination—and the nerve—to launch itself into completely uncharted territory.

With the cooperation of a fuel-oil dealer, and a bold interpretation of the the new Federal Housing Act's home improvement loan clause, the Franklin promptly embarked upon the highly profitable task of financing the replacement of coal furnaces with oil-burning equipment in hundreds of rural Long Island homes. And it was not always a case of replacement. Unable to afford their apartments in the city, many families had taken to living all year round in the dilapidated wooden shacks beside their summer vegetable plots. Later, as light industries like printing, clothes manufacturing and food canning moved out from the nearby metropolis, Roth used other stipulations in the

Housing Act to provide millions of dollars worth of mortgage financing, 80 percent of whose value was guaranteed by the FHA, for the storekeepers, farmers, mechanics and fishermen of Nassau County.

Most established banks, badly burned in the early years of the Depression, were suspicious of anything that had the appearance of novelty. The conventional mortgage of the day generally ran for a maximum of three years and required five payments of interest before final repayment of the entire principal; then, with the bank's approval, the mortgagor could renegotiate his loan for another three years at a higher or lower rate of interest. In contrast, the FHA Title II mortgages were written for an unprecedented period of twenty years and were paid off in fixed monthly installments that included varying portions of interest, taxes, fire insurance and principal. Most of Roth's fellow bankers looked with disdain upon the prospect of such a clientele. As one banker of the old school opined to the *American Banker*: "Good borrowers can get the necessary credit anyway, and the FHA program is not needed by them."

But Roth had built his career on challenging such conventional attitudes. The son of an emigrant housebuilder from Bavaria, Roth had grown up in the Bronx, and for a while he, too, had worked in home construction. At first many banks across New York State, including the Chase, the Manufacturers Trust and First National City, stayed clear of the government-backed mortgages for fear that they would be ruled unconstitutional. But Roth, unlike many Old School Tie bankers, fully understood the economic potential of ordinary people who worked with their hands. Such people wore ties only at funerals and weddings, but they were proud. While the breath was in them they could be trusted to pay their debts. And Roth was quick to grasp that the three-room shack and outdoor privy of today's young production-line worker would soon be transformed into the eight-room residence of the plant foreman.

From the outset Roth and Franklin Square had more business than they could handle, and by 1936 they had loaned out some $1.2 million in FHA mortgages. Fearful that it might overstep its lending limits, Franklin then began to package the mortgages and resell them to larger banks, insurance companies, and savings and loan associations. "They turned to us," Roth explained, "because of the innate conservatism of bankers, and because they wouldn't take the trouble to learn how the papers were handled."

Franklin would collect a sizable initiation fee on each mortgage and undertake to service the mortgage for an annual fee of about .05 percent of principal. "Much of our early success," explained Roth, "was based on my hunch that if the government undertook to guarantee some portion of an obligation—even something as minimal as the interest on a bond—then it would, in a crisis or a default, inevitably be drawn into backing that obligation 100 percent."

With the coming of war, many of Nassau's sleepy villages became outriders in a huge new complex of industrial production. Besides the two major aircraft manufacturers, Grumman and Republic, hundreds of smaller satel-

lite plants sprang up to produce machine parts, communications equipment, cockpit hoods, radar scanners and calibrating instruments. The ensuing influx of highly skilled workers from all over the United States provoked a dramatic increase in home construction. Franklin made numerous RFC business loans, 75 percent of whose value was backed by government, yielding 4 percent annual interest. The remainder of the loan was taken up by the bank, which was generally able to charge an annual interest rate of about 6 percent, thereby yielding a 4 percent spread on the 2 percent interest paid on time deposits. Many of these business loans were to companies in home construction—a Roth specialty—which soon came to be one of the leading industries on Long Island. The Franklin's freewheeling style led many working families to believe it was on their side and genuinely dedicated to improving the community. But it also resulted in frequent clashes with the comptroller of the currency whose office at that time, in Roth's view, seemed to be "stuffed with men who had little or no practical banking experience." The deputy comptroller, he declared, "wanted us to go back to the ways of the past that had got so many banks in so much trouble."

Also, as the war progressed, Roth noticed that an increasing proportion of Franklin Square's customers were women; these included many young mothers whose husbands were overseas or working double shifts on the production lines. Roth and his staff never ceased searching for ways to make the visits of this new type of customer, often with two small children in tow, both convenient and pleasant.

As a result, Franklin Square found itself pioneering a whole new approach to commercial banking. The bank would not seek to attract by its prestige and the awesome size of its vaults, but by the friendliness of its staff and the efficiency of its service. From the beginning, Franklin adopted a softer, more humane style of architecture. Gone were the stone and concrete fortresses

Despite strict sugar rationing, Roth arranged for every child who visited his bank to receive a free lollipop. (Franklin National Bank)

favored by the Old School Ties down on Wall Street. For the head office, and its branches in nearby Elmont and in the emerging community of Levittown, Roth erected single-story brick structures with weather-vanes and clapboard trim in the style of colonial Williamsburg. No longer did tight-lipped tellers peer out-from heavily barred cages. Now they did business across open counters made of pastel-tinted formica. Sunlight and carpets replaced gothic gloom and echoing marble floors.

"We wanted to emphasize the idea that coming in and applying for a loan was not the act of a wastrel or a confirmed sinner," said Roth. "It was a normal, everyday event." Franklin reviewed and streamlined its chain of paperwork again, and yet again. The application time for home mortgages was cut from thirty days to three.

HOW TO USE YOUR GASOLINE RATION BOOK

This book has six pages of eight coupons each. Each coupon is nu[...] and is good only as follows: Coupons numbered 1, during first and [...] months. Coupons numbered 2, during third and fourth months. C[...] numbered 3, during fifth and sixth months. Coupons numbered 4, [...] seventh and eighth months. Coupons numbered 5, during ninth an[...] months. Coupons numbered 6, during eleventh and twelfth month[...]

Each coupon is good for *ONE UNIT* of gasoline. The number of [...] which each coupon gives you the right to buy will depend upon the a[...] supply of gasoline; therefore, the value of the unit may be changed. Any change in value will be publicly announced by the Office of Price Admin- istration.

Do not loosen or tear coupons from the book. Detached coupons will not be honored. When buying gasoline, hand the book to the service station attendant. Only he is allowed to remove coupons. He must remove enough coupons to cover the number of gallons of gasoline purchased. If your purchase is less than one unit, the attendant must nevertheless remove an entire coupon.

The station attendant is permitted to deliver gasoline only into the tank of a vehicle for which you are entitled to use this book. Do not ask him to violate the law.

Typical ration book issued by the federal Office of Price Administration. Previously, a pilot operation run by eighteen banks in the Albany area had helped work the kinks out of a nationwide rationing program for meat, shoes, sugar, and gasoline. (Bettmann Archive)

By today's standards some of Roth's innovations seem obvious, even banal. Yet it was only after another bruising face-off with the comptroller that he obtained permission to provide free customer parking in open lots adjacent to Franklin's offices. But not even the dread comptroller —who for years prevented the bank from dropping the word "Square" from its title— voiced objection to Roth's plan to landscape the approaches to his offices with grassy walkways and beds of blooming flowers. And he raised only an eyebrow when Roth, despite strict sugar rationing, made an under-the-counter deal with Schrafft's, the restaurant chain, to acquire thousands of lollipops; one of these was thereafter presented to every child who entered the bank.

In the face of war, however, the banks of New York also had to contend with sterner problems. President Roosevelt announced that "Dr. New Deal had been dismissed and that Dr. Win-the-War was now in charge." A whole new lexicon of government agencies—including the War Production Board (WPB), the Office of Price Administration (OPA) and the War Food Administration (WFA)—came into being to allocate resources, stimulate production and control prices and wages. Personal income tax went from 4 percent to 6 percent for married couples making more than $1,200. For the first time employers were now made responsible for withholding a portion from the worker's pay from the weekly check. Additional "surtaxes" ranged from 13 percent to 82 percent on income between $2,000 and more than $200,000. Corporations paid up to 40 percent on net income, and so-called "excess profits" were taxed at the rate of 90 percent.

As in World War I, New York's banks became leading partners in the purchase and sale of U.S. war bonds; such purchases, it was believed, provided the best bulwark against untoward inflation by decreasing the volume of currency in circulation. In Albany, eighteen area banks were used as guinea pigs in a pilot test of a bank-supervised rationing program set up by the Office of Price Administration. "The trial took a lot of work," recalls Hollis Harrington, the future chairman of the State Bank of Albany. "But we

HOW MILEAGE IS RATIONED

This poster outlining gas regulations limited the typical family auto to a total of 240 miles a month, of which at least 150 miles must be for journeys to and from work. (Bettmann Archive)

The basic ration for passenger cars

A ration for holders of passenger car registration cards. Each page of 8 coupons is valid for 2 months.

The gallon value of the coupons is fixed by the Office of Price Administration.

The A ration is designed to provide an average of 240 miles per month; of this 150 miles is for occupational use and 90 miles is for family convenience. This is based on average of 15 miles per gallon.

Supplemental ration for passenger cars

An extra ration for those who must drive more than 150 miles a month for occupational purposes. This ration allows a maximum of 470 miles a month for such purposes.

Holders of B books must carry 3 or more passengers or prove that they cannot, and that other transportation is inadequate.

B drivers receive A and B rations. The B book contains 16 coupons and is valid for 3 to 12 months depending on proven needs.

Supplemental ration for essential passenger cars

An extra for special classes of drivers whose work is most essential to the war effort and who must use their cars more than 470 miles a month for occupational purposes.

C books are valid for 3 months.

Qualified applicants receive both A and C books, providing them with enough gasoline for proven occupational use.

The ration for motorcycles

A ration for holders of motorcycle registration cards. Coupons are good until July 22, 1943.

The D ration is designed to provide an average of 240 miles per month, 150 miles for occupational use, 90 miles for family convenience.

Supplemental D books are issued for proven needs in the same way as B or C books.

T The transport ration for all commercial vehicles (except motorcycles) and military vehicles. They receive a T ration but no A ration.

E R The E and R books provide a ration for non-highway equipment and purposes. The E book is for small users, the R for large users.

TO QUALIFY FOR MILEAGE RATIONS, YOU MUST COMPLY WITH TIRE REGULATIONS

quickly developed the ability to run ration accounts parallel to checking accounts, whose basic operations everybody understood."

After the kinks were worked out, the Albany trial was deemed a success and applied nationwide. Retailers of sugar, meat, processed foods, gasoline and footwear across the country received a license from the OPA and were allocated a number of units, or points, each month based on past sales. They also had to open a Ration Banking Account at a convenient bank; as the retailer sold the gas to the public on payment of cash and a specified number of ration stamps, he brought the stamps to the bank and, if all was in order, the retailer would be permitted to apply for new supplies of gasoline. "The primary purpose of the program," recalls Harrington, "was to help prevent counterfeiting and misuse of stamps." In the last year of the war the State Bank of Albany was supervising more than six hundred accounts and processing stamps for a total of 300 tons of sugar, 3.7 million gallons of gas and 29,000 pairs of leather shoes. Other commercial banks across the breadth of New York now shouldered the responsibility for issuing ration coupons. This task, noted the president of the Cattaraugus County Bank (established 1902, current assets $66.6 million), "substantially increased the workload of employees, with little or no additional compensation."

Down on Long Island, Arthur Roth added a new twist to resolving the problems of shortages by setting up a so-called Purchase Club. Consumer items like kitchen appliances, television sets and washing machines were, of course, almost unobtainable even many months after the end of the war. Club members were urged to invest $5 a month to accumulate the necessary funds for such appliances when they became available. More than three hundred other banks around the state, and the country, followed Franklin's lead. Not long after founding the club, Franklin attached a kind of department store showroom to the bank and filled it with display models of appliances that would soon be available for purchase on installment loan.

It was a cardinal tenet in Roth's philosophy that "the best way for a bank to build up its business was to help build up the community in which it resides." As the war came to a close he made a point of addressing store owners in neighborhoods throughout Nassau County and beyond. After projecting slides of drab rundown sidewalks, telegraph poles festooned with overhead cables and storefronts with peeling paint, he would then unveil a carefully prepared architect's impression of how that same neighborhood might look with a major facelift. In this bright postwar scenario Franklin Square, of course, stood ready to help the storekeepers finance these improvements. And it would even provide a list of approved carpenters and electricians; if their work proved defective the bank would get the problem corrected, free of charge. Everything was, in the slang of the day, copasetic. As a result of these presentations Franklin acquired many new customers. And as the stores and offices fixed up their neighborhoods their business increased, along with the size of their accounts at Franklin.

Roth emphasized the Franklin's community spirit in every way possible. Most commercial banks, he noted, demanded full disclosure of a company's finances before granting it a loan. "Many bankers were aloof," he said. "They felt such disclosures were beneath them." In its efforts to "lift the veil of secrecy from the counting house" and enlist its customers as partners, Franklin began to distribute a simplified version of the bank's annual report to all account holders.

The bank's customers seem to have welcomed Roth's refusal to stand on ceremony. The immediate postwar period saw Franklin's total resources increase at the rate of 20 percent and even 30 percent a year, to top $52 million by 1950. The bank—finally permitted to shorten its name to the Franklin National—boasted an annual return on capital of 18 percent, or three times that of the average commercial bank. Though he continued to receive criticism from regulatory authorities for his unorthodox methods, Roth's application of retail sales techniques to commercial banking continued to attract national attention. Many banks from upstate and across the country asked for permission to send teams of experts to study Franklin's paper flow, its floor layouts, and its employee training programs. Even the Bank of America, another pioneer in consumer banking, sent several teams to study Franklin's operation. "They used to call us the Bank of America—

East," said Roth with a chuckle, "and we called them Franklin National Bank—West."

Articles about Franklin appeared in such publications as *Reader's Digest*, *Fortune* and *Newsweek*. Lowell Thomas, the celebrated war correspondent, broadcast a show for NBC from one of the bank's offices. The national media began to refer to Franklin as, simply, the People's Bank.

Many Old School Tie bankers may not have been amused by Franklin's promotional stunts and his idea of making a bank look, and operate, like a department store. But Arthur Roth reveled in the publicity and hired a public relations specialist at the unheard of salary of $4,500 to keep it coming. "Our purpose wasn't self-aggrandizement but an attempt to demonstrate to other banks that such an attitude was appreciated by the public," Roth later explained. "We hoped that all banks would shuck their traditional posture of mystery and secrecy and look their communities in the eye and talk common sense. That way, banking might recoup some of the respect it once had."

While Roth's exuberant campaigns disconcerted the traditionalists, they struck a chord with the next generation of bankers coming up through the ranks. "He's a tall, impressive individual," noted Robert H. Fearon, Jr., now chairman of Oneida Valley National Bank (total assets: $182 million) "He knew what he was doing and could respond convincingly in front of those Congressional committees. Most of all he wasn't afraid to speak his mind. There's no question Roth was something of an inspiration to a lot of younger bankers like me, particularly in the question of tax equity with the thrifts and on the importance of serving the customer and the community."

Even some of the preeminent Old School Ties came to acknowledge the importance of Franklin's efforts. "You know, Arthur," said Horace Flanagan, the head of Manufacturers Trust, after Roth had addressed the leaders of the New York Clearing House, "the banking business needs young fellows like you to shake it up, and make it fly right."

In the years ahead Roth continued to shake up the financial community with an idea for a national credit card for banks (the concept was judged to be ahead of its time, and rejected). He led a drive to strengthen the office of comptroller of the currency (accepted). His bank, with the support of the New York State Bankers Association, fought the savings institutions in court for the right of commercial banks to use the word "savings" in their advertising and promotions (the U.S. Supreme Court eventually voted 8 to 1 in Franklin's favor). He led the charge, again in company with the NYSBA, to make savings banks shoulder a greater portion of the nation's tax burden (partially successful). And, when the thrifts balked on paying the same tax as commercial banks, he spearheaded a nationwide drive to expel them from the American Bankers Association (eventually successful).

Alas, like many of the leading figures in the history of banking in New York, Arthur Roth's career as chairman of Franklin National did not end as he would have liked. In the mid-1960s the bank opened merger talks with the Federation Bank & Trust Co. of New York. By 1969 the newly combined

Michele Sindona, alleged to be "The Vatican's Banker," acquired control of Franklin National in 1972, after Roth resigned. Despite Roth's protests to U.S. regulatory agencies, Sindona overextended the bank, speculating heavily in foreign exchange. In 1974 Franklin collapsed and became the biggest bank failure in U.S. history. Sindona was charged with numerous crimes, including murder, and died in an Italian prison in 1986, claiming with his last breath that he had been poisoned. (AP/Wide World Photos)

board of directors had decided that the father of consumer banking was "a bit too controversial for a bank with close to $2.5 billion in assets" and Roth resigned his position. The new management, however, lacked Roth's incisive intelligence and his flair for innovation. By 1972 Franklin was in trouble, and a block of stock amounting to 21 percent of the bank's capital stock was sold to an Italian national named Michele Sindona. Though reputed to be "the Vatican's Banker," Sindona used his authority to trade heavily in overseas currencies; on occasion the bank found itself holding more than $3 billion in foreign exchange. Though no longer associated with the bank, Arthur Roth laid detailed complaints about such unsound practices before the comptroller of the currency and other federal authorities. Early in 1974 the bank's trading losses amounted to more than $45 million and on May 3 the National Westminster Bank of London refused to clear any more trades by Franklin. One week later the SEC suspended trading in Franklin stock. After borrowing some $2 billion from the Federal Reserve, the bank was finally declared insolvent in October 1974. The Franklin's demise was heralded as the biggest bank failure in American history. All depositors and creditors were paid in full but five of the bank's top executives, including the Italian financier, were sent to jail. Sindona was later charged with additional crimes, including murder, and died in an Italian prison in 1986, claiming with his last breath that he had been poisoned.

For his part Arthur Roth has a full and prosperous life and continues to live with his wife Genevieve in the house they built together more than half a century ago in Rockville Center, on the southern shore of Long Island.

12

The Territorial Imperative

AS WORLD WAR II drew to a close and twelve million Americans in uniform were demobilized, the country was propelled into a period of unparalleled prosperity. This process was further stimulated, in 1948, by Congress's approval of the $15 billion Marshall Plan for the reconstruction of Western Europe. Much of this aid was used in credits to purchase U.S. food, petroleum products, and new industrial machinery. In the wake of these events came an extraordinary demographic phenomenon that would soon become known as "the baby boom." *McCall's* magazine shrewdly endorsed the concept of "togetherness," and the family—split for so long by the vicissitudes of depression and war—once again became the focus of American life.

As the new babies began to walk, and then to run, their proud parents forsook their apartments and their cramped urban dwellings for the green spaces that lay upon the city's fringe. The search for grass and trees, coupled with expanded railroad and highway facilities, would eventually double and triple the populations of neighboring counties like Westchester, Nassau, Suffolk and adjoining areas in New Jersey and Connecticut. With the completion of the Taconic Parkway the eastern bank of the Hudson experienced a major surge in residential development. The Bank of Millbrook, founded in 1891 in the heart of Dutchess County, now began to enjoy the prosperity of its downstate neighbors. Today, it boasts total current assets of more than $60 million.

Numerous medium-sized businesses, exasperated by the crowding and the traffic jams of Manhattan, also pulled up stakes and joined the exodus to the suburbs. A similar movement, albeit on a lesser scale, was also taking place in the larger urban centers of Buffalo, Rochester, Syracuse, Binghamton and Albany.

Such sweeping changes in the American way of life were to have a profound impact on the business of banking throughout the state. While suburban banks like the Westchester County Trust Co. and the Franklin National rode the bonanza of "consumer banking," many money center banks and the giant thrifts headquartered in Manhattan feared that they might come to resemble huge armor-plated dinosaurs, trapped in the big city by an impenetrable wall of federal and state regulation. Their continued success, they believed, depended upon their ability to break through the glass wall and "follow our customers" into the suburbs, and beyond. Such a grim territorial imperative, inevitably, placed them on a collision course with the small and medium-sized independent banks, many of which had grown and flourished upon that same stretch of turf for half a century or more.

Sometimes, at the approach of these juggernauts, the state's smaller banks would run up the white flag and surrender gracefully. But on most occasions they fought what they deemed to be a threat to their very existence with a ferocity that startled the erstwhile invaders, many of whom took pride in their ability to play hardball. This grim struggle for territorial rights would run for more than three decades and extend to the farthest corners of the state. It would swirl through boardrooms, courthouses, convention halls, and legislatures as the various protagonists—small banks, big banks, commercial banks, savings banks, wholesale banks, retail banks—maneuvered for position and combined, split, and then recombined in an ever-shifting kaleidoscope of alliance. Often the issues were so complex that even the regulators, be they the Federal Reserve, the FDIC, the comptroller of the currency, the state superintendent or the Justice Department, could not agree on the right course or, for that matter, any course at all.

A detailed account of these fascinating but often convoluted disputes is beyond the scope of this volume. A brief summary of the highlights, however, is appropriate. The bank legislation of the 1930s had undermined the financial premise of "wholesale banks" like the Central Hanover, Bankers Trust and George Baker's First National Bank. They had been forbidden to underwrite or market securities. And they had lost much of their *cachet* as the ultimate bastions of financial security with the advent of federal deposit insurance; that perennial rib crusher, the "run on the bank," was a thing of the past. Also, in the postwar years it seemed that the basic pattern of corporate borrowing was changing. Now major customers, if they were to restructure the domestic economy and participate in European exports, needed larger sums over longer terms. If the wholesale banks could not gain access to substantial new resources, then companies like General Motors and Du Pont would not be shy of going to securities markets when they needed to build a new plant or set up a new production line. Alternatively, they might be tempted to venture into the hinterland, where many of their plants

were located, and tap the resources of regional banks whose deposits had continued to grow at a vigorous rate.

As a result of these changes the most prestigious "wholesale" banks sought to increase their access to lendable funds by merging with a major "retail" institution. The decade of the 1950s, like that of the 1920s, would become a banker's marriage mart. First National merged with National City, to become First National City. Bankers Trust merged with Public National Bank, which had the fourth largest retail chain in the city. Chemical Bank joined with the Corn Exchange Bank. Hanover linked up with Manufacturers Trust, with the largest number of branches in New York, while Chase National merged with the Bank of the Manhattan Company to become the Chase Manhattan, the largest bank in New York, and in assets second only to California's Bank of America.

But as the Old School Ties tied knot after knot down in the city, they encountered two major problems. First, they discovered that many of the retail deposits they so eagerly sought had, in fact, melted away to the suburbs where they could not be reached, due to the limitations of the McFadden Act of 1927 and the Stephens Act of 1936. Second, they also discovered that their giant new combinations were generating an unprecedented volume of paperwork. As late as the mid-1950s most banks in the state were still using office machinery that showed little advance on that used in the days of Gradgrind and poor Bob Cratchit. As each day dawned clerical employees prepared to grapple with the vagaries of the fearsome Bookkeeping Machine, described by eyewitnesses as a monstrous "combination of adding machine and typewriter." This device was used to enter dates, banks symbols, and amounts paid or received on the ledger card that listed all transactions in a particular account. Each entry, even in the hands of a skilled operator, might take twenty seconds or more. Pocket calculators were as yet unheard of and complex calculations had to be made on something called the Punched Card Tabulating Machine, a version of which had been used, as one bank vice president proudly noted, in "processing the U.S. Census of 1890."

The processing of checks, as always, presented the banks with their biggest paperwork challenge. As consumer banking flourished, and almost every citizen over the age of 18 opened his or her own checking account, the burden increased exponentially. Between 1950 and 1960 the blizzard of checks written by both business and private individuals increased by 75 percent, so that big banks like Chase and First National City found themselves processing, on average, between one and two million checks every working day. Each of these checks, typically, passed through 2.5 banks and was handled by various clerks on ten occasions before it was mailed back to the account holder. Inevitably the biggest logjam came at the moment when the check entered the system at the payee's bank; even the most skilled operator of the electrically powered Proof Machine took at least four seconds to record the account number of the recipient and the dollar sum paid. By 1960 the tidal wave of incoming paper was such that, on average, between 40 and 50 percent of a bank's staff was engaged in the task of processing checks.

If the big banks were to expand in the years ahead, they had to get a firmer handle on such back office operations. In 1954 a technical subcommittee of the American Bankers Association had strongly recommended development of a process called MICR—magnetic ink character recognition—that would enable the critical data on a check to be read by a machine. The basic financial and routing information would be encoded in series of blocklike numbers printed along the bottom of the check in ink containing minute particles of iron. An incoming check would be fed into a reader-sorter machine and transported past a "head" that magnetized the code numbers at the rate of two thousand or more a minute. Then recorded data could be "read" by a magnetic sensor and passed to a computer that automatically entered it on the bank's central books.

By 1961, the first such system in New York was up and running at Chase Manhattan. Other big banks quickly followed suit and the computer revolution was underway. By the mid-1960s Chase had twenty-seven different computer systems at work in every facet of its operations, from stock transfer services and payrolls to installment loans and mortgages. These early days, however, were not without their setbacks and snafus. Once, when an expensive new computer went on line, there were huge disparities between its response to manual and automated commands. "We had garbage in, garbage out, and a backlog of garbage," recalled Barry Sullivan, then executive vice president of Chase. Most banks experienced major problems in data retrieval. Officers knew what information they needed. It was in the computer— somewhere! Without effective video screens and comprehensive access codes, files often had to be laboriously printed out in full before the relevant data could be located.

The five Rockefeller brothers at an awards ceremony in 1967. Nelson, as governor of New York (second from right), and David, as chairman of the Chase Manhattan (far left), made a formidable combination when it came to restructuring the state's banking industry in the 1960s and early 1970s. (AP/Wide World Photos)

The new technology also exerted unexpected gravitational pulls upon the institution's management structure so that executives of the marketing, servicing and operations departments sometimes functioned at cross purposes, to the irritation of customers. Eventually the bank evolved the highly effective concept of "matrix management" under the leadership of Arthur F. Ryan, who subsequently became president of Chase.

The speed and precision of computerized operations gave banks new ways of transacting business, particularly in the international arena. But this potential could not be fully exploited without access to new sources of credit, and the big city banks began, once again, to seek ways of extending their territorial imperative to the rich deposits accumulating in the suburbs. In 1956 First National City believed it had the answer as to how this could be done. The new federal Bank Holding Company Act, it argued, permitted it to merge with Westchester's County Trust Co. (with thirty-nine branches and assets of $382 million) under the umbrella of a holding company. Though Marine Midland had, over the years, established a presence in most of New York's upstate districts, the smaller independent banks in Westchester County saw National City's move in a different light and opposed it with vigor.

Governor Averell Harriman, then running a tight race for reelection against the GOP candidate Nelson Rockefeller, called for a temporary "freeze" on the formation of bank holding companies until the state could draw up a new omnibus banking bill. His proposal was supported by both the legislature and the superintendent of banks, who declared that "the dangers inherent in this proposal—a breaching of banking district lines and a threat to the survival of smaller independent banks—were such as to require immediate remedy by the Legislature." Later the Federal Reserve Board, which had to pass on all mergers involving bank holding companies, also forbade the merger.

The next attempt by the big-city banks to tap the mother lode in the suburbs came—after much high-powered lobbying by both major thrifts and money-market banks—with the passage of the New York Omnibus Banking bill in 1960. This legislation was aggressively opposed by independent bankers across the state, including Arthur Roth. The Franklin and other suburban banks like the Meadow Brook National had taken the risks and built up their communities by the sweat of their brow, and they were not about to let the big thrifts and the big city banks "muscle in" on their success.

"This was the most flagrant example you ever saw of the Old School Tie at work," Roth later noted. "David Rockefeller, then the vice chairman of Chase, was the brother of the new governor, who had himself until recently owned 18 percent of the National Bank of Westchester." Roth, at his happiest when treading on the toes of important personages, now brought a suit charging that the omnibus law was, among other things, unconstitutional. Roth's suit was successful and, to the consternation of the Manhattan banks, a new version of the bill had to be drafted, and then reintroduced in March 1961. After that, whenever Governor Rockefeller encountered the president of the Franklin at a dinner or a reception he would ask Roth, only half in jest, "What are you suing me for now?"

The new omnibus law, delayed but not derailed, permitted the Manhattan banks and the big thrifts like the Dime and the Bowery to merge with banks in both Westchester and Nassau counties. By now, however, the partners in the mating dance had changed. Fickle Westchester County Trust had slipped from the embrace of First National City to begin a slow waltz with Bankers Trust. National City, undismayed by the rebuff, now bent its knee to National Bank of Westchester, with twenty-two branches across the county. In Nassau County, Chemical paired off with Long Island Trust, while Chase sought to merge its assets with those of the Hempstead Bank. Even Morgan Guaranty, the quintessential money market bank, sought an alliance with six leading upstate banks.

Alas, the Federal Reserve and James Saxon, recently appointed comptroller of the currency by President Kennedy, were not in a romantic mood. None of the five marriages, they ruled, could be consummated. While the Manhattan banks were forbidden to merge their way into the suburban market, Saxon permitted them to establish their presence in adjoining counties by opening so-called *de novo* branches, from scratch. Such a process was generally viewed as both slower and more expensive than taking over an existing bank, with its established customers. Chase normally required a *de novo* branch to become profitable within five years; by 1964 it had opened only eleven new branches in Westchester and Nassau, while pushing its profitability deadline back to eight years. First National City, determined to reclaim its title of largest bank in the state, opened no fewer than thirty-seven suburban branches in the same period. Arthur Roth decided to counterattack into the enemy's territory. Within the space of a few months Franklin National opened three Williamsburg-style *de novo* branches in Manhattan.

Not all banks, however, felt the necessity of breaking through the glass wall into the suburbs. The Sterling National Bank & Trust Co. of New York had been established in 1929, just a few months before the market crash, to serve the garment district; even when its clients became very successful and branched into different fields, including legal services, factoring and light manufacturing, they did not, by and large, migrate to the suburbs; the bank's current assets amount to $500 million. Other institutions, like the Merchants Bank of New York, just had to move a few blocks to stay in touch. Founded as Markel Brothers on Canal Street in 1881 to serve immigrants on the Lower East Side, the private bank soon developed a specialty in the diamond and gem trade. In 1926 it was incorporated in its present form to serve as a kind of American version of the ancient Banque Diamantaire in Antwerp, Belgium.

"This is a very close-knit business," noted Rudolf H. Hertz, vice chairman of Merchants. "Since no accountant can certify the precise value of our collateral—the boxes of diamonds and gems being traded—our loans to buyers have to be made primarily on the basis of family connections and, of course, character, character, character."

During the 1930s and 1940s, however, many people on the European side of the business emigrated and chose to establish themselves in the midtown section of Manhattan. To stay with its customers, Merchants opened its first uptown office on 47th Street in 1953; today the bank's total assets amount to more than $700 million.

In a reverse twist, the growing cosmopolitanism of higher finance was underscored by the founding of the Republic National Bank of New York in 1966; much of the bank's initial $11 million capital came from the Trade Development Bank of Geneva, Switzerland, owned by the international financier Edmond J. Safra. By 1993 the bank and its U.S. parent company, the Republic New York Corporation, operated several dozen domestic offices in New York and Florida, and eight overseas branches—including ones in London, Tokyo, Singapore and Buenos Aires—with total assets in excess of $34 billion.

As their *de novo* branches in Westchester and Nassau struggled to accumulate assets and become profitable, many money center banks began to bid aggressively for the use of the overnight balances left in the Federal Reserve by national banks across the country. Though this so-called federal funds market gave Manhattan banks some access to the deposits they sought, the process was indirect and placed the banks second in line for the balances they needed to bid effectively for corporate loans.

In a further effort to solve its funding squeeze, First National City began to work through its London office to acquire Eurodollars. This currency originated in the mid-1950s when the Communist-dominated nations of Eastern Europe, fearful the United States might block their accounts in any Cold War crisis, deposited their dollars in West European banks. Such funds, when advanced to New York by the banks' London offices, were not subject to reserve requirements. In 1961, under the leadership of Walter Wriston, the head of First National City's Overseas Division, the bank introduced the concept of negotiable Bankers Certificates of Deposit (BCD).

These would be issued only to prime corporate customers in units of not less than $1 million. Such a CD could be sold, and resold, in the market created by the Discount Corporation of New York, a prominent dealer in securities.

The new BCDs were a typical product of Wriston's imaginative approach to banking. After receiving his master's degree from the Fletcher School of International Law and Diplomacy, Wriston had served in the Supply Division of the State Department during the war years. Tall, puck-nosed and cerebral, Wriston was known—and feared—for his brusque manner with colleagues who failed to grasp all the ramifications of a problem first time out. After he became president of First National City in 1967 at the age of 48, he seemed to personify the new face of big banking: bold, imaginative and, particularly on the international scene, ever ready to use "muscle" if reasoned persuasion failed to achieve the desired objective.

With efficient CD and Eurodollar markets, writes Harold van B. Cleveland in his *Citibank, 1812–1970*, New York's largest banks would now "be able to shift their asset portfolios away from low-yielding but highly liquid U.S. government securities toward higher-yielding but less liquid assets such as loans and municipal securities." In effect, he notes, such "market funding would come to serve the purpose Frank Vanderlip had once hoped the

Federal Reserve's discount window would serve. It would make banks liquid, without sacrificing yield on assets."

The growing global network of computers, aided in no small way by the almost punitive regulations imposed by many governments upon their own nationals, was creating an immense free-floating pool of cheap international credit. Such funds, instantly accessible at any time of night or day, would shortly be augmented by billions of "petrodollars" derived from the sale of Middle Eastern oil. Soon the prefix *Euro-* on any financial instrument—as in Eurodollars, Eurobonds, Euromarks and Eurocurrency—no longer meant it originated in Europe; it simply indicated that the securities existed offshore, somewhere in the great global limbo that lay beyond the regulatory controls of any specific government. In the years ahead the Manhattan banks, instead of making deposit-based loans premised on the United States' domestic prime rate, shifted increasingly to variable rate loans based on borrowed money keyed to the London Interbank Offering Rate (LIBOR) of the Euromarket. As a result, many domestic credits then moved offshore, to be financed with Eurodollars.

As the 1960s drew to a close it was clear to many banks that the city of New York, never a paradigm of civic efficiency, was becoming close to unmanageable. Between 1965 and 1975 the face of the metropolitan area changed radically, for the worse. Unemployment, racial tensions, the growing use of drugs and violent dissent over the war in Southeast Asia placed enormous new stresses on urban communities across the land. Such tensions, when coupled with the numerous Great Society programs, pushed New York City's operating budget from $3.3 billion to more than $11 billion over the decade. The number of civil service workers more than doubled, and their unions drove increasingly hard bargains with City Hall. To balance its budget, the city's managers resorted to increasingly dubious accounting devices.

In early 1975 two issues of city notes and bonds failed to sell in their entirety, and their underwriters, including many major banks, took a loss. Serious divisions of opinion arose between Mayor Abe Beame and the major banks, which now held $1.2 billion, or 20 percent of their equity, in city paper. The situation was a familiar one for many New York banks. On no fewer than three occasions in this century—in 1907, 1914, and 1933—the banks of New York had been called upon to use their financial resources to bail the city out of its financial crises. Though circumstances had changed markedly, the financiers now buckled on their armor again. A blue-ribbon advisory group, under the leadership of David Rockefeller of Chase, Walter Wriston of Citicorp and Ellmore Patterson of Morgan Guaranty, was set up to seek some kind of resolution with both city and state authorities.

When the city lost its single A bond rating, this group pressed City Hall to restore public confidence by reorganizing its finances and accounting procedures and by making major cuts in personnel and programs. In May 1975 the state came to the city's aid by chartering the Municipal Assistance

President Ford attempted to force New York City into straightening out its finances, but the resulting backlash, expressed in headlines like these, probably brought about his defeat in the election of 1976. (AP/Wide World Photos)

Corporation. Big MAC, as it was called, had the right to issue bonds, control proceeds of the city's 4 percent sales tax, and restructure the city's accounting system. The plan was to take the pressure off the city by substituting $3 billion worth of low-interest MAC bonds for the city's high-interest obligations. However, despite the best efforts of Felix Rohatyn, partner in Lazard Freres, and such men as Wallace Sellers of Merrill Lynch and Thomas Labrecque of Chase, MAC sold only $350 million of its first $1 billion bond issue, leaving the underwriters holding the remaining $650 million.

Startled by this poor reception, Mayor Beame now dismissed some 19,000 city employees, including 5,000 policemen. The circle became vicious. Beame's firings provoked a new round of highly publicized strikes and angry demonstrations, which further reduced the chances of selling MAC's remaining $2.6 billion worth of bonds. Even a further cut of 8,000 employees, and a promise to increase transit fares and have the state take over some city costs, failed to make the bonds more appealing. Continued shortfalls in sales raised questions about the state of New York's ability to make good on its own obligations. Only a guarantee by the federal government, it seemed, could make the bonds sell. All eyes turned to President Ford in Washington, but both he and Congress resolutely refused to approve a realistic rescue package.

"It's the classic quart of bourbon handed to the alcoholic on his promise he won't drink any more," declared one congressman from the rural South. In a speech that October, the president declared that New Yorkers, having made the mess, must now figure out a way to clean it up. No federal aid of any sort would be forthcoming. "Ford to City: Drop Dead" was the resulting headline in the *Daily News.*

This, in many respects, represented the darkest moment of the crisis. A number of money center banks, led by Felix Rohatyn, now produced a plan to reschedule the city's debts over a longer period. In return, the city must agree to impose new taxes, and the federal government would be asked to guarantee a loan of $2.3 billion, to be renewed every year, for three years. Much of these guaranteed funds would be used to bridge the city over the seasonal gap that annually opened up between tax expenditure and tax income. The new proposals were accepted in Washington, but many New Yorkers were to remember Gerald Ford's curt dismissal when they went to the polls in the presidential election of 1976.

As the city seemed to crumble about their ears, many of the money market banks became increasingly concerned about their ability to keep up with their multinational clients and compete effectively with such megabanks as Barclays and Credit Lyonnais in the emerging global marketplace. It was essential, they believed, for America's preeminent banks to extend their financial base beyond the confines of a single city and its immediate environs. Since the Federal Reserve still seemed cool to the idea of active interstate banking, the big banks felt renewed pressure to establish a broader territorial base throughout the state of New York. Such a concerted drive also appealed to the savings banks, who were increasingly eager to acquire the right to offer traditional commercial services like checking and high-interest savings accounts.

In 1971, after many months of intensive lobbying, the New York legislature finally passed a new omnibus banking bill. This would, among other things, permit complete statewide branching in 1976, the year of the nation's bicentennial celebration. In the meantime, the money center banks would be permitted to establish pilot operations, either by merger or by *de novo* branching, in each of the state's nine banking districts. At the same time, upstate banks would be permitted to establish new concentrations of banking power under the umbrella of regional or statewide holding companies. The big banks moved in fast.

"It was like the Day of the Locust," recalled Henry Schramm, vice president of First Trust & Deposit in Syracuse. "In the space of a few months we saw the arrival of Chase Manhattan, First National City (soon to be renamed Citibank), Chemical Bank, Manufacturers Hanover and the Bank of New York. Several New York area savings banks were also circling overhead."

The best defense is a strong offense, and Schramm's First Trust joined with the National Commercial Bank & Trust Co. of Albany to establish a multibank holding company entitled First Commercial Banks, Inc. The new group, with combined assets of $1.3 billion, was soon joined by the National Bank of Homer (total assets: $18 million) and the Oystermen's Bank &

Trust Co. of Sayville, Long Island (total assets: $53 million). This new conglomeration of banking power formed the foundation stone of the Key Bank group, which today has operations in nine states and total assets of more than $18.3 billion. In a parallel move, Hollis Harrington, chairman of the State Bank of Albany, combined his bank with Liberty Bank of Buffalo under the multibank holding company, United Bank Corporation of New York. With the addition of the Syracuse Savings Bank (founded 1849), the Security Trust Co. of Rochester (founded 1882) and the Hempstead Bank of Long Island (founded 1887), the UBCNY would become the Norstar Bank of Upstate New York and, eventually, the Fleet Bank of New York.

The urge to affiliate under the roof of a holding company swept across New York. Historically, the Federal Reserve had rejected proposed mergers when the combination included a major Manhattan bank. But the Central Trust Co. of Rochester (total assets: $283 million) was permitted to join the Charter New York Corporation, a holding company in which Irving Trust was dominant, after it sold off four of its branches to Bankers Trust. Also, the Bank of New York (assets: $1.1 billion) joined with the County Trust Co. of White Plains (assets: $844 million), which had sixty branches through the southern region of the state.

To small independent banks in towns like Oneonta, Norwich, Mattituck and Richmondville, the omnibus bill of 1971 was an abomination. Many had faithfully served their communities for a century and more. And a fair number were family owned and managed, and the torch had been passed on to the third and fourth generation. Often their fathers and grandfathers had known, and done business with, the fathers and grandfathers of their present customers. Their forebears had, by prudent management and a little bit of luck, survived the crises of 1873, 1893, 1907 and 1933. Now, it seemed, the historic chain had been abruptly snapped.

"The big banks came in very fast," recalls Robert Fearon, Jr., then president of Oneida Valley National Bank. "We knew they were using those pilot branches to size us up before deciding to make us an offer, or to just run us into the ground. It was like hearing footsteps in the night."

The same eerie experience was replicated in scores of small cities throughout upstate New York. Teams of youngish research people would canvass the community asking questions such as "Where do you bank?" "What's your household income?" and "What would you like to see changed in your present service?"

Often the big-city researchers would visit the bank's commercial customers and ask them if they were interested in renegotiating their 6.5 percent loan at 5 percent. "We knew the out-of-town bank would have to be taking a loss to make an offer like that," said James A. Whelden, chairman of the Ballston Spa National Bank (established 1838, currents assets $110 million). "It was like living in the shadow of the hangman."

The apprehension of many upstate bankers was further heightened as the big money market banks, once so eager to cultivate their upstate correspondents, began to let things slide. The correspondents were no longer wined

and dined at conventions. And they were no longer invited to send their young executives down to Manhattan for training seminars.

For three years it was open season on the state's small and medium-sized banks. Their only chance of reprieve from the hangman's noose, they believed, lay in somehow modifying the omnibus law's companion legislation, the New York State Financial Reform bill, scheduled for passage in 1974. However, when Harry W. Albright, the superintendent of banks, appointed an advisory committee on the bill it contained no one who worked for an institution with total assets of less than $100 million. Here, once again, Arthur Roth's Old School Ties were out in force. Albright, himself a Yale graduate with a law degree from Cornell, was a thoughtful and precise individual. He had served for many years as an executive assistant to Governor Rockefeller. But he had never served as an officer of a bank.

When the executives of smaller institutions stood up at hearings around the state, Superintendent Albright seemed to brush them off or, as Edward Litchhult, president of North Fork Bank & Trust Co. of Mattituck discovered, was "unable to answer the questions asked by [me] or other independent bankers present." The independents, whose total assets collectively amounted to more than $2 billion, were beginning to smolder.

Not only did they fear that the big commercial banks would drive them to the wall by offering loans below cost. They were also perturbed that the large savings banks, with their less exacting charters and their right to offer higher interest rates under Regulation Q, would drain away the deposits that enabled the independents to make both commercial and mortgage loans in their communities. Their resources would be sucked dry.

Worse, a report by a previous superintendent of banks had revealed that many of the large thrifts had taken the money of their New York depositors and invested it, not in their own community, but in home construction in states like California, where looser regulations enabled them to charge a higher rate of interest, and as many as eight points up front. Indeed, one well-researched study showed they had denied their own depositors FHA and GI government guaranteed mortgages so that they could invest in California.

By the late 1950s "flight money" from New York thrifts amounted to close to $7 billion. What, the small independent bankers now wanted to know, would the superintendent do to prevent the drain of their "lifeblood deposits out of the area to serve distant housing markets and foreign markets solely for high return on their money?"

"We were getting the brush-off," recalled James Whelden, who would one day serve as a director of the Federal Reserve Bank of New York. "It was as if we were too inconsequential for the big guys to notice us. Our problems were just not real to them."

The state of New York, declared Joseph E. Fersch, president of the Sullivan County National Bank of Liberty, was "already overbanked." Yet at the superintendent's hearings, high-powered counsel for the big banks said there was "a real need" for another bank. Though there were more than one hundred independent banks across the state, as things stood each one was forced to fight off the big institutions singlehanded. There was no statewide organization that could speak for them with a single clear voice and demand that the concerns of each individual be addressed.

Robert Fearon, Jr., a career officer in the air force before he returned home to help his father manage the Oneida Valley National Bank in 1956, is a pretty relaxed fellow. Each morning, before turning to the financial pages, he gets the world into focus by reading the cartoon strip "Calvin & Hobbes." Yet one night in March 1974 Fearon became so incensed by the treatment being meted out to the independents that he got up at 3 A.M. and, sitting at his kitchen table, drafted a formal nine-paragraph resolution addressed to Governor Malcolm Wilson, Superintendent Albright and the entire legislature of the State of New York. Preparations for the nation's bicentennial celebration were already underway at that time, and Fearon admits that he "began to feel a bit like old Thomas Paine as I sat there scribbling away, watching the sun come up over the snow." Later that day Fearon had the resolution typed up and distributed to several fellow bankers, with a proposal that all 100-odd independents in New York be invited to a general meeting.

On April 17, 1974, Fearon and his wife Ada May greeted fifty-five bankers from across the state at the Hilton Inn at Syracuse. After declaring their opposition to Albright's bill, the Syracuse group endorsed Fearon's resolution to the governor and agreed to establish a statewide organization, to be called the Independent Bankers Association of New York State (IBANYS).

Some believed the emergence of this feisty new group presented the NYSBA with its most profound crisis since its formation in 1894. Frederick Gardner, at that time executive vice president of the NYSBA, expressed the fear that the independent group, which represented nearly half his entire membership, might diminish, disrupt or even destroy the effectiveness of the larger organization. Fearon and other influential independents sought to assure Gardner that they "would in no way encourage banks to leave" the NYSBA. But the thought that the independents were little more than a disruptive "splinter group" continued to linger for many years.

Though the executive committee of IBANYS met Superintendent Albright—accompanied, somewhat ominously, by his chief examiner—in June, few significant changes were made in the Financial Reform bill. The independent banks, now unified under a common banner, prepared to endure a prolonged siege by the big-city banks.

For the first three or four years the battle hung in the balance. Some independents received an offer they couldn't refuse and sold out, as did the Hayes National Bank of Clinton, which was bought by Irving Trust. Others fought tooth and claw.

Many used the new holding company law to erect their own defensive stockade. Such companies, which generally had the word *bancshares* in the title, were supervised not by the comptroller of the currency but by the more sympathetic Federal Reserve Board. Most required approval by a "supermajority" of 75 percent of the stockholders before any action could be taken on an offer to purchase. Similarly, many of the one-bank holding companies established a "classified board" that prevented more than one-third of the directors from being up for election at any single time. Stock of these holding companies was ostensibly traded over-the-counter, but when an outsider sought to purchase shares he or she would be politely told, "We have no stock for sale at the moment, but if you should wish to *sell* any stock in that company we're prepared to buy it at $38.45 a share."

Fedline terminal, operated here by clerk at Oneida Valley National Bank, enabled small and medium-sized banks to trade directly in Federal Funds with other banks through their accounts at the Federal Reserve Bank of New York. The service also enabled clients of upstate banks to transmit large cash balances to other accounts throughout the U.S. almost instantaneously. Generally, overseas transfers could be executed on a same-day basis. (Photo J. T. W. Hubbard)

The competitive edge enjoyed by most big banks was further blunted when much of the exotic electronic technology they had developed at such expense became available, in miniature form, to many resourceful community banks. Computerized check sorting and monthly balance statements were, of course, commonplace. But now small banks had the equipment to trade directly, should they choose to do so, in the federal funds market. A small bank could also now provide its customers with a MasterCard or VISA credit card that was just as sound as that offered by the money market banks—and, perhaps, at a significantly lower interest rate and annual fee. Soon, also, the small banks' customers could use automatic teller machines (ATMs) to gain access to their accounts at any time of day or night from the corner supermarket or, if they were prepared to wait a few seconds, from the cashier's desk of the Raffles Hotel in downtown Singapore.

While the big banks had far larger advertising budgets and could sometimes offer significantly lower rates on commercial loans, they also had to contend with difficulties of their own. No amount of prestige could offset the fact that their hastily acquired offices were often located a critical three or four blocks away from the mainstream of a city's lunch-hour pedestrian traffic. In consequence those shiny new offices often remained shiny and new—and antiseptically empty.

"Competition was tougher in the area of commercial accounts," recalled Robert Fearon. "Sometimes we could talk our customers into staying with us, but we lost some big ones, too. We attempted to counter-attack by opening branches—six in all—at strategic locations within a twenty mile radius. We knew the territory and the demographics since we'd been living with them all our lives." Many other small banks across the state also sought to strengthen customer loyalties by establishing new branches, sometimes within the county and often across the line in neighboring counties. The Cattaraugus County Bank, headquartered in Little Valley, situated about 40 miles due south of Buffalo, established additional branches in the nearby villages of Franklinville and Randolph in 1978. Similarly, the National Bank & Trust Co. of Norwich expanded out of Chenango County down into the Southern Tier counties of Broome, Tioga and Delaware; by 1980 it had a total of seventeen offices in its four-county region.

The battle hung in the balance. Then, recalls Fearon, "about the fourth year out, the independent banks sensed a kind of change in the wind. We were winning more than we were losing. I suspect it had a lot to do with the big banks' rotation of personnel; now, when a commercial customer went into the bank he'd find a new face behind the desk, and he'd have to tell his whole story from the beginning. And then, a little while later, he'd have to tell it all over again."

Though the big banks undoubtedly had the muscle to push their way into the smallest communities, the stubborn opposition of a few determined independents made the proposition increasingly less cost-effective. Then the slow withdrawal began. The Bank of New York withdrew from such regional upstate communities as Syracuse; in 1980 it merged with Empire National Bank in Newburgh, with thirty-eight branches and assets of $500 million. Then Irving Trust vanished from the scene when it was also acquired, in a hostile takeover, by the Bank of New York. Merchants Bank, Irving's outpost in Syracuse, was then sold to MidLantic Corp. of New Jersey. Chase merged its upstate interests with a long-established regional to become Chase Lincoln First in 1984. Citibank pulled back and, before closing its downtown offices, handed its residual customers and business over to Chase Lincoln. Later, when Manufacturers Hanover merged with Chemical Bank, its thirty-one upstate branches would be acquired by Fleet Norstar.

The message was plain. Both the money center banks and the independents could function better if they sought to supply complementary rather than directly competitive services. Perhaps the new *modus vivendi* was best summed up by Walter Wriston. When the dust of disputation had settled, he was asked what had happened to the big drive north. "Simple," he replied with a rueful chuckle. "We went upstate like gangbusters to capture their markets and they kicked our ass right out of there."

Only after they fought it out toe-to-toe did it become clear that what the large banks could offer by way of price and global reach was, in certain circumstances, no match for the attentive service that a well-run independent could offer its customers over a sustained period of time. While the IBANYS may not have been able to modify the stipulations of the Financial Reform bill, "the arrival of the big banks upstate fostered competition, and the smaller banks survived by being competitive," said Ernest Ginsberg, vice chairman of the Republic New York Corporation and the president of the NYSBA in 1993–1994. "That, after all, is the way the system should work."

Ultimately, the statewide branching experience led to an era of renewed cooperation among banks throughout the state. In 1976, under the leadership of its president, William B. Webber of the Lincoln First Bank of Rochester, the NYSBA brought in a new management team and adopted a new governance structure. The first significant test came in 1981 at the NYSBA's annual legislative policy meeting. In a show of unity, NYSBA's members unanimously approved legislation putting New York in the vanguard of the developing interstate banking movement. A decade later, the NYSBA took the lead in supporting interstate branching, first through successful legislation in New York State and ultimately through federal legislation that passed in 1994. "With the signing of the federal interstate bill by President Clinton," noted Michael P. Smith, the NYSBA's executive vice president, "the long process of banking reform begun with New York's Free Banking Act of 1838 finally came full circle."

"The upstate banks saw that they could better than hold their own against the New York City giants," noted James P. Murphy, then the association's executive vice president and now an executive vice president for the Fleet Financial Group. "So why should they be afraid of competition from Connecticut, New Jersey or Pennsylvania?" Equally important, New York's bankers had recognized that continuing to squabble among themselves would only help their nonbank competitors. "Like Pogo," Murphy added, "we realized that we had met the enemy, and he was us."

13

The Discipline of Debt

PAUL VOLCKER—shoes off, the stub of a 20-cent Cleopatra Grenadier cigar clamped between his teeth—had spent the first part of August sitting beside a river in Wyoming, vainly attempting to catch a fish. Any fish. By August 10, 1982, the only thing the chairman of the board of governors of the Federal Reserve System had reeled in was a disquieting telephone message. "My office called to tell me that Mexico was out of money," Volcker noted subsequently, "so I hurried back to Washington, almost fishless." If Mexico were about to default on its $60 billion worth of debt to foreign banks, Volcker asked himself, could the rest of Latin America, with its additional $300 billion in foreign debt, be far behind?

The debt crisis of 1982 had been long in the making. The first seed of trouble was sown in August 1971, when President Nixon, in an attempt to get a handle on the Vietnam war debt, suspended the right of foreign central banks to obtain gold for their dollars. Over the next eight years the value of paper money underwent massive inflation as the price of bullion rose from the previously mandated $35 an ounce to $450 an ounce. Later it would briefly spike up to $850 an ounce.

This monetary inflation was further exacerbated by so-called credit inflation as banks and other financial institutions eased lending requirements and the American public became increasingly enamored of the plastic credit provided by MasterCard, American Express and VISA. Middle-class families who at the beginning of the 1970s had employed their cards to purchase a

winter coat and a few accessories were, at its end, using plastic promises to finance European vacations and down payments on a new car.

Since the Yom Kippur War in 1973, and the quadrupling of oil prices by OPEC in 1974, vast quantities of petrodollars had flowed into the world's money market banks. Eager to put such resources to work, leading financial institutions across the country—actively encouraged by the U.S. government—had increased their foreign loans, particularly to less developed countries (commonly referred to as LDCs), hard hit by the rise in oil prices. In addition, many smaller banks all over the United States and upstate New York opened "International Departments," hired lesser lights from bigger banks, and made or participated in LDC loans. Swarms of bright young M.B.A.s waving lending agreements from the nation's largest banks flew south to the humorously designated "M.B.A. countries"—Mexico, Brazil and Argentina—to initiate a swelling tide of loans. Over the next five years LDC loans from American banks increased fivefold, from about $17 billion to $82 billion.

The rigorous standards applied to domestic borrowers were shelved in the rush to do business. A few skeptics, like George Champion of the Chase, urged caution but many leading bankers argued that it was impossible for a sovereign government to default, since it could always refinance its way out of trouble. And there were further "safeguards." Most of the loans from private banks were scheduled for repayment not in pesos but in U.S. dollars, at a rate of interest keyed to LIBOR and the U.S. prime. Competition for such "foolproof" loans was intense, and the resources available spiked up sharply with a new gush of petrodollars in the oil crisis of 1979. By the spring of 1982 U.S. loans to LDCs amounted to some $120 billion. Perhaps, also, an element of altruism was involved. "One by one," noted Walter Wriston, chief of Citibank, "we are seeing developing countries finally breaking through the vicious cycles of poverty. Far from despairing, I have great hopes for the future of the LDC in the remaining years of the century."

That, however, was reckoning without inflation. By the last year of the Carter presidency (1976–1980) the annual rate of inflation stood at 21.5 percent. The prime rate, like the rate on residential mortgages, stood at 18 percent. The fear that prices might increase at a yet steeper rate had the effect of pushing purchasers ever deeper into debt. Buy something of tangible worth now, said the voice of popular wisdom, and pay later in sharply inflated dollars. Such inflation had a corrosive effect on both the domestic and the international marketplace. With many Third World loans keyed to the U.S. prime, an increase in America's domestic inflation rate would force up the LDCs' monthly interest payments. By 1982 Mexico was forced to allocate more than one-third of her total export earnings to servicing interest on foreign loans. "It was clear they were on a trajectory—they were going broke—but what could you do about it?" noted Paul Volcker. "You just sat there and wondered: when is Mexico going to blow?"

Now, in mid-August 1982, Mexico had blown. Grupo Industrial Alpha, the nation's largest corporation, was on the verge of default. The peso was inflating at the rate of 60 percent per year. Already, several billion dollars' worth of the country's private capital had migrated north to find safety in the real estate investments and the banks of Florida and California. The rumor mills along Wall Street churned with the word that if Mexico defaulted then Citibank and Bank of America (whose exposure amounted to about $2.5 billion apiece) would be in serious trouble; the impact on Manufacturers Hanover and Chase Manhattan (with an exposure of $1.5 billion) might be even more severe. For the nine U.S. money center banks, loans to Mexico averaged about 45 percent of their capital, while loans to all of Latin America averaged close to twice their capital.

Fed chairman Volcker's first act on returning from his fishing expedition in Wyoming was to summon the leaders of all affected banks to a meeting. Within a week representatives of 850 banks from around the industrial world gathered in the main auditorium of the Federal Reserve Bank of New York. From the first the cerebral and somewhat disheveled Volcker urged caution upon all parties. Default by a foreign government was not like a domestic default. If a bank attempted to foreclose on a soured loan, that government could press its case aggressively in its own courts, or it could "nationalize" assets as it saw fit. In his opening address Volcker finessed the issue by characterizing the situation as a "standstill" rather than a default. Then, after lining up a $3.5 billion bail-out package, Volcker asked the Mexican delegates, in conjunction with an elected committee of bankers, to get behind an International Monetary Fund plan for the restructuring of their economy.

At first Mexico, under the leadership of its populist president Lopez Portillo, objected. The president had lived under IMF strictures before. Their rules, he believed, were too stringent and inherently exploitive. "The speculator has already plundered us," Portillo told his people on television. "But Mexico is not finished. They will never plunder us again." As the last credits ebbed away, however, it became clear Mexico had no choice in the matter, and she finally bowed her head to what was euphemistically referred to as "the discipline of debt."

Volcker also made a concerted effort to forestall the so-called contagion effect that would cause other hard-pressed LDCs to demand Mexico's liberalized terms for themselves. Events, however, quickly wrenched matters out of the Fed's hands. Though Brazil then had foreign debts of $87 billion, she had twice the population of Mexico, and had managed her finances more effectively. Yet hundreds of banks around the world, jarred by Mexico's near default, now refused to extend further credits to Brazil. The biggest private creditor of all was Citibank, with a total of $5 billion invested, a sum so large that it exceeded the bank's shareholder equity by 15 percent. A $6 billion rescue package was quickly assembled at the IMF and Brazil, after its own strident objections, also submitted itself to the unpleasant—some said demeaning—discipline of debt.

Still farther south the military junta of Argentina, burdened with some $30 billion of its own foreign obligations, sought to distract its citizens from their troubles by staging an abortive invasion of the Falkland Islands. But soon even the junta was seeking relief in company with a host of smaller LDCs like Zaire, the Sudan and Bolivia. The loans of most were quietly rolled over and "renegotiated." Schedules for repayment were extended outward from the customary two to ten years and, in some cases, to seventeen years. It became clear to the banks holding LDC claims that chances of recovering their principal were increasingly slim. As the distinguished economist J. M. Keynes had once observed: "If you owe your bank manager a thousand pounds, you are at his mercy; if you owe him a million pounds, he is at your mercy." In the years that followed the banks of the industrialized nations found themselves drawn, ineluctably, into the deepening swamp of Third World debt. As with their plunge into Cuba more than half a century before, the American banks now found themselves at the mercy of those who owed them money. And, in the years ahead they, too, would come to understand the anguish suffered by those who labor under the discipline of debt.

For its part the American public was curious to know how such colossal miscalculations could have occurred. Editors of the *Wall Street Journal* and many magazines ran lengthy articles about the twin evils of rampant inflation

and "The Debt Bomb." *Bonfire of the Vanities*, Tom Wolfe's dramatic portrayal of a fictional bond trader named Sherman McCoy, became an international best-seller. And, on a more serious note, the famous New York publishing house of Farrar Straus & Giroux decided to reissue Dr. Charles Mackay's classic study *Extraordinary Popular Delusions and the Madness of Crowds*, first published in 1841. The collective insanities delineated by Mackay included such wonders as the disastrous Mississippi Scheme, the Tulip Craze, the Children's Crusade and—most telling of all—the South Sea Bubble of 1720, a scam in which the Earl of Oxford and his cronies nearly broke the Bank of England and, in all, bilked the British public out of a cool £13 million. From his researches into a multitude of panics and manias Dr. Mackay concluded that crowds, just like individuals, have their own mental dynamics. "Men," declared the learned doctor, "think in herds; it will be seen that they go mad in herds, while they only recover their senses slowly, and one by one."

During the decade of the 1980s the financial community spawned a whole stampede of more or less crazed herds, each bent on going mad in its own way. The frenzy over Third World debt was just the beginning. On Wall Street a whole generation of young investment bankers could take home a million dollars a year in salary and bonuses, and still consider themselves

The people of London—rich and poor, drunk and sober—crowd around a stock promoter before pledging their fortunes and pawning their possessions to invest in South Sea Company stock, which has already risen "1,000 Per Cent." When the bubble of speculation finally exploded in 1720 the British public found that it had been bilked of more than £13 million. (Bettmann Archive)

The Discipline of Debt

Junk bond king Michael Milken, left, enters court for sentencing on securities and tax violations. Earlier, he master-minded the notorious Predators' Ball and boasted, "We're going to tee-up GM, Ford and IBM and make them cringe."
(AP/Wide World Photos)

hard done by. In the South and West, and in upstate New York, too, the thrifts were gripped in their own special brand of collective insanity, just as the commercial and investment banks sent the wholly pernicious LBO craze into top gear. Soon the "Predators' Ball," a lavish function thrown for corporate raiders at the Beverly Hills Hotel by the junk bond king Michael Milken, became an annual fixture for hundreds of takeover enthusiasts.

Most of these financial manias had a uniquely American caste. Each fad had it own peculiar dynamics, but often as not it was fueled, like the activities in any American high school, by peer pressure: if everyone else was doing something—no matter how dumb—then it must be okay. In 1990 the managing director of IBCA, a respected European credit-rating agency, looked back on the decade and tentatively allowed that American banks "do seem prone to being crazy." *Fortune* magazine was less polite. American lenders, it told its readers, "have a well-earned reputation throughout the world of being mismanaged risk-seeking institutions."

In truth, the decade of the 1980s was as garish, as greedy, and as laced with uncertainty as the era in which Jay Gould and Jim Fisk flourished after the Civil War. It was a decade in which the terms *junk bond, arbitrage, leveraged buy-out, hostile takeover,* and *forebearance* could appear without need of explanation on page one of almost any newspaper in the nation. It was a time in which blue chip corporations like IBM, General Motors, and AT&T found themselves beset by smaller, more nimble competitors. It was a time that witnessed the stock-market drop five hundred points in a single day, and a time in which a bulky Texan named Bunker Hunt came close to cornering the silver market. Many of the wounds were self-inflicted. The prestigious investment bank of Salomon Brothers, already rich beyond measure, would be accused of rigging the market for U.S. Treasury bonds. The officers of several investment banks were sentenced to prison on charges of massive insider trading. And Clark Clifford, a respected advisor to presidents of both political parties, became caught up in the machinations of BCCI, a Third World bank accused of arms dealing and the laundering of drug money.

As the decade of the 1980s progressed, the financial frenzies in the worlds of real estate and leveraged buy-outs (LBOs) began to coalesce. Michael Milken, a West Coast partner of Drexel Burnham Lambert, had completed several historical studies of high-yield bonds purporting to show that the likelihood of their default had been, in fact, greatly exaggerated. His presentations were so convincing that many established investors and financial institutions around the country began to place a substantial portion of their assets in high-yield bonds. Within days, and sometimes just a few hours, Milken's sales staff could sell one or two or four billion dollars' worth of high-yield bonds for an S & L's new shopping mall, or a corporate raider's next LBO. To many it seemed that Milken and his fellow junk bond kings had created a whole new economic order. As one Drexel associate declared, it was the firm's role to "finance the robber barons who would become the owners of the major companies of the future." No company was too big or too prestigious to be invulnerable to a guerrilla attack launched with lowly junk bonds. "We're going to tee-up GM, Ford and IBM," an exuberant Milken once told his assistants. "And make them cringe."

Most of all, however, the decade of the 1980s was a time of steadily accumulating debt—personal, corporate, state, national and international. Debt was everywhere, piling up like sacks of uncollected garbage. For the ordinary citizen new plastic cards with "preapproved" credit lines of $5,000 and $10,000 arrived in the mail. Debt tempted, like a serpent. But, as many learned to their dismay, debt also had its spartan virtues. When debt reached a certain magnitude, it could impose discipline. Often the discipline of debt became so powerful that it could bring hopeless spendthrifts, highly leveraged corporations and even whole nations to heel.

There were many reasons why the major banks of New York were forced to become, in *Fortune*'s damning phrase, "risk-seeking institutions." Their traditional domain had suffered many encroachments. "Boundaries between commercial banks and other financial institutions," noted John D. Wilson, author of *The Chase*, "were becoming increasingly blurred or nonexistent." Many brokerage houses now offered money market mutual funds which, while secure and offering checking account facilities, allowed the customer to receive handsome interest on his or her "deposit." Such accounts, which held more than $180 billion by 1981, permitted the customer, by means of a single phone call, to transfer a portion of those assets into any one of a substantial array of mutual funds—growth, income, bonds—listed by the brokerage. In addition, national department store chains like Sears and Penney's—nemeses of small-town banks earlier in the century—were also providing their customers with loans and other financial services. As if all this were not enough, commercial banks of New York were now fated to watch their old rivals, the highly politicized thrifts, acquire a host of new competitive powers.

Traditionally savings institutions had been known in the industry as "the 3-6-3 crowd" due to their penchant for borrowing at 3 percent, lending at 6 percent and being out on the golf course by 3 P.M. Now, hit by the worst inflation of the century, they believed themselves to be on the brink of extinction. With long-term low-interest mortgages already on their books, many were caught in the vise of having to borrow short, with high-cost certificates of deposit, to lend long. In 1980 Congress and President Carter sought to make the playing field more level for all financial institutions with the passage of the Depository Institutions Deregulation and Monetary Control Act. This legislation, which has been described as "the first major banking reform since the 1930s," required all financial institutions, including state-chartered banks and savings and loan associations, to maintain reserve account balances with the Federal Reserve System. Besides offering thrifts opportunities for income beyond mortgage loans, the act gave all institutions the right to (a) have access to the Fed discount window, (b) offer Negotiable Order of Withdrawal (NOW) accounts, (c) phase out Regulation Q, which gave the thrifts their quarter percent edge on interest-bearing accounts, over a period of six years, (d) offer residential mortgages at interest rates above the ceilings decreed by state usury laws and (e) increase federal deposit insurance coverage from $40,000 to $100,000, even though the average deposit by consumers amounted to a lowly $6,000.

It took more than a level playing field, however, to transform yesterday's afternoon golfer into tomorrow's financial skydiver. In 1981 serious doubts arose in the minds of the braintrusters of the Reagan administration (1980–1988) as to whether the cautious thrift managements had either the temperament or the ability to take advantage of this cornucopia of new opportunity. In consequence the president's men decided to push the S & Ls out into the real world of supply-side economics by appointing Richard Pratt, a brash forty-one-year-old professor of finance at the University of Utah, to the chairmanship of the Federal Home Loan Bank Board (FHLBB). Just as the comptroller of the currency oversaw the nation's commercial banks, so the head of the FHLBB held sway over the nation's thrifts. But Dick Pratt, though fervent in his fashion, was not a typical deregulator. He was articulate

and outspoken, and on weekends he liked to boot up in black leather and race huge Harley-Davidsons across the sand flats near Salt Lake City—just the man, the GOP braintrusters decided, to get the thrifts up and running.

If the savings institutions were to survive as financial entities, Pratt told an incredulous crowd of S & L executives in San Francisco, then they must get used to assuming some measure of entrepreneurial risk. "One approach would be to start ten or fifteen thrift institutions or commercial banks and engage in the the most risky activities legally allowed." To survive the present crisis, he told his audience, they must adopt a whole new outlook. "If you believe that return is related to risk, the expected value of your returns would be higher than any other approach, while at the same time you could buy your funds on a risk-free basis through offering US government obligations in the form of insured savings accounts."

Risk free! It was simple. The skilled player in such a game could have one institution bet on *rising* money rates while a sister organization was choreographed to bet on *falling* rates. After a period of time one bet would prove right, the other wrong. The successful institution would then cash in its winnings, while the unsuccessful one would, through deposit insurance, lay off its losses on the government. Such a fail-safe strategy would undoubtedly become the wave of the future. Indeed, Pratt argued, in their present competitive environment the S & Ls had little choice. "That is a scenario,"

The Discipline of Debt

he concluded, "that we, as regulators, and that you, as management, are going to have to operate under, because that opportunity is a realistic one."

In a further attempt to break the grip of high interest rates, Pratt's FHLBB also gave S & Ls the right to offer their customers adjustable rate mortgages. And it lowered the eligibility requirements for S & Ls to obtain deposit insurance with the Federal Savings and Loan Insurance Corporation (FSLIC). Historically, to prevent its assets from being manipulated by a small clique of insiders, an S & L was required to demonstrate that it had at least four hundred bona fide stockholders before it could become eligible for deposit insurance under the Federal Savings and Loan Insurance Corporation (FSLIC). Pratt and his board now quietly eliminated this requirement. At the same time the FHLBB also reduced the capital requirement (which S & L accountants generally termed "net worth") from 4 to 3 percent of insured deposits.

Pratt sought to further consolidate the competitive power of the thrifts by helping to draft the Garn–St Germain Depository Institutions bill which, on its passage in 1982, abolished Regulation Q and the additional quarter point of interest. In return it gave the thrifts the power to offer their customers checking accounts and commercial loans, and to make direct investments worth up to 40 percent of total assets in nonresidential real estate ventures such as the construction of downtown office buildings and suburban shopping malls.

For a while the new measure appeared to be a masterpiece of deregulation. "I think we hit a home run," President Reagan cheerfully announced at the signing ceremony in October 1982. But the new law, when coupled with the stipulations of the Carter law of 1980, had the unexpected effect of punching the home run right out of the ball park to produce a debacle that the author of *The Madness of Crowds*—were he alive—would undoubtedly describe as the most outrageous and most expensive example of herd insanity known to history. By the time the savings and loan scandal was set to rights it would, in all, cost the American taxpayers in excess of $160 billion.

While Dick Pratt's "fail-safe" investment formula produced only a smattering of interest among old-time thrift executives, his bold talk did arouse the curiosity of the more risk-minded managerial talent in the arena of real estate development. Promoters of shopping malls, condominiums and downtown office buildings were more than happy to take the S & Ls out into the fast lane. And if they couldn't acquire an existing institution, numerous syndicates of venture capitalists and developers were prepared to go ahead and start their own thrifts from scratch. In the next few years state banking authorities granted scores of new charters for S & Ls in Florida, Texas and Colorado. In California, the state commissioner issued charters for no fewer than 210 new S & Ls in a period of eighteen months. Few of these swashbucklers had previous experience in banking, but they liked the mathematics which, on paper at least, said it was possible to parlay $2 million of capital into control of $1.3 billion worth of S & L deposits in the space of five years.

The rush was on. Almost overnight the drowsy marble-faced lobbies of the traditional S & L s were transformed into a single giant casino. Since their depositors were protected up to $100,000, the new supercharged thrifts began to issue high yield certificates of deposit, investing the proceeds in speculative commercial real estate ventures and in the even higher yielding "junk" bonds. Emboldened by their apparent success, some large thrifts— like Charles Keating's Lincoln Savings & Loan and Thomas Spiegel's Columbia Savings & Loan—used the services of brokerages like Drexel Burnham Lambert to issue millions of dollars worth of such junk bonds in their own name.

Despite office vacancy rates that topped 20 percent in many communities across the country, developers now embarked upon one of the biggest building sprees in history. Indeed, statistics would later show that one-third of all office space ever built in America was erected in the decade of the 1980s. U.S. pension funds, normally the most cautious of investors, increased their real estate portfolios from $25 to $125 billion. But the enthusiasm was short lived. The boom in commercial real estate peaked in 1987; five years later *Fortune* magazine would estimate that it had, on average, decreased in value by 45 percent. Indeed, the losses were so staggering that, in the opinion of James Grant, author of the book *Money of the Mind*, by the end of the decade "real estate was eclipsing Third World debt as the nation's top banking problem." These two problems would entwine to produce a feeling in the boardrooms of New York's banks that they were, step by breathless step, being crushed to death by boa constrictors.

The speculative frenzy was further stimulated as the more unscrupulous S & Ls in the South and West created so-called daisy-chains that, by unspoken agreement, traded properties and parcels of land back and forth at prices determined by increasingly inflated appraisals. In Texas this procedure had long been known as "trading a dead horse for a dead cow." Inevitably, numerous accountancy firms, including some of the so-called Big Eight, were drawn into the game. If a firm finally balked at giving its imprimatur to the deception, that firm would be quietly dismissed. Then another firm, with a higher fee scale and a blinder eye would be invited to pronounce the books in good order. It should be noted that in *The Madness of Crowds*, Dr. Charles Mackay identified the Willful Distortion of Fact as an important archway that human herds must pass through on their journey into a state of collective insanity.

For their part most local and regional banks in upstate New York were able to cash in quite smartly on what became known as "the Casino Society." By the end of 1986 the average American family was using 18 percent of its disposable income to service debt. "That's an all-time record," acknowledged a senior economist at Morgan Stanley. As prices of residential real estate rocketed upward, established mortgage holders became eager—with the help of strong promotional advertising from the banks—to leverage the value of their home by taking on a second mortgage in the form of a home equity loan (or HEL). The funds could be used to refurbish the kitchen, but they were more likely to be used to consolidate debt, or invest in the stock market.

Terms were easy. So-called drive-by appraisals became commonplace on the grounds that the property had already been fully appraised at inception. Most banks did not charge "points." While one Pennsylvania institution urged its customers to "take an African safari," a bank headquartered in Buffalo offered low, low interest of 6.9 percent and a major New York bank appealed to its mortgage-holders with the offer of "Prime plus 1.4 percent, with no fees or points." As a further inducement banks often stressed that under the new tax law the interest on such HELs remained fully deductible. Between 1982 and 1987 the value of home equity loans in force increased from $60 billion to $270 billion. But, as ever, there was a downside. "In a long-term sense, real estate is the last bastion of savings in this country," noted one perceptive bank economist at the time. "Now we're eating into it." Soon, a whole new segment of society would find that it, too, must learn to live with the discipline of debt.

Just as upstate suburbanites began to celebrate the casino life-style, however, the money market banks in Manhattan were finding themselves increasingly hard pressed. Indeed, many wondered if their financial premise had not been pulled out from under them. "ARE BANKS OBSOLETE?" was the question *Business Week* magazine posed to its readers in the spring of 1987. The banks' traditional role as middleman between depositors and borrowers was eroding, with their share of the market declining from 85 percent to 60 percent over the two previous decades. The big banks were the hardest hit. In 1975 such banks might have lent to a corporate customer at 2 percent over the cost of obtaining funds. Now this spread had been cut to 0.5 percent and many big corporations, just as they had done in the Great Bull Market of the 1920s, were selling the commercial paper directly to major investors. Credit subsidiaries of major automakers often lured customers by offering low interest or interest-free financing for the first few months of the loan. "The banking business is on a declining path," noted Robert L. Clarke, comptroller of the currency, and "if we don't do something about it, five or ten years down the road we'll end up with a banking industry that's truly a dinosaur."

The banks found themselves under increasing competitive pressure from more lightly regulated foreign giants like Barclays and Sumitomo, which had a market capitalization six times bigger than New York's Citibank. Between 1983 and 1988 the total loans of U.S. banks increased 11 percent, to $675 billion, while those of Japanese banks increased 240 percent, from $500 billion to $1.7 trillion. A significant part of the problem was the cost of deposit insurance and the cost of meeting reserve requirements, which together added an estimated 1.25 percent to the interest charged by New York banks, a price disparity that had driven U.S. corporations to borrow $4 abroad for every $10 they borrowed from American banks. Since the passage of the Community Reinvestment Act (CRA) in 1977, banks were further burdened, noted Michael P. Smith, executive vice president of the NYSBA, with "a massive commitment of time, money and resources to achieve a social mandate." Added to this was the growing debt of the Third World. In the three years following its near default, Mexico's foreign debt had ballooned from $60 billion to $96 billion. The other "M.B.A. nations" were not far behind and several were speaking openly of staging "a debtors' rebellion." Peru in particular had sought to place creditors at its mercy by figuring its own interest payments, and then offering to pay them on a take-it-or-leave-it basis.

When Brazil defaulted on its interest for $68 billion of loans in February 1987, Citicorp decided that it had had enough. John Reed, its chairman, ordered that $3 billion be taken from the bank's revenue stream and channeled to reserves so that the most flagrant Third World debtors could be threatened with cancellation of their loans if they didn't, finally, submit to the discipline of debt. "With the leading U.S. bank strengthened," commented one Wall Street insider, "negotiations [with Third World defaulters] could become much tougher." Though most of Citibank's fellow lenders could not afford to make a similar move, opposition to lending new money to keep LDCs' interest payments current became firmer.

At the beginning of the decade all New York's money market banks had Triple A credit ratings. By 1987 all except one—Morgan Guaranty—had been downgraded to the point where their capital stock was now traded at an average discount of 75 percent of book value. However, many regionals and midsized upstate bankers were prosperous and had little trouble raising capital; often their stock, when available to the public, was selling at two and three times book value.

As the decade progressed, noted a report to the House Committee on Banking, Finance and Urban Affairs, even the healthier big banks found it progressively more difficult "to earn sufficient returns to attract new capital." As high quality borrowers were drawn to the buoyant market in commercial paper, consumer loans and residential mortgages were, with increasing frequency, packaged and "securitized" for sale to pension plans and insurance companies. As a result, stated the House report, "Increasingly banks—espe-

cially the largest banks—have no other way to regain the 'spreads' they once earned except by taking more risks."

The temptation for commercial banks to take an additional risk was also fostered by the new—and often highly destructive—opportunities for gain in the realm of corporate mergers and acquisitions. Since J. P. Morgan, Sr., assembled his great steel and railroad trusts at the turn of the century, takeovers of one corporation by another generally had been financed out of the acquisitor's accumulated earnings and his ability to obtain loans from investment banks like Morgan's and commercial banks like George Baker's First National.

In the 1980s this traditional mode of financing was still available, and had been used by Du Pont in its $7.8 billion acquisition of Conoco Oil. But in the previous decade a new mode of financing called the "leveraged buy-out" had become increasingly popular, particularly among those who lacked the financial base of a corporate giant. Basically, the LBO was a process by which a corporation's own management, or perhaps an outsider, used the *potential* of the target's own resources—its assets and its cash flow—as a *lever* with which to raise the funds for the purchase of a controlling portion of the company's outstanding stock. The LBO was a powerful tool and it became increasingly powerful when it was combined with the public's willingness to purchase huge quantities of high-yield bonds.

Between 1984 and 1987 the dollar volume of LBOs nearly quadrupled, from $4.8 billion to $16.6 billion. In all these transactions, noted Burrough and Helyar in their *Barbarians at the Gate*, "Citibank, Manufacturers Trust Co. [*sic*] and Bankers Trust formed a powerful triumvirate with loose control over the spigots through which flowed the billions of dollars in money necessary to fuel Wall Street's takeover machine." This Niagara of cash was supplemented, particularly in the case of hostile buy-outs, by junk bonds bought from such firms as Drexel Burnham. Often these banks, with their less dominant colleagues, might find themselves handling the affairs of competing bidders; in an effort to allay any talk of conflict of interest these institutions sought to erect so-called Chinese walls between the bank executives working on competing bids. Some, like Bankers Trust, might end up holding a major segment of the new organization's stock.

A typical case was that of the legendary department store Macy's. In 1986 the top executives at the store arranged to float a huge issue of high-yield bonds and used the proceeds to buy out the company's common stockholders. The management buy-out was a mixed blessing, to say the least. The chief beneficiaries of the move were the store's managers, seventy of whom became instant millionaires, while the value of the stock held by Macy's chairman, Edward K. Finkelstein, increased from about $4.4 million to more than $120 million two years after the buy-out. Goldman, Sachs, the investment bank, received a fee of $31 million for its services, plus 2 percent of the new stock issued by the store, worth about $50 million in 1988. The store itself, of course, did not fair so well. Before its loyal management subjected it to the LBO, the store had ten dollars worth of equity for every dollar of debt; it could not have been healthier. After the buy-out this ratio was reversed, with the store now owing ten dollars in debt for every dollar of equity it held. With so much of its earning power devoted to servicing debt, even the slightest dip in sales might dissolve that wafer-thin cushion of equity, thereby causing the corporation to default on its bonds and declare bankruptcy, a fate that actually befell the store in January 1992.

The LBO mania provided a field day for an exotic financial service called arbitrage. Originally "the arbs" had derived their livelihood from reconciling the small discrepancies in the prices of stocks traded on the floor of more than one exchange. In recent years, however, the arbs had used their skills to trade in the stock of companies that were the targets (or potential targets) of takeover bids. When Du Pont sought control of Conoco in 1981 it had outmaneuvered four rival suitors. As the battle swung one way, and then another, an obscure arbitrageur named Ivan Boesky was said to have made a killing of close to $40 million.

The restructuring of Macy's was a so-called *management* buy-out. Other corporations frequently became target of a *hostile* LBO, mounted by outsiders unwelcome to current management. The biggest hostile LBO of the era was that involving the food and tobacco giant RJR Nabisco. In 1988 Nabisco's management sought to take the company private under the leadership of its president Ross Johnson, but at the last moment they were outbid by a hostile counteroffer from a consortium assembled by the leveraged buy-out specialists, Kohlberg Kravis Roberts. In this battle of the titans most of the major banks in Manhattan were lined up on one side or another—or, in some cases, on both sides! The winning bid of $20 billion approximated the gross national product of Pakistan, and *Time* magazine echoed the thoughts of many with its cover story entitled "A Game of Greed." The magazine then went on to wonder, "Has the buyout craze gone too far?"

Though corporate raiders tended to stress the "improvements" that their stewardship might produce, in many LBOs the chief beneficiaries seemed to be the investment banks which, besides interest, might receive between one and two percent of the purchase price in fees and commissions. Fees charged in the leveraged buy-out of Borg Warner Holdings Corp. in 1987 exceeded the equity remaining in the company when the process was complete. As a result of such perverse incentives, some LBO targets were forced to go through the wringer more than once. The experience of the soft-drink bottler Dr. Pepper, which underwent three leveraged buy-outs in the space of four years, was typical. When the investment firm of Forstmann Little & Co. staged its initial $520 million leveraged buy-out of the bottler in 1984, the price seemed high. Yet under its new management the company, while selling off real estate and its subsidiary Canada Dry, was able to service its newly acquired debt with revenues from its core bottling business. Indeed, the prospect seemed so good that in 1986 British soft-drink giant Cadbury Schweppes, with the assistance of Shearson Lehman, made a successful bid for Dr. Pepper. In this second highly leveraged takeover Forstmann sold the block of stock for which it paid $30 million two years previously for a total of $270 million, a 900 percent markup. By now Dr. Pepper's debt amounted to 90 percent of its capitalization. Cadbury Schweppes merged the bottler with 7-Up, another of its subsidiaries, only to have its new creation fall prey, in 1988, to a third highly leveraged takeover bid led by the investment firm of Prudential Bache Securities. This new corporate entity was so heavily encumbered that its total debt now constituted 180 percent of its capitalization.

For a while the commercial banks had believed that they might be able to restore their fading fortunes by running an aggressive mergers and acquisitions department. But experiences like that endured by Dr. Pepper suggested that LBOs, for all their financial glamor, seldom strengthened business. In fact LBOs often crippled their targets, leaving them little better than wounded beasts in the international marketplace. Ironically, IRS regulations acted as a stimulus to such corporate looting; though it was forbidden, of course, to deduct stock dividends on company tax returns, a corporate raider, after saddling a company with debt, was permitted to deduct the interest paid on that company's newly acquired bonds.

Due to pressure from their established corporate customers—the natural target of raiders—most commercial banks and some of the more upstanding investment banks like Goldman, Sachs began to limit their work to defensive financing, helping a target fight off an erstwhile raider or, if that scenario seemed doomed, helping it find a white knight. But even that guarded stance began to erode with the case of Burlington Industries, the largest textile manufacturer in the United States. In the spring of 1987 rumors reached Wall Street that a corporate raider from Canada was seeking to acquire

Burlington. At the time the company was profitable, with a recently opened high-tech denim factory and debt that amounted to less than one half of its stockholder equity. Eager to remain independent, Burlington initiated a search for a white knight to defend it from the raider, who was said to represent the giant Dominion Textile of Canada. After hasty negotiations Morgan Stanley, the Wall Street investment bank, agreed to unsheath its sword and protect Burlington from Dominion. But the services of the white knight did not come cheap. In return for a promise to retain company's present management, Morgan Stanley would help that management stage its own $2.4 billion leveraged buy-out of Burlington.

After the details of this corporate drama were described a few weeks later in a *Barron's* cover story, the management takeover of Burlington came to symbolize the unchivalrous greed of the 1980s, a time in which the difference between black knight and white knight had worn thinner than a coat of enamel. For riding to the rescue of Burlington, Morgan Stanley earned $80 million, which included the profits for underwriting some $2 billion in junk bonds. In addition, for the picayune expenditure of $125 million, it acquired control of one-third of Burlington's stock. Bankers Trust also eventually acquired some 24 percent of Burlington's nonvoting stock.

Under the white knight's scenario, Burlington was asked to shoulder $3 billion worth of new debt, a sum thirty times larger than its equity. Soon the vaunted "discipline of debt" began to assert itself. With annual interest payments of $264 million to service its huge new obligations, Burlington was forced to dismiss hundreds of experienced middle managers, close its research center, and sell off its prized new denim factory to—of all people—Dominion Textile, the black knight whose approach had precipitated Burlington's difficulties in the first place. The message was clear. In the magical kingdom of LBOs, the kiss of the white knight was often just as lethal as that of the black.

As the decade of the 1980s came to a close, and the New York State Bankers Association approached the hundredth anniversary of its founding, the state's big commercial banks, in Dr. Mackay's famous phrase, "began to recover their senses slowly, and one by one." It was now clear that the willingness to take high risks had seldom benefited the balance sheet. In fact, "losses on loans to Latin American governments have wiped out nearly every dollar [the banks] made in their foreign businesses in the 1980s," noted *Fortune* magazine. And the sensational plays of the LBO craze, when averaged out, had boosted the big banks' return on equity by a paltry 1.2 percent. Attempts to raise new capital had fizzled, as when a major bank in the fall of 1990 had to step in and buy back $275 million worth of its own recently issued stock. Pessimism was further strengthened by the Federal Deposit Insurance Corporation Improvement Act of 1991 (FDICIA), which sharply tightened accounting procedures and required all banks whose capital stood below 2 percent of assets by the end of 1992 to be taken over by federal regulators. It was estimated that some sixty weak institutions, with total assets of $25 billion, would fall below the line. In 1993, however, the more rigorous accounting schedules would drive a further one hundred banks, with total assets of $76 billion, into the arms of the FDIC.

Many wondered if commercial banks, with their tightening noose of federal regulation, might not—like dinosaurs—become obsolete. Or could their financial premise be redefined in some way that would enable them to provide American society of the twenty-first century with some form of service that would be unique, substantive and profitable? During the Bush administration (1988–1992) several legislative packages had languished in congressional committees. Almost all proposals for "reform" sought to have banks in some fashion or other restore and enhance their capital position while obtaining the right to reenter fields denied them by the Glass-Steagall Act of 1933. Most challenging of all, the beleaguered banks sought the right to branch nationwide. Though New York State had passed an interstate banking bill in 1982 and an interstate branching bill ten years later, both of these laws depended upon reciprocal action by other states, and the branching law only applied to state-chartered banks that were not Federal Reserve members. Ultimately, therefore, the branching question could be resolved only by legislation at the federal level.

While many of New York's larger banks continued to fall short of the mark, the Federal Reserve and the comptroller of the currency had long urged banks—in accordance with a plan endorsed by the Group of Ten central bank governors at Basel, Switzerland, in 1988—to increase their capital/assets ratio to at least 3 percent by the mid-1980s, to 4 percent by 1992, and then, it was hoped, have a chance of meeting the internationally agreed upon 8 percent of risk-adjusted assets by the turn of the century. To meet such an elevated standard American banks would require some $81 billion in new capital, two-thirds of which would have to be provided by the nation's forty-five largest banks.

In contrast, some experts argued that the industry did not need more capital. What it required, asserted Robert Reischauer, director of the Congressional Budget Office, was, quite simply, "fewer banks." Such a goal could be achieved by so-called *in-market* mergers, like the 1991 marriage between Chemical and Manufacturers Hanover, in which seventy overlapping branches were scheduled to be closed and six thousand people terminated, for a savings of $650 million a year. As John McGillicuddy, the combination's new leader, noted, "We recognize that our first, second and third challenge is to put the ship in order." In contrast, the KeyCorp. of Albany had sought to establish *new market* mergers by acquiring banks in different geographic regions. Income stability was greatly enhanced. While its branches in New England suffered in the 1990–1992 recession, Key's branches in the Pacific Northwest produced solid profits.

Another appealing idea for making U.S. banks more competitive was to tailor the cost of deposit insurance to risk, with no individual depositor receiving more than $100,000 worth of coverage at any particular bank. Sophisticated depositors, like pension funds, would no longer be covered.

Insurance premiums for strong, well-managed banks would be lower, while banks with a poor track record would pay more. Such disparities might, in the end, cause the weaker bank to be acquired by an efficient, stronger bank. Some legislative plans would grant banks, depending on their strength and efficiency, the privilege of selling securities and insurance. But it was far from clear that entry into those highly competitive businesses would be a panacea in the long run, even if it could be achieved in the face of staunch opposition from the securities and insurance industries. Meanwhile, banks received a welcome, if temporary, boost to their earnings in 1992 when, in an effort to get the economy moving again, the Federal Reserve's discount rate was lowered to 3 percent. Instead of making new loans, many New York banks decided to recharge their batteries by investing in medium-term Treasuries at 6 percent, giving them a risk-free spread of 3 percent as lenders' holdings of federal securities increased 23 percent to $630 billion.

Much about the conditions in which the banks of New York operated during the 1990s might have impressed, or surprised, William Cornwell, founder of the New York State Bankers Association. If he were alive one hundred years after he and his fellow Signers of the Call first met in his offices in Buffalo one wintry day in March 1894, he would surely have been awed by the technology of the computer, with its extraordinary powers of assimilation and display. Cornwell would have been startled by the speed with which multibillion dollar deals could be set up, and closed. He would, also, have been startled by the magnitude of debt, both personal and national. And it is probable that he would be both perplexed and intrigued by the megabillions of electronic cash that now sloshed around the globe, seemingly depatriated and ownerless, and tagged with a single imperative: maximize returns.

There are some things, however, that would be all too familiar to William Cornwell. Preeminent among them would be what he was wont to call "the human element." Cornwell had witnessed, first hand, the panics and frenzies of 1873 and 1893. On the latter occasion conditions were far worse than anything experienced by the bankers of the 1920s, or those of today. In the crisis at the end of the previous century, 93 railroads, 500 banks and 15,000 businesses nationwide had failed. In the state of New York, one man in three was out of work, and there was a strong whiff of revolution and anarchy in the air. The sanctioned processes of democracy, however, seemed inadequate for the task of resolving the crisis. As a last resort, it seemed, the nation had been forced to depend on a few public-spirited individuals—giants like Pierpont Morgan, George Baker and James Stillman—to use their own resources in an effort to set things right.

After much cogitation Cornwell had concluded that the only effective counterpoint to panic and commercial disorder lay in forming an association of well-informed banking men that, after reasoned discussion, would then seek to exercise "the wisdom of concerted action in monetary affairs." With the founding of the New York State Bankers Association, cashiers in adjoining counties need no longer know each other "by signature alone." At their face-to-face meetings they could devise and then push hard for programs that, ultimately, would have far more long-term influence than those mustered by the Great Triumvirate down on Wall Street.

Contrary to the prediction of one comptroller of the currency, the formation of the NYSBA has enabled the banks of New York to avoid the fate of the dinosaurs. In the first century of its existence the association has produced solutions to a host of seemingly intractable problems, from providing a more stable currency based on real value to establishing a central banking structure that, while more or less independent of party politics, provided leadership and liquidity in times of crisis. Though members of the association were prone to disagree with one another from time to time on matters of policy and procedure, their mutual respect and the need for tangible results had always drawn them together again.

In the second and third centuries of its existence the association will, in all likelihood, have to confront problems just as complex and as challenging as those encountered in its first one hundred years of life. But so long as the future deliberations of the New York State Bankers Association continue to be based, as they have been in the past, upon shrewd judgment, mutual respect and the idea of *concerted* action, then each member will retain the protective strength of all, and the dream of William Cornwell and the other Signers of the Call will undoubtedly live on.

Appendix

Presidents of the NYSBA

1894–95	William C. Cornwell, President, The City Bank, Buffalo
1895–96	James G. Cannon, Vice President, Fourth National Bank, New York City
1896–97	Seymour Dexter, President, Second National Bank, Elmira
1897–98	A. B. Hepburn, Vice President, Third National Bank, New York City
1898–99	Charles Adsit, President, First National Bank, Hornellsville
1899–1900	Henry C. Brewster, President, Traders' National Bank, Rochester
1900–01	John B. Dutcher, President, National Bank of Pawling, Pawling
1901–02	A. D. Bissell, Vice President, People's Bank, Buffalo
1902–03	Stephen M. Griswold, President, Union Bank of Brooklyn, Brooklyn
1903–04	Lewis E. Pierson, Vice President, New York National Exchange Bank, New York City
1904–05	Charles H. Sabin, Vice President, National Commercial Bank, Albany
1905–06	Alfred H. Curtis, President, National Bank of North America
1906–07	Elliott C. McDougal, President, Bank of Buffalo
1907–08	Charles Elliot Warren, Cashier, Lincoln National Bank, New York City
1908–09	E. S. Tefft, Cashier, First National Bank, Syracuse
1909–10	Ledyard Cogswell, President, New York State National Bank, Albany
1910–11	Luther W. Mott, Vice President, First National Bank, Oswego

1911–12	Walter H. Bennett, Vice President and Cashier, American Exchange National Bank, New York City
1912–13	Cornelius A. Pugsley, President, Westchester County National Bank, Peeksill
1913–14	Robert H. Treman, President, Tompkins County National Bank, Ithaca
1914–15	James H. Perkins, President, National Commercial Bank, Albany
1915–16	John A. Kloepfer, President, Union Stock Yards Bank, Buffalo
1916–17	Benjamin E. Smythe, President, Gramatan National Bank, Bronxville
1917–18	John H. Gregory, President, Central Bank, Rochester
1918–19	Delmer Runkle, President, Peoples National Bank, Hoosick Falls
1919–20	D. Irving Mead, Vice President, Irving Trust Company, Brooklyn
1920–21	S.G.H. Turner, President, Second National Bank, Elmira
1921–22	Jacob H. Herzog, Vice President, National Commercial Bank & Trust Company, Albany
1922–23	Howard Bissell, President, Peoples Bank of Buffalo, Buffalo
1923–24	Willis G. Nash, Vice President, Irving National Bank, New York City
1924–25	Charles E. Treman, President, Ithaca Trust Company, Ithaca
1925–26	William S. Irish, Vice President, First National Bank, Brooklyn
1926–27	Carleton A. Chase, President, First Trust & Deposit Company, Syracuse
1927–28	John McHugh, President, Chase National Bank, New York City
1928–29	Michael E. Cahill, President, Utica National Bank & Trust Company, Utica
1929–30	William K. Payne, President, Cayuga County National Bank, Auburn
1930–31	Mark M. Holmes, President, Exchange National Bank, Olean
1931–32	J. Stewart Baker, President, Bank of Manhattan Trust Company, New York City
1932–33	H. H. Griswold, President, First National Bank & Trust Company, Elmira
1933–34	George V. McLaughlin, President, Brooklyn Trust Company, Brooklyn
1934–35	William L. Gillespie, President, National Commercial Bank & Trust Company, Albany
1935–36	S. Sloan Colt, President, Bankers Trust Company, New York City
1936–37	Raymond N. Ball, President, Lincoln-Alliance Bank & Trust Company, Rochester
1937–38	Frank K. Houston, President, Chemical Bank & Trust Company, New York City
1938–39	Thomas A. Wilson, President, Marine Midland Trust Company, Binghamton
1939–40	Joseph E. Hughes, President, Washington Irving Trust Company, Tarrytown
1940–41	W. Randolph Burgess, President, National City Bank of New York, New York City
1941–42	Eugene C. Donovan, President, Auburn Trust Company, Auburn

1942–43	John P. Meyers, President, Plattsburg National Bank & Trust Co., Plattsburg
1943–44	E. Chester Gersten, President, Public National Bank and Trust Company, New York City
1944–45	C. George Niebank, President, Bank of Jamestown, Jamestown
1945–46	Bernard Finucane, President, Security Trust Company, Rochester
1946–47	Chester R. Dewey, President, Grace National Bank, New York City
1947–48	William A. Kielmann, President, Peoples National Bank of Lynbrook, Lynbrook
1948–49	Burr P. Cleveland, President, First National Bank of Cortland, Cortland
1949–50	Harry W. Davies, President, The Syracuse Trust Company, Syracuse
1950–51	Herbert J. Kneip, President, The National Commercial Bank and Trust Company of Albany, Albany
1951–52	William T. Taylor, Vice President and Director, Bankers Trust Company, New York City
1952–53	Ernest H. Watson, President, First National Bank of New Rochelle, New Rochelle
1953–54	Stanley A. Neilson, Vice President, The Marine Trust Company of Western New York, Gowanda
1954–55	Hulbert S. Aldrich, President, New York Trust Company, New York City
1955–56	William F. Ploch, President, Nassau County Trust Company, Mineola
1956–57	Vernon Alexander, Vice President, National Bank of Geneva, Geneva
1957–58	Richard S. Perkins, Vice Chairman, First National City Bank, New York City
1958–59	Crandall Melvin, President, Merchants National Bank and Trust Company, Syracuse
1959–60	J. Henry Neale, President, Scarsdale National Bank and Trust Company, Scarsdale
1960–61	Albert C. Simmonds, Jr., Chairman, Bank of New York, New York City
1961–62	George A. Newbury, President, Manufacturers and Traders Trust Company, Buffalo
1962–63	Clarence M. Brobst, President, Chemung Canal Trust Company, Elmira
1963–64	George A. Murphy, Chairman, Irving Trust Company, New York City
1964–65	Wilmot R. Craig, Chairman of the Board & President, Lincoln Rochester Trust Company, Rochester
1965–66	Hollis E. Harrington, President, State Bank of Albany, Albany
1966–67	Howard W. McCall, Jr., President, Chemical Bank New York Trust Company, New York City
1967–68	Robert B. Hole, President, National Bank of Auburn, Auburn
1968–69	Patrick J. Clifford, Chairman & President, Security National Bank of Long Island, Huntington
1969–70	John A. Kley, President, The County Trust Company, White Plains

1970–71	Lewis A. Lapham, Chairman, Bankers Trust Company, New York City
1971–72	Claude F. Shuchter, President, Manufacturers & Trades Trust Co., Buffalo
1972–73	Charles E. Treman, Vice President and Trust Officer, Tompkins County Trust Company of Utica, Utica
1973–74	Howard D. Crosse, Vice Chairman, Franklin National Bank, New York City
1974–75	Kenneth E. Buhrmaster, Chairman, First National Bank of Scotia, Scotia
1975–76	William B. Webber, Chairman, Lincoln First Bank of Rochester, Rochester
1976–77	(Charles F. Mansfield, Marine Midland-resigned), H. Russell Johnson, Chairman, The Oneida National Bank & Trust Co. of Central New York, Utica
1977–78	H. Russell Johnson, Chairman, The Oneida National Bank & Trust Co. of Central New York, Utica
1978–79	Peter D. Kiernan, Chairman, United Bank Corp. of New York, Albany
1979–80	Richard K. LeBlond, II, Vice Chairman, Chemical Bank, New York City
1980–81	Edwin J. Lyons, President, St. Lawrence National Bank, Canton
1981–82	John R. Torrell, President, Manufacturers Hanover Trust Co., New York City
1982–83	Robert W. Moyer, President, Wilber National Bank, Oneonta
1983–84	Victor J. Riley, President & CEO, KeyBank, N.A., Albany
1984–85	Peter Herrick, President, The Bank of New York, New York City
1985–86	Robert H. Fearon, Jr., Chairman, President & CEO, The Oneida Valley National Bank, Oneida
1986–87	Daniel P. Davison, Chairman & CEO, U.S. Trust Company of New York, New York City
1987–88	Raymond Van Houtte, President, Tompkins County Trust Co., Ithaca
1988–89	Arthur F. Ryan, President, The Chase Manhattan Bank, N.A., New York City
1989–90	William L. Bitner, III, Chairman & President, The First National Bank of Glens Falls, Glens Falls
1990–91	Robert F. Wallace, President, National Westminster Bancorp, New York City
1991–92	John A. Kanas, President & CEO, North Fork Bank, Mattituck
1992–93	George W. Hamlin, IV, President & CEO, The Canandaigua National Bank & Trust Company, Canandaigua
1993–94	Ernest Ginsberg, Vice Chairman, Republic New York Corporation, New York City
1994–95	Edward D. Miller, President, Chemical Banking Corporation, New York City

Executive Officers of the NYSBA

Name	Title	From	To
Michael P. Smith	Executive Vice President	1989	Present
James P. Murphy	Executive Vice President	1976	1989
Anthony Loiaconí	Acting Executive Manager	1975	1976
Frederick K. Gardner	Executive Vice President	1970	1975
Albert Muench	Executive Vice President	1944	1970
Harold J. Marshall	Secretary	1941	1944
W. Gordon Brown	Executive Manager	1932	1940
Clifford F. Post	Secretary	1930	1931
Edward J. Gallien	Secretary	1917	1929
William J. Henry	Secretary	1909	1916
E. O. Eldredge	Secretary	1900	1908
W. I. Taber	Secretary	1898	1898
Walter E. Frew	Secretary	1897	1897
John A. Kennedy	Secretary	1896	1897
Ledyard Cogswell	Secretary	1895	1896
Charles Adsit	Secretary	1894	1895

Notes

1 • Signers of the Call

1 **five men who assembled** . . . : Primary source, New York State Bankers Association, *Secretary Book*, 1894, 25. The time of the meeting on March 15 is not specified, but the same group met again in the same place on July 7 at 10 A.M., 29. Cornwell, according to newspaper accounts of July 1, 1901, had his office on the ground floor, front, leaving little space for a boardroom. I have therefore situated the boardroom on second floor front. The likelihood of this being the site of the boardroom is further borne out by a photo that shows this room to have a huge window, 20 feet across and 12 feet high, facing west onto Main Street, a most appropriate setting for directors and other visiting dignitaries to meet.

1 **Statistics on Buffalo** . . . : See Albert A. Woltge's *Buffalo Directory*, 1895. Cleveland had been mayor of Buffalo before becoming governor of New York; see *Grover Cleveland* by Allan Nevins, New York, 1932.

1 **319 Main Street** . . . : *The Buffalo Directory*, compiled by Albert A. Woltge, for the Courier Co., 1893–1896.

1 **Henry Brewster** . . . : Data with portrait appears in Pioneer Publishing's *Rochester & Monroe County*, 1908, 35–37.

2 **Avery** . . . : A shadowy figure. His positions and affiliations both listed in NYSBA, *Secretary Book*, and in *Proceedings of the NYSBA, 1894*. Avery continues to be listed in subsequent *Proceedings* and then vanishes from the Oneida County Historical Society's Directory of Residents in 1906.

2   **Barker** . . . : See file in Onondaga Historical Association, Syracuse, N.Y., and obituary in Syracuse *Herald*, May 1, 1935. File includes several photos.

3   **Cornwell** . . . : See biographical notes and photo portrait in John Devoy's *History of Buffalo and Niagara Falls*, Buffalo, N.Y., 1893, 136–138. There is additional biographical material in *The National Cyclopedia of American Biography*, published by James White Co., 1918, vol. 61, 258–259. See biography of father Francis Cornwell in *History of Buffalo & Erie County*, 2 vols., edited by Perry Smith, published Syracuse, N.Y., 1884. Francis Cornwell moved from Wayne County to Buffalo in 1857 and was described as a "sound and painstaking lawyer, a gentleman of culture and refinement, and a quiet, genial friend." He was also the author of a book on decisions made by courts of last resort in New York State; Smith, *History*, vol. 2, 483. The older Cornwell was struck down on Nov. 2, 1869, the night of his election to the Supreme Court of New York. His son William was then eighteen years old.

5   **Academie Julien** . . . : William Cornwell must have attended the academy between January 1871, when Paris fell to the invading Prussian army, and 1873, when the school was closed. Some fascinating insights into life at the Académie are offered by George Moore in his *Confessions of a Young Man*, reprint, Montreal, 1972, 56–57. Cornwell was one year older than Moore, both were relatively well off (Moore even had a manservant in tow), and it is likely that they spent some of their evenings together at the Café de la Nouvelle Athènes. See also William Gaunt's *The Aesthetic Adventure*, London, 1945, for background on artists.

5   **minutes** . . . : See NYSBA, *Secretary Book*, 1894, 25–26. All of Cornwell's statements are direct quotations from speeches, articles, and books he published within a few months of the March 15 meeting in Buffalo. I think it is fair to assume that they (further bolstered by the signed letter dated March 15, 1894, addressed to William Seymour, cashier of the First National Bank of Hudson, New York, pasted into the back of the *Secretary Book*) are accurate and lifelike representations of the thoughts and opinions Cornwell expressed to his fellow bankers in the boardroom of the City Bank.

5   **banks . . . suspended** . . . : There are varying figures of the number of banks involved, but the figure of seven hundred is from Wilbert M. Schneider, *The American Bankers Association Past and Present*, Washington, D.C., 1956, 15–17. Totals were taken at different times in the crisis; on occasion savings banks were added into the total without acknowledgment. Charles Hoffmann, in *The Depression of the Nineties*, Westport, Conn., 1970, 57–58, puts the total at 583 failures in 1893; he breaks them down as follows: 158 national banks (all but five of which were in the South and West), 172 state banks, 177 private banks, 47 savings banks, 13 loan and trust companies, and 61 mortgage companies. Frank B. Latham, *The Panic of 1893*, New York, 1971, 4, speaks of 574 banks failing in 1893. Others failed in the early months of 1894. W. Jett Lauck, *The Causes of the Panic of 1893*, Boston, 1907, 107, quoting a report by the comptroller of the currency, puts the number of all kinds of banks suspended by Sept. 1, 1893, at 415.

6   **unemployment in New York** . . . : Hoffmann, *Depression*, 106–122.

6   **Flower** . . . : *Public Papers of Governor Flower*, 1893, Albany, N.Y., 1894, 345.

6   **depressed farm prices** . . . : See Latham, *Panic of 1893*, 5–7.

6   **"pounding along"** . . . : The quote is from Cornwell's book, *The Currency*

and Banking Law of the Dominion of Canada, published by Putnam's in 1894, 3.

6   **Coxey's army** . . . : Left Massillon, Ohio, March 25, 1894, I. Kull and N. Kull, *An Encyclopedia of American History*, New York, 1965, 278.

6   **Pullman** . . . : May 11, strike began in Chicago; Kull and Kull, *History*, 278.

6   **Henry Frick** . . . **Emma Goldman** . . . : Anarchist Alexander Berkman, a paramour of Emma Goldman, shot Frick twice in his office. See Page Smith, *A People's History: The Rise of Industrial America*, 471–476; for an account of Goldman's speech, see pp. 505–506.

7   **Paris Commune** . . . : *Concise Columbia Encyclopedia*, New York, 1983, 186.

7   **Henry Adams** . . . : Page Smith, *A People's History*, New York, 1919, vol. 6, 488.

8   **534 banks** . . . : Numbers used in a canvass letter to NYSBA; see minutes of meeting, with sample letter last page.

8   **"The Fiat principle"** . . . : Cornwell, *Greenbacks: The Source of Our Troubles*, pamphlet, Buffalo, 1893, 6.

8   **George Levi** . . . : Quotes come from his remarks in *Proceedings* of the NYSBA, 1894, 50.

9   **$900 million** . . . : The figure is derived by Cornwell, *Greenbacks*, 10. In circulation were $346 million worth of greenbacks, $156 million of Treasury notes, and $378 million in silver dollars, a precise total of $880 million.

10   **"fear about Gold Reserve"** . . . : Cornwell, *Greenbacks*, 3, 12.

10   **below $100 million** . . . : Lauck, *Causes*, 95, and Hoffmann, *Depression*, 55, put the date at April 22, but Kull and Kull's generally authoritative *History*, 277, puts the date at April 15. For railroad failures, see Latham, *Panic*, 4. Hoffmann says by June 30, 1894, more than 192 railroad companies, holding one-fourth of all trackage, were in receivership; *Depression*, 63.

11   **"magnificent fiascos"** . . . : *Bankers Magazine*, London, vol. 56, September 1893, 371.

11   **"mild amusement"** . . . : Cornwell, *Greenbacks*, 13.

11   **Frederick Barker** . . . : Incident related in newspaper clipping dated Feb. 26, 1879, found in Barker file at the Onondaga Historical Association. It did not specify the name of the publication.

11   **Empire State Express** . . . : Stewart H. Holbrook, *The Story of American Railroads*, Crown, 1947, 95. The run was made on Sept. 14, 1891.

12   **Antwerp, Wilmurt banks** . . . : Taken from William H. Dillistin, *Historical Directory of the Banks of the State of New York*, New York, 1946.

12   **Brewster background** . . . : Source, *Rochester & Monroe County, N.Y.*, 35–37. His house was at 353 East Ave., just opposite the George Eastman residence; see *Rochester City Directory*, 1894. Brewster's house still stands, but the number has been changed to 901 East Ave. Source, Dr. Karl Kabelac, Rare Books Room, Rush Rhees Library, University of Rochester.

14   **"Big Three"** . . . : *New York Times*, May 3, 1991, 1, 28. In the accompanying picture Baker is referred to as "the Sphinx of Wall St." The Morgan quote is from V. P. Carosso, *The Morgans*, Cambridge, Mass., 1987, 433. Stillman quote from Burr, see below.

14   **"religion/Temple"** . . . : Anna R. Burr, *Portrait of a Banker*, New York, 1927, 96, 191. Frederick L. Allen is harsher. In his *The Lords of Creation*, New York, 1935, 83, he calls Stillman "cold-blooded."

14   **100% dividend** . . . : *New York Times*, May 3, 1931, 1, 28. Sheridan A.

Logan, *George F. Baker and His Bank*, New York, 1981, 127, reports the 100 percent dividends began in 1899. In spring of 1931 the bank's unlisted stock was selling in the region of $8,000 a share.

14   **"silence"** . . . : *New York Times*, May 3, 1931, 1, 28. Also *Dictionary of American Biography*, supp. 5, New York, 1931, 44–45.

15   **lunch at Robinson, White Elephant** . . . : See *Buffalo Directory*, 1895.

15   **names of porter and detective** . . . : All listed in *Buffalo Directory*, 136. Name of Patrick Grady, the elevator boy, is also given. The visiting bankers probably exchanged pleasantries with young Grady on their way up to the boardroom.

16   **Buffalo Evening News** . . . : See issue for March 15, 1894, Buffalo and Erie Historical Society.

16   **horse and trap** . . . : Contemporary map shows it was two miles from railroad station on Main and Whaley to Rushing Water, too far for Cornwell to travel it twice daily on foot. Source, Warren Moffett, Village Historian, on location of station and time to run from Buffalo.

16   **house built in 1885** . . . : Came from Warren Moffett, Village Historian. He also provided the fact that Rushing Water was advertised for rent in the summer of 1905.

17   **Rushing Water** . . . : House visited by author on afternoon of Dec. 20, 1990, in company of Warren Moffett of East Aurora.

17   **Elbert Hubbard** . . . : Did not start the Roycroft Community until 1895, but he lived in East Aurora since 1884. He is, incidentally, *absolutely* unrelated to this author.

17   **Turner** . . . : Delivered address to American Historical Association on July 17, 1893, in Chicago; see Kull and Kull, *History*, 277, and Ray A. Billington, *Westward Expansion*, New York, 1949, 1.

18   **Hydro-electric, Lexow, Hawaii, Ford, Edison** . . . : Kull and Kull, *History*, 275–278.

18   **Social Darwinism** . . . : The best account of political impact of this, in my opinion, is in Herbert Agar, *The Price of Union*, Boston, 1950, 551–552.

18   **Rockefeller's rose** . . . : Agar, *Price*, 552.

19   **"violence of crises"** . . . : Clement Juglar, *Des Crises Commerciales*, Paris, 1889, 44.

19   **always "different"** . . . : Logan, *Baker*, 249.

20   **"extreme measure"** . . . : Lauck, *Causes*, 102–103.

20   **$38 million certificates** . . . : Lauck, *Causes*, 104.

20   **"young ladies . . . at war"** . . . : Cornwell, "Should the Government Retire from Banking?" an article in a book entitled *Sound Money Monographs*, New York, 70.

21   **171 responses etc.** . . . . : NYSBA, *Secretary Book*, 1894, 28. Note that the minutes of the various meetings are not presented in chronological order.

21   **more than eighty banks** . . . : From NYSBA, *Proceedings*, 1894, 73–76.

21   **mild, cloudy** . . . : Data on weather in 1894 from the Department of Soil, Crop and Atmospheric Sciences at Cornell University, phone interview Feb. 14, 1991.

21   **Grand Union Hotel prices** . . . : NYSBA, *Secretary Book*, 1894, 33.

22   **Eckles speech** . . . : NYSBA, *Proceedings*, 1894, 8–11.

23   **Cornwell's inaugural speech** . . . : NYSBA, *Proceedings*, 1894, 23–25.

23   **Preston speech** . . . : NYSBA, *Proceedings*, 1894, 25–33.

25   **council met repeatedly** . . . : NYSBA, *Secretary Book*, 1894, 40.

25 **results membership drive** . . . : NYSBA, *Secretary Book*, 1894, 42. The total of 389 for 1895 found in *Proceedings*, 1895, 14.

25 **"A Way Out"** . . . : The text was reprinted by Cornwell in his article, "A Way Out," *Sound Money Monographs*, 79–91. It was also subsequently taken up in an editorial of the *New York Times*, Dec. 31, 1894. The notion of a three-tiered banking structure is expounded in "Thirty Years of War Currency," *Sound Money Monographs*, 18.

26 **Walker speech** . . . : NYSBA, *Proceedings*, 1895, 26–38.

26 **City National Bank** . . . : Dillistin, *Historical Directory*, 106.

26 **collapse City National** . . . : *Buffalo Evening News*, June 6, 1901, gives a statement of the bank's condition as of June 4. On Monday, July 1, the *News* announced the bank's suspension in a front-page story. The headline read CITY NATIONAL BANK DID NOT OPEN TODAY.

27 **Cornwell's obituary** . . . : *New York Times*, May 12, 1932, 19.

2 • The Speculators

29 **summer of 1783** . . . : Richard B. Morris, *The Peacemakers*, New York, 1965. It was rumored that George III, irked by the haste of the negotiations, may have caused the Duke of Manchester's secretary to be poisoned, 435.

29 **"to make a tour"** . . . : *Writings of Washington*, ed. John C. Fitzpatrick, Washington, D.C., 1938, vol. 27, 65–66. This was a letter to Philip Schuyler, dated July 15, 1783. Incidentally, E. W. Spaulding, in *His Excellency, George Clinton*, New York, 1938, misquotes this passage; see 232.

30 **occupied Oswego** . . . : S. E. Morison, *Oxford History of the American People*, New York, 1965, 287. The British would not withdraw until 1796.

30 **up the Hudson** . . . : Douglas Freeman, *George Washington*, New York, 1952, vol. 5, 450. Once again, this differs from Spaulding, *Clinton*, see p. 272, but Freeman would seem to be the greater authority.

30 **Clinton's past** . . . : Spaulding, *Clinton*, 9–19, 27–30, 45–49.

32 **"roast in hell"** . . . : D. S. Alexander, *Political History of New York State*, New York, 1906, 2 vols., vol. 1, 23.

32 **springs at Saratoga** . . . : Fitzpatrick, *Writings of Washington*, vol. 27, 501.

33 **"under a silent moon"** . . . : Francis Parkman, *Montcalm and Wolfe*, New York, 1962, 2 vols., 302. This book was originally published in 1884 but Parkman actually made the trip in 1844 while an undergraduate at Harvard; see Francis Parkman, *Journals*, 2 vols., ed. M. Wade, New York, 1947.

34 **Fort Stanwix, etc.** . . . : Freeman, *Washington*, vol. 5, 450. See also, Fitzpatrick, *Writings of Washington*, vol. 27, letter to Lt. Henry Dimler, 67, and to Clinton, 501. Fort Stanwix was subsequently renamed Fort Schuyler.

34 **Clinton's survey** . . . : Spaulding, *Clinton*, 156.

34 **"Prompted by . . . observations"** . . . : Fitzpatrick, *Writings of Washington*, vol. 27, letter to Chevalier de Castellux, 189–190.

35 **"Fatigued horses"** . . . : Fitzpatrick, *Writings of Washington*, vol. 27, letter to Congress, 83.

35 **1,000 acres deal** . . . : Spaulding, *Clinton*, 232.

36 **Morris et al., land speculations** . . . : David M. Ellis et al., *History of New York State*, Ithaca, N.Y., 1967, 150–162.

37 **£1.5 million** . . . : E. W. Spaulding, *New York in the Critical Period*, New York, 1932, 142.

37	**Empress of China** . . . : S. I. Pomerantz, *New York, an American City, 1783–1803*, New York, 1938, 152–153. This "handsome, commodious and elegant ship" was designed by John Peck, born 1725. Though no contemporary portrayal of the ship is extant, it was probably a larger but less heavily gunned version of Peck's famous privateer *Rattlesnake*; see Howard I. Chapelle, *The History of American Sailing Ships*, New York, 1935, 134–141, and Carl C. Cutler, *Greyhounds of the Sea*, Annapolis, Md., 1960, 16–17, 393. Also, Margaret Christman, *Adventurous Persuits*, Washington, D.C., 1984, and Philip C. F. Smith, *The Empress of China*, Philadelphia, 1984.
38	**"dress of women"** . . . : Spaulding, *Critical Period*, 14. Quote by Brissot de Warville.
38	**New tracts, etc.** . . . : Ellis, *History*, 150–162.
39	**dubloons . . . Bank of New York** . . . : Henry W. Domett, *History of the Bank of New York, 1784–1884*, New York, 1884, 4–5.
41	**"tall, handsome"** . . . : D. S. Alexander, *Political History of the State of New York*, vol. 1, New York, 1906, 79.
41	**land banks, 4% to 5%** . . . : Theodore Thayer, "Land Banks . . . in the American Colonies," *Journal of Economic History* 12, 1953, 149–159. Note also, from Spaulding, *Clinton*, 232, that Clinton, acting as a private banker, charged his friend Washington 8.5 percent on money borrowed in the land deal.
41	**"absurdity, etc." . . . meeting** . . . : Domett, *Bank of New York*, 6. See also Herbert S. Parmet, *200 Years of Looking Ahead*, New York, 1984, 11–16.
41	**Hamilton and Burr** . . . : S. H. Wandell and M. Minnigerode, *Aaron Burr*, New York, 1925, 2 vols., vol. 1, 133–134. The quote is from Major William Pierce.
43	**Elizabeth Seaton** . . . : Parmet, *200 Years*, 61.
45	**"a merchants clerk"** . . . : Alexander, *Political History*, vol. 1, 48.
45	**"John Adams, etc."** . . . : Bray Hammond, *Banks and Politics in America*, Princeton, N.J., 1957, 275.
46	**"a monstrosity"** . . . : Hammond, *Banks*, 54.
46	**"Jeffersonians, etc."** . . . : Agar, *Price*, 51.
47	**"directed from Washington"** . . . : Arthur Schlesinger, Jr., *The Cycles of American History*, Boston, 1986, 221.
47	**Clinton and Constitution** . . . : Agar, *Price*, 68–69, 141. Also see Allan Nevins, *History of the Bank of New York and Trust Co.*, New York, 1934, 22–25, and Parmet, *200 Years*, 18–21.
48	**Burr & Manhattan Co.** . . . : Wandell and Minnigerode, *Burr*, 175. See also Robert S. Cole, Chase Manhattan *Special Supplement*, July 1969.
49	**"East India Co."** . . . : Hammond, *Banks*, 153.
49	**"political engines"** . . . : Hammond, *Banks*, 158.
50	**$112,400** . . . : Wandell and Minnigerode, *Burr*, 248.
50	**Merchants Bank denied** . . . : Hammond, *Banks*, 158. See also a pamphlet, *A Concise View of the Late Proceedings of the Clintonian Party . . . for the Suppression of the Merchants Bank*, by A. Spectator, New York, 1804. Spectator blames the rival Manhattan Co. for the Merchants' troubles. Hamilton blamed Burr.
51	**Restraining law** . . . : Azariah Flagg, *A Few Historical Facts Respecting . . . the Business of Banking in the State of New York*, New York, 1868, 8–9. In those days "deposits" was often spelled with an extra e.

51   **$2,000 a case** . . . : Wandell and Minnigerode, *Burr*, vol. 1, 134–136.

51   **Burr's loans** . . . : Wandell and Minnigerode, *Burr*, vol. 1, 139–140.

52   **"embryo-Caesar"** . . . : Schlesinger, *Cycles*, 7.

52   **"dangerous man"** . . . : Wandell and Minnigerode, *Burr*, vol. 1, 276.

52   **"warrant the assertions"** . . . : Wandell and Minnigerode, *Burr*, vol. 1, 277.

53   **"private character"** . . . : Wandell and Minnigerode, *Burr*, vol. 1, 279.

54   **Philip Hamilton** . . . : Broadus Mitchell, *Alexander Hamilton*, New York, 1962, 496–498.

54   **hair trigger pistols** . . . : Chase Manhattan Bank archives.

55   **Hamilton shot** . . . : Wandell and Minnigerode, *Burr*, vol. 1, 288–289.

55   **Burr's demise** . . . : Wandell and Minnigerode, *Burr*, vol. 1, 306–309.

55   **Young men** . . . : Hammond, *Banks*, 156.

3 • The Great Projector

57   **Forman biography** . . . : Clipping, *Syracuse Herald*, June 19, 1882, in files of Onondaga Historical Association.

59   **Albany "extensive business"** . . . : Henry B. Fearon, *Sketches of America*, London, 1819, 126.

60   **"Rivers ungovernable"** . . . : Noble E. Whitford, "The Canal System and Its Influences," in *History of the State of New York*, ed. Alexander C. Flick, vol. 5, New York, 1930, 310.

60   **"good sloop navigation"** . . . : Whitford, *History*, 303.

60   **"wild and visionary"** . . . : Clipping, *Syracuse Herald*, 1882.

61   **quotes on Forman** . . . : Clipping, *Syracuse Herald*, 1882.

61   **"NY . . . never rest, etc."** . . . : Dorothy Bobbe, *DeWitt Clinton*, New York, 1933, 160, for "350 miles" quote. Rest from *Syracuse Herald*, 1882. There is some difference of opinion on the date of the Jefferson interview, but it was probably sometime in 1808 since Jefferson left office early in 1809.

61   **shipping cannons** . . . : Ellis, *History*, 244.

61   **$15 million capital** . . . : Flagg, *A Few*, 69. Flagg uses the figure $21 million but in his footnote on page 4 he suggests that even in 1830 somewhat less than two-thirds of this was actually paid in.

62   **Brougham** . . . : H. J. Carmen, "Beginnings of the Industrial Revolution," in *History of the State of New York*, 1930, vol. 5, 349.

62   **Fulton, Hargreaves** . . . : Carmen, *History*, 342–347. Also, Kenneth O. Morgan, ed., *Oxford Illustrated History of Britain*, New York, 1989, 427.

62   **"strict integrity"** . . . : Agar, *Price*, footnote, 221.

63   **Albany Regency** . . . : Dixon R. Fox, *Decline of the Aristocracy in the Politics of New York*, New York, 1919, footnote, 281; James R. Sharp, *The Jacksonians versus the Banks*, New York, 1970, 297.

64   **loan contractors** . . . : Nathan Miller, *The Enterprise of a Free People*, Ithaca, N.Y., 1962, 87.

64   **Saline salt springs** . . . : Clipping, *Syracuse Herald*, 1882.

65   **$74,000** . . . : Miller, *Enterprise*, 87.

65   **Savings Bank** . . . : Miller, *Enterprise*, 88, footnote, 89. Also, Appendix III, 275.

65   **transfer agent** . . . : Flagg, *A Few*, 2.

66   **premium $4.50** . . . : Miller, *Enterprise*, 91.

66   **"Tis, that Genius"** . . . : Page Smith, *People's History*, vol. 3, 774.

66   **"swarms of fireflies"** . . . : Page Smith, *People's History*, vol. 3, 774–776.

66   **beneficiaries** . . . : Miller, *Enterprise*, 116.

67   **Bank of Salina** . . . : Hanry W. Schramm, *The Dynamic Years*, Syracuse, N.Y., 1976, 17.

67   **Chemung Bank** . . . : Pamphlet, *Chemung Canal Trust Co., 1833–1933*, 9–21.

68   **Herkimer County Bank** . . . : Pamphlet, *Herkimer County Trust Co., 1833–1983*, 2–5.

68   **Brown Brothers** . . . : John Kouwenhoven, *Partners in Banking*, New York, 1968, 21–40; Walter Hubbard and R. F. Winter, *North Atlantic Mail Sailings*, Canton, Ohio, 1988, 95–109.

68   **"hazarded upon, etc."** . . . : Miller, *Enterprise*, 152.

69   **Era of Stock Notes** . . . : Flagg, *A Few*, 3–4.

70   **"usurous interest"** . . . : Robert E. Chaddock, *The Safety Fund Banking System in New York*, Washington, D.C., 1910, 249.

70   **six cent notes** . . . : J. J. Knox, *History of Banking in the United States*, New York, 1900, 398.

70   **Jacob Barker** . . . : Jacob Barker, *Incidents in the Life of Jacob Barker*, Washington, D.C., 1855. Additional insights also in Fritz Redlich, *The Molding of American Banking*, New York, 1968, vol. 2, 317–318.

71   **"my personal friend"** . . . : Martin van Buren, *Autobiography*, Washington, D.C., 1920 (reprint), 75.

71   **lombards, etc.&** . . . : James Buchanan, *Report and Observation on the Banks . . . in the State of New York*, New York, 1828, 10–21.

72   **"solvency of banks"** . . . : Ronald Seavoy, *The Origins of the American Business Corporation, 1784–1855*, Westport, Conn., 1982, 118.

73   **"along the line of canals"** . . . : New York Assembly, *Journal*, 1829, 174.

73   **Table** . . . : Chaddock, *Fund*, 240.

73   **"paid up capital"** . . . : Chaddock, *Fund*, 241.

73   **"emission of currency"** . . . : Chaddock, *Fund*, 272.

73   **seven banks** . . . : Flagg, *A Few*, 69.

73   **"bought by knaves"** . . . : New York Assembly, *Journal*, 1829, 174.

74   **Forman's insights** . . . : New York Assembly, *Journal*, 1829, 176.

74   **five times capital** . . . : Hammond, *Banks*, 143.

74   **Adam Smith** . . . : Hammond, *Banks*, 275.

74   **Hong merchants** . . . : New York Assembly, *Journal*, 1829, 179.

74   **Forman argued** . . . : Hammond, *Banks*, 557.

75   **banking commissioners** . . . : For fuller discussion of implications, see Fritz Redlich, *The Molding of American Banking*, New York, 1968, vol. 1, 91–93.

75   **Catskill Bank** . . . : Flagg, *A Few*, 6.

76   **"foreshadowed . . . insurance"** . . . : Richard Sylla (with S. Ratner and J. Soltow), *Evolution of the American Economy*, New York, 1979, 172.

76   **"ignorant . . . community"** . . . : Flagg, *A Few*, 19. To take care of this new obligation, Safety Fund contributions should have been raised, realistically, from 3 percent to at least 10 percent of members' capital. In fact, eleven Safety Fund banks went under in the panic of 1837 and its ensuing depression. After the survivors had their premiums increased, the Fund was still $1 million short, a sum that was covered by the floating of a state bond issue at 6 percent. See Chaddock, *Fund*, for details.

76   **Merchants Bank** . . . : Chaddock, *Fund*, 238–239.
76   **"levelled"** . . . : Jabez Hammond, *History of Political Parties in the State of New York*, Syracuse, N.Y., 1852, 300.
77   **Regency informed** . . . : Flagg, *A Few*, 4.
77   **"intelligent understanding"** . . . : Hammond, *Banks*, 558–559.
77   **Vermont, Indiana** . . . : Benjamin J. Klebaner, *Commercial Banking in the United States*, New York, 1974, 23.
77   **"expectations" and Founder** . . . : Clipping, *Syracuse Herald*, 1882.

4 • The New Breed

79   **Corning's background** . . . : Irene Neu, *Erastus Corning*, Ithaca, N.Y., 1960, chapters 1 and 2.
81   **"self-sustaining growth"** . . . : Schlesinger, *Cycles*, 227.
81   **convention to revise** . . . : Fox, *Decline*, 251.
81   **truly democratic country** . . . : Schlesinger, *Cycles*, 229.
81   **Jackson's inaugural** . . . : J.T.W. Hubbard, co-author, *200 Years*, Washington, D.C., 1973, vol. 1, 215.
82   **"these immunities"** . . . : Schlesinger, *Cycles*, 226.
83   **canal versus railroad** . . . : See comment by Richard Sylla in *Evolution of the American Economy*, 118: "The railroad's inherent advantage over canal and steamboat lay partly in its greater speed and regularity of operation, but more importantly in the flexibility that allowed it to serve areas away from the natural waterways or where high costs made canal building prohibitive."
83   **Utica and Schenectady RR** . . . : Neu, *Corning*, 30, and footnote, 62–63.
84   **"only recompense"** . . . : Alvin F. Harlow, *The Road of the Century*, New York, 1947, 75.
84   **subscriptions** . . . : Neu, *Corning*, 67.
84   **Corning shutout** . . . : The City Bank of Albany clearly believed—though I question the claim's validity—that it was the only Democratic bank in town; at the end of 1835, seeking favors from the Jackson administration, its cashier claimed that all the other banks in Albany were "of a political character" and "hostile to the administration." See quote in Neu, *Corning*, 97.
84   **City Bank opens** . . . : Neu, *Corning*, 89–93, footnote 95.
85   **Astor deal** . . . : Neu, *Corning*, 67–68.
85   **Corning investments** . . . : Neu, *Corning*, 101.
85   **corresponding agent** . . . : Neu, *Corning*, 98, and Ruth W. Roerig, *History of Ballston Spa National Bank*, Ballston Spa, New York, 1988, 38.
86   **new state charters** . . . : Chaddock, *Fund*, 247.
86   **City Bank of New York** . . . : Dilliston, *Directory*, and Hammond, *Banks*, 163–164.
87   **"uniform and sound currency"** . . . : Hubbard, *200 Years*, 232–233.
87   **$15 million tariff** . . . : Miller, *Enterprise*, 166. In 1833 Flagg put this at $15 million.
87   **peremptory demand** . . . : Hammond, *Banks*, 356.
87   **"encroachments"** . . . : Van Buren, *Autobiography*, 184.
88   **United States Bank struggles** . . . : Hubbard, *200 Years*, 233.
89   **"Bank won't break"** . . . : Miller, *Enterprise*, 161.
89   **"Money scarce"** . . . : Miller, *Enterprise*, 165.
89   **Flagg resumes** . . . : Miller, *Enterprise*, 163.

90   wave of credit . . . . : Hubbard, *200 Years*, 234.

91   **Tompkins County Bank** . . . : Pamphlet, *150 years of Trust*, Tompkins County Trust Co., Ithaca, N.Y., 1986, and J. M. Dieckmann, *Short History of Tompkins County*, Ithaca, N.Y., 1986, 82–83.

91   **deposits double** . . . : Dilliston, *Directory* (see lists for each city), and Chaddock, *Fund*, 296–297.

91   **sales public lands** . . . : Denis T. Lynch, *An Epoch and a Time*, New York, 1929, 406.

91   **Corning plans** . . . : Neu, *Corning*, 67, 74.

91   **"quite wild"** . . . : Daniel James, a metal merchant, quoted by Miller, *Enterprise*, 198–199.

91   **British central bank** . . . : Douglass North, *Economic Growth of the United States, 1790–1860*, New York, 1961, 200; Hammond, *Banks*, 547.

91   **Specie Circular** . . . : Kull and Kull, *History*, 163.

91   **bad harvest** . . . : Reginald C. McGrane, *The Panic of 1837*, New York, 1965, 103.

91   **Briggs & Co.** . . . : Hammond, *Banks*, 459.

91   **five million loan** . . . : Flagg, *A Few*, 27–28; see also footnote.

92   **Dry Dock Bank** . . . : Parmet, *200 Years*, 42, and Page Smith, *People's History*, vol. 4, 168.

92   **"pay, pay"** . . . : Philip Hone quoted by Page Smith, *People's History*, vol. 4, 166.

92   **"resume specie payments"** . . . : Miller, *Enterprise*, 205.

92   **Brown Brothers etc.** . . . : Sir John Clapham, *The Bank of England*, Cambridge, U.K., 1966, vol. 2, 152–158.

92   **Safety Fund failures** . . . : Chaddock, *Fund*, 309–340.

93   **Loco-focos** . . . : Martin Gelber, *Dictionary of American History*, NY, 1978, 371.

94   **"major impulses"** . . . : James R. Sharp, *The Jacksonians versus the Banks*, New York, 1970, 301.

94   **Millard Fillmore** . . . : *Report of the Comptroller of the State of New York, 1849*.

94   **Faustian bargain** . . . : Buchanan, *Report*, 6–7.

94   **popular revulsion** . . . : Richard E. Sylla, *The American Capital Market, 1846–1914*, New York, 1975, 32.

95   **free banking passes** . . . : Hammond, *Banks*, 583.

95   **"American system"** . . . : Bray Hammond, "Free Banks and Corporations: The New York Free Banking Act of 1838," *Journal of Political Economy* 44, 1936, 184.

95   **clauses new law** . . . : Chaddock, *Fund*, 380–381.

95   **Ballston Spa Bank** . . . : Roerig, *History*, 11–12, 230–231.

95   **Bank of Angelica, etc.** . . . : See Dilliston, *Directory*, in community sections.

95   **4,050 year charter** . . . : Hammond, *Banks*, 596.

96   **Bank of Vernon** . . . : Pamphlet, *The National Bank of Vernon, 1839–1989*, Vernon, N.Y., 1989.

96   **Delaware Bank of Delhi** . . . : Dilliston, *Directory*, and brochure and clippings sent August 1991.

96   **70 cents on dollar** . . . : Chaddock, *Fund*, 381.

96   **Bank of New York** . . . : Parmet, *200 Years*, 43.

96   **"surrendered to democracy"** . . . : Hammond, *Banks*, 549.

96   **"medium required reserves"** . . . : Hammond, *Banks*, 596.

96   **"bold step"** . . . : Hammond, *Banks*, 680.

96   **Albany City Bank** . . . : Neu, *Corning*, 99, mentions a premium of 8 percent, while Flagg, *A Few*, footnote, 28, says such issues commanded a 12 percent premium. Miller, *Enterprise*, cites instances of premiums on the six percents going as high as 18 percent.

97   **feeder lines** . . . : Edward Hungerford, *Men and Iron*, New York, 1938, 28–32, 68.

98   **herd of cattle** . . . : Stewart H. Holbrook, *The Story of American Railroads*, New York, 1947, 85.

98   **common policy** . . . : Neu, *Corning*, 72.

98   **Bank of Lyons** . . . : New York Superintendent of Banking, *Annual Report*, 1853, 41.

98   **Oneida Valley Bank** . . . : Employee Handbook, Oneida Valley National Bank.

99   **impact of banks** . . . : James S. Gibbons, *The Banks of New York*, NY, 1859, 12–13.

99   **Marine Bank** . . . : Charles H. Diefendorf, *The Marine Trust of Buffalo*, New York, 1951.

99   **Jamestown Bank** . . . : New York Superintendent of Banking, *Annual Report*, 1855, 57. The *Reports* do not break out the figure for capital until 1855, but using the figures for the ammount of stock deposited with the superintendent and the amount of currency in circulation listed in previous years, it is possible to make an accurate estimate of the figure for initial capital.

99   **Glens Falls banks** . . . : Champlain canal was completed in 1823; see Whitford, in *History of the State of New York*, vol. 5, 319. Start of two banks, Joseph E. Barnes, *Profiles in Banking*, Glens Falls, N.Y., 9–23. In the old days, Glens Falls was spelled Glen's Falls. The Superintendent of Banking *Report* in 1851, 21, shows the Glens Falls Bank, with a total of $75,300 worth of stock pledged to the superintendent. This implies a capital of close to $100,000.

99   **Bank of Norwich** . . . : Ellis, *History of New York State*, 246–247, and Lee Morgan-Davy, *National Bank & Trust Co of Norwich, 1856–1981*, Norwich, N.Y., 1981, 1–3.

100   **Banks on east bank of Hudson** . . . : New York Superintendent of Banking, *Annual Reports*, and Dilliston, *Directory*, by community.

100   **"The mill-dam"** . . . : Gibbons, *Banks*, 13.

5 • The Great Leap Forward

101   **"most remarkable era"** . . . : Page Smith, *People's History*, vol. 4, xv.

101   **economic statistics** . . . : See *U.S. Census for 1870*, and Douglass North, *Economic Growth of the United States, 1790–1860*, New York, 1961, v, 205–206.

102   **financed by Britain** . . . : George van Vleck, *The Panic of 1857*, New York, 1967, 9, 13.

103   **"promissory notes"** . . . : Gibbons, *Banks*, 214.

103   **"notes predicated"** . . . : Gibbons, *Banks*, 214–215.

103   **Brown Brothers** . . . : Edwin J. Perkins, *Financing Anglo-American Trade*, Cambridge, Mass., 1975, 238–239.

103   Toulmin Hazards . . . : Perkins, *Financing*, 246.

104   foreign currency . . . : Perkins, *Financing*, 147–149, 219.

104   "get in, get out" . . . : Kouwenhoven, *Partners*, 25.

105   discount days . . . : Gibbons, *Banks*, 26.

105     $500,000 . . . : Gibbons, *Banks*, 200–201.

105   "good as wheat" . . . : Gibbons, *Banks*, 52, 41, 78.

105   "a general wrangle" . . . : Gibbons, *Banks*, 32.

105   "notch too low" . . . : Gibbons, *Banks*, 37.

105   California . . . : Gibbons, *Banks*, 34.

106   "done" . . . : Gibbons, *Banks*, 208.

106   "deposits down" . . . : Gibbons, *Banks*, 209.

106   accommodation paper . . . : Gibbons, *Banks*, 41.

107   tellers . . . : Gibbons, *Banks*, 159.

107   tickler . . . : Gibbons, *Banks*, 189.

107   porters . . . : Gibbons, *Banks*, 267–268.

108   statistics, 1834–54 . . . : John J. Knox, *History of Banking*, New York, 1900, 41. Also, New York Superintendent of Banking, *Report*, dated Dec. 31, 1854. Knox's figures for 1854 are 312 banks with a capital of $79 million.

108   comptroller . . . : Knox, *History*, 405.

108   "fraudulent" . . . : Knox, *History*, 419.

108   superintendent . . . : William G. Sumner, *History of Banking in the United States*, New York, 1896, 422.

108   salaries . . . : New York Superintendent of Banking, *Report*, 1857, 57.

108   free-charter banks . . . : New York Superintendent of Banking, *Report*, Dec. 31, 1851.

108   upstate banks . . . : New York Superintendent of Banking, *Report*, Dec. 31, 1854.

109   "the porters" . . . : Gibbons, *Banks*, 292.

109   clearinghouse . . . : Gibbons, *Banks*, 292–308. He says (p. 304) the packages contained "money" but the constitution of the Clearing House calls them "exchanges," formal parlance for checks. Also, Gibbons himself (p. 114) says most transactions in the city were "by check."

110   carts of specie . . . : Gibbons, *Banks*, 316.

110   examinations . . . : Gibbons, *Banks*, 319–320.

111   model for Fed . . . : Hammond, *Banks*, 707.

112   Old Bullion . . . : *History of the Chemical Bank, 1823–1913*, New York, 1913, 48–50. This agrees with the version given by N. Baxter Jackson, chairman of the Chemical Bank in the late 1940s. In a pamphlet for the Newcomen Society, Pamphlet No. 145, Princeton, N.J., 1949, 15, Jackson wrote: "Your own Bank had maintained redemption in gold throughout the Panic of '57, earning thereby the name 'Old Bullion'." Both accounts, however, differ from that of Bray Hammond, who asserts (*Banks*, pp. 710–713) the bank suspended specie payments a mere two days after the other Manhattan banks. It apparently also suspended in 1861 — for twelve years.

113   banks 'fortify' . . . : Gibbons, *Banks*, 338.

113   "office of gold" . . . : Gibbons, *Banks*, 394.

116 **$49.7 million gold** . . . : Nevins, *History*, 70–71.
117 **$1,000 breakfast** . . . : F. J. Blue, *Salmon P. Chase*, Kent, Ohio, 1987, 146; and, for slightly different version, David Donald, *Inside Lincoln's Cabinet*, New York, 1954, 39.
117 **$2 million per day** . . . : John Sherman, *Recollections*, Chicago, 1895, 270.
118 **"ludicrous"** . . . : Sherman, *Recollections*, 286–287.
119 **greenbacks** . . . : Paul B. Trescott, *Financing American Enterprise*, New York, 1963, 46.
119 **five-twenties** . . . : Davis R. Dewey, *Financial History of the United States*, New York, 1922, 284.
119 **Jay Cooke** . . . : E. P. Oberholtzer, *Jay Cooke, Financier of the Civil War*, 2 vols., Philadelphia, 1907, and J.T.W. Hubbard, *Banking in Mid-America*, Washington, D.C., 1969, footnote 99.
120 **forced loan** . . . : Dewey, *Financial History*, 291.
120 **"floated easily"** . . . : Dewey, *Financial History*, 311.
120 **Thompson** . . . : John D. Wilson, *The Chase*, Cambridge, Mass., 1986, 9.
120 **Baker consults** . . . : *Dictionary of American Biography*, New York, 1931, supp. 5, 44–45, and Logan, *Baker*, 67.
121 **J. J. Knox** . . . : Knox, *History*, vii–ix.
121 **Sherman** . . . : Sherman, *Recollections*, 289.
122 **"next fifty years"** . . . : W. J. Shultz and M. R. Caine, *Financial Development of the United States*, New York, 1937, 316.
122 **central reserve cities, etc.&** . . . : See *National Banking Act of 1864*, sec. 31.
122 **national charters** . . . : Knox, *History*, 98.
123 **Thompson** . . . : Logan, *Baker*, 54–56, 301–302. Also Wilson, *Chase*, 9.
123 **Sandwich Islands** . . . : Logan, *Baker*, 34–36, 55. Also see *New York Times*, May 3, 1931, 1, 29, and N.S.B. Gras and H. M. Larson, *Casebook in American Business History*, New York, 1939, 512–527.
125 **First National hassles** . . . : Logan, *Baker*, 298–300.
126 **Table** . . . : Comptroller of the Currency, *Report*, December 3, 1866, III–IV, and 76–101.
127 **Morgan's corner** . . . : Vincent P. Carosso, *The Morgans*, Cambridge, Mass., 1987, 102. Ron Chernow, in *The House of Morgan*, New York, 1990, 22, says they made $160,000.
127 **"touch is death"** . . . : Kenneth Ackerman, *The Gold Ring*, New York, 1988, 29.
127 **Tenth National Bank** . . . : Comptroller, *Report*, 1867, 219.
128 **$132 gold** . . . : Ackerman, *Ring*, 84.
128 **$137–$141** . . . : Ackerman, *Ring*, 149–151.
128 **$180–$200** . . . : Ackerman, *Ring*, 266–267.
129 **$325 million** . . . : Ackerman, *Ring*, 164–165.
129 **no bullion** . . . : Ackerman, *Ring*, 171.
129 **Speyers** . . . : Ackerman, *Ring*, 181–183.
130 **"great evil"** . . . : *The Nation*, quoted by Ackerman, *Ring*, 189.
131 **"pale as ashes"** . . . : Ackerman, *Ring*, 189–191.
131 **"twenty elephants"** . . . : Ackerman, *Ring*, 273.
131 **half normal rate** . . . : Ackerman, *Ring*, 266.
132 **RIP Fisk & Gould** . . . : Ackerman, *Ring*, 283–285.

133 **"going back"** . . . : Chernow, *House of Morgan*, 122; Andrew Sinclair, *Corsair*, New York, 1981, 177. Thomas Lamont, in his *Henry Davison*, New York, 1933, 74, incorrectly had Morgan rushing back from Bar Harbor.

134 **Roosevelt v. Morgan** . . . : Sinclair, *Corsair*, 162, and Chernow, *House of Morgan*, 112.

134 **15% reserve, call money** . . . : Frank Vanderlip, *From Farm Boy to Financier*, New York, 1935, 169–172.

135 **poring over telegrams** . . . : Sinclair, *Corsair*, 178, and Lamont, *Davison*, 73–74.

135 **Morgan's train ride** . . . : Sinclair, *Corsair*, 178.

135 **cannonlike cigars** . . . : Vanderlip, *Farm Boy*, 174.

135 **Morgan Library** . . . : Carosso, *The Morgans*, 143.

135 **George Baker** . . . : Harold van B. Cleveland et al., *Citibank, 1812–1970*, Cambridge, Mass., 1985, 239–242. Chernow, *House of Morgan*, 129, refers to Baker as "Pierpont's chum."

136 **a dozen institutions** . . . : Lamont, *Davison*, 83, quoting Strong, who speaks of "at least twelve institutions."

136 **"my telephone rang"** . . . : Lester V. Chandler, *Benjamin Strong, Central Banker*, Washington, D.C., 1958, 28.

137 **"melody"** . . . : Lamont, *Davison*, 237–238.

137 **"Why, that's an inspiration"** . . . : Lamont, *Davison*, 54.

138 **"good temper never failed"** . . . : Lamont, *Davison*, 83.

138 **$25 million needed** . . . : Lamont, *Davison*, 82.

138 **"consternation"** . . . : Lamont, *Davison*, 80.

138 **King signs** . . . : Lamont, *Davison*, 82.

140 **First National** . . . : Gras and Larson, *Casebook*, 512–527. Also, *Dictionary of American Biography*, New York, 1931, supp. 5, 44–45; *New York Times*, May 3, 1931, 1, 28.

140 **Thompson v. Baker** . . . : Logan, *Baker*, 97–98, 102, 301.

141 **gold certificates** . . . : O.M.W. Sprague, *History of Crises under the National Banking System*, New York, 1968 (reprint), 41.

142 **"cataclysms"** . . . : Lamont, *Davison*, 92.

143 **A. Gilbert** . . . : NYSBA, *Annual Report*, New York, 1908, 47–49.

143 **Aldrich family** . . . : Nathanial W. Stephenson, *Nelson W. Aldrich*, New York, 1930, 15.

143 **"sidetrack"** . . . : Douglas C. West, *Banking Reform and the Federal Reserve, 1863–1923*, Ithaca, N.Y., 1977, 68.

143 **Warburg** . . . : West, *Reform*, 54–55.

143 **Kronprinzessin Cecélie** . . . : *New York Times*, August 1, 1908. The ship was probably of the North German Lloyd Line.

144 **forensic gift** . . . : Lamont, *Davison*, 93.

146 **Reichsbank** . . . : National Monetary Commission, *Interviews of the Banking and Currency Systems*, Washington, D.C., 1910, 356–357.

146 **Aldrich converts** . . . : Stephenson, *Aldrich*, 334–335. West, *Reform*, 70.

147 **"not profound student"** . . . : Lamont, *Davison*, 93.

147 **"haphazard system"** . . . : Vanderlip, *Farm Boy*, 181, 214.

148 **parliamentary duties** . . . : Warburg, quoted by Lamont, *Davison*, 98.

148 **Jekyl Club** . . . : W. B. and J. H. McCash, *The Jekyll Island Club*, Athens,

Ga., 1989, 1, 124–126. The club changed its name from Jekyl to Jekyll in 1929. It is interesting to note that the McCashes, who had access to the Jekyl Island Club's register, put Benjamin Strong in the party. Neither Lamont, West, Stephenson, nor Chandler, Strong's biographer, place him at the scene. Vanderlip, in *Farm Boy*, 210–219, mentions Strong's presence both on the rail trip down and at the Jekyl Club. Davison and Strong "would be up at daybreak to get a horseback ride, or a swim before breakfast" (p. 116).

149 "unobtrusively" . . . : Vanderlip, *Farm Boy* , 211.

149 "intellectual awareness" . . . : Vanderlip, *Farm Boy*, 217.

149 "conduct a conference" . . . : Vanderlip, *Farm Boy*, 215.

149 confederation of branches . . . : West, *Reform*, 72.

150 "enjoyed following him" . . . : Quoted by Lamont, *Davison*, 101.

150 "like a clearinghouse" . . . : Herman E. Kroos and Paul Samuelson, *Documentary History of Banking and Currency in the United States*, New York, 1969, vol. 3, 1202.

150 "damn Yankee!" . . . : Rixey Smith and Norman Beasley, *Carter Glass, a Biography*, New York, 1939, 1–3.

151 "Siamese twins of disorder" . . . : Smith and Beasley, *Glass*, 96.

151 Senator Hitchcock . . . : Richard H. Timberlake, *The Origins of Central Banking in the United States*, Cambridge, Mass., 1978, 193.

151 Jekyl version bill . . . : West, *Reform*, 125–135.

151 "take the night train" . . . : Timberlake, *Origins*, 193.

152 "unorganized mob" . . . : Chandler, *Strong*, 81, 39.

152 Fed "socialism" . . . : Reported in *Commercial Chronicle*, Oct. 18, 1913.

152 Imperial Bank of Germany . . . : Horace White, *Money and Banking*, 4th ed., New York, 1915, 484–486.

153 53 out of 10,000 . . . : Charles S. Tippetts, *State Banks and the Federal Reserve System*, New York, 1929, 64.

153 "unable to assist" . . . : Tippetts, *State Banks*, 61–62.

153 "Panama Canal" . . . : NYSBA, *Proceedings*, 1914, 12–13.

153 "faithfully supported" . . . : NYSBA, *Proceedings*, 1914, 11.

8 • The Shadow War

156 Examiner's troubles . . . : NYSBA, *Proceedings*, 1918, 148–149.

156 "immense banking power" . . . : New York Superintendent of Banking, *Annual Report*, 1915, 49–51.

157 E. L. Richards . . . : *New York Times*, Sept. 18, 1927, obit., 27; *New York State Redbook*, 1915, 46; *Who's Who in New York*, 1924, 1046. W. A. Swanberg, *Citizen Hearst*, New York, 1961, 230–239; Frank G. Menke, *Encyclopedia of Sports*, New York, 1969, 373, 422.

158 "Public Confidence" . . . : *New York Times*, April 26, 1914.

158 Rural problems . . . : L. H. Bailey, *New York State Rural Problems*, Albany, N.Y., 1913, 57–58; Ellis, *History*, 487.

158 "lithe figures" . . . : David B. Greenberg, *Land That Our Fathers Plowed*, Norman, Okla., 1969, 39.

158 7 cents per hour . . . : Benjamin H. Hibberd, *Effects of the Great War on Agriculture*, New York, 1919, 87. Ellis, *History of NYS*, 493, says $15 to $25 a month, slightly below national averages cited by Hibberd.

158   **rates two points high** . . . : George Soule, *The Prosperity Decade*, New York, 1947, 232–244.

159   **Land Bank** . . . : *Documents of the Senate of the State of New York*, 1914, vol. 11, doc. no. 33, 8; NYSBA, *Proceedings*, 1932, 272–289.

159   **Guaranty Trust** . . . : New York Superintendent of Banking, *Annual Report*, 1915, 9.

159   **"Numerous enquiries"** . . . : *New York Times*, Dec. 30, 1914, 12.

160   **USS Tennessee** . . . : William G. McAdoo, *Crowded Years*, Boston, 1931, 294.

161   **Richards's fire** . . . : *New York Times*, June 8, 1914, 1.

161   **Vanderbilt meeting** . . . : McAdoo, *Crowded Years*, 290–292; Vanderlip, *Farm Boy*, 240–242.

162   **"open up"** . . . : McAdoo, *Crowded Years*, 289; Gerald Dunne, "Federal Reserve," *Business Horizons*, Winter 1966, 60.

162   **62 Cedar Street** . . . : Chandler, *Strong*, 65.

162   **Kaiser's attack** . . . : Herman Kinder and Werner Hilgemann, *The Anchor Atlas*, vol. 2, Garden City, N.Y., 1978, 124–125; A.J.P. Taylor, *A History of the First World War*, New York, 1969, 25–26.

163   **$100 million loan** . . . : Chernow, *Morgan*, 18.

163   **"special investigations"** . . . : New York Superintendent of Banking, *Annual Report*, 1915, 5–8.

163   **Deutsch Bros.** . . . : Dilliston, *Historical Directory*, 24.

164   **Bohemia Bank** . . . : New York Superintendent of Banking, *Annual Report*, 1916, 20–21.

164   **Dr. Albert** . . . : New York Superintendent of Banking, *Annual Report*, 1915, 8; McAdoo, *Crowded Years*, 324–330; Barbara Tuchman, *The Zimmerman Telegram*, New York, 1965, 68; S. E. Morison, *Oxford History of the American People*, New York, 1965, 859.

165   **outlaw market** . . . : A. D. Noyes, *The War Period of American Finance*, New York, 1926, 99–100.

166   **Wilson's reverse** . . . : Kull and Kull, *History*, 330–331.

166   **$1.67 wheat** . . . : Noyes, *Finance*, 98.

166   **Davison in England** . . . : Lamont, *Davison*, 188–192.

167   **Morgan/Harjes deals** . . . : Chernow, *Morgan*, 187–188

167   **Propaganda war** . . . : Morison, *American People*, 850–852; Carl Wittke, *German-Americans and the World War*, Columbus, Ohio, 1936, 68.

167   **Lusitania** . . . : A. A. and Mary Hoehling, *The Last Voyage of the Lusitania*, New York, 1956, 41–42, 171–172.

168   **"reversion to barbarism"** . . . : *Journal of Commerce*, March 3, 1915; Harold C. Syrett, "The Business Press and American Neutrality, 1914–1917," *Mississippi Valley Historical Review* 32 (1945), 221.

169   **Dr. Hexamer** . . . : Wittke, *German-Americans*, 36–37, 68–69.

169   **bond issues** . . . : *Wall Street Journal*, Sept. 22 and Sept. 28, 1915.

170   **French advance** . . . : Syracuse *Post-Standard*, Sept. 27, 1915, 1; Taylor, *First World War*, 60–61. It is interesting to note that the Allies lost 240,000 lives in their effort to gain a bond issue of $500 million; putting it another way, the figures indicate a sacrifice of one Allied soldier for every $2,083 worth of bonds sold.

171   **bond ads** . . . : *Wall Street Journal*, Sept. 22, 23, 1915.

171 **$25 million v. $15 million** . . . : Syracuse *Post-Standard*, Sept. 25–Oct. 5, 1915; *Wall Street Journal*, Oct. 5, 1915.

171 **"million share days"** . . . : Noyes, *Finance*, 149; Syracuse *Post-Standard*, Oct. 2, 1915.

171 **$20 billion clearances** . . . : Noyes, *Finance*, 124.

171 **"prolongation of war"** . . . : *Bankers Magazine*, Nov. 1915.

172 **spy at National City** . . . : Vanderlip, *Farm Boy*, 288–190.

172 **U.S. declares war** . . . : Kull and Kull, *History*, 341–342; Tuchman, *Zimmerman Telegram*.

172 **"stream of romanticism"** . . . : McAdoo, *Years*, 374.

172 **"knock him down"** . . . : C. F. Childs, *Concerning U.S. Government Securities*, Chicago, 1947, 120.

174 **Jefferson County drive** . . . : George W. Reeves, *Jefferson County in the World War*, Watertown, N.Y., 1920, 77–80.

174 **Buffalo drive** . . . : Sweeney, *History of Buffalo & Erie County*, 403, 438, 473–480.

174 **"threat to publish"** . . . : Wittke, *German-Americans*, 36.

175 **Bank name changes** . . . : Dilliston, *Historical Directory*.

175 **"wonderful expansion"** . . . : Syracuse *Post-Standard*, 1915, 22; Morison, *American People*, 855; Hibberd, *Effects of War*, 87. In 1918 Congress granted the Farm Loan Board a further sum of $200 million to sustain the federal farm banks.

175 **$2.9 to $3.6 billion** . . . : New York Superintendent of Banking, *Annual Report*, 1917, 5.

175 **NYSBA convention** . . . : NYSBA, *Proceedings*, 1917, 12–15.

9 • Havana-on-the-Hudson

177 **Doughboys return** . . . : *New York Times*, Dec. 3, 1918, 1.

178 **"different planet"** . . . : Page Smith, *A People's History*, vol. 7, 764.

178 **"arbiter of the world"** . . . : Noyes, *Finance*, 127, 142–143.

178 **New patriotism** . . . : Paul Johnson, *Modern Times*, New York, 1985, 204–205; Morison, *American People*, 883.

180 **Jamie Stillman** . . . : Cleveland, *Citibank*, 102.

181 **"striking expansion"** . . . : Clyde W. Phelps, *Foreign Expansion of American Banks*, New York, 1927, 3, 151–159.

181 **sugar at 70¢** . . . : George S. Moore, *A Banker's Life*, New York, 1987, 171–172.

183 **banks to Cuba** . . . : Henry C. Wallich, *Monetary Problems of an Export Economy*, Cambridge, Mass., 1950, 34–36, 52; Phelps, *Expansion*, 143.

183 **$100 million acceptance pool** . . . : Leland H. Jenks, *Our Cuban Colony*, New York, 1918, 212–213, 222; Cleveland, *Citibank*, 106–107.

183 **Durrell and Farnham** . . . : Both named, *New York Times*, Jan. 26, 1922.

184 **executive culture** . . . : Moore, *Banker's Life*, 170–174.

184 **"cloudburst of credit"** . . . : Jenks, *Colony*, 212–213.

184 **Hotel Sevilla** . . . : Basil Woon, *When It's Cocktail Time in Cuba*, New York, 1928, 18–24.

184 **rum runner** . . . : James Barbican, *Confessions of a Rum-Runner*, New York, 1928.

185 **Stillman/divorce/bank** . . . : John K. Winkler, *The First Billion*, Babson Park, Mass., 1951; Cleveland, *Citibank*, 106; Wallich, *Problems*, 57. Wallich puts total investment at $74 million, but perhaps this was for a different quarter.

185 **"sterilize economy"** . . . : W.P.G Harding, *The Formative Period of the Federal Reserve System*, Boston, 1925, 135–137, 187–193; Federal Reserve Bank of New York, *Annual Report*, 1921, 13.

185 **Cuban crash** . . . : Jules R. Benjamin, *The United States and Cuba*, Pittsburgh, 1977, 16.

185 **"worst setback"** . . . : Cleveland, *Citibank*, 106–107.

186 **E. P. Swenson** . . . : Letter to JTWH from grandson, E. P. Swenson, May 6, 1992.

186 **Charles Mitchell** . . . : Winkler, *Billion*, 262; *New York Times*, Sept. 29, 1929, sec. X, 4; *Who's Who in New York*, 1929, 1195.

187 **"ablest banker"** . . . : Cleveland, *Citibank*, 382.

187 **Mitchell in Havana** . . . : *New York Times*, Jan. 27, 1922, 6; Phelps, *Foreign Expansion*, 168–169.

188 **Postwar farms** . . . : Soule, *Prosperity Decade*, 232, 244; H. Thomas Johnson, "Postwar Optimism and Rural Financial Crisis of the 1920s," in *Explorations in Economic History*, New York, 1973–1974, 173–192.

188 **autos tenfold jump** . . . : Ellis, *NYS History*, 563.

188 **"automobiling"** . . . : Hornell, *Evening Tribune-Times*, May 21, 1924, 1.

190 **First National Bank of Groton** . . . : Lee Shurtleff, *History of the First National Bank of Groton*, Groton, N.Y., 1985, 3.

190 **Bank of Utica** . . . : Release and letter to JTWH, dated May 28, 1992, from Roger Sinnott, president, Bank of Utica.

191 **$6 billion credit** . . . : Robert Sobel, *The Great Bull Market*, New York, 1968, 45.

193 **Havana-on-the-Hudson** . . . : Edmund Wilson, the noted literary critic and lifetime resident of upstate New York, characterized the 1920s as "a drunken fiesta."

193 **"Put up more margin"** . . . : Soule, *Prosperity*, 152–155.

193 **750 banks outside city** . . . : NYSBA pamphlet, *Banking Developments in New York State, 1923–1929*, New York, 1935, 1–19.

195 **National City biggest** . . . : *New York Times*, Sept. 29, 1929, sec. X, 4.

196 **investment trusts** . . . : John K. Galbraith, *The Great Crash*, Boston, 1961, 56–67; Sobel, *Great Bull*, 92–93.

196 **coup de whisky** . . . : Johnson, *Modern Times*, 236.

196 **Strong's death** . . . : Chandler, *Strong*, 473; Johnson, *Modern Times*, 236.

196 **"obligation paramount"** . . . : Galbraith, *Crash*, 42.

197 **"Yankee croakers"** . . . : Smith and Beasley, *Glass*, 174, 289–291; Galbraith, *Crash*, 43. The two books offer slightly different wording for Glass's response.

197 **"abandon Fed"** . . . : Sobel, *Great Bull*, 118.

198 **"markets healthy"** . . . : *New York Times*, Oct. 16, 1929, 41.

198 **Urban Diteman** . . . : *New York Times*, Oct. 23, 1929.

10 • The Great Depression

199 **Henry Pomares** . . . : Phone interview with JTWH, June 17, 1992.

202 **rescue committee** . . . : Galbraith, *Crash*, 105–108.

202 Hollis Harrington . . . : NYSBA, *Survey*, May 1992; letter to JTWH dated May 30, 1992, and phone interview June 6, 1992.

203 aftershock tremors . . . : *New York Times*, Oct. 15, 1929, 40–41; Nov. 14, 1929, 37; Kull and Kull, *History*, 378.

204 Hawley-Smoot . . . : Lester V. Chandler, *America's Greatest Depression*, New York, 1970, 5, 100–109.

204 Canandaigua National Bank . . . : Pamphlet, *One Hundred Year History*, New York, 1987, 12–13.

204 Ballston Spa National Bank . . . : Roerig, *History*, 111–116.

205 Wolcott J. Humphrey . . . : Letter to JTWH in response to NYBA *Survey*, May 1992.

206 "unknown foes" . . . : Page Smith, *People's History*, vol. 8, 291.

206 "frightened look" . . . : Page Smith, *People's History*, vol. 8, 395–398.

206 apple sellers . . . : Page Smith, *People's History*, vol. 8, 299.

207 NCC/Home Loan Bank . . . : Chandler, *Greatest Depression*, 88–89; Federal Reserve Board, *Monetary Statistics*, 1943; Paul Studenski and Herman F. Krooss, *Financial History of the United States*, New York, 1963, 367, 354–355, 371.

208 Mitchell v. Glass . . . : Galbraith, *Crash*, 155; Cleveland, *Citibank*, 183.

208 "tax loss" . . . : C. C. Colt and N. S. Keith, *28 Days*, New York, 1933, 21.

209 Albert Wiggin . . . : Galbraith, *Crash*, 153–155.

209 "son of a banker" . . . : *American Mercury*, Sept. 1932.

209 Winthrop Aldrich . . . : Colt and Keith, *28 Days*, 60.

209 FDR . . . : Page Smith, *People's History*, 388–390.

210 gold reserves fall . . . : Colt and Keith, *28 Days*, 67, 47.

210 First National Bank of Glens Falls . . . : Barnes, *Profiles in Banking*, 119.

211 12,817 banks, etc.& . . . : R. M. Robertson, *The Comptroller and Bank Supervision*, Washington, D.C., 1968, 123–124.

212 New Deal finances . . . : Colt and Keith, *28 Days*, 62–82; NYSBA pamphlet, *Banking Developments*, 1923–29, 2.

212 Glass-Steagall Act . . . : The entire Banking Act of 1933 is printed in the Federal Reserve Board, *Annual Reports*, 1933, 275–295. The passage quoted is on p. 276.

213 "plan is dangerous" . . . : ABA, *Journal*, Sept. 1933, 96.

213 "our own appeals" . . . : NYSBA, *Proceedings*, 1934, 14.

213 Bank of Holland . . . : NYSBA, *Survey*, and phone interview of Mr. Hawes by JTWH, May 27, 1992.

213 loss of 107 . . . : NYSBA, *Banking Developments*, 2.

215 causes of collapse . . . : George J. Benston, "Bank Examination," *The Bulletin*, May 1973, 28.

215 "prudent investment value" . . . : Chandler, *Greatest Depression*, 152.

215 Bank of Castile . . . : NYSBA, *Survey*, plus letter to JTWH dated August 13, 1992.

215 Orange County Trust Co. . . . : NYSBA, *Survey*.

216 Albert Merrill . . . : File, Onondaga County Historical Association.

216 $5 billion bank? . . . : Schramm, *Dynamic Years*, 40.

217 $118 million bank . . . : Schramm, *Dynamics Years*, 41–45.

217 "mortgages turned down" . . . : Schramm, letter to JTWH, June 12, 1992, 3.

217 "safeguarding deposits" . . . : Schramm, *Dynamic Years*, 45.

218 **First Trust fights back** . . . : Schramm, *Dynamic Years*, 46–85. Also recollections of Mark Hanlon and Joseph S. Spaid, Sr., top executives at First Trust.

219 **Merrill and NYSBA** . . . : NYSBA, *Proceedings*, 1931, 7.

220 **PWA is "boondoggle"?** . . . : Arthur T. Roth and Walter S. Ross, *People's Banker*, New Canaan, Conn., 1987, 38.

220 **rooming house** . . . : Letter to JTWH from Wolcott Humphrey, May 1992.

221 **Wall Street Journal** . . . : Quoted by Schramm, *Dynamic Years*, 53.

11 • Lollipops and Free Parking

223 **"world turned upside down"** . . . : Roth phone interview with JTWH, Aug. 1, 1992.

223 **"Old School Tie"** . . . : Roth and Ross, *People's*, 50.

225 **"Good borrowers . . . "** . . . : Quote from *American Banker*, quoted in Roth and Ross, *People's*, 27.

225 **Franklin Square Bank** . . . : All quotes from Roth and Ross, *People's*, 34–69, plus phone interviews with JTWH on Aug. 8, Aug. 15, and Aug. 28, 1992.

228 **Dr. Win-the-War** . . . : Oscar T. Barck Jr. and Nelson M. Blake, *Since 1900*, 4th ed., New York, 1968, 652.

228 **personal taxes** . . . : Barck and Blake, *Since 1900*, 640–646.

229 **rationing by banks** . . . : Harrington Survey, letter and phone interviews with JTWH June 6 and Sept. 16, 1992.

229 **Cattaraugus County Bank** . . . : Pamphlet, *Cattaraugus County Bank*, 1992, no page numbers.

230 **Franklin's innovations** . . . : Roth and Ross, *People's*, 60, plus phone interviews with JTWH.

230 **top $52 million** . . . : Roth and Ross, *People's*, 82.

231 **"Franklin—West"** . . . : Confirmed phone interview, Aug. 28, 1992.

231 **"recoup respect"** . . . : Roth and Ross, *People's*, 74.

231 **"He knew his stuff"** . . . : Fearon interview with JTWH, Aug. 10, and confirmed phone talk, Aug. 30, 1992.

231 **"make fly right"** . . . : Roth phone interview with JTWH, Aug. 28, 1992.

232 **Franklin demise** . . . : Roth and Ross, *People's*, 255–261.

12 • The Territorial Imperative

233 **Marshall Plan** . . . : Barck and Blake, *Since 1900*, 676.

235 **Chase Manhattan** . . . : Cleveland, *Citibank*, 240–242.

236 **"US Census 1890"** . . . : Raymond C. Kolb, "Systems for Handling the Paperwork in Banks," *The Bankers Handbook*, ed. William H. Baughn and Charls E. Walker, Homewood, Ill., 1966, 176–194.

236 **2 million checks a day** . . . : Wilson, *Chase*, 307.

236 **"garbage in"** . . . : Wilson, *Chase*, 311.

237 **Harriman's freeze** . . . : Cleveland, *Citibank*, 246–248.

237 **"remedy by the Legislature"** . . . : New York Superintendent of Banking, *Annual Report*, 1957, 61.

238 **"What are you suing me for"** . . . : Roth and Ross, *People's*, 169–172.

238 **Morgan goes upstate?** . . . : *New York Times*, Jan. 26, 1961; May 4, 1962.

238 **thirty-seven branches** . . . : Wilson, *Chase*, 135–138.

239 **Sterling Bank** . . . : NYSBA, *Survey* and phone interview with Edward Lieb-erstein, senior vice president, Sterling Bank, Aug. 19, 1992.

239 **Merchants Bank of New York** . . . : NYSBA, *Survey*, correspondence with JTWH and phone interview, May 5, 1992.

239 **"second in line"** . . . : Cleveland, *Citibank*, 251–253.

241 **"banks liquid"** . . . : Cleveland, *Citibank*, 256.

241 **LIBOR** . . . : Wilson, *Chase*, 357–359.

241 **Bailout NYC** . . . : Wilson, *Chase*, 258–268.

243 **"Day of the Locust"** . . . : Schramm, *Dynamic Years*, 72, plus interview with JTWH, Aug. 14, 1992.

244 **Central Trust Co. of New York** . . . : Deborah F. Abrams, *Partners for the Future*, Rochester, N.Y., n.d., 72–77.

244 **Bank of New York** . . . : Parmet, *200 Years*, 97.

244 **"big banks, very fast"** . . . : Robert Fearon, Jr., interview with JTWH, Aug. 20, 1992.

244 **"shadow of the hangman"** . . . : James Whelden, interview with JTWH, Aug. 20, 1992.

245 **"unable to answer the questions"** . . . : Independent Bankers Association of New York (IBANY), *Minutes*, April 17, 1974.

246 **"flight money"** . . . : Roth and Ross, *People's*, 165–168.

246 **"the brushoff"** . . . : Whelden interview with JTWH, Aug. 20, 1992.

247 **"no way encourage"** . . . : IBANY, *Minutes*, April 17, 1974.

247 **"$38.45 a share"** . . . : Call by JTWH, spring 1991.

248 **"Competition tougher"** . . . : Fearon interview with JTWH, Aug. 20, 1992.

249 **NBT** . . . : Morgan-Davy, *National Bank*, no page numbers.

249 **Bank of New York** . . . : Herbert S. Parmet, *200 Years*, 97.

13 • The Discipline of Debt

251 **"almost fishless"** . . . : Paul A. Volcker and Toyoo Ghoten, *Changing Fortunes*, New York, 1992, 198–200.

251 **gold $450 an ounce** . . . : James Grant, *Money of the Mind*, New York, 1992, 315.

252 **M.B.A. countries** . . . : Volcker and Ghoten, *Fortunes*, 191.

253 **George Champion** . . . : Grant, *Money*, 339.

253 **"cycles of poverty"** . . . : William Greider, *Secrets of the Temple*, New York, 1989, 436.

253 **21% inflation** . . . : *Time*, March 17, 1980, 16–18.

253 **corrosive effect** . . . : *Time*, Aug. 30, 1982, 34, and Sept. 6, 1982, 52.

253 **"on a trajectory"** . . . : Grant, *Money*, 339.

253 **capital heads north** . . . : Portillo estimated this at $45 billion, but that seems excessive; *Time*, Aug. 30, 1982, 34.

253 **Chase imperiled** . . . : *Time*, Aug. 30, 1982, 34.

253 **loans twice capital** . . . : Volcker and Ghoten, *Fortunes*, 198.

254 **"never plunder again"** . . . : *Time*, Sept. 13, 1982, 72.

254 **$6 billion rescue** . . . : *Time*, Dec. 27, 1982, 62.

254 **"at your mercy"** . . . : *Time*, Sept. 6, 1982, 52.

255 **"go mad in herds"** . . . : Charles Mackay, *Extraordinary Popular Delusions and the Madness of Crowds*, New York, 1932 (reprint), xx.

256 **"crazy . . . risk-seeking"** . . . : *Fortune*, May 7, 1990, 102.

256 "robber barons" . . . : Connie Bruck, *The Predators' Ball*, New York, 1983, 149.

257 "tee-up GM" . . . : James B. Stewart, *Den of Thieves*, New York, 1992, 66–67.

258 "boundaries blurred" . . . : Wilson, *Chase*, 337–338.

258 3-6-3 crowd . . . : Michael Lewis, *The Money Culture*, New York, 1992, 109.

258 Act of 1980 . . . : Thomas Fitch, *Barron's Dictionary of Banking Terms*, New York, 1990, 190–191.

259 Pratt quotes . . . : Martin Mayer, *The Greatest Ever Bank Robbery*, New York, 1992, 60–65.

260 Garn–St. Germain act . . . : Fitch, *Barron's Dictionary*, 277–278.

260 $160 billion . . . : *Fortune*, Dec. 14, 1992, 117.

261 real estate down 45% . . . : *Fortune*, Dec. 14, 1992, 123.

261 "eclipsing debt" . . . : Grant, *Money*, 418.

261 blinder eye . . . : Mayer, *Robbery*, 70.

261 "record debt" . . . : *Business Week*, Feb. 1, 1987, 67.

262 "we're eating it" . . . : *Business Week*, Feb. 1, 1987, 65–70.

262 Banks Obsolete? . . . : *Business Week*, April 6, 1987, 74–82.

263 up 240% . . . : *Fortune*, May 7, 102.

263 "massive commitment" . . . : Michael P. Smith, executive vice president, NYSBA, letter dated Nov. 24, 1992.

263 debtors' rebellion . . . : *Business Week*, Sept. 16, 1985, 46.

263 "negotiations tougher" . . . : *Business Week*, June 1, 1987, 42–43.

263 regionals prosper . . . : *Business Week*, April 6, 1987, 75.

264 "regain spreads" . . . : *The Banking Industry in Turmoil*, report to the U.S. House Committee on Banking, Finance and Urban Affairs, Dec. 1990, 18–24.

264 "powerful triumvirate" . . . : Bryan Burrough and John Helyar, *Barbarians at the Gate*, New York, 1991, 207.

264 Macy's buy-out . . . : Lewis, *Money*, 68–71.

265 Macy's bankruptcy . . . : *Wall Street Journal*, Nov. 1, 1992, B5.

266 Boesky's $40 million . . . : Stewart, *Thieves*, 98.

266 Nabisco LBO . . . : Lewis, *Money*, 66–75.

266 Dr. Pepper LBO . . . : Grant, *Money*, 424–26.

267 Burlington LBO . . . : Chernow, *Morgan*, 696–97.

267 24% of Burlington . . . : *Business Week*, April 4, 1988, 88.

267 losses on LDCs/ buyback . . . : *Fortune*, Dec. 3, 1990, 55.

267 paltry 1.2% . . . : *Business Week*, April 6, 1987, 76.

267 FDICIA . . . : *Fortune*, Dec. 14, 1992, 117–120, and *Time*, Nov. 2, 1992, 50–51.

268 upgrade cap/assets ratio . . . : *Governing Banking's Future*, ed. Catherine England, Norwell, Mass., 1991, 15, and *Fortune*, April 8, 1991, 68.

268 "fewer banks" . . . : *Fortune*, April 8, 1991, 68.

269 reforms . . . : *Time*, Nov. 2, 1992, 50–51.

Bibliography

Abrams, Deborah F. *Partners for the Future*. Rochester, N.Y., 1980.

Ackerman, Kenneth. *The Gold Ring*. New York, 1988.

Agar, Herbert. *The Price of Union*. Boston, 1950.

Alexander, DeSalva S. *Political History of New York*. 2 vols. New York, 1906.

Allen, Frederick L. *The Lords of Creation*. New York, 1935.

Bailey, L. H. *New York State Rural Problems*. New York, 1913.

Barbican, James. *Confessions of a Rum-runner*. New York, 1928.

Barck, Oscar T., and Blake, Nelson M. *Since 1900*. New York, 1968.

Barker, Jacob. *Incidents in the Life of Jacob Barker*. Washington, D.C., 1855.

Barnes, Joseph E. *Profiles in Banking*. Glens Falls, N.Y., 1990.

Baughn, W. H., and Walker, C. E., eds. *The Bankers Handbook*. Homewood, Ill., 1966.

Benjamin, Jules R. *The United States and Cuba*. Pittsburgh, 1977.

Billington, Ray A. *Westward Expansion*. New York, 1949.

Blue, F. J. *Salmon P. Chase*. Kent, Ohio, 1987.

Bobbe, Dorothy. *DeWitt Clinton*. New York, 1933.

Bruck, Connie. *The Predators' Ball*. New York, 1983.

Buchanan, James. *Report and Observations on the Banks . . . in the State of New York*. New York, 1828.

Burr, Anna R. *Portrait of a Banker*. New York, 1927.

Burrough, Bryan, and Helyar, John. *Barbarians at the Gate*. New York, 1991.

Carosso, Vincent P. *The Morgans*. Cambridge, Mass., 1987.

Chaddock, Robert E. *The Safety Fund Banking System*. Washington, D.C., 1910.

Chandler, Lester V. *America's Greatest Depression*. New York, 1970.

————. *Benjamin Strong, Central Banker.* Washington, D.C., 1958.

Chapelle, Howard I. *The History of American Sailing Ships.* New York, 1935.

Chernow, Ron. *The House of Morgan.* New York, 1990.

Childs, C. F. *Concerning U.S. Government Securities.* Chicago, 1947.

Christman, Margaret. *Adventurous Pursuits.* Washington, D.C., 1984.

Clapham, Sir John. *The Bank of England.* Cambridge, U.K., 1966.

Cleveland, H. van B., et al. *Citibank, 1812-1970.* Cambridge, Mass., 1985.

Colt, C. C., and Keith, N. S. *28 Days.* New York, 1933.

Cutler, Carl C. *Greyhounds of the Sea.* Anapolis, Md., 1960.

Devoy, John. *History of Buffalo and Niagara Falls.* Buffalo, N.Y., 1893.

Dewey, Davis R. *Financial History of the U.S.* New York, 1922.

Dieckmann, J. M. *A Short History of Tompkins County.* Ithaca, N.Y., 1986.

Diefendorf, Charles H. *The Marine Trust of Buffalo.* New York, 1951.

Dillistin, William H. *Historical Directory of the Banks of the State of New York.* New York, 1946.

Domett, Henry W. *History of the Bank of New York, 1784-1884.* New York, 1884.

Donald, David. *Inside Lincoln's Cabinet.* New York, 1954.

Ellis, David M., et al. *History of the State of New York.* Ithaca, N.Y., 1967.

Fearon, Henry B. *Sketches of America.* London, 1819.

Fitch, Thomas. *Barron's Dictionary of Banking Terms.* New York, 1990.

Fitzpatrick, John C., ed. *The Writings of Washington.* Washington, D.C., 1938.

Flagg, Azariah. *A Few Historical Facts Respecting . . . the Business of Banking in the State of New York.* New York, 1868.

Flick, Alexander C., ed. *History of the State of New York.* New York, 1930 et seq.

Fox, Dixon R. *Decline of the Aristocracy in the Politics of New York.* New York, 1919.

Freeman, Douglas. *George Washington.* New York, 1952.

Galbraith, John K. *The Great Crash.* Boston, 1961.

Gaunt, William. *The Aesthetic Adventure.* London, 1945.

Gelber, Martin. *Dictionary of American History.* New York, 1978.

Gibbons, James S. *The Banks of New York.* New York, 1859.

Grant, James. *Money of the Mind.* New York, 1992.

Gras, N.S.B., and Larson, H. M. *Casebook in American Business History.* New York, 1939.

Greenberg, David B. *Land That Our Fathers Plowed.* Norman, Okla., 1969.

Greider, William. *Secrets of the Temple.* New York, 1989.

Hammond, Bray. *Banks and Politics in America.* Princeton, N.J., 1957.

Hammond, Jabez. *History of Political Parties in the State of New York.* Syracuse, N.Y., 1852.

Harding, W.P.G. *The Formative Period of the Federal Reserve System.* Boston, 1925.

Harlow, Alvin F. *The Road of the Century.* New York, 1947.

Hibberd, Benjamin H. *Effects of the Great War on Agriculture.* New York, 1919.

Hoehling, A. A., and Mary. *The Last Voyage of the Lusitania.* New York, 1956.

Hoffmann, Charles. *The Depression of the Nineties.* Westport, Conn., 1970.

Holbrook, Stewart H. *The Story of American Railroads.* New York, 1947.

Hubbard, J.T.W. *Banking in Mid-America—a History of Missouri's Banks.* Washington, D.C., 1969.

————, co-author. *200 Years.* Washington, D.C., 1973.

Hubbard, Walter G., and Winter, R. F. *North Atlantic Mail Sailings.* Canton, Ohio, 1988.

Hungerford, Edward. *Men and Iron.* New York, 1938.

Jenks, Leland H. *Our Cuban Colony.* New York, 1918.

Johnson, Paul. *Modern Times.* New York, 1985.

Juglar, Clement. *Des Crises Commerciales.* Paris, 1889.

Kinder, H., and Hilgemann, W. *The Anchor Atlas.* Garden City, N.Y., 1978.

Klebaner, Benjamin J. *Commercial Banking in the U.S.* New York, 1974.

Knox, John J. *History of Banking in the U.S.* New York, 1900.

Kouwenhoven, John. *Partners in Banking.* New York, 1968.

Kroos, H. E., and Samuelson, P. *Documentary History of Banking and Currency in the U.S.* New York, 1969.

Kull, Irving, and Kull, Nell. *An Encyclopedia of American History.* New York, 1965.

Lamont, Thomas. *Henry Davison.* New York, 1933.

Latham, Frank B. *The Panic of 1893.* New York, 1971.

Lauck, W. Jett. *The Causes of the Panic of 1893.* Boston, 1907.

Lewis, Michael. *The Money Culture.* New York, 1992.

Logan, Sheridan A. *George F. Baker and His Bank.* New York, 1981.

Lynch, Denis T. *An Epoch and a Time.* New York, 1929.

McAdoo, William G. *Crowded Years.* Boston, 1931.

McCash, W. B., and J. H. *The Jekyll Island Club.* Athens, Ga., 1989.

McGrane, Reginald C. *The Panic of 1837.* New York, 1965.

Mackay, Charles. *Extraordinary Popular Delusions and the Madness of Crowds.* London, 1841.

Mayer, Martin. *The Greatest Ever Bank Robbery.* New York, 1992.

Menke, Frank G. *Encyclopedia of Sports.* New York, 1969.

Miller, Nathan. *The Enterprise of a Free People.* Ithaca, N.Y., 1962.

Mitchell, Broadus. *Alexander Hamilton.* New York, 1962.

Moore, George S. *A Banker's Life.* New York, 1987.

Morgan-Davy, Lee. *National Bank & Trust Co of Norwich, 1856–1981.* Norwich, N.Y., 1981.

Morison, Samuel E. *Oxford History of the American People.* New York, 1965.

Morris, Richard B. *The Peacemakers.* New York, 1965.

Nadler, Paul S. *Commercial Banking in the Economy.* New York, 1979.

———. *The Banking Jungle.* New York, 1985.

Neu, Irene. *Erastus Corning.* Ithaca, N.Y., 1960.

Nevins, Allen. *History of the Bank of New York and Trust Co.* New York, 1934.

New York State Bankers Association. *Annual Proceedings, 1894–.* New York, et seq.

North, Douglass. *Economic Growth of the United States, 1790–1860.* New York, 1961.

Noyes, A. D. *The War Period of American Finance.* New York, 1926.

Oberholtzer, Ellis P. *Jay Cooke, Financier of the Civil War.* Philadelphia, 1907.

Parkman, Francis. *Journals.* 2 vols. New York, 1947.

———. *Montcalm and Wolfe.* 2 vols. Reprinted. New York, 1962.

Parmet, Herbert S. *200 Years of Looking Ahead.* New York, 1984.

Perkins, Edwin J. *Financing Anglo-American Trade.* Cambridge, Mass., 1975.

Phelps, Clyde W. *Foreign Expansion of American Banks.* New York, 1927.

Pomerantz, S. I. *New York, an American City, 1783–1803.* New York, 1938.

Redlich, Fritz. *The Molding of American Banking.* New York, 1968.

Reeves, George W. *Jefferson County in the World War.* Watertown, N.Y., 1920.

Robertson, R. M. *The Comptroller and Bank Supervision.* Washington, D.C., 1968.

Roerig, Ruth W. *History of Ballston Spa National Bank*. Ballston Spa, N.Y., 1988.

Roth, Arthur T., and Ross, Walter S. *People's Banker*. New Canaan, Conn., 1987.

Schlesinger, Arthur, Jr. *The Cycles of American History*. Boston, 1986.

Schneider, Wilbert M. *The American Bankers Association, Past and Present*. Washington, D.C., 1956.

Schramm, Henry W. *The Dynamic Years*. Syracuse, N.Y., 1976/1988.

Seavoy, Ronald. *The Origins of the American Business Corporation, 1784–1855*. Westport, Conn., 1982.

Sharp, James R. *The Jacksonians versus the Banks*. New York, 1970.

Sherman, John. *Recollections*. Chicago, 1895.

Shultz, W. J., and Caine, M. R. *The Financial Development of the U.S.* New York, 1937.

Shurtleff, Lee. *History of the First National Bank of Groton*. Groton, N.Y., 1985.

Sinclair, Andrew. *Corsair*. New York, 1981.

Smith, Page. *A People's History*. 8 vols. New York, 1976–1991.

Smith, Philip C. F. *The Empress of China*. Philadelphia, 1984.

Smith, Rixey, and Beasley, Norman. *Carter Glass*. New York, 1939.

Sobel, Robert. *The Great Bull Market*. New York, 1968.

Soule, George. *The Prosperity Decade*. New York, 1947.

Spaulding, Ernest W. *His Excellency, George Clinton*. New York, 1938.

———. *New York in the Critical Period*. New York, 1932.

Sprague, O.M.W. *History of Crises under the National Banking System*. New York, 1968 (reprint).

Stephenson, National W. *Nelson W. Aldrich*. New York, 1930.

Stewart, James B. *Den of Thieves*. New York, 1992.

Studenski, Paul, and Krooss, Herman F. *Financial History of the United States*. New York, 1963.

Sumner, William G. *History of Banking in the U.S.* New York, 1896.

Swanberg, W. A. *Citizen Hearst*. New York, 196l.

Sweeney, Daniel J. *History of Buffalo & Erie County, 1914–1919*. Buffalo, N.Y., 1919.

Sylla, Richard. *The American Capital Market, 1846–1914*. New York, 1975.

——— (with Ratner, S., and Soltow, J.). *Evolution of the American Economy*. New York, 1979.

Taylor, A.J.P. *A History of the First World War*. New York, 1969.

Timberlake, Richard H. *Origins of Central Banking in the United States*. Cambridge, Mass., 1978.

Tippetts, Charles S. *State Banks and the Federal Reserve System*. New York, 1912.

Trescott, Paul B. *Financing American Enterprise*. New York, 1963.

Tuchman, Barbara. *The Zimmerman Telegram*. New York, 1965.

Van Buren, Martin. *Autobiography*. Washington, D.C., 1920 (reprint).

Vanderlip, Frank. *From Farm Boy to Financier*. New York, 1935.

Van Vleck, George. *The Panic of 1857*. New York, 1967.

Volcker, Paul A., and Ghoten, Toyoo. *Changing Fortunes*. New York, 1992.

Wallich, Henry C. *Monetary Problems of an Export Economy*. Cambridge, Mass., 1950.

Wandell, Samuel H., and Minnigerode, Meade. *Aaron Burr*. New York, 1925.

West, Douglas C. *Banking Reform and the Federal Reserve, 1863–1923*. Ithaca, N.Y., 1977.

White, Horace. *Money and Banking*. 4th ed. New York, 1915.

Wilson, John D. *The Chase*. Cambridge, Mass., 1986.

Winkler, John K. *The First Billion*. Babson Park, Mass., 1951.

Wittke, Carl. *German-Americans and the World War*. Columbus, Ohio, 1936.

Woon, Basil. *When It's Cocktail Time in Cuba*. New York, 1928.

Index

Index

Index

Index

About the Author

J. T. W. HUBBARD, formerly an editor at *Business Week* and an Associate Professor of Finance at the University of Missouri, is the author of several books, including a scholarly history of frontier banking. *The Race*, his humorous first-person account of what it's like to compete in the Observer Singlehanded Transatlantic sailing race, became a book club main selection. He teaches at Syracuse University's Newhouse School of Public Communications.

MAP
OF THE STATE OF
NEW-YORK
And the Surrounding Country
BY DAVID H. BURR.
Compiled from his large Map of the State.

LAKE HURON

LAKE SIMCOE

Shallow Lakes

C A N A D A

U P P E R

Kingston

LAKE ONTARIO

LAKE ERIE

Welland Canal

Six Nations Indian Rs.

NIAGARA

MONROE

WAYNE

ERIE

GENESEE

ONTARIO

LIVINGSTON

YATES

TOMPKINS

ALLEGANY

STEUBEN

CATTARAUGUS

TIOGA

CHAUTAUQUE

CRAWFORD

WARREN

McKEAN

POTTER

TIOGA

BRADFORD

LYCOMING

P E N N S Y L V A N I A

Meridian of Washington.

Entered according to Act of Congress Jany. 5th 1829 by David H. Burr of the State of New York.